2004 Edition

Children's Book Market

The Writer's Sourcebook

Published by
Institute of Children's Literature

Acknowledgments

The editors of this directory appreciate the generous cooperation of our instructor and student contributors and the children's book editors who made clear their policies and practices.

MARNI MCNIFF, Editor

SUSAN TIERNEY, Articles Editor

BARBARA COLE, Associate Editor

JANINE MANGIAMELE, Assistant Editor

Contributing Writers: Barbara Cole, Vicki Hambleton, Deborah Heinemann, Caroline LaFleur

Cover Design: Joanna Horvath

Contents

Contents (Cont.)

Step-by-Step Through the Submissions Process ▶ ▶ ▶

Ready, Aim . . . Research and Prepare to Sell

Writers are like archers. Our target is to compose the best possible work and find it a home, a market, a bull's-eye. To be a good archer, we first have to have a strong interest, a passion, for the sport. We acquire the best possible equipment, a high-quality of bow and arrows, and maintain them well. We practice our aim and technique, and train with a coach if needed. The better these requirements are followed, the more frequently we hit the bull's-eye. Now substitute the following steps and see if the simile holds for your favorite "sport"—writing.

1 - Target the subject. Is it of personal interest and a subject you feel passionate about? An editor isn't going to be enthusiastic about a book if you're not. What type of research will make it interesting and successful? Children's editors today require first-rate, primary research.

2 - Target the quality. Have you done your best writing? Practiced your skills, gone to writers' conferences, taken courses, joined critique groups, or in some way worked at your craft and gained the right "equipment"?

3 - Target the audience. Can you see it clearly? What is the age? Reading level? Interests? Voice?

4 - Target the competition. Are there other books on comparable subjects? If you're writing in one genre, what else is out there? Do you have a truly different slant to offer?

5 - Target the market generally. Is your book to be trade, mass-market, religious, crossover, educational?

6 - Target the individual publisher and editor. What is this particular company and editor most interested in, most successful with?

We will take you step-by-step through the process of hitting some of these targets. Only you can work on the quality, but we will coach you through subject, audience, competition, and market objectives and how to reach them. You'll come nearer and nearer to a bull's-eye with every arrow—every manuscript sent flying.

Target the Subject

Whether you're finding new ideas, developing a defined project, or searching for markets for your completed manuscript, you can improve the submission process by taking time to do fundamental research. The first step is to select an idea that interests you, that you believe will appeal to readers as much as it does to you, and collect information about it.

This idea and research development step is an important first measure toward selling your book. While most editors and successful writers will tell beginners to focus on writing a good book, not on worrying about what's fashionable in the market and what's not—and they're correct—a good book requires authenticity if it's fiction, and accuracy if it's nonfiction. Subject research is essential in composing the best possible manuscript, whether it's historical background for a novel or a text, geographical information on a region or city, updated data for a scientific principle, or even searches for good character names on a census or genealogical site. Finding and refining your idea with research will strengthen your work, and poise it to sell.

Research resources. Writers have a surfeit of research resources today in the Internet quiver. The Web gives writers access to libraries, research studies, museums, associations, businesses, and a seemingly endless supply of miscellaneous sites available through myriad search engines. You can do this research at your local library if you're not set up at home. Look at:

- encyclopedia sites that might provide links to more detailed pages on other sites.
- university libraries online.

7

- government resources like the Library of Congress, the Smithsonian, NASA.
- museum sites, such as the Metropolitan Museum of Art in New York, the British Museum, and many other world-class museums.
- the sites of smaller, more focused museums, historical sites, even corporations (for that article on sneakers, for example).
- organizations that range from the social to the arts to sports, from the local to the universal.
- journalism and other sites that lead to "experts" for interviews.

Some sites help you to find the existence of material, but you'll need to get it physically from the library or another source. Some sites, however, provide actual content—text, photos, data—online.

Accuracy and annotations. Websites have links to other sites. Follow the trail, the links, and keep clear notes on where you go and what you learn, so you don't lose important resources or unintentionally plagiarize. Narrow your sights in on your topic, and be sure to check and recheck your information against other sources. Take every care with accuracy, since children's editors today want to see primary research sources and they want precision. Keep a running bibliography; you may need it for your submission package and even if you don't, it's a good idea for back-up and additional research, if it's needed. Be sure to check the *Children's Book Market* listings for indications of the kind of bibliographical or other research annotations targeted editors require. (See, for example, the bibliography on page 36.)

Fiction and research. Perhaps you're writing fiction and don't believe you need to do research. You might not, but you very well may. Is your story set in a seaside town you recall from childhood? What's the weather like there when your story is set? Are you sure? Do you need inspiration for character names for a contemporary or historical story? Check local newspapers for stories about children of a particular age and time. Remember that

Internet Research Resources

A list of possible Internet research sites that purports to be comprehensive would take up many pages, but here are broad categories and site examples to start the subject research process.

● **Search engines:** www.google.com and www.dogpile.com are effective search engines because they provide specificity and variety when searching a subject. For a different kind of search, try www.about.com, which offers expert guides to help you navigate through a subject.

● **Government sites:** The U.S. government's sites are a great place to begin research: Look for books, historical archives, photos, and much more at the Library of Congress (www.loc.gov). At NASA (www.nasa.gov), try the Strategic Enterprises sites for space, technology, exploration, earth and physical sciences, and biology. The Smithsonian site (www.smithsonian.org) is divided into Art & Design, History & Culture, Science & Technology. Go to the Government Printing Office (www.access.gpo.gov) and FirstGov (www.firstgov.gov), for everything from government operations to health to mining to special education.

● **Reference sites:** The *Encyclopedia Britannica* (www.britannica.com) site gives brief information on myriad topics, and provides helpful links; a subscriber service allows access to longer articles and more information. The Learning Network's www.infoplease.com is an almanac site with facts on topics from world events to art, architecture, biographies, holiday calendars, weather, health, weights and measures, and much more.

● **Museums:** Large and small museums across the country, and the world, can be indispensable to the writer. Through a search engine, see if local historical societies, for example, have websites. Or try the Metropolitan Museum of Art (www.metmuseum.org), British Museum (www.thebritishmuseum.ac.uk), or try the Virtual Library museums pages (www.icom.org/vlmp) to find museums around the world.

"local" has new meaning on the Internet. You can look up *The Columbus Dispatch* (Ohio) or *The Waterbury Republican* (Connecticut) or *The Mercury News* (San Jose, California). Check a genealogy site for names, or for story ideas, or for nonfiction research. Use all your resources, and of course, turn to print, too. Through your local library you have access to networks of other libraries that will help you borrow virtually any book you need.

Target the Audience

Developing ideas means not only thought and research about your topic or story, but information about the readers. Audience is the meeting place of idea and market research. Who will read this story? Who is this ultimate market (assuming the editor takes the role of the intermediate, not the ultimate market)? What grabs them?

Experts. You know "experts" who can help you find out which books kids are reading at which ages, or what parents or educators are reading, if they're your projected audience. Talk to children's librarians and teachers about the kinds of stories and topics currently, or universally, appealing to young readers. Ask them about curriculum needs, especially for nonfiction. Go to bookstores and speak to managers who specialize in children's books. Online, go to library and reading sites, like those for the American Library Association (ALA) and the International Reading Association (IRA).

Developmental stages. Find out what's happening developmentally at a given age, what's being studied at school, what interests spark your audience. Talk to scout leaders, coaches, music teachers. Observe and talk to the children themselves, especially about books if you can. Go to children's websites to see the topics they cover, and watch television programming and read young people's magazines to learn more about contemporary youth culture. Go to parenting websites to see what problems and joys arise. But remember, you'll need to find your own slants on these subjects—your own way of holding your bow and releasing your arrow.

Age ranges. Use *Children's Book Market*: Browse through

10

Age-Targeting Resources

- **American Library Association (ALA)** and **International Reading Association (IRA):** The lists of books for children compiled by these two organizations will help direct you to age-appropriate writing. (www.ala.org and www.reading.org). The ALA also lists "Great Sites!" for children, which helps writers focus in on kids' interests.
- **American Academy of Pediatrics:** Try the AAP's (www.aap.org) You and Your Family page, or the publications page.
- **Bright Futures:** Available on this organization's website (www.brightfutures.org) are downloads of tip sheets on developmental stages, and a variety of resources on juvenile and adolescent health and behavioral development.
- **National Network for Child Care (NNCC):** The website (www.nncc.org) is divided into early childhood, school age, teens, and evaluation, as well as topics such as intellectual, language, emotional/social, and an Ages and Stages series.
- **Search Institute:** This nonprofit's organization (www.search-institute.org) and website highlight 40 developmental assets for children from grades 6 to 12.

Finding Child and Teen Sites
- **Berit's Best Sites for Children:** A list of 1,000 sites for children, (www.beritsbest.com).
- **KidsClick!:** A librarian-generated list of more than 600 sites for children (http://sunsite.berkeley.edu/KidsClick!). Categories include facts & reference, weird & mysterious, religion & mythology, machines & transportation, and more.
- **The Kids on the Web:** A list of sites compiled since 1994 by the author of *Children and the Internet: A Zen Guide for Parents and Educators;* ALA-recommended site.
- **Surfing the Net with Kids:** A newspaper columnist's recommendations (www.surfnetkids.com), with current topics, a calendar of interesting events, many topics.

the listings to look at the ages covered and review the sample titles. Or start with the Category Index (page 538) and look under "preK" or "middle-grade" or "young adult," and review the publishers listed. Request their catalogues or visit their websites. Catalogues are generally free upon request with a stamped, self-addressed, 9x12 envelope. Examining the catalogues, in print or online, is a very helpful practice even at this stage of research, though it will be essential once you focus in on publishers where you'll target your specific work. See how many titles are published in what genres, for what age ranges, and give you a sense of their subjects and style. What feel do you get for the picture book illustrations, for example, if that is what you want to write, and how is the text likely to reflect that? Is this a wide-ranging publisher, or does it fill a niche?

You might need or want to buy a book to advance your research into what a segment of the children's audience is reading. Amazon.com or Barnesandnoble. com, along with other sites that help you buy books or locate out-of-print titles, have become one of a writer's best friends. Not only do they help you locate children's books you know you want, they give you information on readership ages. Reverse the process and begin your search at one of these sites with a designated age range and see what titles come up. Lots of humor? Nonfiction, but not the fiction you expected? Does this help you in thinking about what you want to write?

Target the Competition
& General Markets

When you're doing your audience or subject research, you might find that two or three large publishers specialize in books for a particular age or field, but the titles they list are old. That's a beginning for your competition research—looking into titles already in the marketplace similar to your idea and finding the publishers that match.

Competitive titles. When you get to the stage of pulling together your submissions package, adding this competition information in a paragraph to your query or proposal, or in a separate one-page summary, will give you a

Competition Research Form

Title	Author	Publisher	Pub. Date	Description/Differences from My Book

definite advantage. It will show editors your professionalism, skills at research, and dedication to your work. If you use the research well, it will also indicate to the editor that you know what that particular company publishes and why your book will fit its list. Doing your competition research, the questions you'll need to ask are:

- What books are in print that are similar to my idea?
- Who are the publishers, and what kinds of companies are they?
- When were they published?
- How are they different in slant, format, audience, etc., from mine?
- If one or more are not different, how will I reslant my idea to make my title more distinct?

This is where you'll need to strike a balance between selecting a subject or a story that is of such significant interest to the audience you're targeting that other authors have addressed it, and the challenge of giving it a new twist. The same subjects will come up over and over again, and there's a reason—a large segment of four-year-olds are always interested in trucks and always will be, for example. But how do you write another picture book on trucks and make sure it's distinct? How do you know that your book on a kindergartener's school tribulations will attract an editor's attention?

Perhaps those kindergarteners are ready for a new book on the subject, because it's been more than five years since the last one was published by one publisher, or any publisher. To find that out, once again you might go to:

- bookstores, to review the selection, put your hands on the books, and peruse them
- *Children's Book Market,* for an overview of companies publishing possibly competitive books
- online booksellers, with subject and age searches
- libraries, whether the catalogues, or *Subject Guide to Children's Books in Print*
- publisher websites and publisher catalogues

At bookstores, ask for a list of all the books on a given subject. They should be able to print one out for you from their computer system. At the library, use the computer database to do a comparable search, or look at the *Subject Guide to Children's Books in Print*.

Market types. Use *Children's Book Market*'s Category Index to generate a list of companies that publish in the category of your book and to start you thinking about the marketplace in general. You might want to use a form like that on page 13. Are the companies with competitive titles generally educational, trade, religious, special interest? Or are they all over the map? Do they have a strong backlist of older titles that they continue to support, or are titles allowed to go out of print?

The individual publisher listings in *Children's Book Market* also give you information on how many books a company publishes each year and how many it accepts from new authors. You're another step closer to selecting the publishers to whom you'll send your submission.

Target the Publisher & Editor

It's time to look more closely at the individual listings in *Children's Book Market* to find out what a company has published and what its editors are currently seeking. *Children's Book Market* can be wonderfully well used to create comparative lists of competitive titles, as above, and even better used to align your work with a publisher who is looking for it.

If you've followed the process here, you've focused in on an idea, determined your readership, and learned what books on that subject and readership are available. But editors' needs change. How do you know who wants what now? The listings in *Children's Book Market* are updated annually, with an emphasis on finding exactly what the editor needs now.

Turn again to the Category Index on page 538, or leaf through the listings themselves, and write down those publishers with interests similar to your own, especially those you didn't find in your earlier research. You've done this in researching the field and competition as a whole, but now you need to focus on the publishers you will pursue for your book. Here's how the listings break down and how to use them best.

- ◆ **Publisher's Interests:** Does the publisher you have in mind produce hardbacks, paperbacks, or both? Is it an imprint of a larger company? Does it publish fiction and/or nonfiction? Does it have a specialization, such as history, regional subjects, educational? Is your book compatible with the publisher's profile?

  Don't stretch to make a match—make it a close one—but if you believe you can slant your book solidly toward a publisher's needs, work toward that in pulling together your proposal. If you've written fiction that just can't be reshaped, be honest, and don't consider a given publisher's needs a good target.

- ◆ **Freelance Potential:** How many books did the publisher produce last year? Of the books published, how many came from unpublished writers? (For an idea of your odds, compare the number of submissions the publisher received last year to the number of titles it published.) What age range does it focus on? Are there particular topics or types of books it specializes in? What genres did the company publish, in fiction or nonfiction?

- ◆ **Editor's Comments:** This section reveals a publisher's current needs, and the types of manuscripts it *doesn't* want to see. It may also give you insight into preferred style or other editor preferences. This information will be one of your best tools in deciding where to submit your work.

You can also keep up with current needs through trade publications like *Children's Writer* newsletter (www.childrenswriter.com or 1-800-443-6078) and *Publishers Weekly* (http://publishersweekly.reviewsnews.com/), which has improved its regular coverage of children's publishing in recent years. *PW* also offers special feature

About Agents

Writers of books at some point face the question of whether or not to look for an agent. Some successful writers never work with an agent, while others much prefer to find a strong representative for their work to deal with the business side. Some publishers, a limited number and usually very large companies, will not accept unsolicited materials except through an agent. But a good manuscript or book proposal will find its home with or without an agent, if you are committed to finding the right publisher to match your work.

How to find an agent: Look at listings in *Literary Marketplace (LMP)*, or the *Writer's Digest Guide to Literary Agents*, or contact the Association of Authors' Representatives or go to their website (www.aar-online.org) for their members list. Identify agents who work with writers for children. Check in your agent guide or go online if the agent has a website for specific contact requirements. If not, send a well-written, professional cover letter describing your work and background, accompanied by an outline or synopsis and sample chapter.

What an agent does: An agent will review your work editorially before deciding to represent you, but the primary work of an agent is to contact publishers, market your material, negotiate for rights and licenses, and review financial statements. In a good working relationship, an agent will offer solid editorial advice on the direction your proposals and stories might take.

Fees: Be careful about agent fees. Increasingly, some will charge for readings and critiques, even without taking you on as a client. Compare the fees, and the commission if you do enter into a contract. A typical rate is 15 percent for domestic sales, 20 percent for foreign.

issues on children's publishing every spring and fall. A *PW* subscription is expensive, but many libraries carry the publication.

Narrow your choices to 6 to 12 publishers, and if you have not yet requested their catalogues, do so, along with their writers' guidelines. Ask a final set of questions—those in the sidebar on page 19.

You're about to pull together your submissions package. First, review the writers' guidelines, if a company has them. Whether or not they do, read the *Children's Book Market* listing closely for specifications, and follow them exactly. Suppose you have completed a biography of Georgia O'Keeffe you'd like to propose to Lerner Publishing. It's ready to go, but it happens to be August. If you check the Lerner listing, and their guidelines, you'll see that the company only accepts submissions in March or October. Don't send your work anyway, assuming they'll hold it until October. They won't. Do exactly what the publisher directs.

Now you're ready to fire your arrow: Submit.

Take Close Aim

When you've narrowed your targeted publishers to a short list, review the individual publishers' catalogues closely or go to their online sites (indicated in the listings) to find out about their overall list and specific titles—dates of publication, slant, format. With even greater focus now as you sight your target, ask:

- Is this a large house, a smaller publisher, or an independent press with 10 or fewer books published yearly?
- How many books are on its backlist?
- What audience does the publisher target?
- Are most books single titles, or does the publisher focus on series books?
- Does it aim for one or two age groups, or does it feature books for all age groups?
- Does the publisher use the same authors repeatedly, or are many different authors featured?
- Are newer authors also represented?
- Is there a mix of fiction and nonfiction books, or is there more of one than the other?
- Is there a range of subject matter? Does my book fit in their range?
- Does the publisher specialize in one or more types of books, such as picture books or easy-to-reads? Is my book one of these, or not?
- Are there books similar to yours? Too similar and too recent, so the publisher might not want duplication?
- Would your book fit in with others this house has published?
- What are the specific requirements of the writers' guidelines and how will I meet them?

Step-by-Step through Query Letters & Proposals

One publisher may prefer to receive a submission consisting of a query letter and nothing else. Another wants an extended proposal packaged in a very specific format: a cover letter, outline, résumé, samples, bibliography, competition research. A query or a cover letter is always required, but many writers find them challenging. How are query letters and cover letters different? How much information should they include? What information? What tone should they take?

Query Letters

The query letter is perhaps the most important component of a book proposal package. It should capture the editor's interest and give a sense of your treatment of the topic. It should also convince an editor that you are the person to write this book. The best advice:

- Be succinct, positive, enthusiastic, and interesting.
- Briefly describe your book proposal.
- Identify the publisher's needs by indicating your familiarity with titles on their list.
- Outline your qualifications to write the book.

Review the query letter samples on pages 28 and 31. Note each of the following elements:

Opener: A direct, brief lead that:
- captures and holds the editor's interest (it could be the first paragraph of your book);
- tells what the subject is and conveys your particular angle or slant;
- reflects your writing style, but is at all times professional; you need not be overly formal, but do not take a casual tone.

Subject: A brief description of your proposed manuscript and its potential interest to the publisher.

Specifications: If applicable, include the following:
- your manuscript's word length;
- number and type of illustrations;
- a brief indication of the research and interviews to be done; if this is extensive, include it on a separate page with a reference to it in your query;
- market information and intended audience; again, if you've done more extensive competition research, attach it separately.

Reader Appeal: A brief description of why your target audience will want to read your proposed book.

Credits: If you have publishing credits, list them briefly, including magazine credits. Don't tell the editor you've read your book to your child's class, or that several teachers have encouraged you to send it in, or that you've taken a writing course. If you have particular qualifications that helped you write the book (e.g., you run obedience classes and have written a book on dog training), say so. Many publishers request résumés. If you're attaching one in your submissions package, your query should mention relevant credits, and then refer to the résumé.

Closing: Let the publisher know if this is an exclusive or simultaneous submission.

Queries are very common for nonfiction submissions, but in the past were very uncommon in fiction. Most editors preferred to see complete manuscripts or several chapters and a synopsis for novels and early fiction. That has changed somewhat in recent years; some editors want a query for fiction before they'll read anything more. Here are some of the distinctions in the queries and packages for nonfiction and fiction:

Nonfiction Query Letter
A nonfiction package may include:

- a query or cover letter (see page 23 for which to use);

- a synopsis (see page 33);
- a detailed outline (topical or chapter) that describes each chapter's contents (see page 34);
- alternatively, a proposal that incorporates the synopsis, outline, and other information, such as the audience targeted (see page 35);
- representative chapters;
- a bibliography, consisting of the books, periodicals, and other sources you have already used to research the project, and those that you will use, including expert sources and interviews (see page 36);
- a résumé (see page 37).

Fiction Query Letters

A fiction query package may also contain any or all of the following:

- one- to two-page synopsis that briefly states the book's theme and the main character's conflict, then describes the plot, major characters, and ending;
- chapter-by-chapter synopsis consisting of one to two paragraphs (maximum) per chapter, describing the major scene or plot development of each chapter. Keep the synopsis as brief as possible. You may either single space or double space a synopsis (see page 32);
- the first three chapters (no more than 50 pages). But check the *Children's Book Market* listing and publisher's writers' guidelines carefully, as some editors prefer to see only the first chapter.

Essentials

Editors need to know from the start that you write well and that you are careful in your work. Many submissions are rejected because queries are poorly written, contain grammatical errors, or show carelessness. Since form as well as content counts, make sure your package:

- is free of spelling, typographical, and grammatical errors;

Query Letter v. Cover Letter

When to use a query letter:

❐ Always when a query is the specific requirement in the publisher's writers' guidelines.

❐ When you are including no other, attached information; the query should be specific, but not exceed a single page.

❐ When you are attaching some additional materials, such as a synopsis or sample chapter.

When to use a cover letter:

❐ When an editor has requested that you send a specific manuscript and it is attached. The cover letter is a polite, professional reminder.

❐ When you have had previous interactions with an editor, who will know who you are. Perhaps you've written something for the editor before, or you had a conversation at a conference when the editor clearly suggested you send your work.

❐ When your proposal package is comprehensive, and explains your book completely enough that a cover letter is all that is needed to reiterate, very briefly, the nature of the proposal.

♦ is cleanly presented and readable, whether typewritten or computer-printed;

♦ includes an SASE—a self-addressed stamped envelope with correct postage, or International Reply Coupons for foreign publishers;

♦ is photocopied for your records.

Query Letter Checklist

Use this checklist to evaluate your query letter before you send it with the rest of your book proposal.

Basics:
- ☐ Address the letter to the current editor, or as directed in writers' guidelines or market listings (for example, Submissions Editor or Acquisitions Editor).
- ☐ Spell the editor's name correctly.
- ☐ Proofread the address, especially the numbers.

Opening:
- ☐ Create a hook—quote a passage from your manuscript, give an unusual fact or statistic, ask a question.

Body:
- ☐ Give a brief overview of what your book proposal is about, but do not duplicate the detailed information you give in the outline or synopsis.
- ☐ List your special qualifications or experience, publishing credits/organization memberships, and research sources.
- ☐ State whether you can or cannot supply artwork.
- ☐ Note if this is a simultaneous submission.

Closing:
- ☐ Provide a brief summation.

Last steps:
- ☐ Proofread for spelling and punctuation errors, including typos.
- ☐ Sign the letter.

Cover Letters

A cover letter accompanies a submitted manuscript and provides an overview of your fiction or nonfiction submission, but it does not go into the same level of detail as a query letter. A cover letter is a professional introduction to the materials attached. It's just the facts. If you are attaching a large package of materials in your submission—a synopsis, outline, competition research, résumé, for example— you don't need a full-blown query, but a cover letter.

Cover letters range from a very brief business format, stating, *"Enclosed is a copy of my manuscript, [Insert Title] for your review"* to something more. In a somewhat longer form, the letter may include information about your personal experience with the topic; your publication credits; if you have them, special sources for artwork; and, if relevant, the fact that someone the editor knows and respects suggested you submit the manuscript.

A cover letter is always included when a manuscript is sent at the request of the editor or when it has been reworked following the editor's suggestions. The cover letter should remind the editor that he or she asked to see this manuscript. This can be accomplished with a simple phrase along the lines of "Thank you for requesting a copy of my manuscript, [Insert Title]." If you are going to be away or if it is easier to reach you at certain times or at certain phone numbers, include that information as well. Do not refer to your work as a book; it is a manuscript until it is published.

Proposals

A proposal is a collection of information with thorough details on a book idea. Arguably, a query alone is a proposal, but here we'll consider the various other components that may go into a proposal package. Always consult—and follow to the letter—writers' guidelines to see what a publisher requires.

Query or cover letter. The descriptions on pages 20–25 should help you construct your query or cover letter.

Synopsis. A brief, clear description of the fiction or nonfiction project proposed, conveying the essence of the entire idea. A synopsis may be one or several paragraphs on the entire book, or it may be written in chapter-by-chapter format. Synopses should also convey a sense of your writing style, without getting wordy. See the samples on pages 32 and 33.

Outline. A formally structured listing of the topics to be covered in a manuscript or book. Outlines may consist of brief phrases, or they may be annotated with one or two-sentence descriptions of each element. See the sample on page 34.

Note that synopses are more common for fiction than outlines. Both outlines and synopses are used to describe nonfiction, but not necessarily both in the same proposal package.

Competition/market research. The importance of researching other titles in the marketplace that might be competitive to yours was discussed earlier (pages 12–15). The presentation of this information to the editor might be in synopsis form or presented as an annotated bibliography.

Bibliography. Bibliographies are important in nonfiction submissions, considerably less so with fiction, except possibly when writing in a genre such as historical fiction. A well-wrought bibliography can go a long way toward convincing an editor of the substance behind your proposal. Include primary sources, which are more and more important in children's nonfiction; book and periodical sources; Internet sources, (but be particularly careful these are well-established); expert sources you've interviewed or plan to interview. For format, use a style reference such as *Chicago Manual of Style, Modern Language Association (MLA) Handbook,* or one of the major journalist references by organizations such as the *New York Times* or Associated Press. See the sample on page 36.

Résumé/publishing credits. Many publishers request a list of publishing credits or a résumé with submissions. The résumé introduces you to an editor by indicating your background and qualifications. An editor can judge from a résumé if a prospective writer has the necessary experience to research and write material for that publishing house. The résumé that you submit to a publisher is different from one you would submit when applying for a job, because it emphasizes writing experience, memberships in writing associations, and education. Include only those credentials that demonstrate experience related to the publisher's editorial requirements, not all of your work experience or every membership. In the case of educational or special interest publishers, be sure to include pertinent work experience.

No one style is preferable, but make sure your name, address, telephone number, and email address (if you have one) appear at the top of the page. Keep your résumé short and concise—it should not be more than a page long. If you have been published, those credits may be included on the one page, or listed on a separate sheet. See the sample on page 37.

Sample chapters or clips. As well-written as a query or even a synopsis might be, nothing can give an editor as clear a sense of your style, slant, and depth of the work you are proposing, or can do, than sample chapters or clips of published work. One of the obvious dilemmas of new writers is that they may not have clips, or they may be few and not suitable to a given proposal. But sample chapters, almost always the first and perhaps one or two others that are representative, help an editor make a judgment on your abilities and the project, or determine how to guide you in another direction—and toward a sale.

Sample Query Letter – Nonfiction

Street Address
City, State ZIP
Telephone Number
Email Address
Date

Ms.Sue Thies
Perfection Learning Corporation
1000 North Second Avenue
Logan, IA 51546

Dear Ms. Thies,

Opener/ Hook

Look, to your left, off the port side of our four-man dinghy. Just below the surface, a giant, black shadow tracks us. Our boat seems tiny, indeed. Salty sea spray stings your eyes. But the V-shaped dorsal fin skimming the water is easy to identify. A lump jumps up your throat. You've heard tales about orcas. Are they ferocious killer whales, all teeth and no brain? Or are they something more? You came on an orca watch to find out. Here you are. But who's watching whom?

Subject/ Reader Appeal

Did you know that orcas are giant dolphins that "see" like Superman? Or that some eat only fish and never stray from their native waters, while others roam, following the small marine mammals that make up their diet? Find out more in *Orca Watch*, a real life high seas adventure for children 8-12.

Orca Watch also explores this question: Could we really "free Willy"? Would he find his family, and would they accept him as their long lost relative? With the move of Keiko, the orca who played Willy in the movie, to his native Icelandic waters, young readers will be especially interested as the world awaits his ultimate release into the wild.

Credits/ Special Experience

I am a freelance writer well published in the children's market, with clips available. Having also written on an adult level for Dr. Randall Eaton, who has studied wild orcas since 1979, I am knowledgeable on the subject and have a number of beautiful photographs. Please let me know if you would like to see an outline, sample chapters, and the photographs for *Orca Watch*.

Closing

Thank you very much for your time and consideration.

Sincerely,

Ellen Hopkins

Sample Cover Letter – Nonfiction

Street Address
City, State ZIP
Telephone Number
Email Address
Date

Laura Walsh, Editor
Millbrook Press
2 Old New Milford Road
Brookfield, CT 06804

Dear Ms. Walsh,

Opener/ Subject

Please find enclosed my proposal for a book on starting seeds indoors. I've enclosed 25 pages of the text of SO YOU WANT TO BE A DRAGON FARMER and an outline of the rest of the book, plus a bibliography.

Market/ Appeal

I've focused specifically on growing snapdragons from seeds, though the principles are applicable to almost any kind of seed starting. The book is intended to fit the science curriculum. And while the text has a kind of wacky voice, the information is sound. A fourth or fifth grader might use SO YOU WANT TO BE A DRAGON FARMER to do an independent science project between mid-February and the end of school. Or the zany style might engage a young reader simply to read the book, without doing any or all of the activities.

Experi- ence

I've gardened for years and am a committed seed starter. I've been asked to speak to garden clubs and other groups about starting seeds indoors. I've done gardening projects with kids and am currently helping a group of inner-city youths with a community garden.

Recently, I've made sales to *Guideposts for Kids*, *Pockets*, *Listen*, *With*, and *Flicker*. I have a Ph.D. and have taught all ages from kindergarten to college.

Submis- sion Status/ Closing

Thank you for considering SO YOU WANT TO BE A DRAGON FARMER. This is an exclusive submission and I am willing to revise. I look forward to hearing from you.

Very truly yours,

Sharelle Byars Moranville

SASE enclosed.

Sample Cover Letter – Fiction

Street Address
City, State ZIP
Telephone Number
Email Address
Date

Liz Flanagan, Managing Editor
Pavilion Children's Books
64 Brewery Road
London, England N7 9NT

Dear Ms. Flanagan,

Opener/Subject

Making friends can be difficult, especially when peers judge one to be "different." From a young age, children struggle with the issues involved in finding, making, and keeping friends.

Ms Enclosed/Synopsis

Please find enclosed a manuscript for a picture storybook, titled *Poetry and Potatoes*. Sonnet returns home after an eventful world tour (racing on camels, outsmarting ostriches, riding in dug-out canoes and on yaks). This feisty and unconventional heroine wants a friend with whom to share her poems and memories of the world. After many attempts to find one, Sonnet concludes that the parochial townspeople are just not ready to broaden their horizons. It seems that loneliness will be Sonnet's fate — yet, if only she knew it, the perfect friend is very near.

Specifications/Appeal

Set in the Edwardian era, this story uses gentle humor to contrast Sonnet's adventurous spirit with society's judgmental views. My story is 1,250 words in length, and targeted toward readers age 7 to 9 years.

Credits

I am the author of 11 books for children and teens. Please see my attached publishing credits. Historical fiction is one of my interests.

Closing

Thank you for your time and consideration.

Best wishes,

Troon Harrison

Enclosed: Manuscript, *Poetry and Potatoes*
          Publishing credits
          SAE with IRC

Sample Query Letter – Fiction

Street Address
City, State ZIP
Telephone Number
Email Address
Date

Stephanie Owens Lurie
President and Publisher
Dutton Children's Books
345 Hudson Street
New York, NY 10014

Dear Ms. Lurie:

Opener/ Subject

I'd like to send you my picture book manuscript, *Fletch: A Cat's Tale*. It's the story of a frazzled cat who takes care of Mr. Munchley, a wonderful cook who can barely see the glasses on the end of his nose or hear the alarm clock ringing next to his ear.

Synopsis

Mr. Munchley thinks he and Fletch live alone. He doesn't notice when a mouse nudges his eyeglasses closer on the dressing table so he can reach them. He doesn't notice when a mouse moves his tea bag into his teacup after he accidentally dunks it in the jelly jar. And he doesn't notice Fletch skittering about the house, hiding the mice and making sure Mr. Munchley didn't notice. For Fletch loves Mr. Munchley, but he can't take care of him alone. And the mice love Mr. Munchley's cooking.

It's a cozy arrangement for everyone, until one day Mr. Munchley stops right in the middle of measuring out cinnamon for his Super-Gooey, Moist-and-Chewy, Butterscotch-Chocolate-Chip-Oatmeal Cookies and says, "I smell a mouse." And suddenly Fletch is more frazzled than ever. Not only does he have to take care of Mr. Munchley, he has to keep Mr. Munchley from finding the mice.

I believe *Fletch: A Cat's Tale* is a funny, kid-friendly story filled with action and illustration possibilities. I hope it fits in with the warm, humorous animal stories Dutton publishes.

Experience

I've published stories in *Cricket*, *Spider*, *Ladybug*, and several anthologies. I've written three books for the Animorphs series and am the co-author of *Kidding Around Kansas City* (John Muir).

Closing

Thank you for your consideration. I look forward to hearing from you.

Sincerely,

Lisa Harkrader

Sample Synopsis – Fiction

Synopsis: The Artemus Anderson Series

Set primarily in the small Texas town of White Rock and the surrounding area, this series covers events in the life of Artemus Anderson at ages 12 and 13. The time is the mid-1870s. Arty and his mother travel from Ohio to take possession of a cattle ranch that Mr. Anderson purchased shortly before his death in a fire. Arty and his mother struggle to overcome the heartache that accompanies their loss. Arty has a personal battle with anger and bitterness toward God. Meanwhile, he faces numerous daily struggles as he finds that life in the West rapidly pushes a boy toward manhood.

As he makes friends, Arty learns about responsibility, sorrow, love, relationship to God, joy. As readers follow Arty through the series, they will learn what life was like in the "Wild West," how kids were much the same as they are today, and that Biblical living, then and now, is rewarding both practically in the world and spiritually.

Chapter Synopses: The Adventures of Artemus Anderson, Book 1

Chapter 1: Arty and his mother, Mrs. Anderson, are on their way by stagecoach to claim their Texas ranch. They are confronted by two villains, whom they manage to defeat by using their wits.

Chapter 2: Arty and Mrs. Anderson arrive in White Rock, Texas, the town closest to their ranch. They have a misunderstanding with the marshal.

Chapter 3: They spend the night in town. The following morning, Arty and his mother go to the ranch, escorted by the marshal and ranch foreman, who has ridden into town to meet them.

Chapter 4: Before they leave town, they are again confronted by the two villains from the stagecoach, but the marshal and foreman intervene and the villains land in jail. At the ranch, the Andersons meet several cowboys, and the old cook, who is the focal point of a funny incident.

Chapter 5: Two months have passed. Arty witnesses to the cook, who is bitter toward God because of past events. Although the cook doesn't share Arty's beliefs, he likes the boy. The cowboys present Arty with a pony, and more humor follows, mixed with a spiritual lesson.

. . .

[The outline continues through Chapter 12. A synopsis for each additional book in the series is included in the proposal package.]

Sample Synopsis – Nonfiction

Name   Address, Telephone, Email

DANGER ON ICE: THE SHACKLETON ADVENTURE

Sir Ernest plans to return to the South Pole with the goal
of traveling across the continent of Antarctica. He must
prepare for the voyage by finding the right crew—men of courage
and adventure—finding a ship, and gathering supplies. On August
8, 1914, five days after World War I is declared, the *Endurance*
leaves England. A stowaway is discovered on board, hiding in a
locker with his cat. After stopping to replenish fuel, the
Endurance leaves South Georgia Island, headed for the Antarctic
Circle.

By December 19, the ship reaches the Antarctic ice pack.
The heavy wooden ship plows through, but soon must sail
through paths in the maze of ice. The ice eventually becomes
so thick the men must walk alongside the ship, breaking up
the ice around and ahead of it. On January 18, 1915, the ice
is too thick to move forward. Shackleton decides to wait for
a path to open. During the night, frigid winds tighten the
ice around the ship, freezing it in place.

The expedition members live on the ship, moving the dog
kennels from the deck to the ice. The scientists study
currents, climate, and the changing ice formations that lift
and tilt their vessel. In August, blizzards add to the
extreme conditions. By October 27, ice pressure begins
crushing the ship. They abandon ship and set up Ocean Camp.
The daytime sun causes ice melt, soaking their tents, bed
rolls, and clothing. Nighttime temperatures freeze everything. When the ice is thin enough for them to feel seasick
with the movement below, they march inland to safer ice. On
December 29, they set up Patience Camp, their home until
April 8, 1916.

Supplies are now running low. They need to change plans
once again, and leave the ice pack for land. They push
lifeboats to the edge of the ice pack, then sail the short
distance to Elephant Island. They prepare the largest
lifeboat, the *James Caird*, for Shackleton and five others to
sail for help. They'll make an 800-mile journey in a 22-foot
boat across some of the most dangerous waters of the south
polar region.

The six leave Elephant Island on April 24. The open boat is
surrounded by whales during the two-week journey through the
. . .

Sample Outline – Nonfiction

Outline of <u>Off-the-Wall Soccer for Kids</u>

I.   Introduction

II.   History and size of competitive youth indoor
        soccer

III.   How indoor soccer differs from outdoor soccer

        A. size of playing surface

        B. number of players

        C. out of bounds

        D. substitutions

        E. uninterrupted play

        F. using the boards as another teammate

        G. quick transitions between offense and
           defense

        H. speed of play

IV.   Basic skills for offense

V.   Using the boards on offense

VI.   Basic skills for defense

VII.   Using the boards on defense

VIII.   Drills for offense

IX.   Drills for defense

X.   Situation strategies for offense

XI.   Situation strategies for defense

XII.   Handling parents and pressure

XIII.   Conditioning requirements for a faster, more
        exhausting game

XIV.   Appendix: Official Rules of Indoor Soccer

Sample Proposal – Nonfiction

```
Date
Mr. Rob Taylor, Editor
McGraw-Hill/Contemporary Books
# 1 Prudential Plaza
130 E. Randolph St., Suite 900
Chicago, IL 60601

Dear Mr. Taylor:
   I am enclosing my proposal for the book Off the Wall Soc-
cer Kids. It is presented in conformance with the McGraw-Hill
submission guidelines.
```

A. Rationales
```
   1. There is no book on coaching youth indoor soccer.
   2. Three million boys and girls play the game—the same num-
ber who were playing Little League baseball when I wrote my
first book on that sport. That book was the first on the
subject, and now 8 publishers offer 11 Little League books.
   3. Youth indoor soccer is a burgeoning sport, organized as a
youth winter sport in 1995, yet it had its first national
championship tournaments in 1997.
```

B. Subject
```
   It is called indoor arena soccer to differentiate it from
futsal, an international version of indoor soccer. The U.S.
version is a hybrid of outdoor soccer and indoor hockey,
i.e., hockey played with a ball, with sidebards, no out-of-
bounds, on-the-fly substitutions, and no time-outs. It is
fast-paced and high scoring. The United States Indoor Soccer
Association reports more than 500 private indoor facilities,
each housing from two to six indoor soccer arenas. In addi-
tion, . . . [continues]
```

C. The Market
```
   1. Three thousand youngsters play youth soccer, supported by
their parents, coaches, officials, and administrators.
   2. There are more than 300,000 websites on the subject of
indoor soccer, and 30,000 for youth indoor soccer.
   3. There are 9 national soccer organizations, four of which
have youth in the title.
   4. There are four national soccer magazines . . .
```

D. Book Competition
```
   No books have been published on coaching youth indoor
soccer. A brief review of 17 books on soccer and coaching
outdoor youth soccer is attached.
```

E. Book Size and Completion
```
   I anticipate 170 to 200 pages, color cover, 30 black-and-
white photos and 200 diagrams inside. I anticipate six
months to complete the writing. . . .
```

Sample Bibliography

SOURCES FOR <u>DANGER ON ICE: THE SHACKLETON ADVENTURE</u>

Alexander, Caroline. "Endurance." *Natural History.* vol. 108, no. 3 (April 1999): 98-100.

_____. *The Endurance: Shackleton's Legendary Antarctic Expedition.* New York: Alfred A. Knopf, 1998.

Armstrong, Jennifer. *Shipwreck at the Bottom of the World: Shackleton's Amazing Voyage.* New York: Crown Publishers, 1998.

_____. *Spirit of Endurance.* New York: Crown Publishers, 2000.

Explorers and Discoverers of the World. Edited by Daniel B. Baker. Detroit: Gale Research, 1993.

Briley, Harold. "Sail of the Century." *Geographical,* vol. 71, no. 4 (April 1999): 48-53.

"The Furthest South." *Geographical,* vol. 68 (February 1996): 30-35.

Hammel, Sara. "The Call of the Sea: It Was a Matter of Endurance." *U.S. News & World Report.* (May 31, 1999: 67)

Kimmel, Elizabeth Cody. *Ice Story: Shackleton's Lost Expedition.* New York: Clarion Books, 1999.

Lane, Anthony. "Breaking the Waves." *The New Yorker* (April 12, 1999): 96-101.

Rogers, Patrick. "Beyond Endurance." *People Weekly,* vol. 51, no. 9 (March 8, 1999): 151-153.

"A Salute to Survival." *USA Today,* vol. 129, no. 2667 (December 2000): 8-9.

Shipwrecks. Edited by David Ritchie. New York: Facts on File, 1996): 74, 117.

Shackleton, Sir Ernest. *South: A Memoir of the* Endurance *Voyage.* (New York: Carroll & Graff, 1999 reissue of 1918 edition).

Shackleton, Sir Ernest. *Shackleton: His Antarctic Writings.* (London: British Broadcasting Corp., 1983).

"Shackleton Expedition." American Museum of Natural History website. www.amnh.org/exhibitions/shackleton

Sample Résumé

Ann Purmell
Address, Telephone Number, Email

Experience

- Writer of inspirational and children's literature.

- Freelance journalist and feature writer for *Jackson Citizen Patriot* (Michigan), a Booth Communications daily. Affiliate newspapers throughout Michigan carry my articles.

- Freelance writer for *Jackson Magazine,* a monthly business publication.

- Guest lecturer for Children's Literature and Creative Writing classes at Spring Arbor College, Spring Arbor, Michigan.

- Performs school presentations for all grade levels.

Publications/Articles

Published numerous articles, including:

- "Prayers to the Dead," *In Other Words: An American Poetry Anthology* (Western Reading Services, 1998).

- "Promises Never Die," *Guideposts for Teens* (June/July 1999). Ghost-written, first-person, true story.

- "Teaching Kids the Financial Facts of Life," *Jackson Citizen Patriot* (July 20, 1999). An interview with Jayne A. Pearl, author of *Kids and Money.*

- "New Rules for Cider? Small Presses Might Be Put Out of Business," *Jackson Citizen Patriot* (December 12, 1999).

- "Jackson Public Schools Prepare for Change: Technology, Ideas Shaping Education," *Jackson Magazine* (December 1999). An interview with Dan Evans, Superintendent of Jackson Public Schools.

Education

- B.S., Nursing, Eastern Michigan University.

- Post-B.A. work, elementary education, Spring Arbor College.

- *Highlights for Children* Chautauqua Conference, summer 1999.

Sample Manuscript Pages

Title Page

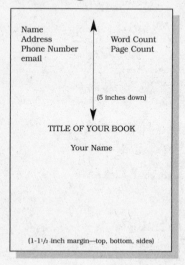

Name
Address
Phone Number
email

Word Count
Page Count

(5 inches down)

TITLE OF YOUR BOOK

Your Name

(1-1½-inch margin—top, bottom, sides)

New Chapter

Last Name/Title

Page No.

(5 inches down)

Chapter Heading

(1-1½-inch margin—top, bottom, sides)

Following Pages

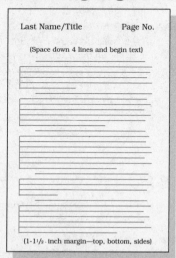

Last Name/Title

Page No.

(Space down 4 lines and begin text)

(1-1½-inch margin—top, bottom, sides)

Manuscript Preparation

Prepare and mail your manuscript according to the following guidelines:

- Use high-quality 8½x11 white bond paper.
- Double-space manuscript text; leave 1- to 1½-inch margins on the top, bottom, and sides. (See page 38.)
- Send typewritten pages, letter-quality computer print-outs, or clear photocopies. You may send a computer disk if the publisher requests one.
- *Title Page.* In the upper left corner, type your name, address, phone number, and email address.

  In the upper right corner, type your word count, rounded to the nearest 10 to 25 words. For anything longer than a picture book, you may also type the number of pages. (Don't count the title page.) Center and type your title (using capital letters) about 5 inches from the top of the page with your byline two lines below it.

  Start your text on the next page. (Note: if this is a picture book or board book, see page 41.)
- *Following Pages.* Type your last name and one or two key words of your title in the upper left corner, and the page number in the upper right. Begin new chapters halfway down the page.
- *Cover Letter.* Include a brief cover letter following the guidelines on page 25.

Mailing Requirements

- Assemble pages unstapled. Place cover letter on top of title page. Mail in a 9x12 or 10x13 manila envelope. Include a same-sized SASE marked "First Class." If submitting to a publisher outside the US, enclose an International Reply Coupon (IRC) for return postage.
- To ensure that your manuscript arrives safely, include a self-addressed, stamped postcard the editor can return upon receipt.
- Mail your submissions First Class or Priority. Do not use certified or registered mail.

Picture Book Dummy

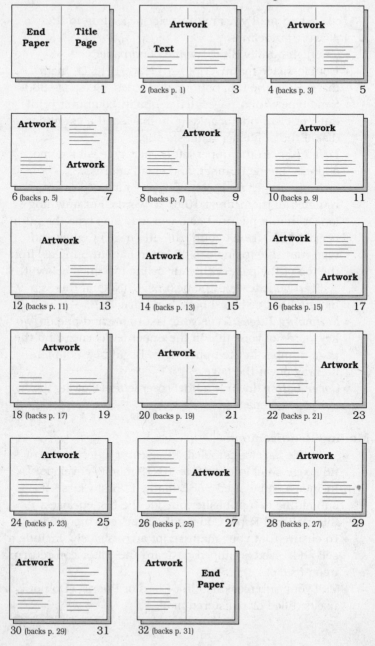

1

2 (backs p. 1)   3

4 (backs p. 3)   5

6 (backs p. 5)   7

8 (backs p. 7)   9

10 (backs p. 9)   11

12 (backs p. 11)   13

14 (backs p. 13)   15

16 (backs p. 15)   17

18 (backs p. 17)   19

20 (backs p. 19)   21

22 (backs p. 21)   23

24 (backs p. 23)   25

26 (backs p. 25)   27

28 (backs p. 27)   29

30 (backs p. 29)   31

32 (backs p. 31)

Picture Book Submissions

Most editors will accept a complete manuscript for a picture book without an initial query. Because a picture book text may contain as few as 20 words and seldom exceeds 1,500 words, it is difficult to judge if not seen in its entirety. Do not submit your own artwork unless you are a professional artist; editors prefer to use illustrators of their own choosing.

Prepare the manuscript following the guidelines for the title page on pages 38–39. Drop down four lines from the byline, indent, and begin your manuscript on the title page. Type it straight through as if it were a short story. Do not indicate page breaks.

Before submitting your picture book, make certain that your words lend themselves to visual representation and work well in the picture book format. Preparing a dummy or mock-up similar to the sample on page 40 can help you.

The average picture book is 32 pages, although it may be as short as 16 pages or as long as 64 pages, depending on the age of the intended audience. To make a dummy for a 32-page book, take eight sheets of paper, fold them in half, and number them as the sample indicates; this will not include the end papers. (Each sheet makes up four pages of your book.) Lay out your text and rough sketches or a brief description of the accompanying illustrations. Move these around and adjust your concept of the artwork until you are satisfied that words and pictures fit together as they should.

Do not submit your dummy unless the editor asks for it. Simply submit your text on separate sheets of paper, typed double-spaced, following the format guidelines given on page 38. If you do choose to submit artwork as well, be sure to send copies only; editors will *rarely* take responsibility for original artwork. Be sure to include a self-addressed, stamped envelope (SASE) large enough for the return of your entire package.

Step-by-Step through the Business of Publishing

Book Contracts

Once a publisher is interested in buying your work, he or she will send a book contract for your review and signature. While book contracts vary in length and precise language from publisher to publisher, the basic provisions of these contracts are more similar than different. All writers should understand publishing contract standards, know enough to acknowledge an offer as appropriate, and recognize when there may be room to negotiate. Remember, the agreement isn't complete until the contract is signed.

In Plain English

The best advice for your first contract reading is not to let the legal terminology distract you. A book contract is a complex legal document that is designed to protect you. It defines the rights, responsibilities, and financial terms of the author, publisher, and artist (when necessary).

Because some publishers issue standard contracts and rarely change wording or payment rates for new writers, you may not need an agent or a lawyer with book-publishing experience to represent you in the negotiation of the contract. But if you choose to negotiate the contract yourself, it is advisable that you read several reference books about book contracts and have a lawyer, preferably with book-contract experience, look it over prior to signing the agreement.

In either case, you should be familiar enough with the basic premises of the contract to communicate what items you would like to change in the document. For your protection, reread the contract at every stage of negotiation.

On the following pages you'll find a primer on the basic provisions of a book contract. If a statement in your contract is not covered or remains unclear to you, ask the editor or an attorney to "translate" the clauses into plain English.

Rights and Responsibilities

A standard book contract specifies what an author and a publisher each agree to do to produce the book and place it in the marketplace. It explicitly states copyright ownership, royalty, advance, delivery date, territorial and subsidiary rights, and other related provisions.

Grant of Rights

A clause early in the contract says that on signing, the author agrees to "grant and assign" or "convey and transfer" to the publisher certain rights to a book. You thus authorize, or license, the publisher to publish your work.

Subsidiary rights are negotiated in a contract. These rights include where a book is distributed, in what language it is printed, and in what format it is published. While most publishers want world English-language rights, some publishers will consent to retaining rights only to the United States, the Philippines, Canada, and US dependencies. With the United Kingdom now part of the European Community, more and more publishers want British publication rights, in English, so they can sell books to other members of the European Community.

Other subsidiary rights often included in contracts are:

- *Reprint Rights:* These consist of publishing the work in magazines (also known as serial rights), book club editions, and hardcover or paperback versions.
- *Mechanical Rights:* These cover audio and video cassettes, photocopying, filmstrips, and other mechanical production media.
- *Electronic or Computer Rights:* More and more contracts include rights to cover potential use on software programs, multimedia packages, online services, etc.
- *Dramatic Rights:* These include versions of the work for film, television, etc.
- *Translation Rights:* These allow a work to be printed in languages other than English.

If you don't have an agent, you may want to assign a publisher broad rights since you may not have the necessary connections or experience to sell them on your own.

If possible, seek a time limit that a publisher has to use subsidiary rights. That way certain rights will revert to you if the publisher has not sold them within a specific period.

Copyright Ownership

According to the Copyright Act of 1976 (which became effective January 1, 1978), you own all rights to your work for your lifetime plus 50 years, until you choose to sell all or part of the copyright in very specific ways. According to this law, your idea is not copyrighted; it is your unique combination of words—how you wrote something—that this law protects and considers copyrighted. A separate clause in a book contract states that you retain the copyright in your name.

Once you complete your manuscript, your work is protected. You don't need to register your work, published or unpublished, with the United States Copyright Office. In most contract agreements, a publisher is responsible for registering the published version of your work. However, registration does offer proof of ownership and a clear legal basis in case of infringement. If you decide to register, send a completed application (obtained from the Copyright Office), a $30 filing fee, and one copy of your unpublished manuscript to the Register of Copyrights, Copyright Office, Library of Congress, Washington, DC 20559.

You should realize that writers who provide a copyright notice on their submitted manuscript may be viewed as amateurs by many editors. If you have registered your unpublished manuscript with the Library of Congress, notify your publisher of that fact once your book is accepted for publication.

Manuscript Delivery

A book-publishing contract sets a due date by which you must complete and deliver an acceptable manuscript of a certain length. This clause allows a publisher to request editorial changes, permits editing of the manuscript with your review and approval, establishes editorial schedules, and indicates how many author's alterations (also known as editorial changes) you may make without cost after the book has been typeset.

Warranty and Indemnification

You will be asked to ensure that the manuscript is your original work; that it contains nothing libelous, obscene, or private; and that you own it. The clause also stipulates that the author must pay the publisher's court costs and damages should it be sued over the book. Publishers do not alter this provision readily, but the author who has written in good faith should not be concerned. Discuss a ceiling on the amount of the author's liability, just in case.

Obligation to Publish

The publisher agrees to produce and distribute the book in a timely manner, generally between one and two years. The contract should specify the time frame and indicate that if the publisher fails to publish the book within that period, the rights return to you (reversion of rights) and you keep any money already received.

Option

The option clause requires the author to offer the publisher the first chance at his or her next book. To avoid a prolonged decision-making process, try to negotiate a set period for the publisher's review of a second book, perhaps 60 or 90 days from submission of the second manuscript.

Payment

Calculations for the amount of money an author receives as an advance or in royalties are fairly standardized.

- ◆ *Advance:* An advance is money the writer receives in a lump sum or installments when a manuscript is accepted or delivered. It is paid "against" royalties coming from anticipated profits.
- ◆ *Royalty:* A royalty is a percentage of sales paid to the author. It is based either on a book's retail price or on net receipts, and it may be fixed or arranged on a sliding scale. Standard royalty is 10% of the retail price for the first 5,000 copies, 12.5% for the next 5,000 copies, and 15% thereafter. A new author may be offered only 10% or the scale may slide at a higher number of copies. Depending on the extent of artwork and who

supplied it to the publisher, author and artist may divide royalties or the artist may be paid a flat fee.

- ◆ *Accounting Statements:* The publisher must provide the author with earning statements for the book. Most companies provide statements and checks semiannually, three or more months after each accounting period ends. Be sure to determine exactly when that is. For example, if the accounting periods end June 30 and December 31, you should receive statements by October 1 and April 1.

Before You Sign . . .

The explanations presented here include suggestions for a reasonable and (we hope) profitable approach to your book contract. Every situation presents distinct alternatives, however. Your agreements with a publisher must be undertaken in good faith on both sides and you should feel comfortable with the deal you strike.

You can find additional information about copyrights and publishing law in *The Copyright Handbook: How to Protect and Use Written Words* (fifth ed) by Stephen Fishman (Nolo Press, 2000) and *Every Writer's Guide to Copyright and Publishing Law* by Ellen Kozak (Henry Holt, 1997).

A Note About Self, Subsidy, and Co-op Publishing Options

When you self-publish your book, you assume the cost of and responsibility for printing and distributing your book. By contrast, subsidy presses handle—for a fee—the production and, to some degree, the marketing and distribution of a writer's book. Co-op or joint-venture publishers assume responsibility for marketing and distribution of a book, while the author pays some or all of the production costs. Based on your own needs and expectations, you may choose to try one of these approaches. If you do, exercise caution. Be sure you understand the terms of any contract, including exactly how much you will be required to pay, the marketing and distributing services the publisher is promising, and the rights you are retaining. It is advisable to consult a lawyer before entering into any arrangement.

Postage Information

When you send a manuscript to a publisher, always enclose a return SASE with sufficient postage; this way, if the editor does not want to use your manuscript, it can be returned to you. To help you calculate the proper amount of postage for your SASE, here are the US postal rates for first-class mailings in the US and from the US to Canada based on the June 2002 increase.

Ounces	8½x11 Pages (approx pgs)	US 1st-Class Postage Rate	US to Canada
5	21–25	$1.26	$1.60
6	26–30	1.49	1.85
7	31–35	1.72	2.10
8	36–40	1.95	2.35
9	41–45	2.18	3.10
10	46–50	2.41	3.10
11	51–55	2.64	3.10
12	56+	2.87	3.10

How to Obtain Stamps

People living in the US, Canada, or overseas can acquire US stamps through the mail from the Stamp Fulfillment Service Center: call 800-STAMP-24 (800-782-6724) to request a catalogue or place an order. For overseas, the telephone number is 816-545-1100. You pay the cost of the stamps plus a postage and handling fee based on the value of the stamps ordered, and the stamps are shipped to you. Credit card information (MasterCard, Visa, and Discover cards only) is required for fax orders. The fax number is 816-545-1212. If you order through the catalogue, you can pay with a US check or an American money order. Allow 3–4 weeks for delivery.

Frequently Asked Questions

How do I request a publisher's catalogue and writers' guidelines?

Write a brief note to the publishing company: *"Please send me a recent catalogue and writers' guidelines. If there is any charge please enclose an invoice and I will pay upon receipt."* The publisher's website, if it has one, offers a faster and less expensive alternative. Many companies put their catalogues, or at least their latest releases and their writers' guidelines on the Internet.

Do I need an agent?

There is no correct answer to this question. Some writers are very successful marketing their own work, while others feel more comfortable having an agent handle that end of the business. It's a personal decision, but if you decide to work through an agent, be an "informed consumer." Get a list of member agents from the Association of Authors' Representatives, 3rd Floor, 10 Astor Place, New York, NY 10003 (available for $7.00 and SAE with $.60 postage).

I need to include a bibliography with my book proposal. How do I set one up?

The reference section of your local library can provide several sources that will help you set up a bibliography. A style manual such as the *Chicago Manual of Style* will show you the proper format for citing all your sources, including unpublished material, interviews, and Internet material.

What do I put in a cover letter if I have no publishing credits or relevant personal experience?

In this case you may want to forego a formal cover letter and send your manuscript with a brief letter stating, *"Enclosed is my manuscript, [Insert Title], for your review."* For more information on cover letters see page 25.

I don't need my manuscript returned. How do I indicate that to an editor?

With the capability to store manuscripts electronically and print out additional copies easily, some writers keep postage costs down by enclosing a self-addressed stamped postcard (SASP) saying, *"No need to return my manuscript. Please use this postcard to advise me of the status of my manuscript. Thank you."*

Do I need to register or copyright my manuscript?

Once completed, your work is automatically protected by copyright. When your manuscript is accepted for publication, the publisher will register it for you.

Should I submit my manuscript on disk?

Do not send your manuscript on disk unless the publisher's submission guidelines note that this is an acceptable format.

When a publisher says "query with sample chapters," how do I know which chapters to send? Should they be chapters in sequence or does that matter? And how many should I send?

If the publisher does not specify which chapters it wishes to see, then it's your decision. Usually it's a good idea to send the first chapter, but if another chapter gives a flavor of your book or describes a key action in the plot, include that one. You may also want to send the final chapter of the book. For nonfiction, if one chapter is more fully representative of the material your book will cover, include that. Send two to three but if the guidelines state "sample chapter" (singular), just send one.

How long should I wait before contacting an editor after I have submitted my manuscript?

The response time given in the listings can vary, and it's a good idea to wait at least a few weeks after the allocated response time before you send a brief note to the editor asking about the status of your manuscript. If you do not get a satisfactory response or you want to send your manuscript elsewhere, send a certified letter to the editor withdrawing your work from consideration and requesting its return. You are then free to submit the work to another publishing house.

A long time ago, in 1989, I was fortunate enough to have a picture book published. If I write a query letter, should I include that information? It seems to me that it may hurt more than it helps, since I have not published anything since that.
By all means include it, though you need not mention the year it was published Any publishing credit is worth noting, particularly if it is a picture book, because it shows you succeeded in a highly competitive field.

How do I address the editor, especially if she is female (e.g., Dear Miss, Dear Ms., Dear Mrs., Dear Editor-in-Chief, or what)?
There is no accepted preference, so the choice is really yours, but in general Ms. is used most frequently. Do use the person's last name, not his or her first. Before you decide which title to use, make sure you know if the person you are addressing is male or female.

If a publisher does not specify that "multiple submissions" are okay, does that imply they are not okay?
If a publisher has a firm policy against multiple submissions, this is usually stated in its guidelines. If not mentioned, the publisher probably does not have a hard and fast rule. If you choose to send a multiple submission, make sure to indicate that on your submission. Then it's up to the publisher to contact you if it prefers not to receive such submissions.

Publishing Terms

Advance: initial payment by publisher to author against future sales

Agent: professional who contacts editors and negotiates book contracts on author's behalf

All rights: an outright sale of your material; author has no further control over it

Anthropomorphization: attributing human form and personality to things not human, for example, animals

Backlist: list of publisher's titles that were not produced this season but are still in print

Beginning readers: children ages 4 to 7 years

Book contract: legal agreement between author and publisher

Book packager/producer: company that handles all elements of producing a book and then sells the final product to a publisher

Book proposal: see **Proposal**

Caldecott Medal: annual award that honors the illustrator of the current year's most distinguished children's book

CD-ROM: (compact-disc read-only memory) non-erasable electronic medium used for digitalized image and document storage

Clean-copy: a manuscript ready for typesetting; it is free of errors and needs no editing

Clip: sample of a writer's published work. See also **Tearsheet**

Concept book: category of picture book for children 2 to 7 years that teaches an idea (i.e., alphabet or counting) or explains a problem

Contract: see **Book contract**

Co-op publishing: author assumes some or all of the production costs and publisher handles all marketing and distribution; also referred to as "joint-venture publishing"

Copyedit: to edit with close attention to style and mechanics

Copyright: legal protection of an author's work

Cover letter: brief introductory letter sent with a manuscript

Disk submission: manuscript that is submitted on a computer disk

Distributor: company that buys and resells books from a publisher

Dummy: a sample arrangement or "mock-up" of pages to be printed, indicating the appearance of the published work

Electronic submission: manuscript transmitted to an editor from one computer to another through a modem

Email: (electronic mail) messages sent from one computer to another via a modem or computer network

End matter: material following the text of a book, such as the appendix, bibliography, index

Final draft: the last version of a polished manuscript ready for submission to an editor

First-time author: writer who has not previously been published

Flat fee: one-time payment made to an author for publication of a manuscript

Front matter: material preceding the text of a book, such as title page, acknowledgments, etc.

Galley: a proof of typeset text that is checked before it is made into final pages

Genre: category of fiction characterized by a particular style, form, or content, such as mystery or fantasy

Hard copy: the printed copy of a computer's output

Hi/lo: high-interest/low-reading level

Imprint: name under which a publishing house issues books

International Reply Coupon (IRC): coupon exchangeable in any foreign country for postage on a single-rate, surface-mailed letter

ISBN: International Standard Book Number assigned to books upon publication for purposes of identification

Letter-quality printout: computer printout that resembles typed pages

Manuscript: a typewritten, or computer-generated document (as opposed to a printed version)

Mass-market: books aimed at a wide audience and sold in super-markets, airports, and chain bookstores

Middle-grade readers: children ages 8 to 12 years

Modem: an internal or external device used to transmit data between computers via telephone lines

Ms/Mss: manuscript/manuscripts

Newbery Medal: annual award that honors the author of that year's most distinguished children's book

Outline: summary of a book's contents, usually nonfiction, often organized under chapter headings with descriptive sentences under each to show the scope of the book

Packager: see **Book Packager**

Pen name/pseudonym: fictitious name used by an author

Picture book: a type of book that tells a story primarily or entirely through artwork and is aimed at preschool to 8-year-old children

Pre-K: children under 5 years of age; also known as preschool

Proofread: to read and mark errors, usually in typeset text

Proposal: detailed description of a manuscript, usually nonfiction, and its intended market

Query: letter to an editor to promote interest in a manuscript or idea

Reading fee: fee charged by anyone to read a manuscript

Reprint: another printing of a book; often a different format, such as a paperback reprint of a hardcover title

Response time: average length of time for an editor to accept or reject a submission and contact the writer with a decision

Résumé: short account of one's qualifications, including educational and professional background and publishing credits

Revision: reworking of a piece of writing

Royalty: publisher's payment to an author (usually a percentage) for each copy of the author's work sold

SAE: self-addressed envelope

SASE: self-addressed, stamped envelope

Self-publishing: author assumes complete responsibility for publishing and marketing the book, including printing, binding, advertising, and distributing the book

Simultaneous submission: manuscript submitted to more than one publisher at the same time; also known as a multiple submission

Slush pile: term used within the publishing industry to describe unsolicited manuscripts

Small press: an independent publisher that publishes a limited or specialized list

Solicited manuscript: manuscript that an editor has asked for or agreed to consider

Subsidiary rights: book contract rights other than book publishing rights, such as book club, movie rights, etc.

Subsidy publishing: author pays publisher for all or part of a book's publication, promotion, and sale

Synopsis: condensed description of a fiction manuscript

Tearsheet: page from a magazine or newspaper containing your printed story or article

Trade book: book published for retail sale in bookstores

Unsolicited manuscript: any manuscript not specifically requested by an editor; "no unsolicited manuscripts" generally means the editors will only consider queries or manuscripts submitted by agents

Vanity press: see **Subsidy publishing**

Whole language: educational approach integrating literature into classroom curricula

Work-for-hire: work specifically ordered, commissioned, and owned by a publisher for its exclusive use

Writers' guidelines: publisher's editorial objectives or specifications, which usually include word lengths, readership level, and subject matter

Young adult: children ages 12 years and older

Young reader: the general classification of books written for readers between the ages of 5 and 8

Gateway to the
Markets ▶▶▶

The Past Perfect: History Writing

By Ellen Hopkins

A small historical moment: Lynne Cheney, wife of the Vice President of the United States, establishes a charitable fund that will finance an annual award for the best work of history written for young people. The James Madison Book Award will have a cash prize of $10,000. Cheney, author of the children's book *America: A Patriotic Primer*, said at the announcement of the fund, "I hope by recognizing books that teach children and young people about our country's past, this award will encourage authors to take up this subject and publishers to seek out writers who can make American history come alive."

You don't have to be a history buff to take up the subject, or to give life to the past. Armed with a solid interest in something that has already happened, you can form a battle plan: One, locate your target. Two, research to find an angle of attack. Three, turn on the computer, and charge!

History is a narrative of past events, usually accompanied

Ellen Hopkins has published 20 nonfiction titles and has a young adult novel under contract with Simon & Schuster. She is also a freelance adult writer and owns Juniper Creek Publishing, which publishes *Three Leaping Frogs, Northern Nevada's Fun Newspaper for Kids.*

by an analysis of causes and effects. It is not only the *who, what, when,* and *where,* but also the *why.* What or who caused the event, when and where? What has happened since, in large part because of this wrinkle in time? Why was the episode important? And why do you want to write about it?

Your Go-for-It Button

Every editor will tell you enthusiasm for your subject is critical. If you don't care about what you're writing about, it's doubtful your readers will either. You will spend weeks, perhaps even months, on this project. Make sure it's something you love. Think about what excites you about history, and whether you're drawn to a certain time period or to learning more about a specific historical person. Maybe you heard about an event and thought, "Wow, that would make a great book." These are fine places to start.

But if none of the above has pushed your go-for-it button, try starting with something you're passionate about. If you love tennis, share that passion with young readers through the history of the game. Talk about where it started, its earliest players, when the sport came to America, how it evolved.

My first nonfiction book took root on a trip to the Smithsonian National Air and Space Museum, in Washington, D.C. I've always loved aviation and while there I saw an exhibit called Women in Flight. My first thought was, "Wouldn't it be great to let young women know they can be more than models and movie stars? They can be pilots and astronauts!" I went home and straight to work on *Petticoat Pilots, How Women Won Their Wings.* That book has yet to find a home, but the one that followed, *Air Devils: Sky Racers, Sky Divers and Stunt Pilots,* did publish and is selling very well.

Once you think you know what you want to write about, research. No, not the subject. Not yet, anyway. First, take a look at who might want a book on this topic. Many publishers maintain established series. If you think your idea is a good fit, query the house regarding your proposed subject, then write to suit their guidelines. With luck, they might send you a contract before you even start the writing process. (If it's your first book, however, you will probably have to write it *on spec*—speculation—to prove you can complete a publishable manuscript, under deadline.)

Air Devils was originally a 2,500-word photo essay for younger readers about the history of air racing. I queried Perfection Learning Corporation. Editorial Director Sue Thies liked the idea, but wanted 10,000 words for their hi-lo middle-grade series. (Hi-lo refers to high interest subject matter, written at a lower vocabulary level to entice reluctant readers.) Thies asked me to write the book to fit, and the rest is—yes, history.

A Hungry Market

Even if you're not writing for a specific series, you must assess market need. Obviously, eras like the American Revolution and the Civil War have been well covered. There are hundreds of books on these broad topics, from biographies to historical romances. If you want to write about these time periods, you'll have to narrow your focus and find a very fresh angle and voice. Mark out a good, solid angle of attack.

What the Editors Say about History

Read what these four editors have to say about the markets for history and about their companies:

- ◆ Marcia Marshall, Senior Editor, Lerner Publishing, page 261.
- ◆ Sue Thies, Editorial Director, Perfection Learning Corporation, page 324.
- ◆ Hope Killcoyne, Managing Editor, Silver Moon Press, page 369.
- ◆ Timothy Travaglini, Publisher, Walker Books for Young Readers, page 405.

Air Devils is really the history of aviation—a very large topic to cover in 10,000 words. I chose to attack it from the angle of man's love of competition. Who was the first to think about flying? Perhaps a caveman trekking across the tundra, envying birds? Who was the first into the air? Did ancient Incas use hot air balloons to track game and enemy movements? My research said maybe!

The Places to Go, the People to Meet

Okay, you've settled on your subject and angle of attack. Now it's time for some serious research on the topic. One reason nonfiction remains a hungry market is we learn new things about old subjects almost daily. Rarely is it a good idea to research using books more than three or four years old. The exception might be autobiographies by an important figure in your story.

Encyclopedias will give you the pertinent facts, but use them cautiously. Again, use only the latest available. Online encyclopedias can be a good choice, as they are updated regularly, but remember even these are only a very first step. And please beware of simply rewording the information you find. Your job is not only to state the facts, but to bring those facts to life.

You can start by using other websites on the Internet as well. You must be very aware of the source of the website and its likelihood of accuracy. Generally, you can rely on Internet addresses with the extensions *edu; gov; mil; org.* Do be leery of *home pages*, unless they belong to experts on your subject, such as academics.

Another valuable resource is Infotrac, a database of articles taken from magazines and periodicals. You can access Infotrac at your library or, if you have a library card, through your home computer. Simply go to your county library's website and ask for the Infotrac link. Type in your subject and refine your search by requesting articles with the full text and the most recent articles first.

Often these articles will lead you to experts in the field. Always try to secure interviews with them if possible. Don't worry. Most people love to talk about their work, and the information and anecdotes you will collect are invaluable.

While researching my book *Countdown To Yesterday, the Earth's Prehistoric Past,* I came across the name of an anthropologist conducting research in Central America. The magazine article pointed me to his university, and his department put me in touch with him. Tom Dillehay was a treasure trove of information about the origins of humans in North America. Much of what he told me he had only recently discovered. My book contained the most up-to-date theories

Research Sites

Free Sites
- **Factmonster.com** Kid-style encyclopedia articles.
- **Discovery.com** Discovery Channel online.
- **Nationalgeographic.com**
- **Howstuffworks.com**
- **SI.edu** Smithsonian Institution.
- **LOC.gov** Library of Congress.

Pay Sites
- **EB.com** Encyclopedia Britannica, with Internet links.
- **Elibrary.com** Book and magazine excerpts.

available at the time I wrote it. That would not have been possible had I used an outdated book as a resource.

Try museums and historical societies, which sometimes house oral histories, recorded by the families of local luminaries. Consider the insights you might gather! You can also query the Library of Congress (LOC). While researching a biography of the Stinson sisters, I was able to access Marjorie Stinson's personal papers, including her diary, through the LOC. Not only did I discover her history, but her feelings. This brought Madge's very own voice to my book, *Storming the Skies.*

Full Circle
So now you've researched and have tons of great information. Time to begin the writing itself. Your lead or opening is crucial to drawing in readers and keeping them reading. One trick of the trade is to begin with a question you feel needs to be answered. Then write full circle. Build your readers' knowledge, step by step, until they can answer the question themselves by the end of your story.

Another idea is to open with an anecdote—a short tale, illustrating the time period and/or person you're writing about. "I think anecdotal information can capture a child's interest," says Ellen Fockler, head librarian for the Washoe County, Nevada, School District. "Kids love learning something specific about a famous person or event. Perhaps that's one reason the stories of Lincoln foreseeing his own death, for example, are so persistent."

Fockler also says it's important for content and language to be age-appropriate, but not watered down. "I've seen some books, fiction and nonfiction, where sentence fragments are used to *simplify* the language; I object to that. Even the youngest students need to read sentences that are correct and complete. Content should be interesting, presented in a readable narrative."

When writing history for younger readers, the order you present information in is usually fairly straightforward, chronologically. But if possible, relate past events to current ones. "Information should be relevant," explains Fockler. "If history can be tied to the things kids see happening around them today, they may find it more memorable."

So consider your passions. Do your research. Outline your battle plan. And off you go. Who knows? Maybe in a year or two, the James Madison Award will be yours.

On Voice

How will you tell your story? Will you write a straight nonfiction piece, or use your research to create historical fiction? You can always do both, and why not? Wouldn't it be awesome to get paid twice to write about your passion?

Of course, you'll have to do one or the other first. Writing the nonfiction book first will give you the solid historical background to wrap your fiction piece around. With a solid feel for the era, your novel or short story will come remarkably to life.

Remember, however, as you move into fiction writing, story is more important than facts. Characters and plot are integral to all great fiction, and more important than place. Use setting and sensory details as tools to give your story shape.

Most editors prefer history to be told in the third person. Be sure to double-check guidelines if you want to tell your story in first person. Many editors also frown on fictional dialogue in a nonfiction story. Be sure to ask before you invent a conversation!

Toddler Books: A World without Limits

By Susan Heyboer O'Keefe

In a time when parents read to their infants while they're still in the womb, it's no wonder that babies and toddlers are a prime segment of the children's book market. From 'zero' to two or three is the age category for toddler books. Many writers wonder what they can write about for children whose world is circumscribed by the bars of a playpen. How can they write for an audience that is pre-verbal, then pre-literate?

Stand Out from the Crowd

Writers who see the toddler market within these limits end up limiting their submissions to a narrow, few topics. Editors readily reveal what they're seeing too much of in their slush piles: "Rhyming manuscripts and ABC and counting books," says Erin Clarke, Associate Editor at Alfred A. Knopf and Crown Books for Young Readers. Of these submissions, Clarke says, very few are accepted for publication, "because the marketplace is teeming with them."

"I see too many bedtime stories for this age group," says Sarah Ketchersid, Candlewick Press Editor. Julie Strauss-

Author of 16 books, Susan Heyboer O'Keefe has written the best-selling *One Hungry Monster,* the upcoming *More Hungry Monsters,* the teen mystery *My Life and Death by Alexandra Canarsie,* and the tentatively titled *Death by Eggplant,* a middle-grade novel to be published by Roaring Brook Press.

Gabel, Editor at Dutton Books for Children, says she sees too much "easy, predictable rhyme," and too many "saccharine-sweet books, too."

Yet look in any publisher's catalogue, season after season, and you will find alphabet, counting, and bedtime books, lots of sweetness, lots of rhyme. How did those writers get past the editorial bias and make it to publication?

Cindy Eng Alvarez, Vice President and Editorial Director of Little Simon Books, explains where many writers go wrong. "While the A to Z concept is an important one for toddlers, I find that authors use it as their main idea or hook and try to combine any theme or subject matter with it. As a result, not all of the words make sense and/or are appropriate for the age group."

What about verse? "A lot of beginning writers feel compelled to copy a master, like Dr. Seuss," says Alvarez. "I often find that writers sacrifice story, sentence and line structure, and language for the sake of rhyme."

What the Editors Say about Toddler Books

Read what these four editors have to say about their companies and this colorful market:

- Sarah Ketchersid, Editor, Candlewick Press, page 117.
- Julie Strauss-Gabel, Editor, Dutton Books, page 173.
- Erin Clarke, Associate Editor, Random House, Alfred A. Knopf & Crown Books for Young Readers, page 254.
- Cindy Eng Alvarez, Vice President and Editorial Director, Little Simon, page 270.

A World of Discovery

If you take away the three most frequently seen topics of bedtime books and ABC and counting books, what's left?

Everything!

"There are so many developmental milestones at this time," says Strauss-Gabel, "so much that is vibrant and exciting to children discovering their world for the very first time. Their books need not be limited to one format or one mood."

Read, Read, Read!

Stephen King makes a living scaring people. True to form, he scared those of us trying to follow in his footsteps when he said you can't write unless you read two hours every day; that two hours of reading gives you the minimum "word tools" you need to write.

Before you throw out your pens and laptop, consider two things: First, two hours of reading a day is a goal, not an instant achievement. Second, you may not be able to read two hours every day, but in no other genre could you read two books a day. Or three. Or four. Toddler books make the ideal real. Visit your local bookstore and in a half hour's browsing you can easily go through a handful of books. Then bring your shopping bag to the library and check out a bundle of favorites and classics every week. Saturate yourself in the art and craft of children's writing, all kinds for all ages.

Our four editors gave their personal picks from their company selections, an excellent starting point for your own reading, as well as a source of insight into each editor's taste. They also provided their favorite classics. Because so many titles were repeated, this list eliminates the duplications.

Julie Strauss-Gabel, Dutton Books

- *All My Little Ducklings*, by Monica Wellington
- *Minerva Louise and the Red Truck,* by Janet Morgan Stoeke
- *Wake Up, Mama,* by Hope Vestergaard, illustrated by Theirry Courtin

Sarah Ketchersid, Candlewick Books

- *I Kissed the Baby*, by Mary Murphy
- *Hug,* by Jez Alborough
- *So Much,* by Trish Cooke, illustrated by Helen Oxenbury
- *Owl Babies*, by Martin Waddell, illustrated by Patrick Benson
- The Maisy titles, by Lucy Cousins

Read, Read, Read!

Erin Clarke, Random House
- *Grow Babies!, Wow Babies!,* and *Baby Talk!,* by Penny Gentieu
- *A Color of His Own* and *Let's Play,* by Leo Lionni
- *My Many Colored Days,* by Dr. Seuss, illustrated by Steve Johnson and Lou Fancher
- *A Countdown to Spring, An Animal Counting Book,* by Janet Schulman, illustrated by Meilo So
- *Hushabye,* by John Burningham

Cindy Eng Alvarez, Simon & Schuster
- *Chicka Chicka Boom Boom,* by Bill Martin Jr. and John Archambault, illustrated by Lois Ehlert
- *Counting Kisses: A Kiss & Read Book* and *Where Is Baby's Belly Button?,* by Karen Katz
- *Blue Hat, Green Hat* and *Moo Moo, Baaa, La La La,* by Sandra Boynton
- *Good Night, Sweet Butterflies: A Color Dreamland,* by Dawn Bentley, illustrated by Heather Cahoon

Classics—Old and New
- *"More More More," Said the Baby,* by Vera B. Williams
- *Winnie the Pooh,* by A. A. Milne
- *The Very Hungry Caterpillar,* by Eric Carle
- *Gotta Go! Gotta Go!,* by Sam Swope
- *Pat the Bunny,* by Dorothy Kunhardt
- *Titch,* by Pat Hutchins
- *Good Night, Gorilla,* by Peggy Rathmann
- *Brown Bear, Brown Bear, What Do You See?,* by Bill Martin Jr. and Eric Carle
- *Richard Scarry's Best Word Book Ever,* by Richard Scarry
- *Humphrey's Corner* and *Humphrey's Bedtime,* by Sally Hunter

This is the age when children are discovering, like explorers in uncharted waters, what it means, what it feels like, to be alive. Just about every aspect of the world around them can be a topic if handled well. Their inner world, too, can be a rich source of subject matter—the senses and the emotions—but give everything a toddler treatment. Describe things broadly and briefly, the word equivalent of bright, bold colors. Toddler books are not the arena for subtlety of feeling, clever wordplay, lengthy stories, or too many characters.

Think of finger painting as a metaphor: Pictures made in finger-paint's primary colors work best when done in simple strokes. Try to get fancy and mix colors as you would oil paints, and you get a muddy mess.

A Toddler's Eye View

Most successful adult fiction stays within the main character's point of view. For a successful toddler book, stay within the toddler's point of view. What's important to the toddler? What makes up his or her day?

"For the most part, a great toddler book is about toddlers," says Ketchersid. "That's what they are most interested in after all—themselves!"

Strauss-Gabel agrees: "As with all picture books, I find books for very young children with an adult, outsider's perspective frustrating—candy-coated or out-of-touch views of toddlers, books about how adults wish children could be. Even the littlest readers need to see themselves and their concerns addressed in books."

The five senses are the toddler's keys to discovery and five roads to fun. But put away laundry list descriptions of "Jane saw the dog. Jane petted the dog. The dog smelled good." *Pat the Bunny* has been written, and even 40 years later, imitators can't come close. Dorothy Kunhardt's book was "interactive" decades before the word was invented.

Yet creativity will always find new ways to make familiar subjects soar. Consider how the sense of touch is explored in the wonderful *Tickle, Tickle,* by Dakari Hru and illustrated by Ken Wilson-Max: "me papa tickle me feet/he call it "finger treat"/me scream and run each time he come/me papa tickle me feet." The toddler's joyous dread of being tickled by a loved one is a universal experience. Add language with island rhythms and vivid art, and you've got a winning book that will not only get repeat requests, it will lead to interaction between child and reader. Other ways to lead to interaction are through simple repetition and perfect rhyme that allow toddlers to anticipate and repeat refrains. A wonderful example of this is Dr. Seuss's *Mr. Brown Can Moo! Can You?*

A Toddler's Day

Toddler routines also make good topics, and not just the simple day presented in the soothing, back-in-print *My World*, by Margaret Wise Brown and illustrator Clement Hurd. For example, the Japanese import *Everyone Poops*, by Taro Gomi and translated by Amanda Mayer Stinchecum, proves that any topic can be a good topic, handled the right way. Many critics panned this book, but parents have bought it by the thousands and kids love it. It's instructive and reassuring but the lessons take a back seat to the outrageous humor. Even parents find it silly and fun, which brings up a good point: Every toddler book has two audiences.

This is a point of agreement among the editors, that a book must appeal to child and reader. On the simplest level, the adult will be reading the book over and over, sometimes over and over in a single sitting, so it has to hold up through repetition. On a higher level, the book should somehow also touch the lives of both child and reader to be truly successful. Books that touch the reader's heart are perhaps the easiest example to give (though not the easiest to write). These include *Guess How Much I Love You*, by Sam McBratney, illustrated by Anita Jeram; *I Love You the Purplest*, by Barbara M. Joosse, illustrated by Mary Whyte; *Love You Forever*, by Robert Munsch, illustrated by Sheila McGraw; and of course, *The Runaway Bunny*, another classic by Brown and Hurd. A title like *Where the Wild Things Are*, by Maurice Sendak has a more subtle and layered adult appeal.

More Than Hugs and Growls

A toddler's day goes far beyond hugs. There is so much for them to see and do and learn. Yet because of the age, many beginning writers think that a lesson for toddlers means writing *down*. "A lot of people think that they need to dumb down concepts for kids, which is a complete misconception," says Alvarez. One way to dumb down a story is to make its moral explicit. "Writers for this age level have the tendency to make the text overly didactic for the audience," says Clarke. Writers seldom pick blunt, moralistic tracts for their own reading. They're simply not enjoyable. The same holds true for both child and adult readers of toddler books.

Nonfiction for toddlers offers both a way to avoid preachiness plus an opportunity to rise above the slush pile, simply because so few beginning writers submit nonfiction manuscripts. The advantages stop there, however. Nonfiction for toddlers is just as difficult to write, since editors are not looking for dictionary-type entries stripped down to one-syllable words. Take a look at some toddler-size bits of information, such as that in the youngest I Spy books, by Jean Marzollo and Walter Wick; *Here Are My Hands,* by Bill Martin, Jr., John Archambault, and Ted Rand; and even *Everyone Poops.* You'll find in these and other nonfiction books many of the same techniques you use in fiction, including verse, narrative, dialogue, but wrapped around information toddlers need and their parents want them to know.

No Limits

Toddler books present a unique challenge to writers, but offer many unique rewards that make the effort well worth it. The writer becomes the map, the native guide, to helping children unlock the wonders of a brand new world. And by making the process engaging and exciting, an author also helps create a future generation of readers.

Whither Thou Goest: Finding Your Way through the Religious Fiction Market

By Sharelle Byars Moranville

The climax of Kimberly Willis Holt's National Book Award winner *When Zachary Beaver Came to Town* comes when Zachary is finally baptized in a Texas pond. The tension of Cynthia Rylant's *A Fine White Dust*, a Newbery Honor Book, comes from the teenage main character's choosing between Preacher Man and his parents. Max Lucado's *You Are Special* never uses the words *baptism, preacher,* or *God,* yet the story is intended to assure children that no matter what travails they experience, they are dear in God's eyes.

On the surface, the first two books would seem more religious and the latter more general. Yet, as it happens, *When Zachary Beaver Came to Town* and *A Fine White Dust* were published by secular publishers, and *You Are Special* was published by a religious press. This suggests that

Sharelle Byars Moranville is the author of *Over the River*, a coming-of-age story, and *The Purple Ribbon*, a chapter book. She writes for *Storydog.com* and is also the author of many stories that have appeared in children's magazines.

much spiritual content finds its way into secular novels, and that many religious or moral messages for the religious market are subtly but beautifully communicated, without the specific mention of religion or morality.

Where does this apparent paradox put writers when they are trying to determine where to send their manuscripts? Should they submit to religious or secular publishing houses? How do writers produce the best possible books that will be saleable in one market or the other?

And—earlier in the creative process—how do writers, especially those just beginning their careers, know what kinds of books they ought to be writing? Mystery novels that incidentally teach the Torah? Chapter books with talking animals? Christian romances?

If a religious publisher specifically says in market directories or writing periodicals that it is looking for board books that teach golden rule behavior, for example, a 50-word book about sharing might seem right. Writing a little story about sharing crayons with big sister couldn't be that hard could it? Many people can write a 50-word book about sharing, but only some can write a saleable one, and you want to be one of them.

Following the Star

The fact is, publishers receive far more manuscripts than they can use—many of them very, very good. Because they are so overwhelmed by manuscripts they can't use, Zonderkidz, a leading publisher of children's religious books, meets this surfeit of manuscripts by asking writers to post their proposals on the Manuscript Service section of the Evangelical Christian Publishers Association (ECPA) website. Zonderkidz Editor Gwen Ellis says that although she has not yet bought any manuscripts from postings on the ECPA site, she thinks that it offers writers hope and an opportunity to show their work.

Even if authors submit directly to a publishing house, the competition is still intense. To succeed, writers need to find their best niches or, within the specific area of religious fiction, a sub-niche. They need to discover what they write best within the category. Most writers have only a few writing categories in which they can truly star. Without that star power, the chance of a manuscript being selected is small.

"Choose to write not what is fashionable or what we think may sell but what comes out of our deepest selves—the sounds from our own particular hearts," writes Katherine Paterson, author of *The Same Stuff as Stars, Lyddie, The Great Gilly Hopkins,* and many other children's books. ("The Responsibility to Write: Stay True to Your Heart and Mind." *The Writer,* March 2003).

How does a writer hear these sounds and ultimately shape them into strong religious fiction manuscripts? Often the answer to the first question is surprisingly close to home.

A list of 10 favorite books is a good starting place. The list should contain books that were cherished in childhood, books that were beloved in adolescence, and books that are still captivating in adulthood. A writer who has a shelf full of dog-eared Christian romances will have a natural affinity for telling that same kind of story.

Susan Heyboer O'Keefe writes both secular and religious fiction, and is author of *Love Me, Love You; My Life and Death by Alexandra Canarsie; What Does a Priest Do? What Does a Nun Do?,* among others, She recommends that writers "look first at the magazines and books you yourself read for spiritual nourishment. Chances are good that you've internalized these beliefs and language."

A thoughtful reading history is a good basis for starting to listen to those "sounds from our own particular hearts." So is the recognition of our passions—who we are deep down. Religious writer Kimn Gollnick, whose work is anthologized in books for the Christian market such as *Chicken Soup for the Christian Woman's Soul* and *God's Abundance for Women,* and has been published in *Pockets* and *R-A-D-A-R,* speaks of her love of God and Jesus Christ: "I spend time studying issues in light of the Bible. It's natural that I write religious fiction," she says.

Woven Naturally
Although personal conviction and lifelong passions are reliable clues to where a writer's true star power lies, they

are not enough. Somewhere along the way, all writers of fiction must master the rudiments of good storytelling.

In religious writing, storytelling may have an extra burden. As Leonard Goss, Editorial Director at Broadman & Holman, says, "The author must communicate in a style that holds one's attention." While that's true for all children's fiction, it is perhaps especially essential in religious writing because the lessons, doctrines, or beliefs are too often conveyed heavy-handedly. Religious publishers want high-quality, professional work, not just conviction. In religious stories, a young main character should realistically figure out the moral of a story independently. A well-intentioned adult character should not be the one to deliver the moral message. Remember that kids like to read about kids, not wise adults, and they like to see fictional kids solve their own problems. There should be no lectures, and the message at the core of the story should be clear.

> ## What the Editors Say about Religious Fiction
>
> Read more about the current needs and perspectives of these editors of religious fiction:
>
> - Michelle Cook, Assistant Managing Editor, Augsburg Books, page 90.
> - Leonard Goss, Editorial Director, Broadman & Holman, page 112.
> - Heather Gemmen, Acquisitions Editor, Faith Kidz, page 188.
> - Gwen Ellis, Editor, Zonderkidz, page 424.

"In a children's story, the theme is based on a biblical principle like forgiveness, being kind, honoring parents, personal sacrifice, and so on, and many times includes a Bible scripture," says Gollnick. "The challenge is to do all this without sounding preachy, but to weave this message through your story as naturally as possible."

Stream of Truth
Once the story is complete and the manuscript is polished to perfection, where should it go—to a religious house or a

secular publisher? Begin with a thoughtful analysis of the manuscript to decide. O'Keefe says, "Know the real point of your story. If it's to explain a specific element of faith or to show God's love, the chances are that you should be looking at religious publishers."

Many children's religious fiction publishers want an expression of a specific belief system. Nachum Shapiro, the Managing Editor of Judaica Press, a prominent Orthodox Jewish publisher, says, "We ask ourselves two things when considering a children's book manuscript. One, will this book accomplish something positive for Jewish children? Two, do we think this book will succeed? If the answer to the first question is no, because the story and/or message teach a lesson that conflicts with Torah values, then we don't even bother asking the second question." But, he adds, "We might also be interested in a book that teaches a more general good lesson, a lesson that Western society may share in common with Torah."

Goss explains that Broadman & Holman's "children's material does not have to be blatantly or overtly Christian, but it does have to stand within the stream of Christian truth and it does have to represent the wider Protestant evangelical children's market."

Michelle Cook, Assistant Managing Editor for Augsburg Books and Acting Children's Acquisitions Editor, says that a manuscript suitable for their house must have Christian content. She recounts a writer sending a wonderful proposal for a book on grief, but the manuscript didn't mention God. "Because we felt so strongly about the subject," Cook says, "we simply asked the author if she would mind adding a spiritual angle to the book. She agreed, and we published it."

When writers are narrowing their market targets down to specific publishers, research is paramount. Good market research takes time. Sometimes inexperienced writers become impatient and start shooting at those targets wildly. Unless they're very lucky, they're not going to hit anything.

O'Keefe gives this advice: "Read actual books or articles from the publisher, not just the guidelines." It will deepen an understanding of what a publisher really means. O'Keefe continues, "For example, the guidelines may read 'interested in Christmas books.' In actuality, this may mean that one publisher would accept a Christmas book in which Santa Claus figures heavily, while another would accept a Christmas book centering on the Incarnation of Christ."

Sometimes a religious publisher's requirements are very specific about sources. Gollnick points out that "many houses specify which Bible translation they prefer, such as King James, New American Standard, New International Version, etc. The major concern of religious publishers is respect for their beliefs, so be sure you understand them."

An Alternative

Once a writer finishes a thoughtful analysis of the story and of the market, and the manuscript is ready to go out, does it need to be essentially "print-ready" when it lands on the editor's desk?

It does need to be a strong manuscript, but many religious fiction publishers expect to work with their authors to perfect the story. Ellis, at Zonderkidz, and Goss, at Broadman & Holman, both say that their editorial staffs make plans to work with writers in very active ways to develop the best books possible.

But if, after several tries, a writer can't make any headway in the book market, Gollnick suggests starting with religious magazine markets. "Religious editors like to see that you've published short fiction in markets like Sunday school take-home papers and children's magazines," she says, "perhaps because this shows your ability to write a story while understanding the religious market. Don't overlook these lower-paying markets. Editors peruse these publications and become familiar with the writers publishing in them, giving you that edge of familiarity with them."

To use a corporate analogy, we don't become vice presidents in the fourth month of employment. Likewise, in writing, it often takes time and work and talent, then more time and work and talent to break into the book market. But don't give up if success seems to come slowly. Make sure you've found the perfect niche—your star place.

Listings ▶▶▶

How to Use the Listings

On the following pages are over 500 profiles of publishers involved in the wide range of children's publishing. Over 50 publishers are new to the directory. These publishing houses produce a variety of material from parenting guides, textbooks, and classroom resources to picture books, photo essays, middle-grade novels, and biographies.

Each year we update every listing through mailed surveys and telephone interviews. While we verify everything in the listing before we go to press, it is not uncommon for information such as contact names, addresses, and editorial needs to change suddenly. Therefore, we suggest that you always read the publisher's most recent writers' guidelines before submitting a query letter or manuscript.

If you are unable to find a particular publisher, check the Publishers' Index beginning on page 578 to see if it is cited elsewhere in the book. We do not list presses that publish over 50% of their material by requiring writers to pay all or part of the cost of publishing. While we cannot endorse or vouch for the quality of every press we list, we do try to screen out publishers of questionable quality.

To help you judge a publisher's receptivity to unsolicited submissions, we include a Freelance Potential section in each listing. This is where we identify the number of titles published in 2003 that were written by unpublished writers, authors new to the publishing house, and agented authors. We also provide the total number of query letters and unsolicited manuscripts a publisher receives each year. When possible, we list the number of books published in 2003 by category (e.g. picture books, young adult novels).

Use this information and the other information included in the listing to locate publishers that are looking for the type of material you have written or plan to write. Become familiar with the style and content of the house by studying its catalogue and a few recent titles.

Denlinger's Publishers

P.O. Box 1030
Edgewater, FL 32132-1030

Editor: Patricia Red

Publisher's Interests
This electronic publisher features fiction for all ages. It welcomes almost any genre, but does not publish poetry, illustrated books, erotica, or textbooks.
Website: www.thebookden.com

Freelance Potential
Published 24 titles (4 juvenile) in 2003: all were developed from unsolicited submissions and 3 were by agented authors. Of the 24 titles, most were by unpublished writers and 12 were by authors who were new to the publishing house. Receives 1,700 unsolicited mss yearly.
- **Fiction:** Published 2 chapter books, 5–10 years; and 2 middle-grade books, 8–12 years. Genres include adventure, fantasy, folklore, and historical and inspirational fiction.
- **Representative Titles:** *Teammates, The Universal Bond* by Bob Weissman is the story of Katie Calhoun and her adventures at a posh girls' school. *An Audience of One* by Beth Staas (12+ years) follows the experiences of a young pianist hoping to become a concert musician and to attend the Julliard School of Music in New York.

Submissions and Payment
Guidelines and catalogue available at website. Send complete ms with market analysis and biography. Accepts disk submissions (WordPerfect text), and email submissions to acquisitions@thebookden.com. SASE. Responds in 3–6 months. Publication in 6–8 months. Royalty.

Editor's Comments
We began as a traditional publishing house based in Virginia in 1926. For years we specialized in nonfiction titles about pets. We began to move into fiction in the 1950s and now focus exclusively on it. Electronic publishing is the way of the future. For now it also represents a "foot in the door" for new authors. For the coming year, we are interested in queries for inspirational fiction and historical fiction, especially with strong female characters. We do not want books under 100 pages.

Icon Key

☆ New Listing   🖱 Epublisher

⊗ Not currently accepting submissions

Abdo Publishing Company

Suite 622
4940 Viking Drive
Edina, MN 55435

Editor-in-Chief: Paul Abdo

Publisher's Interests

Abdo Publishing Company specializes in nonfiction educational materials that meet national curriculum standards for children in preschool through grade eight. Its specialties include biography, history, geography, science, social studies, and sports.
Website: www.abdopub.com

Freelance Potential

Published 200 titles in 2003: 1 was developed from an unsolicited submission. Of the 200 titles, 1 was by an unpublished writer and 3 were by authors who were new to the publishing house. Receives 120 queries yearly.

- **Nonfiction:** Publishes early picture books, 0–4 years; easy-to-read books, 4–7 years; story picture books, 4–10 years; chapter books, 5–10 years; and middle-grade books, 8–12 years. Topics include travel, geography, animals, nature, science, social studies, sports, history, leisure, and multicultural and ethnic subjects. Also publishes reference books and biographies.
- **Representative Titles:** *Golden Gate Bridge* (grades K–4) discusses the construction details and monument features of this national landmark; part of the All Aboard America series. *Tabby Cats* by Stuart A. Kallen (grades K–5) explores the eating habits, growth patterns, communication, and care of tabbies; part of the Cats series.

Submissions and Payment

Query with résumé. No unsolicited mss. Accepts photocopies, computer printouts, and simultaneous submissions if identified. SASE. Responds in 2–4 months. Publication on October 1 of each year. Flat fee.

Editor's Comments

Send us your résumé for future consideration if you are a freelance writer, illustrator, or photographer with the credentials to write for us. Do not submit a complete manuscript—we do not read them, and they will not be returned. Visit our website if you wish to submit your résumé electronically.

Absey and Company

23011 Northcrest Drive
Spring, TX 77389

Publisher: Edward E. Wilson

Publisher's Interests
Now in its eighth year, Absey and Company publishes fiction
and nonfiction for early readers through young adults. Picture books, chapter books, and novels can be found in its
catalogue, along with some language arts resource materials
for teachers.
Website: www.absey.com

Freelance Potential
Published 8 titles (6 juvenile) in 2003: most were developed
from unsolicited submissions. Of the 8 titles, 3 were by
unpublished writers and 2 were by authors who were new to
the publishing house. Receives 1,200 queries yearly.
- **Fiction:** Published 2 story picture books, 4–10 years; 2 chapter
  books, 5–10 years; and 2 young adult books, 12–18 years.
- **Nonfiction:** Publishes educational titles, 0–18 years. Features
  biographies and books about religion and history. Also publishes educational activity books and poetry collections, as well
  as language arts resource titles for educators.
- **Representative Titles:** *Where I'm From* by George Ella Lyon
  (YA) tells how a poet from Kentucky uses her background in
  her work and takes young writers on a journey that leads to
  the creation of a poem. *Dragonfly* by Alice McLerran is an
  adventure story about a boy who is trying to raise a dragon
  in his home without anybody knowing about it.

Submissions and Payment
Guidelines available. Query with résumé, outline, and sample
chapters. Accepts photocopies. No simultaneous submissions. SASE. Responds in 6–9 months. Publication in 1 year.
Payment policy varies.

Editor's Comments
Send us a query that includes information about your relevant
qualifications and previous publishing experience, as well as a
chapter-by-chapter outline and two or three sample chapters.
Send your query directly to us—we don't accept submissions
from literary agents.

Action Publishing

P.O. Box 391
Glendale, CA 91209

Publisher: Michael Metzler

Publisher's Interests
Action Publishing specializes in adventure and fantasy books for children from birth to 18 years. Many of its titles are published as part of popular series.
Website: www.actionpublishing.com

Freelance Potential
Published 12 titles (8 juvenile) in 2003: 10 were by agented authors. Receives numerous queries and mss yearly.
- **Fiction:** Publishes early picture books, 0–4 years; easy-to-read books, 4–7 years; story picture books, 4–10 years; middle-grade books, 8–12 years; and young adult books, 12–18 years. Genres include adventure and fantasy. Also publishes books in series.
- **Nonfiction:** Publishes middle-grade books, 8–12 years; and young adult books, 12–18 years. Topics include nature and the environment.
- **Representative Titles:** *The Family of Ree* by Scott E. Sutton (all ages) introduces the world of Ree, a whimsical land of wizards and giant sea beasties; part of the Family of Ree series. *Merrywinkle* by Anne Fewell (3–10 years) presents the adventures of Santa's big brother.

Submissions and Payment
Guidelines available at website. Accepts queries and mss through literary agents only. SASE. Response time and publication period vary. Royalty; advance.

Editor's Comments
All of our books, no matter what the target age group, must have a fantasy or adventure theme—it's what Action Publishing is all about! We will consider submissions sent by agents only. If you're interested in having your book published by us, you must first get an agent who will adequately and enthusiastically represent you. We are looking for adventure and fantasy books for children of all ages, but are especially interested in books that will work as part of a series, with either a common character or theme tying the titles together.

Africa World Press

Suite B
541 West Ingham Avenue
Trenton, NJ 08607

President & Publisher: Kassahun Checole

Publisher's Interests
Africa World Press has a children's list that includes folk-tales, picture books, and books that address social and cultural issues. All of its juvenile titles have African, African-American, Caribbean, or Latin-American themes. For adults, it publishes scholarly works on Africa and its diaspora. It was launched in 1983.
Website: www.africanworld.com

Freelance Potential
Published 120 titles (16 juvenile) in 2003: 1 was by an agented author. Receives 500 queries yearly.
- **Fiction:** Publishes young adult books, 12–18 years. Features folktales.
- **Nonfiction:** Publishes books about African, African-American, Caribbean, and Latin-American history, culture, and social issues. Also publishes educational and parenting titles.
- **Representative Titles:** *Imani and the Flying Africans* by Janice Liddell is a story about a young boy who learns about his race and familial history from his mother, who tells him the story during a car ride from Detroit to Savannah. *The Legend of the African Bao-Bab Tree* by Bobbi Dooley Hunter tells about a beautiful tree that complains to the Great Spirit of the wild plains about wanting to be the best, brightest, and most hand-some of all the African trees.

Submissions and Payment
Query with outline/synopsis and sample chapter. No unsolicited mss. Accepts photocopies, computer printouts, and simultaneous submissions if identified. SASE. Responds in 2 weeks. Publication in 6–12 months. Royalty; advance.

Editor's Comments
Unlike other small and medium-size presses, which often publish only a handful of books each year, we are dedicated to the publication of as many books as is feasible. Just remember that your book must relate to the African, African-American, Caribbean, or Latin-American experience.

Aladdin Paperbacks

Simon & Schuster Children's Publishing Division
4th Floor
1230 Avenue of the Americas
New York, NY 10020

Submissions Editor

Publisher's Interests
Paperback reprints of hardcovers from Simon & Schuster imprints are the foundation of Aladdin Paperbacks' list. Fiction and nonfiction titles for beginning readers to young adults are all part of the company's publishing program. Many of its titles appear as part of series.
Website: www.simonsayskids.com

Freelance Potential
Published 150 titles in 2003: 15 were developed from unsolicited submissions and 75 were by agented authors.
- **Fiction:** Publishes story picture books, 4–10 years; middle-grade novels, 8–12 years; and young adult books, 12–18 years. Genres include historical and contemporary fiction, mystery, suspense, and adventure.
- **Nonfiction:** Publishes biographies.
- **Representative Titles:** *Harriet Tubman and the Freedom Train* by Sharon Gayle (6–8 years) relates the story of one of the most famous heroes of the Civil War and her underground railroad. *Missing From Haymarket Square* by Harriette Gillem Robinet (9–13 years) is a fictional historical account of one girl and her father who are determined to participate in a demonstration in 1886 Chicago.

Submissions and Payment
Guidelines available. Query with biography, outline/synopsis, and writing sample. No unsolicited mss. SASE. Response time, publication period, and payment policy vary.

Editor's Comments
Competition here for new writers is very tough since most of our list is made up of reprints of previously publishesd books from the imprints of Simon & Schuster's Children's Publishing Division. However, if you feel confident that your book idea will turn heads because of its uniqueness, style, and readability, send us a query that details your plot and shows us what makes it special. We are especially interested in queries for middle-grade mysteries and books in series for young adults.

ALA Editions

American Library Association
50 East Huron Street
Chicago, IL 60611

Editorial Director: Patrick Hogan

Publisher's Interests
As the publishing arm of the American Library Association, ALA Editions offers a list of nonfiction titles written for professional researchers and librarians. Its current list includes titles on library service to young adults, building and maintaining collections, budgeting and finance, resource-based activities, the Internet, storytelling, and cataloguing.
Website: www.ala.org/editions

Freelance Potential
Published 35 titles in 2003: 3 were developed from unsolicited submissions. Of the 35 titles, 12 were by authors who were new to the publishing house. Receives 50 queries yearly.
- **Nonfiction:** Publishes textbooks, resource materials, and reference books for librarians and educators. Also offers children's library programming materials.
- **Representative Titles:** *Developing a Compensation Plan for Your Library* by Paula M. Singer (librarians) offers step-by-step strategies for developing compensation packages that can be tailored to individual libraries. *25 Latino Craft Projects* by Ana-Elba Pavon & Diana Borrego (librarians) features tips for creating and publicizing unique cultural programs for individual communities.

Submissions and Payment
Guidelines available at website. Query with outline/synopsis. SASE. Responds in 2–8 weeks. Publication in 7–9 months from completion of manuscript. Royalty.

Editor's Comments
We strive to bring library professionals and researchers the latest and most innovative materials possible to help make their jobs easier and more successful. We welcome writers with expertise in areas of interest to our audience. We suggest you study our current catalogue to gain a better understanding of the areas we cover. The catalogue will also give you a sense of the broad range of areas our publications cover and help you determine if your expertise meets our needs.

Alef Design Group

4423 Fruitland Avenue
Los Angeles, CA 90058

Submissions Editor: Jane Golub

Publisher's Interests
This publisher offers juvenile fiction and nonfiction about the
Jewish faith and Judaism. Alef Design Group produces books
and novels about Jewish history, holidays and celebrations,
and self-discovery. Its list also includes books about Jewish
family life and parenting.
Website: www.torahaura.com

Freelance Potential
Published 1 title in 2003. Receives 36 queries, 36 unsolicited
mss yearly.
- **Fiction:** Publishes story picture books, 4–10 years; and chapter books, 5–10 years. Genres include historical and religious
  fiction with Jewish themes.
- **Nonfiction:** Publishes chapter books, 8–10 years; middle-
  grade books, 8–12 years; and young adult books, 12–18
  years. Topics include Judaism and Jewish life. Also publishes
  parenting titles.
- **Representative Titles:** *In the Thirteenth Year* by Sandra Satten
  (8–11 years) uniquely blends Torah and science fiction in a
  novel about a boy approaching his bar mitzvah. *Let's Talk
  About the Sabbath* by Dorothy Kripke (6–8 years) offers a young
  person's guide to the Sabbath, from meeting the Queen of the
  Sabbath to celebrating Havdallah.

Submissions and Payment
Prefers query with sample chapters. Accepts complete ms.
Accepts photocopies and computer printouts. SASE.
Responds to queries in 1–2 weeks, to mss in 3–6 months.
Publication in 1–2 years. Royalty, 5–10%.

Editor's Comments
We're always interested in reviewing submissions of well-
crafted Judaica. Most of our juvenile titles are written for
readers in middle school and high school, although we do
occasionally publish a story picture book. We're also interested
in Jewish parenting and family titles from writers who have
qualifications in these fields.

All About Kids Publishing

Suite D
6280 San Ignacio Avenue
San Jose, CA 95119

Editor: Linda L. Guevara

Publisher's Interests

All About Kids Publishing is an independent publisher that produces a list of fiction and nonfiction titles for children up to the age of ten. Its audience includes educators as well as parents.
Website: www.aakp.com

Freelance Potential

Published 9 titles in 2003: all were developed from unsolicited submissions. Of the 9 titles, all were by authors who were new to the publishing house and 7 were by unpublished writers. Receives 7,500 unsolicited mss yearly.

- **Fiction:** Published 7 easy-to-read books, 4–7 years; and 2 story picture books, 4–10 years. Also publishes toddler books, 0–4 years; and chapter books, 5–10 years. Genres include multicultural and inspirational fiction; adventure; fantasy; humor; animal books; and alphabet books.
- **Nonfiction:** Publishes story picture books, 2–10 years. Topics include animals, crafts, history, nature, the environment, mathematics, and science. Also publishes cookbooks.
- **Representative Titles:** *Cinnamon's Busy Year* by Tony Waters (2–8 years) follows Cinnamon and her friends as they find a holiday to celebrate every month of the year. *Magical Thoughts* by Arlene Maguire (2–8 years) describes things to picture in your imagination that tempt the five senses.

Submissions and Payment

Guidelines available by mail and at website. Send complete ms with résumé. No queries or email submissions. Requests digital file with acceptance. SASE. Responds in 2–3 months. Publication in 30 months. Royalty, 3–5%; advance, varies.

Editor's Comments

Our goal is to set the standard in children's and educational publishing. We seek to create innovative books of the highest quality. Our emphasis encompasses multiculturalism, education, and conscience, and we look for books that will open new doors to imagination.

Ambassador-Emerald International

427 Wade Hampton Boulevard
Greenville, SC 29609

Publisher: Tomm Knutson

Publisher's Interests
A Christian publisher, Ambassador-Emerald International offers a variety of fiction and nonfiction titles for children ages six and up. Founded in 1995, it also offers religious, regional titles focusing on the southeastern United States. **Website:** www.emeraldhouse.com

Freelance Potential
Published 55 titles (7 juvenile) in 2003: 10 were developed from unsolicited submissions and 20 were by agented authors. Of the 55 titles, 5 were by unpublished writers and 10 were by authors who were new to the publishing house. Receives 1,800 queries yearly.
- **Fiction:** Published 2 chapter books, 6–10 years; 2 middle-grade novels, 8–12 years; and 1 young adult book, 12–18 years. Also publishes books in series. Genres include religious, historical, and regional fiction.
- **Nonfiction:** Published 1 middle-grade book, 8–12 years; and 1 young adult book, 12–18 years. Topics include religion, history, current events, and regional subjects. Also offers biographies.
- **Representative Titles:** *The Secret Garden* by Lois Gladys Leppard (8–13 years) is a mystery set in Ireland; part of the Janie and Tom Mystery series. *Christian Men of Science* by George Mulfinger & Julia Mulfinger Orozco features 11 short biographies that focus on each scientist's accomplishments and the evidence of his Christian faith.

Submissions and Payment
Guidelines and catalogue available with 9x12 SASE ($1.29 postage) and at website. Query. Accepts photocopies and email to authors@emeraldhouse.com. SASE. Responds in 6 weeks. Publication in 1 year. Royalty, 5–15%; advance, $250–$1,000.

Editor's Comments
We want to see more religious activity books for ages three to six as well as religious fiction for ages six to fifteen. Regional books about the Carolinas' Coast Islands are also needed.

Amsco School Publications

315 Hudson Street
New York, NY 10013-1085

Publisher: Henry Brun

Publisher's Interests
Publishing for nearly 70 years, Amsco School Publications
specializes in educational material on a variety of subjects
including science, mathematics, language arts, and social
studies. Its list includes textbooks and supplementary curriculum-based materials. All of its books are written for high
school students.
Website: www.amscopub.com

Freelance Potential
Published 100 titles in 2003: 1 was developed from an unsolicited submission. Receives 60 queries yearly.
- **Nonfiction:** Publishes educational textbooks, workbooks, and
  teachers' guides. Topics include mathematics, chemistry, earth
  science, economics, history, geography, reading, composition,
  literature, health, and psychology.
- **Representative Titles:** *Achieving Competence in Science* by
  Paul S. Cohen et al. provides a concise review of middle school
  science curriculum including topics in earth, life, and physical
  science, and technology. *Chemistry: A Contemporary Approach*
  by Paul S. Cohen & Saul Geffner serves as a basal text for high
  school chemistry students and includes step-by-step solutions
  and sample problems.

Submissions and Payment
Guidelines available. Query with résumé, outline, prospectus, and sample chapters with activities. Accepts photocopies, computer printouts, and simultaneous submissions
if identified. Availability of artwork improves chance of
acceptance. SASE. Responds in 1 month. Publication in
18–24 months. Royalty.

Editor's Comments
In general, we prefer to work with experienced educators
who can provide the latest information on a given subject.
Interested writers should send a detailed query with an outline, sample chapters, and activities. If you can supply artwork, so much the better.

Annick Press

15 Patricia Avenue
Toronto, Ontario M2M 1H9
Canada

Editors

Publisher's Interests
Annick Press is a Canadian publisher that features a list of fiction and nonfiction books for middle-grade and young adult readers. It is no longer publishing picture books. **Website:** www.annickpress.com

Freelance Potential
Published 30 titles in 2003.
- **Fiction:** Publishes middle-grade books, 8–11 years; and young adult novels, 12–18 years. Genres include contemporary fiction and humor.
- **Nonfiction:** Publishes middle-grade books, 8–11 years; and young adult books, 12–18 years.
- **Representative Titles:** *Ultra Hush-Hush* by Stephen Shapiro & Tina Forrester (10+ years) reports the stories of espionage and special missions of men and women in the Second World War; part of the Outwitting the Enemy: Stories from the Second World War series. *The Three and Many Wishes of Jason Reid* by Hazel Hutchins (10–12 years) is a fantasy about a boy who is offered three wishes, and whose third wish is always for more wishes.

Submissions and Payment
Guidelines available. Query with synopsis and sample chapter. Accepts photocopies and computer printouts. SAE/IRC. Response time, publication period, and payment policy vary.

Editor's Comments
Since we first started publishing 28 years ago, our commitment has been to develop high-quality books that entertain and challenge young readers. Our teen novels capture strong and distinctive contemporary voices. Our nonfiction is characterized by its high degree of originality and by subject matter that has an inherent appeal to our readers. Topics must be thoroughly researched. We are interested in reviewing queries that describe books that pose questions, open doors, encourage discussion, incite laughter and tears, and invite the sharing of emotions. Please note that we are no longer accepting submissions for picture books.

Atheneum Books for Young Readers

1230 Avenue of the Americas
New York, NY 10020

Executive Editor: Caitlyn Dlouhy

Publisher's Interests
A division of Simon & Schuster, Atheneum develops hard-cover picture books as well as middle-grade and young adult novels. Biographies also appear on its list.
Website: www.simonsayskids.com

Freelance Potential
Published 103 titles in 2003: 6 were developed from unsolicited submissions, 40 were by agented authors, and 4 were reprint/licensed properties. Receives 30,000 queries yearly.
- **Fiction:** Published 2 concept books, 10 toddler books, and 25 early picture books, 0–4 years; 8 easy-to-read books, 4–7 years; 12 story picture books, 4–10 years; 2 chapter books, 5–10 years; 16 middle-grade novels, 8–12 years; and 15 young adult books, 12–18 years. Genres include historical and science fiction, mystery, fantasy, and adventure.
- **Nonfiction:** Published 3 young adult books, 12–18 years. Also publishes story picture books, 4–10 years; chapter books, 5–10 years; and middle-grade books, 8–12 years. Topics include science, nature, the environment, history, sports, and multicultural issues. Also publishes biographies.
- **Representative Titles:** *Hatching Magic* by Ann Downer (10–14 years) is a fantasy about a thirteenth-century wizard who is transported to modern Cambridge. *Ellsworth's Extraordinary Electric Ears and Other Amazing Alphabet Anecdotes* by Valorie Fisher (4–8 years) is a three-dimensional picture book about the alphabet.

Submissions and Payment
Guidelines available. Query for nonfiction. Send 3 sample chapters with summary for fiction. Accepts photocopies and computer printouts. SASE. Responds in 3 months. Publication period varies. Royalty.

Editor's Comments
Well-crafted, high-quality books are of more interest to us than books that exploit the latest trends, fads, or gimmicks. We are willing to consider books in a wide range of styles, on virtually any subject.

Further the Mission
Michelle Cook
Augsburg Books

Augsburg Books is an imprint of Augsburg Fortress Publishers, the official publisher of the Evangelical Lutheran Church in America. Michelle Cook, Assistant Managing Editor for Augsburg Books and Acting Children's Acquisitions Editor, says that manuscripts must have Christian content to be considered by their house. "The book must further our mission somehow by enhancing faith and bringing children and families together in their spiritual lives."

Cook says that currently Augsburg is looking for children's books that "retell a Bible story or tell a story about Jesus or God. Generic faith-based stories don't sell as well for us as do the stories that specifically talk about Jesus' life or God's creation."

Augsburg's best-selling children's book to date is *Miss Fannie's Hat*, by Jan Karon—a story about a grandmother "who has lots of hats and offers to give one to her church for an auction. She has a hard time deciding which hat to give, and finally decides to part with her favorite (the pink straw with roses) because she thinks it can make the biggest difference." Cook attributes the book's success partly to Karon's widely recognized name as author of the best-selling adult series The Mitford Years. But the book itself is reason enough. Cook says: It stresses the theme of trusting in God and acting in selfless ways.

Advising authors on submitting their proposals to Augsburg Books, Cook highly recommends acquiring the guidelines and following them exactly. The extent to which writers do or don't follow guidelines gives an editor a clue about "what kind of person this author would be like to work with."

Augsburg Books

P.O. Box 1209
Minneapolis, MN 55440-1209

Submissions Editor

Publisher's Interests

The catalogue of Augsburg Books includes a section devoted to titles for children and families. These books, which focus on Christian heritage, include picture books, story collections, intergenerational activity books, and young adult novels.
Website: www.augsburgbooks.com

Freelance Potential

Published 36 titles (12 juvenile) in 2003: 1 was developed from an unsolicited submission, 6 were by agented authors, and 1 was a reprint/licensed property. Receives 1,000 queries yearly.

- **Fiction:** Published 6 toddler books and 4 early picture books, 0–4 years; and 2 story picture books, 4–10 years. Also publishes easy-to-read books, 4–7 years; middle-grade books, 8–12 years; and young adult novels, 10–15 years.
- **Nonfiction:** Publishes concept books and toddler books, 0–4 years; and story picture books, 4–10 years. Also publishes activity books, devotionals, and educational materials. Topics include Lutheranism, family life, spirituality, prayer, parenting, and Christian education.
- **Representative Titles:** *Cheer Up, Chicken!* by Bob Hartman (4–8 years) is a story of giving and receiving that teaches children to put the needs of others before their own. *In the Beginning* by Steve Turner (3–5 years) is a retelling of the creation story that uses simple words and rhyme.

Submissions and Payment

Guidelines and catalogue available at website. Query with résumé, outline, and synopsis. Accepts photocopies, computer printouts, and simultaneous submissions if identified. SASE. Responds in 1–3 months. Publication in 2–3 years. Royalty, 5–10% of gross.

Editor's Comments

Our children's books draw readers into a God-centered world where they find answers to life's questions and an abiding love. We currently need Bible-based stories for ages three to eight.

A/V Concepts Corporation

30 Montauk Boulevard
Oakdale, NY 11769

Editor-in-Chief: Laura Solimene

Publisher's Interests
This publisher specializes in educational software that helps
students improve their vocabulary and reading skills. It offers
products from original stories to classic novels designed to
meet the needs of teachers and students in high-interest/
low-vocabulary programs. A/V Concepts Corporation is part
of the EDCON Publishing Group.
Website: www.edconpublishing.com

Freelance Potential
Published 12 titles in 2003. Of the 12 titles, 6 were by
unpublished writers and 3 were by authors who were new to
the publishing house. Receives 300 queries, 200 unsolicited
mss yearly.
- **Fiction:** Publishes middle-grade books, 8–12 years; and young
  adult books, 12–18 years. Genres include fantasy, adventure,
  science fiction, and horror. Also publishes biographies and stories about nature.
- **Representative Titles:** *Hamlet* (grade 4 reading level) is an
  easy-reading adaptation of Shakespeare designed to ignite the
  interest of reluctant readers. *Vowel Tricksters* (grades 2–4)
  strengthens recognition and usage of vowel digraphs, r-controlled vowels, and y as a vowel, teaching students not to be
  fooled by vowel sounds that vary with letter juxtaposition.

Submissions and Payment
Guidelines and catalogue available with 9x12 SASE ($1.35
postage). All work is assigned. Submissions are not returned.
Responds in 3–6 weeks. Flat fee.

Editor's Comments
All of our books are written on assignment. We do not accept
unsolicited manuscripts. Send us a résumé that demonstrates your ability to meet our publishing needs, along with
writing samples or published clips. Most of our writers have a
background in education and are familiar with the needs of
hi/lo students of all ages. If we have an appropriate project,
we will contact you.

Avisson Press

3007 Taliaferro Road
Greensboro, NC 27408

Editor: M. L. Hester

Publisher's Interests
This publisher now specializes in biographies for a young
adult audience. Avisson Press features titles on notable
African Americans, women, and minorities, as well as
biographies of scientists and athletes. Collective biographies are also part of its list. It does not accept any fiction
or general nonfiction.

Freelance Potential
Published 8 titles in 2003: 7 were developed from unsolicited
submissions and 1 was by an agented author. Of the 8
titles, 1 was by an unpublished writer and 4 were by
authors who were new to the publishing house. Receives
500 queries each year.
- **Nonfiction:** Published 8 young adult biographies, 12–18 years.
  Topics include history, science, sports, and ethnic and multicultural subjects.
- **Representative Titles:** *Go, Girl!* by Jacqueline Robb (YA) is a
  collective biography of female pop music stars who beat the
  odds and attained their dreams. *Here Comes Eleanor* by Virginia Veeder Westervelt (YA) provides a close look at the fearless
  first lady, Eleanor Roosevelt.

Submissions and Payment
Query with outline, author biography, and sample chapter.
Accepts photocopies, computer printouts, and simultaneous
submissions if identified. SASE. Responds in 2 weeks. Publication in 12 months. Royalty, 8–10%.

Editor's Comments
We prefer submissions of 12,000–25,000 words, or longer,
depending on the subject matter. We will consider a manuscript that is shorter if the author is willing to add material to
the book. We tend to target older readers in the young adult
category—at least 12 years and up. Biographies on individuals
from all walks of life are welcome, although in the past we have
tended to focus on the life stories of significant women and
African Americans.

Baker Book House Company

6030 East Fulton
Ada, MI 49301

Submissions Editor

Publisher's Interests

Baker Book House Company has been publishing true-to-the-Bible stories for children of all ages for over 60 years. Its books range from picture books and storybooks for young children, to middle-grade titles that show older children the importance of God's presence in their lives.

Website: www.bakerbooks.com

Freelance Potential

Published 240 titles (12 juvenile) in 2003: all were by agented authors. Of the 240 titles, 1 was by an unpublished writer. Receives 100 queries yearly.

- **Fiction:** Publishes story picture books, 4–10 years. Genres include inspirational stories with a Christian theme.
- **Nonfiction:** Publishes toddler books and early picture books, 0–4 years; and middle-grade books, 8–12 years. Topics include Bible stories and stories that show the presence of God in our lives. Also publishes parenting titles and homeschooling titles for adults.
- **Representative Titles:** *The Light and the Glory for Children* by Peter Marshall & David Manuel (9–12 years) reveals God's plan for America from the days of Christopher Columbus through the time of George Washington. *Ivy and Allison* by Jane Peart (10–14 years) presents the story of two orphans who were part of the nearly 100,000 children transported across the country between 1854 and 1904 to find new homes.

Submissions and Payment

Guidelines and catalogue available at website. Agented submissions only. No unsolicited mss. Response time varies. Publication in 1–2 years. Royalty.

Editor's Comments

We accept submissions from agented authors only, so if you are interested in having us consider your work, we suggest you contact The Writer's Edge or First Edition, manuscript services of the Christian Publishers Association. We subscribe to both services and regularly review the properties they feature.

Baker's Plays

P.O. Box 699222
Quincy, MA 02269-9222

Managing Director: Kurt Gombar

Publisher's Interests
Dramatic materials of all types are found in this publisher's catalogue. It offers full-length and one-act plays, musicals, drama texts, anthologies, audition materials, and sound-effect and dialect tapes. Baker's Plays markets its materials to high school, university, community, regional, and children's theater groups.
Website: www.bakersplays.com

Freelance Potential
Published 20 titles (7 juvenile) in 2003. Of the 20 titles, 4 were by unpublished writers and 10 were by authors who were new to the publishing house. Receives 50–75 queries, 300+ unsolicited mss yearly.
- **Fiction:** Publishes plays for family, high school, and children's theater groups. Genres include comedy, mystery, folktales, and fairy tales. Also offers holiday plays, classics, and musicals. Religious plays are produced under a separate division.
- **Nonfiction:** Publishes theater texts.
- **Representative Titles:** *Monologues for Teenage Girls* by Roger Karshner (YA) features 30 original speeches that deal with issues relevant to today's teens, including drugs, alcoholism, school, sex, and suicide. *The Cinderella Syndrome* by V. Glasgow Koste is a comedy that takes a fresh look at the nature of kinship, the search for identity, and transformations.

Submissions and Payment
Guidelines available. Query with script history, reviews, and sample pages or synopsis; or send complete ms. Accepts photocopies, laser-quality computer printouts, and simultaneous submissions if identified. SASE. Responds to queries in 1 month, to mss in 3–4 months. Publication period and payment policy vary.

Editor's Comments
We're always looking for new and exciting work, but we strongly favor plays that have had the benefit of a stage reading, workshop reading, or full production.

Bantam Books for Young Readers

1745 Broadway
New York, NY 10019

Editor

Publisher's Interests

An imprint of Knopf Delacorte Dell Young Readers Group, this division of Random House publishes juvenile literature in a variety of genres for all ages. It also publishes nonfiction books for young adult readers. Only agented authors may send queries. Unpublished writers may submit work to its two contests: the Marguerite de Angeli Prize and the Delacorte Press Contest for a First Young Adult Novel.
Website: www.randomhouse.com/kids

Freelance Potential

Published 275 titles in 2003: most were by agented authors and 90 were reprint/licensed properties. Of the 275 titles, some were by unpublished writers. Receives 2,000 queries each year.

- **Fiction:** Publishes early picture books, 0–4 years; easy-to-read books, 4–7 years; story picture books, 4–10 years; chapter books, 5–10 years; middle-grade books, 8–12 years; and young adult novels, 12–18 years.
- **Nonfiction:** Publishes young adult books, 12–18 years.
- **Representative Titles:** *Milkweed* by Jerry Spinelli (10+ years) is a novel about a Jewish boy living on the streets of Warsaw in Nazi Germany. *Who Needs Donuts?* by Mark Alan Stamaty (all ages) is a picture book about a boy whose love of donuts takes him on a journey to the city to meet a collector of donuts.

Submissions and Payment

Submit queries through agents only. New writers may submit middle-grade novels for the Marguerite de Angeli Prize and young adult novels for the Delacorte Press Press Contest for a First Young Adult Novel. See the contests and awards section of this directory. No simultaneous submissions. SASE. Response time varies. Publication in 2 years. Royalty; advance.

Editor's Comments

If you're interested in having us publish your work, you must have your agent contact us. Alternatively, you can submit entries to our contests.

Beach Holme Publishing

226-2040 West 12th Avenue
Vancouver, British Columbia V6J 2G2
Canada

Publisher: Michael Carroll

Publisher's Interests

This Canadian publisher and its imprints, Sandcastle Books, Porcepic Books, and Prospect Books, offer young adult historical novels and adult poetry, fiction, and nonfiction. It works with Canadian authors only, and features books with Canadian themes.
Website: www.beachholme.bc.ca

Freelance Potential

Published 13 titles (5 juvenile) in 2003: 3 were developed from unsolicited submissions and 10 were by agented authors. Of the 13 titles, 2 were by unpublished writers and 7 were by new authors. Receives 1,200 queries yearly.

- **Fiction:** Published 1 chapter book, 5–10 years; and 4 middle-grade books, 8–12 years. Genres include Canadian historical, contemporary, multicultural, and Native Canadian fiction.
- **Representative Titles:** *Death by Exposure* by Eric Walters & Kevin Spreekmeester (YA) follows two teens who discover a man entombed in ice—a photographer whose photos provide a mystery. *Charlotte's Vow* by Marion Woodson (YA), set in a coal mining town in 1912, tells the story of a girl determined to help and protect her family.

Submissions and Payment

Guidelines available. Query with 3 sample chapters, market analysis, and description of intended audience. Accepts photocopies and computer printouts. SASE. Responds in 4–6 months. Publication in 1 year. Royalty; advance.

Editor's Comments

We select books for publication based on originality, plot development, dialogue and narrative, and thematic cohesion. Most of the children's manuscripts we receive have some historical or regional significance and are set in Canada. Canadian historical fiction for middle-grade readers is especially welcome. Include teachers' guides and resources if possible. Note that we no longer publish illustrated children's books, science fiction, mystery, romance, detective, Western, horror, or action books.

Bebop Books

95 Madison Avenue
New York, NY 10016

Editor: Jennifer Frantz

Publisher's Interests

Multicultural material for emergent and beginning readers is published by Bebop Books. Its titles are used by kindergarten and first-grade teachers to help young children develop early reading skills and strategies. The books are designed for use with Fountas and Pinnell's Guided Reading™ and Reading Recovery® leveling systems.
Website: www.bebopbooks.com

Freelance Potential

Published 12 titles in 2003: all were developed from unsolicited submissions. Of the 12 titles, 4 were by unpublished writers and 6 were by authors who were new to the publishing house. Receives 600 unsolicited mss yearly.

- **Fiction:** Publishes emergent and beginning readers, grades K–2, with multicultural and ethnic themes. Features books in English and Spanish.
- **Nonfiction:** Publishes emergent and beginning readers, grades K–2, about multicultural and ethnic subjects.
- **Representative Titles:** *Jump Rope* by Mimi Chapra (Guided Reading Level B) is an illustrated book about young children enjoying this activity. *Moving Day Surprise* by Tina Solberg (Guided Reading Level G) is a story about a child who experiences an unexpected event when she moves to a new home.

Submissions and Payment

Guidelines available at website or with SASE. Send complete ms. Accepts photocopies. SASE. Responds in 4 months. Publication in 10 months. Royalty; advance.

Editor's Comments

We look for realistic fiction and nonfiction that feature young children of color. We prefer stories that are culturally specific; that is, the content of the story relates specifically to a particular culture or ethnic group. Stories about universal childhood experiences are also acceptable. It's a plus if your book incorporates classroom concepts, such as simple math or science. Don't send animals stories, folklore, or fantasy.

Behrman House

11 Edison Place
Springfield, NJ 07081

Acquisitions Editor

Publisher's Interests
Behrman House offers books on a wide variety of Jewish
topics and themes, such as Jewish faith, history, ethics,
and holidays. Its materials are used by Jewish children in
elementary and secondary schools and include Jewish textbooks, teaching guides, teacher resources, and books for
families to use at home.
Website: www.behrmanhouse.com

Freelance Potential
Published 15 titles in 2003: all were developed from unsolicited submissions. Receives 250 queries, 250 unsolicited
mss each year.
- **Nonfiction:** Publishes chapter books, 5–10 years; middle-grade
  books, 8–12 years; and young adult books, 12–18 years. Topics
  include Judaism, religion, theology, prayer, holidays, the Bible,
  the Holocaust, history, liturgy, Hebrew, and ethics. Also offers
  educational resource materials and religious instructional
  materials for adults.
- **Representative Titles:** *Let's Discover the Alef Bet* by Sarah
  Feldman (grades K–2) helps young children learn the names
  and sounds of the 22 letters of the Hebrew language. *Hitler's
  War Against the Jews* by David Altshuler (grades 9–10) presents a young reader's version of the Davidowicz bestseller.

Submissions and Payment
Prefers query with table of contents and sample chapter. Will
accept complete ms with résumé and author biography.
Accepts photocopies, computer printouts, and simultaneous
submissions if identified. SASE. Responds in 2 months. Publication in 18 months. Royalty, 5–10%; advance, $1,500. Flat
fee, to $5,000.

Editor's Comments
Our mission is to bring the Jewish tradition alive for young
readers; we want to inspire them so they embrace Jewish history, faith, and ethics as an important and exciting part of
their daily lives and as a source of strength for their souls.

Benchmark Books

Marshall Cavendish
99 White Plains Road
Tarrytown, NY 10591

Editorial Director: Michelle Bisson

Publisher's Interests
This imprint of the publisher Marshall Cavendish specializes in nonfiction books that are used as supplementary resources in kindergarten through high school classrooms. All titles are produced in series covering a wide range of subject matter, including mathematics, science, social studies, literature, and history.
Website: www.marshallcavendish.com

Freelance Potential
Published 150 titles in 2003.
- **Nonfiction:** Publishes chapter books, 5–10 years; and middle-grade books, 8–12 years. Topics include mathematics, science, animals, social studies, history, and world cultures.
- **Representative Titles:** *The Shoemakers* by Leonard Everett Fisher (grades 4 and up) looks at this early American occupation and the life and times of the colonists who plied this trade; part of the Colonial Craftsmen series. *It's the Wind* by Catherine Nichols (grades 1–2) explores the ways nature creates wind; part of the We Can Read About Nature series.

Submissions and Payment
Query with 1–3 chapters and table of contents. Accepts photocopies and computer printouts. SASE. Responds in 6–8 weeks. Publication in 9–18 months. Payment policy varies.

Editor's Comments
We believe that the foundation of a child's education is the written word. We are always looking for fresh, innovative ways to create and build on that foundation. While we cover many topics, we are especially interested in seeing submissions that fit into one of our series on science, history, or literature. We have numerous series on each topic, so please review our current catalogue to discover where your idea, if it has not already been covered, would best fit in. Keep in mind that our books are designed to act as supplementary sources for topics already covered by school curricula. Please note that we are no longer accepting fiction submissions.

The Bess Press

3565 Harding Avenue
Honolulu, HI 96816

Editor: Revé Shapard

Publisher's Interests
Books for children and young adults that reflect the people
and wildlife of Hawaii and the Pacific Islands are the specialty
of this regional publisher. It also publishes elementary, intermediate, and high school textbooks, and coloring, activity,
and board books about Hawaii.
Website: www.besspress.com

Freelance Potential
Published 9 titles in 2003: 8 were developed from unsolicited
submissions, all were by agented authors, and 1 was a
reprint/licensed property. Of the 9 titles, 4 were by authors
who were new to the publishing house. Receives 125 unsolicited mss yearly.
- **Fiction:** Published 2 story picture books, 4–10 years; and 1
  young adult book, 12–18 years.
- **Nonfiction:** Published 1 young adult book, 12–18 years; and 2
  coloring books. Topics include Pacific studies, language, geography, nature, wildlife, and literature. Also publishes board
  books and activity books.
- **Representative Titles:** *The Shark-Man of Kapu Bay* by P. J.
  Neri (YA) tells the chilling ghost story of a Hawaiian sea monster with a single bulging, black eye; part of the Hawaii Chillers
  series. *The Little Makana* by Helen M. Dano (4–10 years) tells
  about a mother's bond with her unborn baby, and features
  three lullabyes.

Submissions and Payment
Guidelines available. Send complete ms. Accepts photocopies,
computer printouts, and simultaneous submissions if identified. SASE. Responds in 4–6 weeks. Publication in 6–12
months. Royalty, 5–10%.

Editor's Comments
We're looking for books with regional themes based on Hawaii
and the Pacific Islands. We especially need books for emerging
readers that have a distinctly Hawaiian focus, as well as
Hawaiian-themed fiction, board books, and coloring books.

Bethany House Publishers

11400 Hampshire Avenue South
Minneapolis, MN 55438

Submissions Editor

Publisher's Interests
This publisher describes itself as "the premier publisher of youth fiction in the Christian market," and its list includes a number of best-selling fiction series. It also publishes evangelical Christian nonfiction for readers up to the age of 18.
Website: www.bethanyhouse.com

Freelance Potential
Published 31 titles in 2003: 5 were by agented authors. Of the 31 titles, 1 was by an author who was new to the publishing house. Receives 50–75 queries yearly.
- **Fiction:** Published 4 easy-to-read books, 4–7 years; 9 middle-grade novels, 8–12 years; and 14 young adult books, 12–18 years. Also publishes story picture books, 4–10 years; and chapter books, 5–10 years. Genres include adventure; mystery; suspense; and inspirational, contemporary, and historical fiction.
- **Nonfiction:** Published 1 early picture book, 0–4 years; 2 middle-grade books, 8–12 years; and 1 young adult book, 12–18 years. Also publishes concept books, 0–4 years. Topics include contemporary issues, spirituality, theology, family life, and social issues. Also publishes devotionals, curriculum guides, and Christian educational resources.
- **Representative Titles:** *Mandie and the Night Thief* by Lois Gladys Leppard (8–14 years) is a mystery about some missing jewelry; part of the Mandie Books series. *A Growing-Up Guide* by Sandra Byrd (9–14 years) offers a cool alternative to the influences of pop culture.

Submissions and Payment
Guidelines available at website. Query appropriate editor by sending fax to 952-996-1304. Not currently accepting unsolicited mss. Responds in 9–12 weeks. Publication period varies. Royalty; advance.

Editor's Comments
Please note that all of our fiction books are published as part of series. Right now, we are looking for fresh ideas for nonfiction titles. Books that help readers apply Christian principles to their daily lives are most welcome.

Beyond Words Publishing

Suite 500
20827 NW Cornell Road
Hillsboro, OR 97124-9808

Managing Editor: Barbara Leese

Publisher's Interests

This West Coast publisher is known for its books that inspire young people to follow their dreams. Its focus is on nonfiction titles and picture books, and it welcomes submissions from young writers.
Website: www.beyondword.com

Freelance Potential

Published 8 titles in 2003: 3 were developed from unsolicited submissions and 2 were by agented authors. Of the 8 titles, 6 were by unpublished writers and 4 were by authors who were new to the publishing house. Receives 3,000 unsolicited mss each year.

- **Fiction:** Published 2 story picture books, 4–10 years; 2 middle-grade books, 8–12 years; and 4 young adult books, 12–18 years. Genres include fairy tales, folktales, stories about nature, and multicultural fiction.
- **Nonfiction:** Publishes story picture books, 4–10 years; middle-grade books, 8–15 years; and young adult books, 12–18 years. Also publishes middle-grade books written by young authors.
- **Representative Titles:** *Generation FIX* by Elizabeth Rusch features stories from kid activists who have made a difference in the world. *Authors by Request* by Cathy Collison & Janis Campbell features interviews with favorite children's authors and answers readers' most-asked questions.

Submissions and Payment

Guidelines available. Send complete ms with description of market and competition. Accepts photocopies, computer printouts, and simultaneous submissions if identified. SASE. Responds in 4–6 months. Publication in 1 year. Royalty, 5–10%; advance.

Editor's Comments

Our mission statement is "Inspire to Integrity," and every book we publish must fulfill this mission. Please research our previously published books. This will help you to determine whether your book fits in with what we do best.

Blackbirch Press

10911 Technology Place
San Diego, CA 92127

Editorial Director

Publisher's Interests
American history, natural science, social studies, and other curriculum-based subjects are the focus of this education publisher. Blackbirch Press offers an extensive list of nonfiction books for elementary and middle-school students.
Website: www.galegroup.com/blackbirch/

Freelance Potential
Published 50+ titles in 2003. Receives 1,000 queries yearly.
- **Nonfiction:** Publishes story picture books, 4–10 years; chapter books, 5–10 years; middle grade books; 8–12 years; and young adult books, 12–18 years. Topics include science, nature, the environment, ecology, American history, women's history, geography, business, sports, and multicultural subjects.
- **Representative Titles:** *American Inaugurals: The Speeches, the Presidents, and Their Families* (10+ years) offers a unique glimpse of America's leaders through their speeches and includes facts, photographs, and sidebars that help put each inauguration in historical perspective. *Giraffes* (8–10 years) explores the lives of these wild animals and their unique habits; part of the Wild Wild World series.

Submissions and Payment
Guidelines available. Query with résumé. No unsolicited mss. Accepts photocopies and simultaneous submissions if identified. SASE. Responds in 4 months. Publication in 1 year. Royalty; advance.

Editor's Comments
We continue to look for writers whose expertise can help us deliver quality books on a variety of curriculum-based subjects. We are interested in writers who can demonstrate a talent for combining creativity and innovation with the latest information on a given topic. Since our union with the Gale Group, we have been able to expand our list with an increasing number of books on a wide variety of subjects. We look for writers who can present ideas for new series or suggestions for a fresh approach.

Blue Sky Press

Scholastic Inc.
557 Broadway
New York, NY 10012-3999

Acquisitions Editor: Bonnie Verburg

Publisher's Interests

Nonfiction books about nature and history appear on Blue
Sky Press's list along with fiction titles for readers of all ages.
An imprint of Scholastic, it publishes the well-known Captain
Underpants and Ricky Ricotta's Mighty Robot book series.
Blue Sky Press accepts submissions from previously pub-
lished authors only.
Website: www.scholastic.com

Freelance Potential

Published 16 titles in 2003. Receives 5,000 queries yearly.
- **Fiction:** Publishes toddler and early picture books, 0–4 years;
  easy-to-read books, 4–7 years; story picture books, 4–10 years;
  chapter books, 5–10 years; middle-grade novels, 8–12 years;
  and young adult books, 12–18 years. Genres include historical
  and multicultural fiction, folklore, fairy tales, fantasy, humor,
  and adventure.
- **Nonfiction:** Publishes middle-grade books, 8–12 years. Topics
  include nature, the environment, and history.
- **Representative Titles:** *The Adventures of Captain Underpants*
  by Dav Pilkey (7-10 years) is a humorous chapter book about a
  very unconventional superhero; part of the Captain Underpants series. *How Groundhog's Garden Grew* by Lynne Cherry
  (4+ years) is a picture book about a groundhog who learns how
  to grow and care for a garden for himself after he is caught
  stealing food from his friends.

Submissions and Payment

Accepts queries from previously published authors only. No
unsolicited mss. Accepts photocopies. SASE. Responds in 6
months. Publication in 2–5 years. Royalty; advance.

Editor's Comments

We have a very small list, and we receive thousands of queries
each year. For this reason, we can consider only submissions
from writers who have already had their work published. We
strongly suggest that you search the Scholastic website and
study the kinds of books we publish before contacting us.

Borealis Press Ltd.

8 Mohawk Crescent
Nepean, Ontario K2H 7G6
Canada

Senior Editor: Glenn Clever

Publisher's Interests
Borealis Press is a Canadian publisher that offers both fiction
and nonfiction for children of all ages. Its focus is on books
that are concerned with understanding and improving the
human condition.
Website: www.borealispress.com

Freelance Potential
Published 20 titles (4 juvenile) in 2003: 18 were developed
from unsolicited submissions. Of the 20 titles, 2 were by
unpublished writers and 8 were by authors who were new to
the publishing house. Receives 50 queries yearly.
- **Fiction:** Publishes story picture books, 4–10 years; and young
  adult books, 12–18 years. Genres include ethnic and multicultural fiction and fantasy.
- **Nonfiction:** Publishes reference titles about Canadian history.
  Also offers drama, poetry, and books with multicultural
  themes.
- **Representative Titles:** *Mystery at Port Royal* by Barbara Little
  is the story of Gui, a young stowaway pursued by a strange
  man when he gets to Canada. *No Place for a Child* by Donna
  Richards tells the tale of a girl from a remote island sent to live
  in town, where all is new to her.

Submissions and Payment
Guidelines available. Query with outline/synopsis and sample chapter. No unsolicited mss. Accepts photocopies and
disk submissions. No simultaneous submissions. SAE/IRC.
Responds in 3–4 months. Publication in 1–2 years. Royalty,
10% of net.

Editor's Comments
We look for books that explore the human condition, and offer
situations from which we can learn. Many of our titles celebrate the wonder and beauty of life, as well as the cruelties
and sadness that are also a part of nature and humanity. Fiction should focus on dynamic characters and character development. Canadian authored and oriented material is preferred.

BOW Books

Suite 109
803 Forest Ridge Drive
Bedford, TX 76022

Editor: Jennifer Noland

Publisher's Interests

The mission of this children's book publisher is to encourage proper, ethical behavior in everyday life and demonstrate the value of a Christian lifestyle. BOW Books publishes a range of material for children from 3 to 12 years, including picture books, chapter books, audio books, and ancillary products.
Website: www.bowbooks.com

Freelance Potential

Published 6–8 titles in 2003: 1 was developed from an unsolicited submission. Of the 6–8 titles, 1 was by an unpublished writer and 1 was by an author who was new to the publishing house.

- **Fiction:** Publishes easy-to-read books, 4–7 years; story picture books, 4–10 years; and chapter books, 5–10 years. Also publishes books in series, 5–8 years. Genres include adventure and inspirational fiction.
- **Representative Titles:** *Tiny the Bee* by Kelli Chambers (3–8 years) is the story of a small bee, teased about the size of his wings, who grows up to realize all his dreams. *Treetop Clubhouse* by Jeff Carnehl presents the story of three groups of boys growing up in the same town who finally meet.

Submissions and Payment

Guidelines and catalogue available with 6x9 SASE ($.55 postage). Query with information on intended audience, length, and author biography. SASE. Responds in 3 months. Publication in 18 months. Royalty. Flat fee.

Editor's Comments

As a publishing company guided by Christian values, we are interested in books that demonstrate biblical values and truth, and present those principles in an inspirational and enjoyable way. We prefer to focus on the positive aspects of life and the enormous potential we have while here on Earth, so please do not send proposals that dwell on dark or heavy subjects. We advise potential authors to visit our website and become familiar with what we publish before submitting a proposal.

Boyds Mills Press

815 Church Street
Honesdale, PA 18431

Manuscript Tracker: J. DeLuca

Publisher's Interests
This children's publisher offers a variety of fiction and nonfiction titles for readers up to the age of 18. Concept books, picture books, easy-to-read titles, and middle-grade and young adult books can all be found in its catalogue. Its Wordsong imprint publishes five to seven poetry volumes each year.
Website: www.boydsmillspress.com

Freelance Potential
Published 60 titles in 2003: 25 were developed from unsolicited submissions, 10 were by agented authors, and 6 were reprint/licensed properties. Of the 60 titles, 8 were by unpublished writers and 8 were by authors who were new to the publishing house. Receives 2,000 queries, 6,000 unsolicited mss yearly.

- **Fiction:** Publishes concept books and early picture books, 0–4 years; easy-to-read books, 4–7 years; middle-grade novels, 8–12 years; and young adult books, 12–18 years. Genres include multicultural and ethnic books and adventure. Also publishes poetry books.
- **Nonfiction:** Publishes concept books, 0–4 years; easy-to-read books, 4–7 years; and middle-grade books, 8–12 years. Topics include science, nature, geography, and history.
- **Representative Titles:** *Zoe's Hats* by Sharon Lane Holm (2–6 years) introduces young children to the concepts of color and pattern by following a girl who loves hats. *Finding Zola* by Marianne Mitchell (9–12 years) is a mystery in which a wheelchair-bound girl must find her missing caretaker.

Submissions and Payment
Guidelines available. Query with outline; or send ms. Accepts photocopies and computer printouts. SASE. Responds in 1 month. Publication period and payment policy vary.

Editor's Comments
Nonfiction picture books for five- to eight-year-old children are especially welcome this year. We look for titles that will have lasting value for readers.

Boynton/Cook Publishers

Heinemann
361 Hanover Street
Portsmouth, NH 03801-3912

Editorial Assistant: Eric Chalek

Publisher's Interests
Boynton/Cook specializes in English literature, language arts, writing, composition, and drama textbooks for use in high school and college classrooms, as well as professional resources for educators.
Website: www.boyntoncook.com

Freelance Potential
Published 8 titles in 2003: 1 was developed from an unsolicited submission. Receives 1,000+ queries yearly.
- **Nonfiction:** Publishes textbooks, grades 9 and up. Also publishes professional resource materials for educators. Topics include language arts, literature, rhetoric, communication, composition, writing, style, and drama.
- **Representative Titles:** *What to Expect When You're Expected to Teach* by Anne Bramblett & Alison Knoblauch (teachers) is a collection of essays that address the anxieties and problems encountered by first-time teachers and offer helpful solutions. *College Writing* by Toby Fulwiler (college students) walks students through the main elements of writing, from discovery and research to revising and editing, encouraging them to find and celebrate their own voices.

Submissions and Payment
Catalogue and guidelines available at website. Query with cover letter, project description, table of contents, sample illustrations if applicable, chapter summaries, and 3 sample chapters. Accepts photocopies, computer printouts, and simultaneous submissions if identified. SASE. Responds in 6–8 weeks. Publication in 10–12 months. Royalty.

Editor's Comments
Please check out our website to review our guidelines and determine if your proposal is appropriate for our publishing house. We are interested in hearing from new authors with new ideas, but you must be an excellent writer with experience in the area you wish to write about. Keep in mind that we publish both textbooks for students and resources for teachers.

Branden Books

P.O. Box 812094
Wellesley, MA 02482

Editor: Adolph Caso

Publisher's Interests
This publisher features nonfiction and some fiction for children up to age fourteen, focusing primarily on biographies and reference titles for middle-grade readers.
Website: www.branden.com

Freelance Potential
Published 10 titles in 2003. Receives 500 queries yearly.
- **Fiction:** Publishes story picture books, 4–10 years; and middle-grade novels, 8–12 years. Genres include mystery and historical fiction. Also publishes stories about friendship and stories with problem-solving themes.
- **Nonfiction:** Publishes young adult books, 12–18 years. Topics include health, sports, and legal, ethnic, social, and multicultural subjects. Features reference books and biographies.
- **Representative Titles:** *Chicken Pox Explosion* by Laura Caso (7–10 years) is a young girl's story of how her family was besieged by chicken pox while on vacation in Italy. *Mean Mean Madeleen, Sweet Sweet Angeleen* by Elizabeth Burton (all ages) presents the troubled behavior of two sisters and its resolution.

Submissions and Payment
Query with 2-paragraph synopsis. No unsolicited mss. Accepts photocopies and computer printouts. SASE. Responds in 1 week. Publication in 6–10 months. Royalty, 5–10%.

Editor's Comments
We suggest you review our catalogue, available at our website, to see if your proposal is a good fit for us. We publish mostly nonfiction for middle-grade readers, and strive to produce a diverse list of titles that have one thing in common: literary excellence. Please send us a well-written query no more than two paragraphs long. Explain your idea, and tell us why you feel your book will appeal to its target audience. We are always interested in ideas from new writers who can tackle a topic with style and a focus supported by solid research. Unsolicited manuscripts will not be read—do not send them.

Breakwater Books

P.O. Box 2188
St John's, Newfoundland A1C 6E6
Canada

General Manager: Wade Foote

Publisher's Interests
Educational books and resource materials for children and
adults that reflect the people, unique culture, and wildlife of
Newfoundland, Labrador, and the Maritime provinces are the
specialty of Breakwater Books, a regional publisher, which
was established in 1973.
Website: www.breakwater.nf.net

Freelance Potential
Published 12 titles (2 juvenile) in 2003: 6 were developed
from unsolicited submissions. Of the 12 titles, 5 were by
unpublished writers and 5 were by authors who were new to
the publishing house. Receives 600+ queries yearly.
- **Fiction:** Publishes early picture books, 0–4 years; and young
  adult novels, 12–18 years. Genres include adventure, historical
  fiction, and humor.
- **Nonfiction:** Publishes chapter books, 5–10 years; middle-grade
  books, 8–12 years; and young adult books, 12–18 years. Topics
  include history, current events, religion, and social and multicultural issues. Also publishes Canadian history anthologies.
- **Representative Titles:** *Gaddy's Story* by Sally Goddard tells
  the tale of the first weeks of life of an Atlantic cod. *Muinji'j
  Becomes a Man* by Saqamaw Mi'sel Joe is the story of a boy
  who travels with his grandfather from their native village to sell
  animal pelts in the city.

Submissions and Payment
Catalogue available at website. Query with résumé and clips.
No unsolicited mss. Availability of artwork improves chance
of acceptance. SAE/IRC. Responds in 8 months. Publication
in 1 year. Royalty, 10%.

Editor's Comments
We are looking for book ideas that will help students of all ages
appreciate the rich cultural heritage of the provinces of Atlantic
Canada, their people, traditions, and natural resources. Collaboration with educators and students allows us to meet
classroom needs and create excellent resource material.

A Broader Religious Market
Leonard G. Goss,
Broadman & Holman Publishers

Broadman & Holman Publishers, the book publishing division of LifeWay Christian Resources, is one of the world's largest religious publishing houses. Although it is a denominational house, it publishes for the broader Christian market. Its children's books do not have to be overtly Christian, but they do have to fit within the parameters of Christian truth.

Leonard G. Goss, Editorial Director, says that currently the house is "looking for books to sell to the mass-market in the baby/toddler category. Board books seem to outsell traditional flat picture books. Sales of picture books are not that popular in the Christian Booksellers Association (CBA) market unless the book is tied to a name author or can offer perceived value at an extremely low cost. We are also looking for books on prayer—prayer and promises, prayer and poems, etc.—for children. Even though the general and religious children's book markets were flooded with books on prayer after September 11, books in this area still perform well."

A burgeoning publishing program at Broadman & Holman is in books that meet the homeschooling market. Goss says, "Homeschoolers want their kids to read, and they are looking for curriculum tools in all the traditional academic areas, as well as general books, to encourage kids to do that."

Some of its best-sellers in Christian children's fiction are *A Parable About the King*, by Beth Moore; *When the Creepy Things Come Out*, by Melody Carlson and illustrated by Susan Reagan; Stephen Elkins's *The Bible Prayer Collection*, *Special Times Stories for Babies*, and *Special Times Stories for Toddlers*; *Bible Town Detectives*, by Mary Rose Pearson; and *Chip Hilton Sports Series*, by Coach Clair Bee. Many of their books have been finalists in the Evangelical Christian Publishers Association (ECPA) Gold Medallion Awards.

Broadman & Holman Publishers

127 Ninth Avenue North
MSN 198
Nashville, TN 37234-0198

Children's Team

Publisher's Interests
This publisher focuses on nonfiction and fiction books that bring children and young adults a love of reading and an understanding of Christian values. Beginning in 2004, it will review manuscripts for children's books only.
Website: www.broadmanholman.com

Freelance Potential
Published 22 titles in 2003: 8 were developed from unsolicited submissions and 4 were by agented authors. Of the 22 titles, 2 were by authors who were new to the publishing house. Receives 300 unsolicited mss yearly.
- **Fiction:** Publishes story picture books, 4–10 years. Genres include historical and contemporary fiction with biblical themes.
- **Nonfiction:** Publishes toddler and concept books, 0–4 years; easy-to-read books, 4–7 years; and story picture books, 4–10 years. Topics include contemporary issues, traditional and retold Bible stories, and Christianity.
- **Representative Titles:** *Love Your Neighbor* by Melody Carlson is a story of the kid next door and how one can learn to get along with different kinds of people; part of the Just Like Jesus Said series. *God Is in Control* by Stephen Elkins features songs with accompanying stories that deal with topics related to God and His love; part of the Dove Award series.

Submissions and Payment
Guidelines available. Send complete ms for educational resources. Accepts agented submissions only for children's books. Accepts photocopies, computer printouts, and simultaneous submissions if identified. SASE. Responds in 3 months. Publication in 12–18 months. Royalty; advance.

Editor's Comments
For the coming year we are focusing our publishing efforts on children's material. We are interested in fiction and nonfiction. Keep in mind that everything we publish has some connection to Christianity and biblical themes.

The Brookfield Reader

137 Peyton Road
Sterling, VA 20165

Submissions Editor: Dawn Manausa

Publisher's Interests

The Brookfield Reader publishes fiction and nonfiction for children of all ages, from toddlers through young adults. Its books range from picture books to historical novels, to mystery and adventure for middle-grade readers.
Website: www.brookfieldreader.com

Freelance Potential

Published 6 titles in 2003: 5 were developed from unsolicited submissions and 1 was by an agented author. Of the 6 titles, 1 was by unpublished writer and 4 were by authors new to the publishing house. Receives 600 queries yearly.

- **Fiction:** Publishes easy-to-read books, 4–7 years; story picture books, 4–10 years; and young adult books, 12–18 years. Genres include contemporary and historical fiction, mystery, folklore, suspense, adventure, and stories about sports.
- **Representative Titles:** *Double Time* by Vincent E. Sescoe (YA) is a story of suspense that features a brother and sister, transported back in time to 1863, who escape from Confederate troops and become involved with the Underground Railroad. *Jonathan & Papa* by Susan K. Baggette (18 months–pre-K) follows Jonathan as he spends a busy, happy day with his wheelchair-bound grandfather; part of The Jonathan Adventures series.

Submissions and Payment

Guidelines and current topic requests available at website. Query. Accepts email queries to info@brookfieldreader.com. SASE. Responds in 1–2 months. Publication in 18 months. Royalty, 5–10%; advance, $1,000–$2,000.

Editor's Comments

Check our website for updates on the topics currently of greatest interest to us. In general, our mission is to inspire a child's imagination, and to encourage communication between children and adults. Books which explore the world around us, our American heritage, and our family values are tops on our list, and we are always interested in exciting, new ideas.

The Bureau for At-Risk Youth

A Guidance Channel Company
135 Dupont Street
P.O. Box 760
Plainview, NY 11803-0760

Editor-in-Chief: Sally Germain

Publisher's Interests

Materials for guidance education are the specialty of this publisher. It offers books, curricula, booklets, pamphlets, videos, and multi-media products that are used by guidance counselors, parents, and educators working with children in kindergarten through high school. The Bureau for At-Risk Youth's products cover drug abuse and violence prevention, character education, teen sexuality, special needs issues, and general guidance topics.
Website: www.at-risk.com

Freelance Potential

Published 12 titles in 2004.

- **Nonfiction:** Publishes curriculum and classroom materials, activity books, workbooks, and reference titles, grades K–12. Topics include health and social issues, special education, parenting, character education, self-esteem, decision making, teen sexuality, and teen suicide.
- **Representative Titles:** *For Teens Only* is a 42-pamphlet series that addresses substance abuse, anger and conflict, life skills, sexual assault, family issues, personal health, and career development. *YouthLink* is a flexible curriculum for designing a mentoring program for 12- to 18-year-old students that includes a facilitator's guide, youth workbook, and posters.

Submissions and Payment

Query or send complete ms. SASE. Responds to queries in 1–3 months, to mss in 2–6 months. Publication in 6 months. Payment policy varies.

Editor's Comments

Our staff spends many hours creating and choosing the best guidance resources for our customers. If you're interested in submitting material to us, remember that our target audience is professionals who work with young people. Our writers have specific skills and expertise in the areas they write about. Most of the materials we accept are designed to work as part of a series or in a workbook or curriculum format.

Butte Publications

P.O. Box 1328
Hillsboro, OR 97123-1328

Acquisitions Editor

Publisher's Interests
This publisher specializes in resource materials that serve
the deaf and hard of hearing communities. Butte Publications offers several new titles each year, and many of its publications are designed for use by parents and professionals
working with deaf children. Skill building, language, and
recreation are among the topics covered.
Website: www.buttepublications.com

Freelance Potential
Published 8 titles in 2003: all were developed from unsolicited submissions. Receives 30 queries yearly.
- **Nonfiction:** Publishes resource and educational books on signing, interpreting, vocabulary, reading, writing, language skills,
  and speech reading. Also publishes parenting titles.
- **Representative Titles:** *Metaphor Stories for Deaf Children* by
  Bob Rittenhouse (12–16 years) helps students succeed in reading and language development by providing experience in
  working with metaphoric language. *Mystery of the Totems* by
  Jean F. Andrews is a novel about a deaf boy traveling on a lux-
  ury cruise ship that sails up the Inside Passage of Alaska; part
  of the Flying Fingers Mysteries series.

Submissions and Payment
Guidelines available. Query with table of contents, market
analysis, and sample chapters. Accepts computer printouts.
Availability of artwork improves chance of acceptance. SASE.
Responds in 3–6 months. Publication in 1 year. Royalty.

Editor's Comments
While our titles are limited to topics related to deafness, we do
offer a broad spectrum of books on this subject. Our materials
target parents, educators, and professionals in this field, as
well as children. We encourage unsolicited queries—in fact,
most of our books start out this way. In your proposal, include
information on your qualifications for writing for people with
hearing loss and identify any organizations or institutions that
might be interested in your book.

High-Quality Books
Sarah Ketchersid, Candlewick Press

Unlike many children's publishers that are imprints and divisions of larger firms, Candlewick Press is an independent company that publishes just children's books, close to 200 a year. It is completely owned and operated by its employees and has achieved its remarkable success, its editors say, by publishing only high-quality books they completely believe in. The result has been a string of best-sellers and awards any size publisher would envy. Outstanding titles range from the picture book classic *Guess How Much I Love You* to the Newbery Honor novel *Because of Winn Dixie*, with lots of award winners in between.

What does "high quality" mean in a toddler book submission? It means your best work, brilliantly polished and, above all, a story worth reading over and over and over. Candlewick Editor Sarah Ketchersid explains: "Beginning writers often write books for toddlers that are too slight. Very few publishers nowadays are doing original board books, so a toddler text is almost always a picture book. Many of the toddler submissions I receive come up short—in length or in story—for a 32-page, hardcover picture book."

By contrast, her ideal submission has "a playful sense of language and a great read-aloud quality. Also, toddler books should be interactive—I don't mean that they need to have flaps or pull-tabs to be interactive— but they should engage the youngest listeners and encourage them to take part in the story in some way." She adds, "A healthy dose of humor and joy helps, too."

(Listing for Candlewick Press on
following page)

Candlewick Press

2067 Massachusetts Avenue
Cambridge, MA 02140

Acquisitions: Liz Bicknell

Publisher's Interests
In operation for more than 10 years, Candlewick Press develops high-quality fiction and nonfiction titles in hardcover and paperback titles. Publishing only material for children, this publisher targets early, middle-grade, and young adult readers.
Website: www.candlewick.com

Freelance Potential
Published 200 titles in 2003.
- **Fiction:** Publishes early picture books and toddler books, 0–4 years; middle-grade books, 8–12 years; and young adult books, 12–18 years. Genres include contemporary, multicultural, historical and science fiction; adventure; mystery; humor; fantasy; and stories about sports.
- **Nonfiction:** Publishes concept books and toddler books, 0–4 years; story picture books, 4–10 years; middle-grade books, 8–12 years; and young adult books 12–18 years. Topics include animals, history, nature, the environment, and geography. Also publishes biographies for young adults.
- **Representative Titles:** *Billy's Bucket* by Kes Gray (3–6 years) is a story of a boy's birthday that reminds us to never underestimate the power of an empty bucket—or a child's imagination. *Snail Boy* by Leslie McGuirk (3–7 years) features a pony-sized talking snail that befriends a young boy.

Submissions and Payment
Guidelines available at website. Currently not accepting unsolicited manuscripts or queries. All writing is done on assignment. Send résumé with writing samples for future consideration. SASE. Response time varies. Publication period varies. Royalty.

Editor's Comments
Due to an overload of manuscripts, we are not accepting unsolicited queries or manuscripts at this time. We invite you to check our website often for updates to our submissions policy. In the meantime, feel free to send your résumé along with writing samples to be considered for future projects.

Capstone Press

7825 Telegraph Road
Minneapolis, MN 55438

Product Planning Editor: Helen Moore

Publisher's Interests
Capstone Press specializes in nonfiction for beginning, chal-
lenged, and reluctant readers, as well as parenting and edu-
cation titles for adults who interact with children. Numerous
imprints are part of the Capstone family, including A+,
Bridgestone, Capstone High-Interest, Pebble, Blue Earth,
Life Matters, Yellow Umbrella, Let Freedom Ring, and
Picture Window.
Website: www.capstone-press.com

Freelance Potential
Published 100 titles (90 juvenile) in 2003. Receives numerous
queries and unsolicited mss yearly.
- **Nonfiction:** Publishes middle-grade books, 8–12 years; and
  young adult books, 12–18 years. Topics include animals, pets,
  crafts, hobbies, geography, health, fitness, history, science,
  technology, sports, and the military. Also publishes biographies
  and self-help, parenting, and education titles.
- **Representative Titles:** *A Free Black Girl Before the Civil War*
  by Christy Steele & Kerry Graves (YA) is the story of a free
  black teen from Massachusetts who fought to abolish slavery.
  Teen Mothers by Julie Endersbe (YA) presents the many
  issues related to sexuality in ways that make sense to teens.

Submissions and Payment
Guidelines available at website. Query with cover letter,
résumé, and 3 short writing samples. SASE. Responds in 1
month. Publication period varies. Flat fee.

Editor's Comments
We are always interested in receiving material from authors
who understand the needs of our unique audience: children
and teens who are interested in reading, but often struggle
with the mechanics. Our mission is to help people learn to
read and read to learn. We publish and distribute accessible,
accurate, attractive, and affordable books to serve the needs of
readers, educators, and librarians. If you have an idea that
suits us, please follow our guidelines and send it in.

Carolrhoda Books

Lerner Publishing Group
241 First Avenue North
Minneapolis, MN 55401

Fiction Submissions Editor: Zelda Wagner

Publisher's Interests
An Imprint of Lerner Publishing Group, Carolrhoda Books
has been publishing children's trade books for more than 30
years. Its catalogue is filled with storybooks, easy-to-read
books, and novels.
Website: www.lernerbooks.com

Freelance Potential
Published 240 titles in 2003: 1 was developed from an unsolicited submission, 1–5 were by agented authors, and 27–28
were reprint/licensed properties. Of the 240 titles, 1–5 were
by authors who were new to the publishing house. Receives
500 queries, 2,000 unsolicited mss yearly.
- **Fiction:** Published 10 story picture books, 4–10 years; and 2
  young adult books, 12–18 years. Also publishes middle-grade
  novels, 8–12 years. Genres include mystery and contemporary,
  historical, and multicultural fiction.
- **Nonfiction:** Published 40 easy-to-read books, 4–7 years; 30
  chapter books, 5–10 years; and 50 middle-grade books, 8–12
  years. Topics include social issues, life science, geography, history, the environment, and sports.
- **Representative Titles:** *Jennifer Jones Won't Leave Me Alone* by
  Frieda Wishinsky (3–8 years) tells the story of a boy who is
  embarrassed by the amorous attention of a classmate. *Martha
  Washington* by Candice Ransom (6–8 years) is a beginning
  reader biography about the woman who set the standards for
  future first ladies.

Submissions and Payment
Guidelines available. Accepts submissions in March and
October only. Query with outline and sample chapters; or
send complete ms. Accepts photocopies and computer printouts. SASE. Responds in 4–6 months. Royalty; advance.

Editor's Comments
Our needs this year include middle-grade and young adult fiction and picture books. We'll also consider high-quality nonfiction, such as biographies and nature and science books.

Carson-Dellosa Publishing Company

P.O. Box 35665
Greensboro, NC 27425

Editorial Director: Jennifer Weaver-Spencer

Publisher's Interests

Carson-Dellosa's catalogue showcases supplementary educational resource materials for use in kindergarten through eighth-grade classrooms. It offers student workbooks, teacher resource and activity books, charts, manipulatives, flash cards, puzzles, and decorative classroom products. Carson-Dellosa has been in operation for more than 25 years.
Website: www.carson-dellosa.com

Freelance Potential

Published 100 titles in 2003: 5 were developed from unsolicited submissions. Of the 100 titles, 20 were by authors who were new to the publishing house. Receives 150–200 queries yearly.

- **Nonfiction:** Publishes supplementary educational materials, pre-K–grade 8. Topics include language arts, mathematics, science, arts and crafts, and multicultural subjects.
- **Representative Titles:** *Daily Math Warm-Ups* (grades 1–5) offers teachers an effective structure for introducing, reinforcing, and assessing student's math skills and is based on NCTM standards. *Writing* by Kelley Wingate (grades 1–5) improves composition skills with age-appropriate activities that emphasize writing building blocks.

Submissions and Payment

Guidelines available. Query with outline and representative pages. Accepts photocopies, computer printouts, and simultaneous submissions if identified. SASE. Responds in 6–8 weeks. Publication in 1–2 years. Flat fee.

Editor's Comments

Please note that we do not accept works of fiction, including children's storybooks. However, ideas for supplementary educational products and books from writers and teachers *are* welcome. In your proposal include a summary of your idea and the book's or product's objectives. State the intended audience or grade level and tell us how this product would stand out from its competition.

Cartwheel Books

Scholastic Inc.
557 Broadway
New York, NY 11105

Executive Editor: Grace Maccarone

Publisher's Interests
This division of Scholastic Inc. publishes a wide variety of books for children up to the age of 10. It considers the work of previously published or agented authors only.
Website: www.scholastic.com

Freelance Potential
Published 100 titles in 2003: 10 were developed from unsolicited submissions, many were by agented authors, and 4 were reprint/licensed properties. Receives 800–1,000 queries, 500–800 unsolicited mss yearly.

- **Fiction:** Published 20 concept books, 20 toddler books, and 20 early picture books, 0–4 years; 20 easy-to-read books, 4–7 years; 10 story picture books, 4–10 years; and 5 chapter books, 5–10 years. Genres include humor and stories about families, friendship, holidays, and animals.
- **Nonfiction:** Publishes concept books, toddler books, and early picture books, 0–4 years; easy-to-read books, 4–7 years; and story picture books, 4–10 years. Topics include mathematics and science.
- **Representative Titles:** *Little Bear Gets Dressed* by Jane Brett (3+ years) teaches young children how to dress themselves. *Barnaby's Bunny* by Wendy Rouillard (4–8 years) is about a young bear who would like to have a class pet, but first must learn responsibility for his teacher to agree. *A Nose Like a Hose* by Jenny Samuels (2–5 years) is a rhyming picture book about an elephant who flaunts his long nose.

Submissions and Payment
Accepts submissions from agents and previously published authors only. Accepts photocopies and computer printouts. SASE. Responds in 3–6 months. Publication period varies. Payment policy varies.

Editor's Comments
We are always interested in easy-to-read fiction for children between the ages of four and eight, and we especially need novelty books designed to appeal to toddlers that can help them learn basic skills.

Charlesbridge

85 Main Street
Watertown, MA 02472

Submissions Editor

Publisher's Interests

Charlesbridge is the nonfiction imprint of Charlesbridge Publishing that focuses on appealing and educational nature, science, social studies, and multicultural books. Other imprints include Talewinds, publishing picture books, and Whispering Coyote, with stories in verse or prose for young children and parents to share.
Website: www.charlesbridge.com

Freelance Potential

Published 28 titles in 2003: 3 were developed from unsolicited submissions, 2 were by agented authors, and 3 were reprint/licensed properties. Of the 28 titles, 2 were by unpublished writers and 3 were by authors who were new to the publishing house. Receives 2,400 unsolicited mss yearly.

- **Nonfiction:** Publishes concept books and toddler books, 0–4 years; and story picture books, 4–10 years. Topics include art, ecology, history, social studies, math, multicultural issues, science, nature, and social issues. Also publishes biographies and poetry.
- **Representative Titles:** *Frogs Sing Songs* by Yvonne Winer (4–9 years) offers young readers a close-up look at some of nature's most musical creatures. *Face-to-Face with the Cat* by Stéphanie Frattini (3–7 years) uses simple text and vivid photographs to present facts about the life cycle of cats.

Submissions and Payment

Guidelines available. Send complete ms. Accepts photocopies and computer printouts. No simultaneous submissions. SASE. Responds in 2–6 months. Publication in 2–5 years. Royalty. Flat fee.

Editor's Comments

We're always interested in fresh, entertaining books, but stress that we review exclusive submissions only. Please be sure to write "Exclusive Submission" on all envelopes and cover letters. Visit our website to view our complete catalogue, the latest version of our guidelines, and tips from our editors.

Charles River Media

10 Downer Avenue
Hingham, AL 02043

President: Dave Pallai

Publisher's Interests
The titles published by Charles River Media cover topics from
computer graphics and animation to networking, game pro-
gramming, and virtually anything related to the Internet. Its
CyberRookies™ series targets readers from 12 to 18 years.
Charles River Media publishes both books and CD-ROMs.
Website: www.charlesriver.com

Freelance Potential
Published 50 titles (10 juvenile) in 2003: 3 were developed
from unsolicited submissions and 6 were by agented authors.
Receives 100 queries yearly.
- **Nonfiction:** Publishes how-to and informational books and CD-
  ROMs about computer graphics, animation, game programming,
  the Internet, and networking.
- **Representative Titles:** *Creating 3D Comix* by R. Shamms
  Mortier (YA) gives tips and tricks for bringing pen and ink char-
  acters to life using 3D art and effects. *Game Programming
  Gems* by Mark DeLoura (YA) offers comprehensive coverage of
  all the major technologies used in game development.

Submissions and Payment
Guidelines and catalogue available on website or with #10
SASE ($.76 postage). Query. Accepts photocopies. Availability
of artwork improves chance of acceptance. SASE. Responds
in 1 month. Publication in 4 months. Royalty, 5–15% of net;
advance, $1,000–$7,500.

Editor's Comments
All of our material is targeted to readers age 11 or older who
have some experience with computers and electronics and are
looking for useful, accurate information that will help them
expand their knowledge and learn new skills. If you have the
expertise to write knowledgeably on topics such as graphics,
animation, game programming, and networking, send us a
query explaining your idea for a book or CD-ROM. Please go to
our website to review our guidelines and catalogue carefully
before sending your submission.

Chelsea House Publishers

Suite 400
1974 Sproul Road
Broomhall, PA 19008-0914

Editorial Assistant

Publisher's Interests
This well-known educational publisher produces curriculum-based titles for use in the school and library markets. It publishes nonfiction for middle-grade and young adult readers, and the majority of books found in its catalogue are published in series.
Website: www.chelseahouse.com

Freelance Potential
Published 300 titles in 2003: 75 were reprint/licensed properties. Of the 300 titles, 73 were by unpublished writers and 110 were by authors who were new to the publishing house. Receives 300 queries, 50 unsolicited mss yearly.
- **Nonfiction:** Publishes middle-grade books, 8–12 years; and young adult books, 12–18 years. Topics include American history, world history, African-American studies, the classics, criminal justice, sports, popular culture, science, travel, drug education, and Christian studies. Also publishes books about parenting, literary criticism, and reference titles for adults.
- **Representative Titles:** *Discovering Antarctica: The People* by June Loves follows the earliest explorers to the region and their race to explore the South Pole. *Maya Angelou* by Miles Shapiro tells the story of this well-known poet who has inspired people of all ages with her work.

Submissions and Payment
Guidelines available. All books are assigned. Send résumé with clips or writing samples. No queries or unsolicited mss. SASE. Publication period varies. Flat fee.

Editor's Comments
Our mission is to bring librarians and media specialists the highest-quality nonfiction books for children and young adults. We are always willing to review résumés from writers with demonstrated expertise in one of the areas we cover. Keep in mind that most of our series are developed in-house and that we usually assign projects to authors familiar to us. But if your qualifications meet our needs, get in touch.

Chicago Review Press

814 North Franklin Street
Chicago, IL 60610

Editorial Director: Cynthia Sherry

Publisher's Interests
This nonfiction publisher offers children's activity books for a
variety of age ranges, as well as how-to titles, biographies,
nature writing, and books about parenting. Chicago Review
Press is now in its thirtieth year.
Website: www.ipgbook.com

Freelance Potential
Published 42 titles (8 juvenile) in 2003: 5 were developed
from unsolicited submissions, 10 were by agented authors,
and 6 were reprint/licensed properties. Of the 42 titles, 8
were by unpublished writers and 15 were by authors who
were new to the publishing house. Receives 600 queries, 400
unsolicited mss yearly.
- **Nonfiction:** Published 8 middle-grade books, 8–12 years. Also
  publishes toddler books, 0–4 years; primary books, 6–9 years;
  and young adult titles, 12–18 years. Topics include science,
  mathematics, social issues, history, literature, and art.
- **Representative Titles:** *The Wright Brothers for Kids* by Mary
  Kay Carson (9+ years) is an activity book that highlights the
  Wright brothers' ingenuity and problem-solving skills. *Rain-
  forests: An Activity Guide* by Nancy F. Castaldo (6–9 years)
  takes kids through the common layers of the rainforest, from
  the forest floor to above the canopy.

Submissions and Payment
Guidelines available. Query with 1–2 sample chapters and/or
projects; or send complete ms with résumé. Accepts photocopies, computer printouts, and simultaneous submissions if
identified. SASE. Responds in 8–10 weeks. Publication in
1–20 months. Royalty, 7–10%; advance, $1,500.

Editor's Comments
Activity books for readers ages six through nine remain a top
editorial priority. In your submission, include information
about your credentials. It's also a good idea to describe the
book's competition and market. Are there possibilities of sales
to organizations or institutions?

Children's Book Press

2211 Mission Street
San Francisco, CA 94110

Editorial Submissions

Publisher's Interests
Now in its twenty-ninth year, Children's Book Press is dedicated to providing elementary school children with books about contemporary life in the Latino/Chicano, African-American, Asian-American, multi-racial, and new immigrant communities.
Website: www.cbookpress.org

Freelance Potential
Published 4 titles in 2003: 1 was developed from an unsolicited submission. Receives 1,200 unsolicited mss yearly.
- **Fiction:** Publishes story picture books, 4–10 years. Genres include ethnic, multicultural, and social fiction.
- **Nonfiction:** Publishes story picture books, 4–10 years. Topics include social issues and ethnic and multicultural communities and culture.
- **Representative Titles:** *My Diary from Here to There* by Amada Irma Pérez (6+ years) is a bilingual storybook about a young girl's journey with her family from Ciudad Juárez, Mexico, to their new home in Los Angeles. *Bears Make Rock Soup* by Lise Erdrich (6+ years) is a collection of Native-American stories that pay homage to the people, animals, forests, and rivers that live in harmony beneath the wide skies of the Plains.

Submissions and Payment
Guidelines available at website. Send complete ms. Accepts photocopies, computer printouts, and simultaneous submissions if identified. SASE. Responds in 2+ months. Publication in 12–18 months. Royalty; advance.

Editor's Comments
Our mission is to broaden the base of children's literature by publishing multicultural and bilingual stories that reflect the diversity and experiences of minority and new immigrant communities in the United States. We like to see children in active roles in stories, and we like stories that are told from the children's point of view. We favor material that encourages critical thinking about social or personal issues.

Children's eLibrary

24 West 25th Street
New York, NY 10010

Submissions Editor: Jim Kirchman

Publisher's Interests

Formerly known as iPicturebooks, Inc., Children's eLibrary specializes in picture books for young readers. All of its material is published exclusively on the Internet. Both fiction and nonfiction titles on a wide range of subjects are featured at its website. In addition to original titles, the publisher also licenses rights to out-of-print titles. The site is powered by ipicturebooks.com, an affiliate of the AOL Time Warner Books Group.
Website: www.childrenselibrary.com

Freelance Potential

Published 600 titles in 2003: 90 were developed from unsolicited submissions. Receives 2,000 queries yearly.
- **Fiction:** Publishes stories about nature and the environment; humor; historical, multicultural, and ethnic fiction; fantasy; fairy tales; folklore; and folktales.
- **Nonfiction:** Publishes books about nature, the environment, animals, pets, science, technology, and multicultural and ethnic subjects. Also features biographies.
- **Representative Titles:** *A Beautiful Seashell* by Ruth Lercher Bornstein (3–4 years) is the story of a grandmother recalling her youth in a house by the sea. *Water* by Nicola Edwards explores the qualities of water, where it comes from, and what can be done with it; part of the Science Explorers series.

Submissions and Payment

Guidelines available at website. Query via email following instructions at website. SASE. Responds in 1–2 weeks. Publication in 1 year. Royalty.

Editor's Comments

Our site is designed to appeal to teachers and librarians seeking original or out-of-print material for use on school networked computers. New books that work well in electronic form are always of interest to us. If you are curious about what we produce and want to join our site, we ask you to visit first. We have specific instructions about submitting work.

Childswork/Childsplay

A Guidance Channel Company
135 Dupont Street
P.O. Box 760
Plainview, NY 11803-0760

Editor: Karen Schader

Publisher's Interests
With a focus on the social and emotional needs of children and adolescents, this publisher creates books for teachers, therapists, and parents that will help them positively influence children's lives. Childswork/Childsplay publishes a wide range of books, games, audio and video tapes, and creative software programs.
Website: www.childswork.com

Freelance Potential
Published 7 titles in 2003: 1 was developed from an unsolicited submission. Of the 7 titles, 1 was by an unpublished writer and 1 was by an author who was new to the publishing house. Receives 200 queries, 175 unsolicited mss yearly.

- **Nonfiction:** Publishes informational titles, games, and activity books, 6–12 years.
- **Representative Titles:** *The Bear Who Lost His Sleep* by Jessica Lamb-Shapiro (4–8 years) helps children reduce their anxiety by reasoning out their concerns. *Calm Down & Play* by Loretta Oleck-Berger (5–12 years) is an activity book designed to help impulsive children learn to control their behavior and play productively with others.

Submissions and Payment
Guidelines available. Query with clips or writing samples. Accepts photocopies and computer printouts. No simultaneous submissions. SASE. Responds in 1 month. Publication in 6 months. Flat fee.

Editor's Comments
The products we publish and produce must first and foremost be fun to read, play with, listen to, or view. Our target audience is therapists and teachers, but the end-user of everything we create is a child, so products must have a distinctive appeal to children. We urge you to familiarize yourself with our materials before sending a submission. If you have an idea you think would interest us, send a query with a cover letter describing the market for your product.

Child Welfare League of America

3rd Floor
440 First Street NW
Washington, DC 20001

Acquisitions Editor: Peggy Tierney

Publisher's Interests
The Child & Family Press imprint of this publisher offers children and parents books that will help them cope with issues like separation anxiety and disabilities. Its CWLA Press imprint offers books and training materials for professionals who work with children and families.
Website: www.cwla.org/pubs

Freelance Potential
Published 25 titles (4 juvenile) in 2003: 22 were developed from unsolicited submissions and 3 were by agented authors. Of the 25 titles published, 12 were by previously unpublished writers and 13 were by writers who were new to the publishing house. Receives 1,500 unsolicited mss yearly.
- **Fiction:** Published 3 story picture books, 4–10 years; and 1 chapter book, 5–10 years. Also publishes middle-grade novels, 8–12 years.
- **Nonfiction:** Publishes titles for parents, professionals, and volunteers in the fields of social work, human services, child welfare, and child care. Topics include adoption, foster care, child abuse and neglect, and teen pregnancy.
- **Representative Titles:** *The Kissing Hand* by Audrey Penn is the story of Chester Raccoon and his mother, and the ways they reassure each other at separations. *Learning How to Learn: Getting Into and Surviving College When You Have a Learning Disability* by Joyanne Cobb (YA) offers resources and practical tips in an inspirational and LD-friendly format; includes a guide to LD-friendly colleges and universities.

Submissions and Payment
Send complete ms. Accepts photocopies, computer printouts, and email submissions to ptierney@cwla.org. SASE. Responds in 3–6 months. Publication in 2 years. Royalty.

Editor's Comments
We are seeking books that help children and adults deal with life's challenges. Titles for children should be engaging and original. Titles for professionals should be well researched.

Christian Ed. Publishers

P.O. Box 26639
San Diego, CA 92196

Assistant Editor: Janet Ackelson

Publisher's Interests

Christian Ed. Publishers is an independent, evangelical publishing company, producing curriculum materials based on the Word of God. Its mission is to introduce young people to a personal faith in Jesus Christ. Its list includes both fiction and nonfiction for preschool through high school students. **Website:** www.christianedwarehouse.com

Freelance Potential

Published 80 titles in 2003: 6 were by unpublished writers and 10 were by authors who were new to the publishing house. Receives 300 queries yearly.

- **Fiction:** Publishes religious fiction, pre-K–grade 12.
- **Nonfiction:** Publishes Christian educational titles, Bible-based curriculum, and Bible club materials, grades K–12.
- **Representative Titles:** *Honeybees for Jesus* (2–3 years) helps the very young learn simple Bible concepts, that God loves them, and that Jesus is their friend. *All-Stars for Jesus–Middlers* (grades 3–4) helps children learn how to live according to God's Word and how to grow spiritually.

Submissions and Payment

Guidelines and catalogue available with 9x12 SASE (4 first-class stamps). All work by assignment only. Publication in 12–18 months. Flat fee, $.03 per word.

Editor's Comments

All of the people who write for us are spiritually dedicated and help assist in their ministries. They have hands-on experience in writing for children and young adults and agree with our statement of faith. If you are an experienced writer who meets these requirements, we'd welcome your request for a freelance writer application. After we review your application, if you are right for us, we will place you on our list of available writers. All work is done by assignment only. Keep in mind that the type of material we publish is very specific. We are currently looking for curriculum books for preschoolers, church-wide special events programs, and Bible-teaching crafts.

Christian Focus Publications, Ltd.

Geanies House, Fearn by Tain
Ross-shire IV20 1TW
Scotland

Children's Editor: Catherine Mackenzie

Publisher's Interests
Christian Focus Publications offers biblically-accurate
books for adults and children. Its children's titles help
young readers discover Christ, teach them about God, and
inspire them to become lifelong Bible readers. As an evangelical, reformed, non-denominational company, Christian Focus
Publications believes that God's Word is true.
Website: www.christianfocus.com

Freelance Potential
Published 100 titles (35 juvenile) in 2003: 2 were developed
from unsolicited submissions and 1 was by an agented
author. Receives 360 queries, 240 unsolicited mss yearly.
- **Fiction:** Publishes chapter books, 7–10 years; middle-grade
  books, 9–13 years; and young adult books, 12+ years. Genres
  include contemporary fiction.
- **Nonfiction:** Publishes Bible story books, devotionals, biographies, puzzle books, and activity books.
- **Representative Titles:** *Amazon Adventures* by Horace Banner
  describes the culture of the Amazon Rain Forest through stories that include a Bible verse and a lesson for the reader to
  take away. *The Caring Creator* by Carine MacKenzie (6–9 years)
  tells the story of how God created the world and how He continues to look after it.

Submissions and Payment
Guidelines available at website. Query with author information sheet, synopsis, chapter headings, and 3 sample chapters. Send complete ms for works shorter than 10 chapters.
Accepts email submissions to Catherine.Mackenzie@
christianfocus.com. SAE/IRC. Does not return mss to
authors outside the UK. Response time, publication period,
and payment policy vary.

Editor's Comments
We need authors for our Torchbearers series. Aimed at 8- to
11-year-old readers, the style of this series is fictional, but
each book focuses on a real martyr from history.

Christopher-Gordon Publishers

Suite 12
1502 Providence Highway
Norwood, MA 02062

Vice President: Susanne F. Canavan

Publisher's Interests

This publisher caters to the educational market with assessment and instructional books on reading, writing, math, science, and general education. It also offers titles related to self improvement.
Website: www.christopher-gordon.com

Freelance Potential

Published 25+ titles in 2003: 4 were developed from unsolicited submissions. Receives 150 queries, 50 unsolicited mss yearly.

- **Nonfiction:** Publishes in-service development materials for educators at all grade levels. Topics include assessment and instruction, children's literature, teaching literature, supervision and school improvement, professional self-development, technology, math, and education law.
- **Representative Titles:** *Literature Circles in Middle School: One Teacher's Journey* by Bonnie Campbell et al. (educators) features ready-to-use materials for improving literature circles in the classroom. *Making Facts Come Alive* by Rosemary A. Bamford and Janice V. Kristo (teachers, grades K–8) helps teachers evaluate and choose the best in nonfiction literature and examines the role nonfiction plays in the curriculum.

Submissions and Payment

Guidelines and catalogue available with #10 SASE ($.57 postage). Query with table of contents, sample chapters, and market analysis; or send complete ms. Accepts photocopies. SASE. Response time varies. Publication in 18 months. Royalty, varies; advance, varies.

Editor's Comments

We are looking for educators who can bring us books that offer innovative techniques and ideas that will bring teachers concrete ideas they can use in the classroom. Include a market analysis with your query, tell us how your book will be used as a learning tool, and explain what makes it better than others currently available.

Chronicle Books

6th Floor
85 Second Street
San Francisco, CA 94105

Submissions Editor: Dora Bolgar

Publisher's Interests
Chronicle Books publishes a range of books for children up
to the age of 14, as well as fine art books for adults. Founded
in 1966, it focuses on picture books for children up to age
eight and nonfiction for middle-grade readers.
Website: www.chroniclekids.com

Freelance Potential
Published 175 titles (45 juvenile) in 2003: 12 were developed
from unsolicited submissions, 8 were by agented authors,
and 18 were reprint/licensed properties. Receives 2,500
queries, 20,000 unsolicited mss yearly.
- **Fiction:** Publishes concept books, toddler books, and early picture books, 0–4 years; easy-to-read books, 4–7 years; and story
  picture books, 4–10 years. Genres include folktales and contemporary, multicultural, and ethnic fiction.
- **Nonfiction:** Publishes chapter books, 5–10 years; and middle-grade books, 8–12 years. Topics include nature, science,
  history, and social issues. Also publishes fine art titles about
  design, art, architecture, and photography for adults.
- **Representative Titles:** *Ruby's Wish* by Shirin Yim Bridges (4–8
  years) is the story of a young Chinese girl determined to go to
  the university rather than get married as tradition dictates. *The
  Moon Ring* by Randy DuBurke (4–8 years) tells about a girl who
  finds a magical moon ring in the grass one special night.

Submissions and Payment
Guidelines available. Send complete ms for picture books.
Query with outline/synopsis and 3 sample chapters for
longer works. Accepts photocopies and simultaneous submissions if identified. SASE. Responds in 4–6 months. Publication in 1–4 years. Royalty; advance. Flat fee.

Editor's Comments
We specialize in high-quality books that have a unique and
vibrant spirit our readers will enjoy. Our primary interests
right now are fiction and nonfiction picture books for young
children, and middle-grade chapter books.

Clarion Books

Houghton Mifflin Company
215 Park Avenue South
New York, NY 10003

Editorial Director/Associate Publisher: Dinah Stevenson

Publisher's Interests
This widely recognized imprint of Houghton Mifflin targets
children of all ages with fiction and nonfiction picture books
and chapter books, as well as titles for middle-grade and
young adult readers.
Website: www.hmco.com

Freelance Potential
Published 60 titles in 2003: 6 were developed from unsolicited submissions, 20 were by agented authors, and 6 were
reprint/licensed properties. Receives 500 queries, 2,500
unsolicited mss yearly.
- **Fiction:** Publishes picture books, 3–8 years; chapter books,
  7–10 years; middle-grade novels, 8–12 years; and young adult
  novels, 12–18 years. Genres include adventure, folktales, fairy
  tales, and historical and science fiction.
- **Nonfiction:** Publishes picture books, 3–6 years; middle-grade
  books, 8–12 years; and young adult books, 12–18 years. Topics
  include biography, nature, ecology, history, holidays, and multicultural and ethnic issues.
- **Representative Titles:** *Clarabella's Teeth* by An Vrombaut (3–6
  years) is a picture book about a crocodile and her animal
  friends who learn about the importance of taking care of their
  teeth. *Bound for the North Star* by Dennis Brindell Fradin (YA)
  features 12 accounts of runaway slaves who successfully
  escaped and includes archival photographs and prints.

Submissions and Payment
Guidelines available. Query for chapter books and novels;
send complete ms for picture books. Accepts photocopies and
computer printouts. SASE. Responds in 4 months. Publication in 2 years. Royalty.

Editor's Comments
Our list features quality fiction and nonfiction for very
young readers through teenagers. We consider unsolicited
submissions, but please don't send computer disks, faxes,
or email submissions.

I. E. Clark Publications

P.O. Box 246
Schulenburg, TX 78956-0246

General Manager: Donna Cozzaglio

Publisher's Interests

This publisher's catalogue of plays and musicals includes many suitable for children's theater and school classrooms. Both classical and contemporary plays are available from I. E. Clark, and it also offers plays about holidays, religion, and multicultural subjects.

Website: www.ieclark.com

Freelance Potential

Published 5 titles in 2003: 1 was developed from an unsolicited submission and 2 were by agented authors. Of the 5 titles, 2 were by unpublished writers and 1 was by an author who was new to the publishing house. Receives 500+ unsolicited mss yearly.

- **Fiction:** Publishes middle-grade plays, 8–12 years; and young adult plays, 12–18 years. Features drama classics, musicals, religious and holiday plays, and plays with bilingual and multicultural themes.
- **Representative Titles:** *Toys in the Haunted Castle* by Pat Zawadsky is a children's theater play, inspired by Oscar Wilde's "The Canterville Ghost," about a doll and a Jack-in-the-Box who have been left in a deserted castle for years. *Juvie* by Jerome McDonough (YA) is a play about juvenile delinquents who have committed crimes or are hooked on drugs.

Submissions and Payment

Guidelines available. Send complete ms with reviews, programs, or other proof of production. Accepts photocopies, computer printouts, and simultaneous submissions if identified. SASE. Responds in 6+ months. Publication in 6–12 months. Royalty.

Editor's Comments

You should make every effort to get your play produced before sending it to us. If your play has been produced, send newspaper reviews and photographs. Good reviews won't guarantee publication and bad reviews won't guarantee rejection. We make up our own minds regarding the marketability of a play.

Clear Light Publishers

823 Don Diego
Santa Fe, NM 87505

Publisher: Houghton Harmon

Publisher's Interests
This publisher's books explore Southwestern, Native American, and Hispanic themes. Offering both fiction and nonfiction, it has a juvenile list that includes picture books, novels, and nonfiction.
Website: www.clearlightbooks.com

Freelance Potential
Published 10 titles (2 juvenile) in 2003. Receives 250+ unsolicited mss yearly.
- **Fiction:** Publishes story picture books, 4–10 years; and young adult books, 12–18 years. Genres include historical, regional, multicultural, and inspirational fiction.
- **Nonfiction:** Publishes middle-grade books, 8–12 years; and 2 young adult books, 12–18 years. Topics include nature, religion, history, multicultural and ethnic subjects, social issues, health, and fitness. Also publishes biographies.
- **Representative Titles:** *Children's Book of Yoga* by Thia Luby (3–12 years) is a new program of yoga designed to appeal to children and includes six complete workouts with more than 40 poses. *Circle of Wonder: A Native American Christmas Story* by N. Scott Momaday (all ages) is the story of one lonely child's experience of Christmas that takes the reader into a world of spiritual magic created by faith and love.

Submissions and Payment
Send complete ms. Accepts photocopies, computer printouts, and simultaneous submissions if identified. Availability of artwork improves chance of acceptance. SASE. Responds in 3 months. Publication in 1 year. Royalty.

Editor's Comments
Our purpose is to enrich the lives of our readers by offering stories and nonfiction titles that accurately portray the culture of Native Americans and Hispanics. We offer many retold stories and legends as well as original writing that captures the essence of these cultures. Books that can be published in a bilingual format are an ongoing need.

Concordia Publishing House

3558 South Jefferson Avenue
St. Louis, MO 63118-3968

Acquisitions Editor: Peggy Kuethe

Publisher's Interests
Nonfiction books for children and adults that relate to some
aspect of the Christian faith are the specialty of this publisher, which is a division of the Lutheran Church-Missouri
Synod. All work is now being assigned; unsolicited freelance
work is no longer considered.
Website: www.cph.org

Freelance Potential
Published 40 titles (25 juvenile) in 2003: 4 were developed
from unsolicited submissions, 1 was by an agented author,
and 10 were reprint/licensed properties. Of the 40 titles, 4
were by authors who were new to the publishing house.
- **Nonfiction:** Publishes early picture books, 0–4 years; easy-to-
  read books, 4–7 years; and story picture books, 4–10 years.
  Topics include religious issues.
- **Representative Titles:** *3 in 1* by Joanne Marxhausen (4–9
  years) explains the concept of the Trinity to young children by
  using an apple and relating its skin, flesh, and seeds to the
  Father, Son, and Holy Spirit. *Send a Baby* by Mary Manz
  Simon (2–6 years) presents the story of the birth of John the
  Baptist in a classroom-size version teachers can read aloud.

Submissions and Payment
No longer accepting unsolicited submissions. All work is now
done by assignment only. Query or send résumé.

Editor's Comments
If you are interested in writing for us, you need to send us a
résumé that lists your qualifications and specifies the writing
you have done in the past. Familiarize yourself with our publishing interests to make sure your background is appropriate
for us. There are only a few opportunities for new writers at
Concordia Publishing. Since we are no longer accepting freelance submissions and have several authors with whom we
have worked in the past, we are most likely to assign work to
them first. All unsolicited manuscripts will be returned without
being read.

Contemporary Drama Service

Meriwether Publishing Ltd.
885 Elkton Drive
Colorado Springs, CO 80907

Associate Editors: Theodore Zapel & Rhonda Wray

Publisher's Interests

Dramatic material for children ages eight and up is available from this publisher. Its catalogue is filled with plays, skits, musicals, and speech resource materials that are used by middle and high school drama programs, community theaters, and churches.
Website: www.contemporarydrama.com

Freelance Potential

Published 70 titles in 2003: 50 were developed from unsolicited submissions and 5 were by agented authors. Of the 70 titles, 15 were by authors who were new to the publishing house. Receives 1,600 queries yearly.

- **Fiction:** Publishes middle-grade plays, 8–12 years; and young adult plays, 12–18 years. Publishes musicals, folktales, and fantasies. Also offers skits, adaptations, novelty plays, parodies, and social commentaries.
- **Nonfiction:** Publishes young adult books, 12–18 years. Features books about improvisations, theater games, speech, acting techniques, and theater arts.
- **Representative Titles:** *Plays for Young Audiences by Max Bush* by Roger Ellis, ed. includes 10 full-length plays by Max Bush, including adaptations of classics, heroic fantasy adventures, and dramas that deal with social issues. *You Can Do Christian Puppets* by Bea Carlton explains how to create papier-mache and cloth puppets as well as a folding stage.

Submissions and Payment

Guidelines available. Query with outline/synopsis. Accepts photocopies, computer printouts, and simultaneous submissions if identified. SASE. Responds in 6 weeks. Publication in 6 months. Royalty. Flat fee. Special projects, negotiable.

Editor's Comments

Play submissions should include cast and prop lists, information on costumes, and set specifications. Queries on theatercraft books should define the book's market. Please include a list of your publishing credits and/or experience.

Cook Communications Ministries

4050 Lee Vance View
Colorado Springs, CO 80918-7100

Editorial Assistant

Publisher's Interests
Educational and entertaining fiction and nonfiction—all with
Christian themes—can be found in Cook Communications
Ministries' catalogue. Its juvenile list includes concept books,
picture books, and books for early and middle-grade readers.
Website: www.cookministries.com

Freelance Potential
Published 75 titles (30 juvenile) in 2003: 5 were developed
from unsolicited submissions and 49 were by agented
authors. Of the 75 titles, 1 was by an unpublished writer and
5 were by authors who were new to the publishing house.
Receives 1,500 queries yearly.
- **Fiction:** Publishes concept books, toddler books, and early picture books, 0–4 years; easy-to-read books, 4–7 years; chapter
  books, 5–10 years; and middle-grade books, 8–12 years. Also
  publishes books in series, 8–12 years. Genres include inspirational and religious fiction.
- **Nonfiction:** Publishes concept books and early picture books,
  0–4 years; story picture books, 4–10 years; and middle-grade
  books, 8–12 years. Topics include religion and social issues.
  Also publishes self-help titles and reference books for adults.
- **Representative Titles:** *The Non-Praying Mantis* by Matt Whit-
  lock (4–7 years) features a bug's view on prayer, pride, and per-
  severance. *Jesus' Early Years* (6–12 years) focuses on Jesus'
  birth and Christmas and Advent activities; part of the Creative
  Bible Activities for Children series.

Submissions and Payment
Guidelines available. Query with clips. Accepts photocopies
and simultaneous submissions if identified. SASE. Responds
in 2 weeks. Publication in 2 years. Payment policy varies.

Editor's Comments
For the coming year, we need board books for toddlers and
chapter books for middle-grade readers. New writers should try
to submit a picture or board book that presents a basic Bible
story or addresses an overtly Christian theme.

Corwin Press

2455 Teller Road
Thousand Oaks, CA 91320

Editorial Department

Publisher's Interests
Corwin Press publishes books for educators in kindergarten
through grade 12 to help them with their daily responsibilities and offer new and innovative teaching techniques they
can put to work in the classroom.
Website: www.corwinpress.com

Freelance Potential
Published 6 titles in 2003.
- **Nonfiction:** Publishes books for educators of children in grades
  K–12 on topics such as administration, assessment and evalu-
  ation, professional development, curriculum development,
  classroom practice, special education, gifted and talented edu-
  cation, bilingual learners, counseling, school health, and using
  technology in the classroom.
- **Representative Titles:** *What's So Funny About Education?* by
  Lou Fournier and Tom McKeith (educators) is a playful and
  humorous satire that offers fresh insights on education. *Time-
  Saving Tips for Teachers* by Joanne C. Wachter and Clare
  Carhart (educators) offers practical ideas that work.

Submissions and Payment
Guidelines available. Query with outline and prospectus
including alternative titles, rationale, prospective market, and
competitive analysis. SASE. Response time varies. Publication
in 7 months. Royalty.

Editor's Comments
We're looking for books based on theory, research, and practical experience that our readers can learn from and put into
practice in their lives and in their classrooms. Books should
offer practical, hands-on advice to educators who want to be
successful in their chosen careers, and should be user-friendly
with a style and format tailored to suit the busy schedule all
educators have. We are not interested in books that simply
summarize existing knowledge. We want books that offer fresh
insights, conclusions, and recommendations for action—sub-
stantive and practical books that are readable and useful.

Coteau Books

401-2206 Dewdney Avenue
Regina, Saskatchewan S4R 1H3
Canada

Managing Editor: Nik L. Burton

Publisher's Interests
Coteau Books publishes titles written by Canadian authors.
A literary publisher, it offers quality chapter books for mid-
dle-grade and young adult readers.
Website: www.coteaubooks.com

Freelance Potential
Published 20 titles (10 juvenile) in 2003: 20 were developed
from unsolicited submissions. Of the 20 titles, 6 were by
unpublished writers and 6 were by authors who were new to
the publishing house. Receives 500–700 queries, 200–300
unsolicited mss yearly.
- **Fiction:** Publishes chapter books, 5–10 years, middle-grade
  books, 8–12 years; and young adult novels, 12–18 years.
  Genres include regional, contemporary, and historical fiction;
  adventure; mystery; suspense; and humor. Also publishes
  stories about nature and the environment
- **Representative Titles:** *Come Like Shadows* by Welwyn Wilton
  Katz (YA) tells how an ancient curse on the play Macbeth
  threatens two young actors as they stage a modern production. *Tunnels of Time* by Mary Harelkin Bishop (11+ years) is
  about mysterious tunnels that take a girl back in time to the
  dangerous past.

Submissions and Payment
Canadian authors only. Guidelines available with 9x12 SASE
($.90 Canadian postage). Query with summary, writing sam-
ples, and curriculum vitae; or send complete ms. Accepts
photocopies and computer printouts. No simultaneous submissions. SASE. Responds in 3–6 months. Publication in 1–2
years. Royalty; 10%.

Editor's Comments
We are a serious, literary publisher, and many of our books
have won awards. The manuscripts we will consider must be
of the highest quality, and we will consider work from Canadian authors only. At this time, we are interested in fiction
for middle-grade readers, and young adult novels.

Covenant Communications

Box 416
American Fork, UT 84003-0416

Managing Editor: Shauna Nelson

Publisher's Interests

This publisher offers books, audio tapes, and video products for all ages—all of which support the doctrines and values of The Church of Jesus Christ of the Latter-day Saints.
Website: www.covenantcom-lds.com

Freelance Potential

Published 120 titles in 2003: 15 were developed from unsolicited submissions and 4 were reprint/licensed properties. Of the 15 titles, 12 were by unpublished writers and 17 were by authors who were new to the publishing house. Receives 600 unsolicited mss yearly.

- **Fiction:** Published 1 early picture book, 0–4 years; 2 story picture books, 4–10 years; and 3 young adult books, 12–18 years. Genres include adventure, humor, suspense, romance, science fiction, and inspirational and historical fiction.
- **Nonfiction:** Published 1 concept book and 3 toddler books, 0–4 years; 2 easy-to-read books, 4–7 years; and 1 story picture book, 4–10 years. Also publishes biographies, activity books, novelty and board books, photo essays, and reference titles. Topics include history, religion, and regional subjects.
- **Representative Titles:** *Tower of Thunder* by Chris Heimerdinger is an adventure story set in biblical times about a brother and sister who save a baby from a power-hungry king; part of the Tennis Shoes Adventure series. *My Little Book About Prayer* by Val Chadwick Bagley (3–5 years) is a board book that uses simple words to express the power of prayer.

Submissions and Payment

Guidelines available at website. Send ms with summary. Accepts photocopies, computer printouts, disk submissions, and email to tylerm@covenant-lds.com. SASE. Responds in 3 months. Publication in 6–12 months. Payment policy varies.

Editor's Comments

Please review the author guidelines on our website before submitting your manuscript. We look for work that is original, insightful, thorough, and well-written.

Creative Bound

P.O. Box 424
151 Tansley Drive
Carp, Ontario K0A 1L0
Canada

Editor: Jill Grassie

Publisher's Interests
This Canadian publisher specializes in nonfiction titles that focus on personal growth and enhanced performance. Now in its nineteenth year, it develops parenting titles, self-help books, and books dedicated to the exploration of body, mind, and spirit. In 2004 it will begin accepting submissions for children's books.
Website: www.creativebound.com

Freelance Potential
Published 4 titles in 2003: 1 was developed from an unsolicited submission. Of the 4 titles, 2 were by unpublished writers and 2 were by authors who were new to the publishing house. Receives 120 queries yearly.
- **Nonfiction:** Publishes informational and self-help books. Topics include parenting, personal growth, health, fitness, spirituality, recovery, healing, business, motivation, and teaching.
- **Representative Titles:** *Feeling Great: Teaching Children to Excel at Living* (parents) by Dr. Terry Orlick offers ideas and more than 100 activities designed to help children cope with stress and act on good decisions. *Who's in Charge? A Guide to Family Management* by Dr. Maggie Mamen (parents) uses the metaphor of running a small company to provide a troubleshooting approach for parents who want to regain control.

Submissions and Payment
Guidelines available with 6x9 SAE/IRC. Accepts photocopies and IBM disk submissions. SAE/IRC. Responds in 1 month. Publication in 6–12 months. Royalty.

Editor's Comments
We continue to look for quality titles that offer innovative ideas for parents. Books that deal with personal growth and the development of body, mind, and spirit are also always needed. Our mandate is to "help experts get their message out." To that end, we now provide publication services to self-motivated authors of nonfiction products. We will also begin reviewing ideas for children's books this year.

The Creative Company

123 South Broad Street
Mankato, MN 56001

Editor: Aaron Frisch

Publisher's Interests

This publisher targets the school and library markets with
nonfiction titles that are part of a series. It also offers a variety of books for the trade market. The Creative Company primarily publishes books for children in kindergarten through
grade six, and covers such topics as animals, science, sports,
and geography.

Freelance Potential

Published 100 titles in 2003: 8 were developed from unsolicited submissions and 4 were by agented authors. Of the
100 titles, 1 was by an unpublished writer and 4 were by
authors who were new to the publishing house. Receives 200
unsolicited mss yearly.

- **Fiction:** Publishes story picture books, 4–10 years; and young
  adult books, 12–18 years.
- **Nonfiction:** Publishes story picture books, 4–10 years; chapter books, 5–10 years; and young adult books, 12–18 years.
  Topics include nature, science, the environment, animals,
  sports, geography, endangered species, astronomy, the arts,
  literature, humanities, world history, and explorers. Also
  publishes poetry.
- **Representative Titles:** *Little Red Riding Hood* by Charles Per-
  rault and Sarah Moon (14+ years) retells the classic tale with
  haunting photography. *Cheetahs* by Jill Kalz (4–10 years) presents facts about these intriguing big cats; part of the Let's
  Investigate series.

Submissions and Payment

Guidelines available. Send complete ms. Accepts photocopies.
SASE. Responds in 10–12 weeks. Publication in 2 years.
Flat fee.

Editor's Comments

Unlike many other publishers, we do not rely on a committee
to select what we publish. Our publisher and art director make
every selection, and continue to shepherd it through the publishing process, ensuring a level of quality rarely found today.

Creative Editions

123 South Broad Street
Mankato, MN 56001

Managing Editor: Aaron Frisch

Publisher's Interests
Creative Editions, an imprint of The Creative Company, publishes fiction, nonfiction, poetry, and picture books for children of all ages on a wide range of topics.

Freelance Potential
Published 5 titles in 2003: 3 were by agented authors.
Receives 50 queries yearly.
- **Fiction:** Publishes story picture books, 4–10 years; and young adult books, 12–18 years. Genres include fairy tales and folktales. Also publishes poetry.
- **Nonfiction:** Publishes young adult books, 12–18 years. Topics include nature, the environment, animals, and sports. Also features biographies.
- **Representative Titles:** *I Met a Dinosaur* by Jan Wahl & Chris Sheban (4–8 years) is the rhyming tale of a girl whose imagination is sparked by a visit to The Museum of Natural History. *The Last Resort* by J. Patrick Lewis (9–14 years) is the story of an artist who goes on a search for his lost imagination and ends up at The Last Resort, a mysterious seaside hotel.

Submissions and Payment
Query with 500-word sample from manuscript. Accepts photocopies and computer printouts. No simultaneous submissions. SASE. Responds in 4–6 months. Publication in 4 years. Royalty; advance.

Editor's Comments
We are always interested in new authors and new ideas, but we are very selective, and insist on excellent writing, truly unique story ideas, and creative, distinctive design and illustration. Prospective writers should look at our current catalogue and the titles on our list before sending us their proposal. If you feel you have a unique book idea that our readers will cherish for years to come, send us a 500-word sample. With over 70 years in the publishing business, only a few books make it through our review process every year, and the books we publish are of the highest quality.

Creative Education

123 South Broad Street
Mankato, MN 56001

Managing Editor: Aaron Frisch

Publisher's Interests
Creative Education, an imprint of The Creative Company,
publishes books for libraries and schools to use as resource
materials in the classroom. Many of its titles are published as
part of a series. Books for readers from eight to eighteen
years are its specialty, and topics range from animals and
nature, to the arts, literature and history.

Freelance Potential
Published 55–60 titles in 2003: 10–20 were developed from
unsolicited submissions and 5 were by agented authors.
Receives 100–150 queries yearly.
- **Fiction:** Publishes story picture books, 4–10 years.
- **Nonfiction:** Publishes story picture books, 4–10 years; middle-
  grade books, 8–12 years; and young adult books, 12–18 years.
  Topics include nature, science, geology, endangered species,
  Native Americans, astronomy, the arts, humanities, literature,
  world history, and explorers. Also publishes biographies.
- **Representative Titles:** *Anaheim Angels* by Wayne Stewart is
  the story of the players and coaches on the World-Series-win-
  ning team; part of the Baseball: The Great American Game
  series. *Air* by Maria Hidalgo (4–8 years) presents facts about
  air; part of the Let's Investigate series.

Submissions and Payment
Guidelines available. Query with manuscript sample. Accepts
photocopies and computer printouts. No simultaneous submissions. SASE. Responds in 4–6 months. Publication in 4
years. Payment policy varies.

Editor's Comments
Since most of what we publish is for the school and library
markets, make sure you tailor your idea and sample to match
the curriculum of the grades you are writing for. Most of what
we publish is nonfiction, and fits into a series. We are always
interested in receiving new ideas from qualified writers, but
review our guidelines and list first to be certain your idea will
work for us.

Creative Learning Press

P.O. Box 320
Mansfield Center, CT 06250

Editor: Kris Morgan

Publisher's Interests
This publisher provides teachers and parents with educational resources for use in homes and classrooms. Its textbooks, activity books, and how-to titles cover a broad range of curriculum areas, including math, science, language arts, and history. Creative Learning Press also offers materials for teaching gifted students.
Website: www.creativelearningpress.com

Freelance Potential
Published 50 titles in 2003: 5 were developed from unsolicited submissions. Receives 100 queries, 100 unsolicited mss each year.
- **Nonfiction:** Publishes textbooks, educational materials, how-to titles, teaching resources, and audio cassettes, grades K–12. Topics include science, mathematics, language arts, geography, history, research skills, business, fine arts, and leadership. Also offers materials for gifted students.
- **Representative Titles:** *Enrichment Clusters: A Practical Plan for Real-World Student-Driven Learning* by Joseph S. Renzulli et al. (teachers, grades K–9) discusses how enrichment clusters offer both students and teachers opportunities to delve into areas of strong interest. *12 Easy Steps to Successful Research Papers* by Nell W. Meriwether (grades 7–12) helps students through the process of writing a research paper, from choosing a subject to taking notes and preparing the final copy.

Submissions and Payment
Query with sample pages; or send complete ms with résumé and artwork. Accepts photocopies, computer printouts, and email to clp@creativelearningpress.com. SASE. Responds in 1 month. Publication period varies. Royalty.

Editor's Comments
We continue to develop our line of book and activity titles for teachers who work with gifted students, but all types of creative, how-to books are welcome. It's important to include detailed, concrete examples to illustrate your ideas.

Creative Teaching Press

P.O. Box 2723
Huntington Beach, CA 92647

Director of Product Development: Carolea Williams

Publisher's Interests
Creative Teaching Press publishes educational resource
materials for teachers to use in preschool through eighth-
grade classrooms, including bulletin board sets, puzzles, educational wall borders, and charts. Many of this publisher's
products have been created by teachers for their peers.
Website: www.creativeteaching.com

Freelance Potential
Published 70+ titles (12 juvenile) in 2003: 25 were developed
from unsolicited submissions. Of the 70+ titles, 5 were by
unpublished writers and 5 were by authors who were new to
the publishing house. Receives 150 queries, 100+ unsolicited
mss yearly.
- **Fiction:** Publishes easy-to-read books, 4–7 years. Genres
  include ethnic and multicultural fiction, fantasy, and folktales.
- **Nonfiction:** Publishes easy-to-read titles, 4–7 years. Topics
  include history, social issues, arts and crafts, and mathematics.
  Also features special education and multicultural titles.
- **Representative Titles:** *Be a Friend* (grades K–3) teaches children about friends and fairness; part of the Character Education series. *Earth Book for Kids* (grades 3–6) presents ideas for
  experiments, arts and crafts projects, and ways for kids to
  understand and participate in the healing of the environment.

Submissions and Payment
Guidelines available. Prefers complete ms; accepts query with
outline. Accepts photocopies, computer printouts, and simultaneous submissions if identified. SASE. Responds in 1–2
months. Publication period and payment policy vary.

Editor's Comments
We are always looking for new and innovative teaching ideas
that have been put to the test in the classroom. Many of our
writers are teachers themselves who want to let their peers
know about methods that have worked well for them. We publish a range of books for emergent and struggling readers, as
well as our teacher resource materials.

Creative With Words Publications

P.O. Box 223226
Carmel, CA 93922

Editor & Publisher: Brigitta Geltrich

Publisher's Interests
Creative With Words Publications specializes in thematic anthologies for all ages. Some of the topics recently covered include school, travel, love, friends, values, and folklore. It publishes fiction and nonfiction as well as poetry.
Website: http://members.tripod.com/CreativeWithWords

Freelance Potential
Published 12 titles in 2003. Receives 800–1,000 queries, unsolicited mss yearly.
- **Fiction:** Publishes anthologies for all ages. Genres include fairy tales, folktales, romance, and humor, as well as stories about nature, the environment, animals, sports, holidays, and school issues.
- **Nonfiction:** Publishes educational anthologies for all ages. Topics include animals, pets, nature, sports, and humor.
- **Representative Titles:** *Animals Our Friends* explores the many ways animals become part of our lives. *Human Emotions* takes a look at the many different emotions we experience during our lifetimes.

Submissions and Payment
Guidelines available. Query or send complete ms. Accepts photocopies and computer printouts. No simultaneous submissions. SASE. Responds to queries in 1–4 weeks, to mss in 1 month after anthology deadline. Publication in 1 month. No payment; 20–40% discount on 10+ copies purchased.

Editor's Comments
We are always interested in seeing the work of new writers who want to be part of one of our anthologies. We look for prose submissions of up to 990 words, and poetry up to 26 lines. Please visit our website for the themes we are covering in the coming year. Remember that we cannot accept multiple submissions. Our stories are meant to cater to readers young and old, and therefore we will not accept any material that includes inappropriate material such as excessive violence, racial slurs, or pornography.

Cricket Books

Suite 1100
332 South Michigan Avenue
Chicago, IL 60604

Submissions Editor

Publisher's Interests
A publisher of both fiction and nonfiction, Cricket Books features chapter books, middle-grade titles, and young adult books in its catalogue. An imprint of the Cricket Magazine Group, it is currently not accepting unsolicited submissions.
Website: www.cricketbooks.net

Freelance Potential
Published 18 titles in 2003: 3 were developed from unsolicited submissions, 3 were by agented authors, and 1 was a reprint/licensed property. Of the 18 titles, 2 were by unpublished writers and 12 were by authors who were new to the publishing house. Receives 1,500 queries, 5,000 unsolicited mss yearly.
- **Fiction:** Publishes chapter books, 5–10 years; middle-grade books, 8–12 years; and young adult books, 12–18 years. Genres includes fantasy and contemporary, historical, and multicultural fiction. Also publishes poetry books, bilingual books, picture books, and humor.
- **Nonfiction:** Publishes books about history, mathematics, science, technology, social issues, and sports.
- **Representative Titles:** *Freedom Roads* by Joyce Hansen & Gary McGowan (10–14 years) shows how archaeologists and historians use the latest technology to reconstruct the heroic journeys of the slaves who used the Underground Railroad. *Seek* by Paul Fleischman (YA) is a coming-of-age story about a teen's search for the disk jockey father who abandoned him.

Submissions and Payment
Guidelines and catalogue available. Not accepting unsolicited submissions at this time; check website for updates. SASE. Responds in 4–6 months. Publication in 18 months. Royalty, up to 10%; advance, $2,000+.

Editor's Comments
We have announced a moratorium on unsolicited manuscripts. Unfortunately, our small staff is unable to handle the increasing number of submissions. Watch our website for updates.

Critical Thinking Company

P.O. Box 448
Pacific Grove, CA 93950

Managing Editor: Cheryl Black

Publisher's Interests
This publisher's mission is to provide easy-to-use products that empower the mind. It provides supplemental education materials that are designed to develop thinking skills and improve learning in reading, writing, math, science, and social studies, and its products are used in kindergarten through college classrooms.
Website: www.CriticalThinking.com

Freelance Potential
Published 24 titles in 2003. Of the 24 titles, 2 were by unpublished writers and 4 were by authors who were new to the publishing house. Receives 25–30 unsolicited mss yearly.
- **Fiction:** Published 2 concept books, 0–4 years. Also published 12 activity books, grades 3–12. Offers reading series that promote critical thinking skills.
- **Nonfiction:** Published 2 concept books, 0–4 years; 4 easy-to-read books, 4–7 years; and 4 chapter books, 5–10 years. Publishes supplemental educational materials in all curriculum areas with an emphasis on critical thinking, grades K and up.
- **Representative Titles:** *Math Detective* (grades 3–6) uses a broad range of math concepts and thinking skills to prepare students for advanced math courses and assessments that measure reasoning and comprehension in math. *Can You Find Me?* (pre-K–K) develops skills in reading readiness, science, and math while also covering basic thinking skills, such as sequence, analogy, and classification.

Submissions and Payment
Guidelines available. Send complete ms. Accepts photocopies, computer printouts, and Macintosh and DOS disk submissions. SASE. Responds in 6–9 months. Publication in 1–2 years. Royalty, 10%.

Editor's Comments
We are currently expanding our preschool and primary-grade materials for the parent market. Remember, we don't want books that teach through drill and memorization.

Crocodile Books, USA

Interlink Publishing Group, USA
46 Crosby Street
Northhampton, MA 01060

Editor: Pamela Thompson

Publisher's Interests
This imprint of Interlink Publishing Group offers children up to the age of 12 a variety of story picture books, both fiction and nonfiction. Its fiction list includes fantasy, adventure, and folktales, while its nonfiction titles focus on animals, nature, and the environment.
Website: www.interlinkbooks.com

Freelance Potential
Published 6 titles in 2003: all were by agented authors. Receives 500 unsolicited mss yearly.
- **Fiction:** Publishes story picture books, 3–12 years. Genres include multicultural and ethnic fiction, fantasy, adventure, and folktales.
- **Nonfiction:** Publishes story picture books, 3–12 years. Topics include animals, nature, pets, and the environment.
- **Representative Titles:** *Rescuing Einstein's Compass* by Shulamith Levey Oppenheim (3–8 years) is the story of a boy who meets the famous scientist and rescues his lost compass while on a sailing trip. *Nico's Octopus* by Caroline Pitcher (3–8 years) follows the adventures of a boy who finds an octopus in his fishermen's net and learns about this mysterious creature from the sea.

Submissions and Payment
Query with up to 10 ms pages, illustration sample, synopsis, and author biography. Accepts photocopies and computer printouts. SASE. Responds in 1–2 months. Publication in 18 months. Royalty, 6–7%.

Editor's Comments
If you study our catalogue you'll see that our illustrated picture books come from writers and artists from all over the world. Many of our books have international themes. We also have a strong focus on nature and the environment. We don't consider unsolicited manuscripts that are not illustrated—that is, we don't match authors with illustrators because there are too many wonderful complete manuscripts already out there.

Crossquarter Publishing Group

P.O. Box 8756
Sante Fe, NM 87504

Submissions Editor: Tony Ravenscroft

Publisher's Interests
Established in 1986, Crossquarter Publishing Group is an electronic publisher offering science fiction, biographies, and autobiographies, as well as nonfiction titles covering such topics as fitness, health, and cultural issues. Its audience comprises both young adult and adult readers.
Website: www.crossquarter.com

Freelance Potential
Published 6 titles (1 juvenile) in 2003: each was developed from an unsolicited submission. Of the 6 titles, 5 were by unpublished writers and all were by authors who were new to the publishing house. Receives 150+ queries yearly.

- **Fiction:** Publishes young adult books, 12–18 years. Genres include science fiction.
- **Nonfiction:** Publishes young adult books, 12–18 years. Topics include health, fitness, metaphysics, healing techniques, the environment, and cultural issues. Also publishes New Age titles for adults.
- **Representative Titles:** *Merlyn's Magick: The Wizard's Secret Notebooks* by Joshua Free (YA–Adult) finds the notebooks of Merlyn from ancient times reappearing with another Merlyn, living in the city of Denver. *Shyla's Initiative* by Barbara Casey (YA–Adult) is an occult romance about a 35-year-old novelist whose life changes dramatically when she becomes entangled in a soul transference.

Submissions and Payment
Guidelines available at website. Query. Accepts photocopies and simultaneous submissions if identified. SASE. Responds in 2–3 months. Publication in 9 months. Royalty, 8–10%.

Editor's Comments
Our goal is to help to promote cultural awareness and environmental awareness through our ebooks. Science fiction novels are always of interest as are nonfiction titles concerned with balancing the body, mind, heart, and spirit. Please take the time to review our guidelines before contacting us.

Crossway Books

Good News Publishers
1300 Crescent Street
Wheaton, IL 60187

Editorial Administrator: Jill Carter

Publisher's Interests
Evangelical Christians read Crossway's Bibles and books. Its juvenile list caters to toddlers through preteens and includes story picture books and novels. For adults, Crossway Books offers books about parenting and family life, as well as titles appropriate for Christian homeschooling.
Website: www.crosswaybooks.org

Freelance Potential
Published 90 titles (10 juvenile) in 2003: 2 were developed from unsolicited submissions, 6 were by agented authors, and 4 were reprint licensed properties. Of the 90 titles, 4 were by unpublished writers and 20 were by new authors. Receives 1,000 queries yearly.
- **Fiction:** Published 2 toddler books and 2 early picture books, 0–4 years; 3 story picture books, 4–10 years; and 3 chapter books, 5–10 years. Genres include historical and contemporary fiction and adventure, all with Christian themes.
- **Nonfiction:** Publishes adult parenting and educational books on home and family life, Christian living, homeschooling, health, the Bible, and church issues.
- **Representative Titles:** *Best of All* by Max Lucado is a picture book that teaches children that you don't have to be famous to be special. *God Knows My Name* by Debby Anderson is a simple story that explains to children the lessons of more than 12 Scripture verses.

Submissions and Payment
Guidelines available. Query with outline/synopsis and 2 sample chapters. No email queries or unsolicited mss. Accepts photocopies and simultaneous submissions if identified. SASE. Responds in 6–8 weeks. Publication in 12–18 months. Payment policy varies.

Editor's Comments
Our mission is to make a difference in people's lives through Christ. Send us children's books that will help us fulfill that mission. Picture books are not being accepted at this time.

Crown Books for Young Readers

1745 Broadway
New York, NY 10019

Submissions Editor

Publisher's Interests
Hardcover nonfiction books are the specialty of Crown Books
for Young Readers. A division of Random House Children's
Books, it develops books for the very young, beginning readers,
middle-schoolers, and young adults on a variety of topics,
including science, social issues, and history.
Website: www.randomhouse.com/kids

Freelance Potential
Published 25 titles in 2003: 11 were by agented authors and
4 were reprint/licensed properties. Receives 500 queries,
1,000 unsolicited mss yearly.
- **Nonfiction:** Publishes concept books and toddler books, 0–4
  years; story picture books, 4–10 years; chapter books, 5–10
  years; middle-grade books, 8–12 years; and young adult books,
  12–18 years. Topics include science, nature, sports, history,
  and social issues.
- **Representative Titles:** *First to Fly* by Peter Busby (8+ years)
  tells how, through trial and error, two boys from Dayton, Ohio,
  built the plane that would change the world. *Me and My
  Senses* by Joan Sweeney (4–8 years) includes easy-to-understand text and bright illustrations to introduce young readers
  to the five senses; part of the Me and My . . . series.

Submissions and Payment
Guidelines available. Accepts submissions from agented
authors only. Accepts photocopies, computer printouts, and
simultaneous submissions if identified. Availability of artwork
improves chance of acceptance. SASE. Responds in 3
months. Publication period varies. Royalty; advance.

Editor's Comments
Because we receive so many submissions, we have recently
decided that we can only consider submissions that come
through literary agents. If you have a nonfiction title that
you think would be right for us, review our guidelines and
have your agent submit your work. Ideas for illustrations are
strongly encouraged.

CSS Publishing Company

P.O. Box 4503
517 Main Street
Lima, OH 45802-4503

Submissions Editor: Stan Purdum

Publisher's Interests
CSS Publishing is a Christian publisher that creates books
and resource materials for religious leaders and educators to
use with their congregations and students.
Website: www.csspub.com

Freelance Potential
Published 180 titles in 2003: 100 were developed from unsolicited submissions, 2 were by agented authors, and 10 were
reprint/licensed properties. Of the 180 titles, 25 were by
unpublished writers and 80 were by authors who were new
to the publishing house. Receives 1,000 unsolicited mss
each year.

- **Nonfiction:** Publishes story picture books, 4–10 years; and
  young adult books, 12–18 years. Topics include religious education, prayer, worship, and family life. Also publishes resource
  materials, program planners, newsletters, and church supplies
  for Christian educators.
- **Representative Titles:** *The Giant Book of Children's Sermons*
  by Wesley T. Runk (teachers) offers 260 object lessons from
  every book of the New Testament to share with children.
  Keepin' It Real by Sandra McLeod Humphrey (YA) uses a young
  teen's letters to God to demonstrate how faith can help overcome life's everyday frustrations and obstacles.

Submissions and Payment
Guidelines and catalogue available at website. Send complete
ms with résumé. Accepts photocopies, computer printouts,
and simultaneous submissions if identified. SASE. Responds
in 6 months. Publication in 6 months. Royalty. Flat fee.

Editor's Comments
We publish practical resource material for educators and families interested in raising Christian children. Our books include
parish-tested materials that can be put to use by Lutheran,
United Methodist, and Episcopal congregations, and address
the issues of youth ministry, stewardship, Christian education,
and other topics for promoting an active Christian lifestyle.

Dandy Lion Publications

Suite L
3563 Sueldo
San Luis Obispo, CA 94301-7331

Editor: Dianne Draze

Publisher's Interests
Educational resource materials on mathematics, science, language arts, and critical and creative thinking are offered by Dandy Lion Publications. Its materials are used by kindergarten through eighth-grade teachers who work in regular, special education, and gifted classrooms.
Website: www.dandylionbooks.com

Freelance Potential
Published 6 titles in 2003: 3 were developed from unsolicited submissions and 3 were by agented authors. Receives 20 queries yearly.
- **Nonfiction:** Publishes educational resource materials, grades K–8. Features books that include educational activities, exercises, games, or instructional procedures. Topics include literature, language arts, research, mathematics, science, and critical and creative thinking.
- **Representative Titles:** *Mystery Disease* by Mark A. Bohland (grades 5–8) is a problem-based unit that helps students combine science, social studies, math, research, and group collaboration to solve a problem and present their findings. *Math-a-Logic* (grades 4–8) uses eight areas of logic to provide practice in math computations and thinking skills.

Submissions and Payment
Guidelines available. Accepts queries from practicing teachers only. Query with sample chapters. No unsolicited mss. Accepts photocopies, computer printouts, and simultaneous submissions if identified. SASE. Responds in 2–4 weeks. Publication in 6–9 months. Royalty; advance.

Editor's Comments
We have been working hand-in-hand with teachers for more than 25 years to provide motivating, challenging educational experiences for students in the primary, intermediate, and middle school grades. Most of our materials focus on developing creative and critical thinking skills, and many of our products are designed for above-average students.

May Davenport, Publishers

26313 Purissima Road
Los Altos Hills, CA 94022

Publisher & Editor: May Davenport

Publisher's Interests

This small, family-owned publisher is currently interested in contemporary, fictional novels for teachers to use to motivate teens to read. It is not accepting fiction for younger children at this time.
Website: www.maydavenportpublishers.com

Freelance Potential

Published 4 titles in 2003: all were developed from unsolicited submissions. Of the 4 titles, most were by unpublished writers and all were by authors who were new to the publishing house. Receives 1,000+ queries yearly.

- **Fiction:** Published 4 young adult books, 15–18 years. Genres include adventure, humor, mystery, and historical fiction. Also publishes read-and-color books, 6–8 years; story picture books, 4–10 years; and middle-grade novels, 8–12.
- **Representative Titles:** *Drivers' Ed is Dead* by Pat Delgado (15–18 years) is a farcical story about how a misfit teacher and two infuriated teens had to solve their own problems when their school dropped drivers' education. *Tug of War* by Barbara A. Scott (15–18 years) presents the dilemmas faced by three children in Kansas during the American Civil War.

Submissions and Payment

Guidelines available. Query. SASE. Responds in 1–2 weeks. Publication in 1–2 years. Royalty, 15%. Flat fee.

Editor's Comments

We're always interested in books that serve as supplementary novels to high school English and creative writing courses. Material that motivates reluctant readers will always be considered. We'd like to see humorous fiction for 15- to 18-year-old readers, as well as fiction that deals with today's teenage conflicts, solutions, joys, and activities. A hint for writers who want to submit to us—use your literary tools purposefully so your teenage audience can read silently and imagine what's happening in your story. Our objective is to expose teens to models of writing beyond the Internet "chat room" style.

Jonathan David Publishers

68-22 Eliot Avenue
Middle Village, NY 11379

Editor-in-Chief: Alfred J. Kolatch

Publisher's Interests
The focus of Jonathan David Publishers is popular Judaica.
While most of its books are nonfiction and aimed at adult
readers, children's titles—both fiction and nonfiction—also
appear on its list.
Website: www.jdbooks.com

Freelance Potential
Published 22 titles (2 juvenile) in 2003. Receives 1,200
queries yearly.
- **Fiction:** Publishes easy-to-read books, 4–7 years; and story
  picture books, 4–10 years. Genres include folktales and
  Jewish culture.
- **Nonfiction:** Publishes easy-to-read books, 4–7 years; and middle-grade books, 8–12 years. Topics include religion, Judaica,
  history, culture, and multicultural issues.
- **Representative Titles:** *My Baby Brother: What a Miracle!* by
  Sylvia Rouss is the story of a young girl who wonders why her
  family is making a huge fuss over her newborn brother; part of
  the Growing Up Jewish with Sarah Leah Jacobs series. *The
  Jewish Puzzle Book* by Sylvia & Arthur Levinsohn includes
  puzzles that range from simple rebuses for the very young to
  crosswords and acrostics that challenge adults.

Submissions and Payment
Guidelines available. Query with résumé, table of contents,
synopsis, and sample chapter. No unsolicited mss. Accepts
photocopies and computer printouts. No simultaneous submissions. SASE. Responds in 1–2 months. Publication in 18
months. Royalty; advance. Flat fee.

Editor's Comments
While our catalogue does feature backlist titles on a wide range
of topics, our current focus is on popular Judaica only. Submissions that do not relate to Jewish life and culture are inappropriate for us. Please limit your initial contact with us to a
query letter sent through regular mail only—no emails or
phone calls, please.

DAW Books

375 Hudson Street
New York, NY 10014

Associate Editor: Peter Stampfel

Publisher's Interests
In operation for more than 25 years, DAW Books caters to
teens and adults who like to read science fiction, fantasy,
and thriller novels. It publishes fiction only, and a number of
its titles are published in series.
Website: www.dawbooks.com

Freelance Potential
Published 48–50 titles in 2003: 20 were by agented authors.
Of the 48–50 titles, 5 were by authors who were new to the
publishing house. Receives 1,000+ unsolicited mss yearly.
- **Fiction:** Publishes science fiction, thriller, and fantasy novels
  for young adults and adults.
- **Representative Titles:** *The War of the Flowers* by Tad Williams
  (YA and up) features a 30-year-old singer in a not-so-success-
  ful rock band who retreats to an isolated cabin and finds himself drawn to a place beyond his wildest dreams. *The Gates of
  Sleep* by Mercedes Lackey (YA and up) is a story about a 17-
  year-old girl who is the ward of bohemian artists in turn-of-
  the-century England; part of the Elemental Masters series.

Submissions and Payment
Guidelines available. Send complete ms. Accepts photocopies
and computer printouts. No simultaneous submissions.
SASE. Responds in 3 months. Publication in 8–12 months.
Royalty, 6%; advance.

Editor's Comments
At DAW Books we are committed to finding and developing
new talent in the science fiction, fantasy, and thriller genres.
In the past we have often published first novels that demonstrated the writers' exceptional talents. A literary agent is
not required for submission, but we will not consider manuscripts that are currently on submission to another publisher. The average length of the novels we publish varies
but is never less than 80,000 words. Don't send novellas,
short stories, short story collections, or poetry. And please
don't send any type of nonfiction.

Dawn Publications

12402 Bitney Springs Road
Nevada City, CA 95959

Editor: Glenn Hovemann

Publisher's Interests
This publisher focuses on the wonders of nature and tries to teach children about the world around them through high-quality picture books, including trade books that are suitable for classroom use.
Website: www.dawnpub.com

Freelance Potential
Published 8 titles in 2003: all were developed from unsolicited submissions, 6 were by agented authors, and 4 were reprint/licensed properties. Of the 8 titles, 2 were by authors who were new to the publishing house. Receives 2,000–3,000 unsolicited mss yearly.

- **Nonfiction:** Publishes story picture books, 4–12 years. Topics include the environment, conservation, ecology, family relationships, personal awareness, and multicultural and ethnic issues. Also offers teacher guides.
- **Representative Titles:** *Okomi, The New Baby* by Helen & Clive Dorman (2–5 years) is a story about a new baby chimpanzee and what happens when his powerful father arrives. *Born with a Bang* by Jennifer Morgan (7+ years) is the first book of a trilogy in which the Universe tells its own life story of chaos and creativity, science and struggle, beginning in the very beginning and ending with the formation of Earth.

Submissions and Payment
Guidelines available at website. Query or send complete ms. Accepts photocopies, computer printouts, and simultaneous submissions if identified. SASE. Responds in 2–3 months. Publication in 18–24 months. Royalty; advance.

Editor's Comments
We are a nature awareness publisher for adults and children. Our goal is to teach children about the beauty and fascination of nature and to inspire them to explore, appreciate, and respect their world. We accept only a few of the thousands of submissions we receive, so follow our guidelines, read some of the books we've published, and send only your best work.

Denlinger's Publishers

P.O. Box 1030
Edgewater, FL 32132-1030

Editor: Patricia Red

Publisher's Interests
This electronic publisher features fiction for all ages. It welcomes almost any genre, but does not publish poetry, illustrated books, erotica, or textbooks.
Website: www.thebookden.com

Freelance Potential
Published 24 titles (4 juvenile) in 2003: all were developed from unsolicited submissions and 3 were by agented authors. Of the 24 titles, most were by unpublished writers and 12 were by authors who were new to the publishing house. Receives 1,700 unsolicited mss yearly.
- **Fiction:** Published 2 chapter books, 5–10 years; and 2 middle-grade books, 8–12 years. Genres include adventure, fantasy, folklore, and historical and inspirational fiction.
- **Representative Titles:** *Teammates, The Universal Bond* by Bob Weissman is the story of Katie Calhoun and her adventures at a posh girls' school. *An Audience of One* by Beth Staas (12+ years) follows the experiences of a young pianist hoping to become a concert musician and to attend the Julliard School of Music in New York.

Submissions and Payment
Guidelines and catalogue available at website. Send complete ms with market analysis and biography. Accepts disk submissions (WordPerfect text), and email submissions to acquisitions@thebookden.com. SASE. Responds in 3–6 months. Publication in 6–8 months. Royalty.

Editor's Comments
We began as a traditional publishing house based in Virginia in 1926. For years we specialized in nonfiction titles about pets. We began to move into fiction in the 1950s and now focus exclusively on it. Electronic publishing is the way of the future. For now it also represents a "foot in the door" for new authors. For the coming year, we are interested in inspirational fiction and historical fiction, especially with strong female characters. We do not want books under 100 pages.

Dial Books for Young Readers

Penguin Group (USA) Inc.
345 Hudson Street
New York, NY 10014

Submissions Editor

Publisher's Interests
This imprint of the Penguin Young Readers Group includes fiction and nonfiction for preschool through high school readers, including concept and toddler books, chapter books, and middle-grade titles.
Website: www.penguinputnam.com

Freelance Potential
Published 41 titles (40 juvenile) in 2003: 25 were developed from unsolicited submissions, 16 were by agented authors, and 3 were reprint/licensed properties. Receives 2,000+ queries, 1,000+ unsolicited mss yearly.
- **Fiction:** Publishes concept books, toddler books, and early picture books, 0–4 years; easy-to-read books, 4–7 years; story picture books, 4–10 years; chapter books, 5–10 years; middle-grade novels; and young adult books, 12–18 years.
- **Nonfiction:** Publishes concept and early picture books, 0–4 years; easy-to-read books, 4–7 years; story picture books, 4–10 years; middle-grade books, 8–12 years; and young adult titles, 12–18 years.
- **Representative Titles:** *Katie's Wish* by Barbara Shook Hazen (5+ years) is the story of a young Irish girl who lived during the potato famine. *The Village That Vanished* by Ann Grifalconi (5+ years) follows young Abekenile and the villagers of Yao who unite to hide from the slavers coming their way.

Submissions and Payment
Guidelines and catalogues available with SASE. Query with up to 10 pages; send complete ms for picture books. SASE. Response time, publication period, and payment policy vary.

Editor's Comments
Competition here is very tough and we strongly urge writers to take the time to send us a query that truly describes their book and why it will work for us. We look for books with strong story lines and memorable characters. If you are a new writer, you may want to consider submitting to other houses that receive fewer submissions.

Didax

395 Main Street
Rowley, MA 01969

Vice President: Martin Kennedy

Publisher's Interests
Didax specializes in instructional materials for use in preschool through high school classrooms. Its catalogue offers manipulatives and educational games in addition to books that cover all curriculum areas.
Website: www.didaxinc.com

Freelance Potential
Published 50 titles in 2003: 10 were developed from unsolicited submissions. Of the 50 titles, 2 were by unpublished writers and 8 were by authors who were new to the publishing house. Receives 100 queries, 80 unsolicited mss yearly.
- **Nonfiction:** Publishes reproducible activity books and teacher resources, grades pre-K–12. Topics include grammar, phonics, spelling, writing, reading, science, art, music, social sciences, basic math, fractions, geometry, algebra, and probability.
- **Representative Titles:** *Poetry Writing for the Early Grades* (grades 2–4) introduces a variety of poetic forms, including shape poems, acrostics, string poems, limericks, haiku, and cinquains. *Magic with Math* (grades 5–8) uses tricks and games to build students' problem-solving, reasoning, calculating, and algebra skills.

Submissions and Payment
Guidelines available. Query with résumé and outline; or send complete ms. Accepts photocopies, computer printouts, disk submissions (Microsoft Word), email submissions to development@didaxinc.com, and simultaneous submissions if identified. SASE. Responds to queries in 2 weeks, to mss in 1 month. Publication in 1 year. Royalty; advance.

Editor's Comments
The works we accept for publication provide practical information for teaching a concept or skill in an original manner. They all incorporate hands-on or multi-sensory learning and demonstrate a strong theoretical or research basis. Familiarize yourself with our publications before you submit your work, which may address any area of the curriculum.

Discovery Enterprises

31 Laurelwood Drive
Carlisle, MA 01741

President: JoAnne Weisman-Deitch

Publisher's Interests

American history is the focus of all the publications offered by
Discovery Enterprises. It publishes plays for students in grades
four through ten that are based on letters, diaries, journals,
and government documents. It also publishes history books
based on primary source materials for readers between the
ages of four and twelve.
Website: www.ushistorydocs.com

Freelance Potential

Published 12 titles in 2003: 2 were developed from unsolicited
submissions. Of the 12 titles, 3 were by authors who were
new to the publishing house. Receives 50–60 queries yearly.

- **Fiction:** Publishes plays, grades 4–10. Also publishes middle-
  grade novels, 8–12 years; and young adult books, 12–18 years.
  Genres include historical fiction.
- **Nonfiction:** Publishes easy-to-read books, 4–7 years; chapter
  books, 5–10 years; and middle-grade books, 8–12 years. Features educational books about American history.
- **Representative Titles:** *California Gold Rush* by Phyllis Raybin
  Emert (grades 6 and up) is a reproducible play in which Sutter
  and other historical figures recount the early days of the gold
  rush and life in mining towns. *A Different Drummer: Thoreau
  and Will's Independence Day* by Claiborne Dawes (7–12 years)
  introduces readers to Thoreau's search for independence from
  material possessions and his respect for nature through the
  words of a Concord boy, Will Crawford.

Submissions and Payment

Guidelines available. Query with résumé, outline, and nonfiction clips. No unsolicited mss. Accepts photocopies and
simultaneous submissions if identified. SASE. Responds in 3
months. Publication in 2–8 months. Royalty.

Editor's Comments

We are interested in plays that have a reading time of about 40
minutes; the performance time will be longer. We're currently
only accepting submissions about American history.

DiskUs Publishing

P.O. Box 43
Albany, IN 47320

Submissions Editor: Holly Janey

Publisher's Interests
Now in its seventh year, DiskUs Publishing is an epublisher
that offers fiction and nonfiction for children of all ages. Its
site includes concept and toddler books, books for early and
middle-grade readers, and titles for teens. Its publications
may be purchased through the mail or downloaded.
Website: www.diskuspublishing.com

Freelance Potential
Published 60–70 titles (10 juvenile) in 2003: 30 were developed from unsolicited submissions. Receives 12,000 queries
each year.
- **Fiction:** Publishes concept and toddler books, 0–4 years; easy-
  to-read books, 4–7 years; middle-grade novels, 8–12 years; and
  young adult books, 12–18 years. Publishes all genres.
- **Nonfiction:** Publishes concept and toddler books, 0–4 years.
  Also features adult self-help books, books about religion, and
  puzzle books.
- **Representative Titles:** *Little Chick & Mr. Worm* by Cia Leah
  is the story of chick who hatches out of his shell on Easter
  morning only to find that he is the last chick to hatch and
  his mother is gone. *The Little Dragon Without Fire* by Laraine
  Anne Barker tells about a dragon who is miserable because
  he can't breathe fire and can't join in dragon games.

Submissions and Payment
Guidelines available at website. Query with résumé, word
count, synopsis, and first 3 chapters. Accepts email queries
to editors@diskuspublishing.com. SASE. Responds in 3–6
months. Publication in 5 months. Royalty.

Editor's Comments
Please remember that if you query us via email, you must
include a subject head that reads "DiskUs" followed by your
subject. Other queries will not be opened and will be deleted.
Log on to our website before contacting us for complete
instructions. We will consider submissions of virtually all
genres, for readers of all ages.

Domhan Books

Suite 514
9511 Shore Road
Brooklyn, NY 11209

Young Adult Editor

Publisher's Interests

Founded in 1998, Domhan Books offers middle-grade and
young adult novels of many genres. It also offers informational
and how-to books for teens. While it accepts manuscripts
from writers from all over the world, it is now accepting submissions from previously published authors only.
Website: www.domhanbooks.com

Freelance Potential

Published 50 titles (20 juvenile) in 2003: 48 were developed
from unsolicited submissions and 12 were by agented
authors. Of the 50 titles, 25 were by unpublished writers and
25 were by authors who were new to the publishing house.
Receives 500+ queries, 1,500+ unsolicited mss yearly.
- **Fiction:** Publishes middle-grade novels, 8–12 years; and young
  adult books, 12–18 years. Genres include adventure, fantasy,
  folktales, mystery, suspense, romance, Westerns, and contemporary, historical, inspirational, multicultural, religious, and
  science fiction.
- **Nonfiction:** Publishes young adult books, 12–18 years. Features how-to and informational books.
- **Representative Titles:** *Obstacles of Love* by Tonya Taylor
  Ramagos (YA) is novel about a girl who develops romantic feelings toward a student she is tutoring. *God's Children* by
  Clarence Guenter (10–12 years) tells about the life of a Men-
  nonite boy growing up in Canada in the 1940s.

Submissions and Payment

Guidelines and catalogue available at website or with 9x12
SASE ($.55 postage). Query with clips for nonfiction; send
complete ms for fiction. Accepts disk submissions (RTF or
ASCII). SASE. Responds to queries in 1–2 weeks, to mss in
4–6 weeks. Publication in 6 months. Royalty; 30–50% net.

Editor's Comments

Due to the overwhelming number of manuscripts we have
recently received, we are closed to submissions from new
authors. Visit our website for updates on this policy.

Dorling Kindersley

375 Hudson Street
New York, NY 10014

Submissions: Beth Sutinis

Publisher's Interests
This publisher is best known for its distinctive, highly visual
style of books for adults and children. Its goal is to develop
high-quality, innovative books that enrich the reader's
lifestyle. Its catalogue offers both fiction and nonfiction titles
for all ages.
Website: www.dk.com

Freelance Potential
Published 250 titles in 2003: 3 were by agented authors and
50 were reprint/license properties. Receives 1,000 queries
each year.
- **Fiction:** Publishes concept books, toddler books, and early
  picture books, 0–4 years; chapter books, 5–10 years; middle-
  grade books, 8–12 years; and young adult novels, 12–18
  years. Genres include contemporary and historical fiction,
  science fiction, fairy tales, folktales, humor, mystery, stories
  about nature, and romance.
- **Nonfiction:** Publishes concept books and toddler books, 0–4
  years; easy-to-read books, 4–7 years; middle-grade books, 8–12
  years; and young adult titles, 12–18 years. Topics include
  geography, health and fitness, history, current events, crafts,
  computers, animals, history, religion, and science. Also publishes bilingual titles and activity books.
- **Representative Titles:** *Children's Encyclopedia of American
  History* is published in conjunction with the Smithsonian Institution and offers a unique survey of the story of America.
  Mammals discusses various species with text and illustrations
  specifically designed to build a foundation for advanced exploration; part of the Eye Wonder series.

Submissions and Payment
Guidelines available. Accepts queries through agents only. No
unsolicited mss. SASE. Responds in 6 months. Publication in
2 years. Royalty, 10%; advance, varies.

Editor's Comments
We will consider queries from agented authors only; please do
not submit completed manuscripts.

Dover Publications

31 East 2nd Street
Mineola, NY 11501-3582

Editor-in-Chief: Paul Negri

Publisher's Interests
This publisher features coloring books, activity books, and sticker books for readers of all ages. It also publishes fiction reprints for children, as well as juvenile titles on math, science, and music.
Website: www.doverpublications.com

Freelance Potential
Published 650 titles (140 juvenile) in 2003. Receives 400 queries, 400 unsolicited mss yearly.
- **Fiction:** Publishes reprints of children's classics and story-books. Genres include folktales, fantasy, and fairy tales. Also publishes animal stories.
- **Nonfiction:** Publishes educational titles, anthologies, and biographies. Also publishes activity, craft, and coloring books. Topics include Native Americans, ancient history, animals, dinosaurs, science, mythology, Americana, American history, needlework, fashion, languages, literature, hobbies, adventure, and fine art.
- **Representative Titles:** *Learning About Wild Cats* by Jan Sovak describes characteristics of lions, tigers, cheetahs, and other wild cats. *Puzzling Questions About the Solar System* by Martin Gardner presents fascinating facts about the sun, planets, moons, comets, asteroids, and space flight in an easy-to-follow question-and-answer format.

Submissions and Payment
Catalogue available at website. Query or send complete ms. SASE. Response time varies. Publication period varies. Flat fee.

Editor's Comments
We publish a wealth of fun and educational sticker and activity books with great appeal to young readers. We encourage you to visit our website to see the variety of topics we cover. Projects that families can do together are always of interest. We also publish quality, educational books for adults and children on a variety of historical topics. Historical accuracy is a must!

Down East Books

P.O. Box 679
Camden, ME 04843

Production Editor: Michael Steere

Publisher's Interests

A regional publisher, Down East Books offers a list that
includes titles on art, nostalgia, history, photography, natural
history, and gardening, all with Maine or New England
themes. It also publishes regional children's books, both fiction and nonfiction. 2% self-, subsidy-, co-venture, or co-op
published material.
Website: www.downeastbooks.com

Freelance Potential

Published 25 titles (10 juvenile) in 2003: 12 were developed
from unsolicited submissions and 4 were reprint/licensed
properties. Of the 25 titles, 4 were by unpublished writers
and 2 were by authors who were new to the publishing
house. Receives 1,000 queries, 700 unsolicited mss yearly.

- **Fiction:** Published 2 toddler books, 0–4 years; 2 easy-to-read
  books, 4–7 years; 1 chapter book, 5–10 years; and 1 middle-
  grade novel, 8–12 years. Genres include adventure, mystery,
  humor, and contemporary fiction with New England settings.
- **Nonfiction:** Published 2 toddler books, 0–4 years; and 2 easy-
  to-read books, 4–7 years. Topics include life and nature in
  Maine and New England.
- **Representative Titles:** *Brown Cow Farm* by Dahlov Ipcar (3+
  years) is a counting book that looks at the animals that live on
  a farm in Maine. *The Henhouse* by Carol Dean (4–8 years)
  relates the author's experiences growing up on a chicken farm.

Submissions and Payment

Guidelines available. Query with clips or writing samples; or
send complete ms. Accepts photocopies, computer printouts,
and simultaneous submissions if identified. SASE. Responds
in 2–8 weeks. Publication in 1 year. Royalty, 9–12%; advance,
$300–$600.

Editor's Comments

A Maine or New England subject and setting is required of all
the children's books we publish, and the setting itself must be
integral to the work.

Dramatic Publishing

311 Washington Street
Woodstock, IL 60098

Acquisitions Editor: Linda Habjan

Publisher's Interests
This publisher offers one-act and full-length plays and musicals for use by professional, stock, community, school, and children's theater groups. It also publishes resource materials and reference texts about the theater arts.
Website: www.dramaticpublishing.com

Freelance Potential
Published 50 titles in 2003. Receives 250 queries, 600 unsolicited mss yearly.
- **Fiction:** Publishes full-length and one-act plays, musicals, and anthologies.
- **Nonfiction:** Publishes books about the theatre arts and production guides. Topics include stagecraft, audition techniques, and directing.
- **Representative Titles:** *House of Seven Gables* by Vin Morreale Jr. is adapted from the novel by Hawthorne and follows the demise and resurrection of the once-prosperous Puncheon clan. *The Twits* by David Wood is adapted from the Roald Dahl book and is set in a circus ring where Mr. and Mrs. Twit play a series of tricks on each other.

Submissions and Payment
Guidelines available. Send complete ms with résumé, synopsis, production history, reviews, cast list, and set and technical requirements; include audiocassette for musicals. Accepts photocopies and computer printouts. SASE. Responds in 10–12 weeks. Publication in 18 months. Royalty.

Editor's Comments.
We are interested in any production that explains human behavior in new and insightful ways. We are looking for original plays that will appeal to families and children, as well as one-act plays with large casts that would be appropriate for school groups to perform. Always send a properly bound script, preferably with a hard cover. Do not send loose pages or pages held together with an elastic band or paper clip. Musicals must be accompanied by a cassette.

Originality
Julie Strauss-Gabel
Dutton Books

Dutton Books for Children publishes more than 100 books a year. Editor Julie Strauss-Gabel is looking for originality—originality in content, originality in style. Selling the book to a publisher is only the first step. It then has to sell to parents and teachers, and the usual toddler book submission is often simply not strong enough to do both.

"Unoriginal books that cover very familiar territory (without looking at an idea in some new way) aren't going to survive in today's competitive market," Strauss-Gabel says. "This is especially true of basic concept books that don't add anything to the many already on the shelves." She advises writers to look at toddler life from the child's perspective. "What else is happening beyond bedtime or tantrums? What format, style, language, story, etc. will appeal to toddlers and the adults in their lives?"

This connection to both child and adult is important. Strauss-Gabel wants to see books that touch the lives of both, the child as audience and the adult as the person buying the book then reading it over and over again.

What is she looking for specifically in toddler books?

"An original idea, a great story, and a tight, lyrical text," she says. "I want a manuscript that can be read aloud over and over again and that offers something that no book already on the market can offer. I want beautiful language and great illustration potential. I want a manuscript that reflects the experience of a multifaceted universe of real kids."

While Dutton's general policy is to query first, Strauss-Gabel's personal policy is to read complete picture book manuscripts addressed to her.

(See listing for Dutton Children's Books
on following page)

Dutton Children's Books

Penguin Young Readers Group
14th Floor
345 Hudson Street
New York, NY 10014

Queries Editor

Publisher's Interests
This division of Penguin Young Readers Group offers quality fiction and nonfiction for children of all ages.
Website: www.penguin.com

Freelance Potential
Published 105 titles in 2003: 6 were developed from unsolicited submissions, 29 were by agented authors, and 30 were reprint/licensed properties. Of the 105 titles, 12 were by unpublished writers and 16 were by authors who were new to the publishing house. Receives 3,500 queries yearly.

- **Fiction:** Published 13 concept books, 7 toddler books, and 10 early picture books, 0–4 years; 3 easy-to-read books, 4–7 years; 36 story picture books, 4–10 years; 13 middle-grade books, 8–12 years; and 7 young adult books, 12–18 years. Genres include adventure, mystery, suspense, fantasy, and humor.
- **Nonfiction:** Published 9 story picture books, 4–10 years; 4 middle-grade books, 8–12 years; and 3 young adult books, 12–18 years. Topics include history and nature. Also publishes biographies and interactive nonfiction.
- **Representative Titles:** *Skippyjon Jones* by Judy Schachner (5–8 years) is about a hyper, endearing kitty with a Zorro-like alter-ego who can't resign himself to being just an ordinary cat. *The Boy Who Spoke Dog* by Clay Morgan (10–14 years) is about an orphan shipwrecked on an island near New Zealand and the wild sheepdogs who help him learn to survive.

Submissions and Payment
Guidelines available. Query with brief synopsis, sample pages (up to 10 for novels, up to 5 for picture books), and publishing credits. No unsolicited mss. SASE. Responds in 2–3 months. Publication in 1+ years. Royalty; advance.

Editor's Comments
We're especially interested in fiction for ages eight to twelve, and twelve to sixteen. We no longer accept unsolicited manuscripts, so please adhere to our specifications: query with sample pages only.

Eakin Press

Sunbelt Media, Inc.
P.O. Box 90159
Austin, TX 78709-0159

Publisher: Virginia Messer

Publisher's Interests

With a juvenile list that includes picture books, chapter books, and middle-grade novels, Eakin Press focuses on Texas and the American Southwest. Books about the region's history, geography, and culture can be found in this independent, regional publisher's catalogue.

Website: www.eakinpress.com

Freelance Potential

Published 80 titles in 2003: 72 were developed from unsolicited submissions, 1 was by an agented author, and 4 were reprint/licensed properties. Of the 80 titles, 8 were by unpublished writers and 40 were by authors who were new to the publishing house. Receives 2,500 queries yearly.

- **Fiction:** Publishes picture books, 4–10 years; easy-to-read books, 4–7 years; chapter books, 5–10 years; and middle-grade novels, 8–12 years. Genres include historical and multicultural fiction, folklore, and stories about animals.
- **Nonfiction:** Publishes easy-to-read titles, 4–7 years; story picture books, 4–10 years; chapter books, 5–10 years; and middle-grade books, 8–12 years. Features biographies and books on regional history.
- **Representative Titles:** *Ima and the Great Texas Ostrich Race* by Margaret McManis is the story of the daughter of Governor James Stephen Hogg and her determination to prove her brothers wrong. *New Life, New Land* by Ann Fears Crawford is an easy-to-read chapter book about Texas women.

Submissions and Payment

Guidelines available. Query with résumé, sample chapter, and clips or writing samples. Accepts photocopies, computer printouts, and simultaneous submissions if identified. SASE. Responds in 6 months. Publication in 1–2 years. Royalty.

Editor's Comments

Good stories about the Southwest for readers ages five to fourteen will make it out of the slush pile. Please familiarize yourself with our publishing program before contacting us.

ebooksonthe.net

Write Words, Inc.
2934 Old Route 50
Cambridge, MD 21613

Publisher: Constance Foster

Publisher's Interests
This epublisher devotes about one-third of its publishing program to children's titles. It offers juvenile fiction and nonfiction on a variety of subjects and in a number of genres. It also publishes self-help and psychology for adults.
Website: www.ebooksonthe.net

Freelance Potential
Published 20–25 titles (5 juvenile) in 2003: 8 were developed from unsolicited submissions. Receives 1,200 queries, 1,500 unsolicited mss yearly.
- **Fiction:** Publishes fiction for all ages. Genres include mainstream, experimental, historical, Western, and science fiction; adventure; horror; and mystery.
- **Nonfiction:** Publishes nonfiction for all ages. Topics include psychology, money, and business. Also offers self-help titles, inspirational titles, and books of international interest and subject matter.
- **Representative Titles:** *The Queen Bee* by Ann Herrick is a retelling of a fairy tale about seeking fortune, breaking a spell, and discovering the identity of a real prince. *Winter Shaker* by Louise Ulmer is a historical fiction book about a girl who moves with her aunt to a Shaker settlement after her mother dies and her father joins the army.

Submissions and Payment
Guidelines available at website. Query or send complete ms. Accepts disk submissions and email submissions to publisher@ebooksonthe.net (attach RTF files). SASE. Responds to queries in 1 day, to mss in 3 months. Publication in 3 months. Royalty, 40%.

Editor's Comments
We encourage and support submissions from unpublished writers, but we suggest you review the guidelines on our website before contacting us. We prefer to see narrative fiction written in the past tense. Craft and how-to books for all ages are still of special interest.

Educational Ministries

165 Plaza Drive
Prescott, AZ 86303-5549

Submissions Editor: Linda Davidson

Publisher's Interests
This publisher targets Christian educators and worship leaders who work for mainline Protestant churches. It offers activity books, books about prayer, worship, and the Bible, and material about Christian holidays and celebrations. It also produces parenting titles and videos that are used in religious education classes.
Website: www.educationalministries.com

Freelance Potential
Published 2–3 titles (1 juvenile) in 2003: 1 was developed from an unsolicited submission. Receives 190 unsolicited mss yearly.

- **Fiction:** Publishes toddler books, 0–4 years. Features books with Christian themes, educational fiction, and adult fiction.
- **Nonfiction:** Publishes educational resource materials for use by Protestant denominations.
- **Representative Titles:** *Growing with the Bible* by Elaine M. Ward (all ages) features 50 stories drawn from the New and Old Testaments that are written in a way that even young children can understand and gain meaning from. *Teaching to Wonder: Spiritual Growth Through Imagination and Movement* by Judy Gattis Smith (teachers) offers practical ideas and activities that use movement and rhythm to teach children about God and creation.

Submissions and Payment
Guidelines available. Send complete ms. Accepts photocopies, computer printouts, and simultaneous submissions if identified. SASE. Responds in 6–8 weeks. Publication in 1–4 months. Flat fee.

Editor's Comments
We're seeking practical, innovative, and creative resources. Materials should be easy to use and list everything a teacher would need for a session, with step-by-step instructions for leading the class. Our theology leans to the liberal side; we would not be classified as conservative or fundamental.

Educators Publishing Service

P.O. Box 9031
Cambridge, MA 02139-9031

Vice President, Publishing: Charlie Heinle

Publisher's Interests

This publisher helps educators teach reading, reading comprehension, grammar, vocabulary, spelling, and math. Many of its products are used to develop the skills needed for state assessment tests and college entrance exams. It also offers materials for students who have learning disabilities.
Website: www.epsbook.com

Freelance Potential

Published 30 titles in 2003: 10 were developed from unsolicited submissions. Of the 30 titles, 5 were by unpublished writers and 5 were by authors who were new to the publishing house. Receives 200 unsolicited mss yearly.

- **Fiction:** Publishes easy-to-read books, 4–7 years; chapter books, 5–10 years; and middle-grade novels, 8–12 years. Genres include multicultural and ethnic fiction.
- **Nonfiction:** Publishes reading, writing, vocabulary, grammar, comprehension, and elementary math workbooks, grades K–12. Also publishes educational materials for students with learning disabilities.
- **Representative Titles:** *Beyond the Code* by Nancy M. Hall (grades K–2) includes stories that are preceded by writing and spelling activities designed to introduce new sight words and teach phonetic patterns. *Right into Reading* by Jane Ervin (grades 1–2) offers a solid foundation in basic phonics sounds and a variety of readings from the earliest level.

Submissions and Payment

Send complete ms with résumé, outline, sample chapter, and table of contents. Accepts photocopies, computer printouts, and simultaneous submissions if identified. SASE. Responds in 2 months. Publication in 1 year. Royalty.

Editor's Comments

Most of our writers are teachers. If you have created lessons that have been successful, we're interested in hearing from you. Ideas for books or workbooks that are appropriate for kindergarten through high school classrooms are welcome.

Edupress

208 Fabricante, #200
San Clemente, CA 92675

Product Coordinator: Amanda Meinke

Publisher's Interests

Preschool through eighth-grade teachers and homeschoolers
use products from Edupress. It features classroom resources,
activity books, and educational materials on language arts,
math, science, social studies, and art. Titles on early childhood skills and curriculum development are also available
from this publisher.
Website: www.edupress.com

Freelance Potential

Published 30 titles in 2003: 3 were developed from unsolicited submissions. Receives 30 queries yearly.
- **Fiction:** Publishes easy-to-read books, 4–7 years.
- **Nonfiction:** Publishes books and resource materials for educators, pre-K–grade 8. Topics include social studies, science, language arts, mathematics, art, early childhood skills, and curriculum development.
- **Representative Titles:** *Ancient Egypt Activity Book* (grades 2–6)
  includes historic and cultural arts, crafts, games, and cooking
  activities that can be used across the curriculum. *Biographies
  That Build Character* (grades 4–6) helps students develop key
  language arts skills through reading, writing, and discussion
  while also building their understanding of good character.

Submissions and Payment

Guidelines available. Query with outline and sample pages.
Accepts photocopies and computer printouts. SASE.
Responds in 4–5 months. Publication in 1 year. Flat fee.

Editor's Comments

Our motto is "education with imagination." Peruse our catalogue and you will see that we set very high creative standards
for the classroom products we develop and market. We're looking for quality materials that will expand our offerings in the
areas of reading, phonics, grammar, and mathematics—but
anything that will help teachers meet assessment standards
while making learning fun will be considered. Most of the
material we accept comes from experienced teachers.

Eerdmans Books for Young Readers

255 Jefferson Avenue SE
Grand Rapids, MI 49503

Children's Books Publisher: Judy Zylstra

Publisher's Interests
The mission of Eerdmans Books for Young Readers is to foster faith in God by publishing picture books, middle-grade and young adult fiction and nonfiction titles that will inspire their readers.
Website: www.eerdmans.com

Freelance Potential
Published 15 titles in 2003: 5 were developed from unsolicited submissions, 6 were by agented authors, and 4 were reprint/licensed properties. Of the 15 titles, 1 was by an unpublished writer and 3 were by authors who were new to the publishing house. Receives 5 unsolicited mss yearly.

- **Fiction:** Publishes easy-to-read books, 4–7 years; story picture books, 4–10 years; middle-grade novels, 8–12 years; and young adult novels, 12–18 years. Genres include inspirational and religious fiction. Also publishes retellings of classic tales.
- **Nonfiction:** Publishes early picture books, 0–4 years; and middle-grade books, 8–12 years. Topics include Christian living, the Bible, and prayer. Also publishes educational titles and biographies.
- **Representative Titles:** *One Fine Day* by Elizabeth Van Steenwyk (all ages) tells the story of the day the Wright brothers first flew, using an old-time radio play as its format. *Silent Dreams* by Dandi Daley Mackall (all ages) is the tale of an orphaned girl who finds solace at the silent movie theater.

Submissions and Payment
Guidelines available. Send complete ms for picture books. Query with 3–4 sample chapters for longer works. Accepts photocopies, computer printouts, and simultaneous submissions if identified. SASE. Responds in 3–4 months. Publication period varies. Royalty.

Editor's Comments
We are always interested in books that will inspire children and young people to celebrate and appreciate the wonders of God's world and the joys of leading a spiritual, Christian life.

Eldridge Publishing

P.O. Box 14367
Tallahassee, FL 32317

Editor: Susan Shore

Publisher's Interests
Full-length and one-act plays and youth theater plays and
musicals are found in Eldridge Publishing's catalogue. Its
dramatic materials are used by community theaters, as well
as by junior and senior high schools. It also publishes a
smaller line of nondenominational religious plays. Eldridge
Publishing has been in operation since 1906.
Website: www.histage.com

Freelance Potential
Published 70 titles in 2003: 2 were by agented authors.
Receives 500+ unsolicited mss yearly.
- **Fiction:** Publishes full-length and one-act plays, skits, and
  musicals, grades 6–12. Genres include contemporary and classical drama, humor, folktales, melodrama, Westerns, and Bible
  stories. Also publishes plays about holidays and adult drama
  for community theater.
- **Representative Titles:** *Case of the Missing Homework* by Gary
  H. Smith (grades 5–6) is a melodrama about a boy who steals a
  classmate's homework to give to his girlfriend. *Mr. Wiggins' Toy
  Shoppe* by Kathy Montgomery (all ages) is a lighthearted play
  about a group of toys in a Christmas window display that
  encounters some unusual visitors.

Submissions and Payment
Send complete ms stating play length and age ranges for
actors and audience. Include cassette and sample score with
musical submissions. Accepts photocopies, computer printouts, and simultaneous submissions if identified. SASE.
Responds in 2 months. Publication in 6–12 months. Royalty,
varies. Flat fee for religious plays.

Editor's Comments
Please note that we prefer to receive plays that have been per-
formed at least once. Holiday plays and children's plays with
religious themes are always needed. Comedies, mysteries, and
musicals for junior and senior high schools are also welcome.
Flexible casting is a plus.

Encore Performance Publishing

P.O. Box 692
Orem, UT 84059

President: Michael Perry

Publisher's Interests
Encore Performance Publishing offers full-length and one-act plays, skits, musicals, and monologues, as well as books about theater arts, from set design to stage makeup, for school and community theater groups who put on performances for children, families, and adults.
Website: www.encoreplay.com

Freelance Potential
Published 15 titles (5 juvenile) in 2003: 1 was by an agented author. Of the 15 titles, 1 was by an unpublished writer and 7 were by authors who were new to the publishing house. Receives 100 queries yearly.
- **Fiction:** Publishes plays and dramatic series, 5–18 years. Features dramas with multicultural, religious, and ethnic themes, as well as educational, bilingual, and humorous plays.
- **Nonfiction:** Publishes books about theater arts, all ages. Topics include acting, auditions, improvisation, stage management, set design, lighting, and makeup.
- **Representative Titles:** *Snow Child* by J. D. Davidson (all ages) is the story of a childless couple whose ice sculpture of a little girl comes to life when a fairy grants their New Year's wish. *Shusha and the Story Snatcher* by Shirley Barrie (grades K–2) tells how a young girl's doll saves her from the story snatcher.

Submissions and Payment
Guidelines available. Query with résumé, synopsis, and production history. Accepts photocopies and computer printouts. SASE. Responds in 2 weeks. Publication in 2 months. Royalty, 50% performance, 10% book.

Editor's Comments
We are especially interested in plays that deal with topical and moral issues to provide an uplifting and edifying message for children, families, and adults. Challenging plays that will encourage both actors and audiences to become more actively involved in the process of creating a theatrical production are always welcomed.

Enslow Publishers, Inc.

Box 398
40 Industrial Road
Berkeley Heights, NJ 07922-0398

Editor: Brian Enslow

Publisher's Interests
Enslow Publishers, Inc., has been producing educational books for use in grades two through twelve for more than 25 years. Its specialty is nonfiction, and all of its titles are curriculum-based. Areas covered include social studies, history, and science. Most of its books are part of series.
Website: www.enslow.com

Freelance Potential
Published 200 titles in 2003: 25 were developed from unsolicited submissions. Of the 200 titles, 50 were by authors who were new to the publishing house. Receives 1,000 queries yearly.
- **Nonfiction:** Publishes middle-grade books, 8–12 years; and young adult books, 12–18 years. Topics include social issues, health, history, the environment, science, and multicultural issues. Also publishes biographies.
- **Representative Titles:** *The Aaron Burr Treason Trial* by Eileen Lucas (grade 6 and up) discusses the legal intricacies of the case and its political impact; part of the Headline Court Cases series. *AIDS In The 21st Century* by Michelle Houle (grade 6 and up) gives an in-depth description of the AIDS epidemic and what is being done to combat the illness.

Submissions and Payment
Guidelines available. Query with outline and market analysis. Accepts photocopies and computer printouts. SASE. Responds in 1–6 months. Publication in 1 year. Royalty; advance. Flat fee.

Editor's Comments
New ideas for our established series, as well as suggestions for new series, are always of interest. Most of our authors are teachers, but writers with expertise in a given subject area are welcome as well. Our goal is to provide the best materials possible for our audience. Tell us how you can help meet this goal with your book and why it is special. Give us a query that demonstrates your ability to make information fun.

ETC Publications

700 East Vereda del Sur
Palm Springs, CA 92262

Senior Editor: Richard W. Hostrop

Publisher's Interests
Academic reference books for educators and school administrators are the centerpiece of this publisher's list. It also produces materials for homeschooling parents as well as educational titles written for students at the middle school and
high school levels.

Freelance Potential
Published 3 titles in 2003: 1 was developed from an unsolicited submission. Of the 3 titles, 1 was by an unpublished
writer and 1 was by an author who was new to the publishing house. Receives 50+ queries yearly.
- **Nonfiction:** Published 1 middle-grade book, 8–12 years. Also
  publishes young adult books, 12–18 years. Publishes reference
  books for school educators and administrators and parents
  who homeschool. Topics include history, education, and curriculum development.
- **Representative Titles:** *Bite the Wall* by Victor J. Ross (school
  administrators) is a firsthand account by a school superintendent that captures the conflict, tension, and humor that go along
  with the job. *The Internet for Educators and Homeschoolers* by
  Steve Jones (teachers) describes the second phase of the Internet's evolution and explains ways to best use the Internet to
  teach children.

Submissions and Payment
Query with 2 sample chapters. No unsolicited mss. Accepts
photocopies, computer printouts, and simultaneous submissions if identified. Availability of artwork improves chance of
acceptance. SASE. Responds in 1 month. Publication in 9
months. Royalty, 5–15%.

Editor's Comments
While we're always interested in reviewing top-notch reference
titles for educators, we would also like to review materials
with a Christian slant that are written specifically for homeschoolers. We also continue to seek state histories for use in
elementary classrooms.

Evan-Moor Educational Publishers

18 Lower Ragsdale Drive
Monterey, CA 93940

Editorial Assistant: Lisa Mathews

Publisher's Interests
Serving teachers and homeschoolers working with preschool
through sixth-grade students, Evan-Moor offers educational
resources that focus on the major curriculum areas—language arts, mathematics, science, and social studies—with
an emphasis on the primary grades. It now offers some software to accompany its products.
Website: www.evan-moor.com

Freelance Potential
Published 55 titles (3 juvenile) in 2003: 9 were by authors
who were new to the publishing house. Receives 200 queries,
150 unsolicited mss yearly.
- **Nonfiction:** Publishes classroom and homeschooling resources,
  teaching materials, and activity books, pre-K–grade 6. Topics
  include social studies, mathematics, science, technology, reading, writing, language arts, early learning, arts and crafts, and
  thematic units.
- **Representative Titles:** *Readers' Theater* (grades 1–6) is a
  series of six books that provide the fun and interest of full-
  scale dramatic productions without the staging challenges.
  Basic Math Skills (grades 1–3) is a comprehensive resource for
  students who need additional skill practice; it corresponds to
  the strands of the NCTM content standards.

Submissions and Payment
Guidelines available at website. Query with outline and sample pages; or send complete ms. Accepts photocopies and
computer printouts. SASE. Responds in 3 months. Publication in 1–2 years. Flat fee.

Editor's Comments
If you peruse our catalogue or visit our website, you'll see that
most of our titles target the early grades, rather than the intermediate grades. We also have a strong emphasis on language
arts, and most of our products are published as part of a
group or series. Before contacting us, research the market
and make sure your idea fits with our mission.

Exclamation! Publishers

P.O. Box 664
Phoenixville, PA 19460

President & Publisher: Denise E. Heap

Publisher's Interests
Exclamation! Publishers develops historical fiction titles, as
well as well-researched straight nonfiction and creative nonfiction. Its list also features poetry and cookbooks.
Website: www.deheap.com

Freelance Potential
Published 8 titles in 2003: 1 was developed from an unsolicited submission. Of the 8 titles, 1 was by an author who
was new to the publishing house. Receives 250 queries
each year.
- **Fiction:** Published 2 young adult books, 12–18 years. Genres
  include historical fiction.
- **Nonfiction:** Published 1 middle-grade book, 8–12 years; and 3
  young adult books, 12–18 years.
- **Representative Titles:** *Friendship of the White Rose* by Lilo
  Ramdohr discusses the activities of a little-known resistance
  movement known as the White Rose. *Roses at Noon: Coming
  Together* by Ruth Sachs is a factual novel about the early
  years of the White Rose movement as they started on their
  path to resistance.

Submissions and Payment
Guidelines available at website. Query with author biography
or résumé. No unsolicited mss. Email queries to dheap@
deheap.com (no attachments). SASE. Responds in 4–6 weeks.
Publication period varies. Royalty, 15%.

Editor's Comments
We publish materials for students, young adults, and adults.
Our primary interests are in the areas of historical fiction, creative nonfiction, straight nonfiction, and poetry. For us to consider children's poetry, however, it must be excellent. We're
especially interested in projects that can stand alone and that
can be easily transformed into textbooks. If you'd like to write
for our newsletter, the History Project, which covers history,
civics, and international politics for middle school and high
school students, query with your credentials.

Facts on File

17th Floor
132 West 31st Street
New York, NY 10001

Editorial Director: Laurie Likoff
Senior Editor, Young Adult: Nicole Bowen

Publisher's Interests
This well-known reference publisher has been producing
titles for schools and libraries since 1941. Facts on File publishes nonfiction titles on a variety of subjects for readers
ages five and up. Most of its titles are published as parts of
series. It also offers material online and on CD-ROMs.
Website: www.factsonfile.com

Freelance Potential
Published 240 titles (75 juvenile) in 2003: 5 were developed
from unsolicited submissions, 60–75 were by agented
authors, and 15 were reprint/licensed properties. Of the 240
titles, 120 were by unpublished writers. Receives 150 queries
each year.

- **Nonfiction:** Published 25 middle-grade books, 8–12 years; and
  50 young adult books, 12–18 years. Also publishes chapter
  books, 5–10 years. Topics include history, social issues, current affairs, politics, multicultural issues, mathematics, science, and the environment.
- **Representative Titles:** *Technology in Action* by Sally & Adrian
  Morgan (grades 4–9) links concepts in the physical sciences to
  principles in the biological sciences; part of the Designs in Science series. *Hurricanes* by Michael Allaby (grades 6–12) tells
  how a hurricane begins and talks about storm surges and predicting damage; part of the Dangerous Weather series.

Submissions and Payment
Query with outline, sample chapter, description of audience,
competitive titles, and marketing ideas. Accepts photocopies,
computer printouts, and simultaneous submissions if identified. SASE. Responds in 2 months. Publication in 1 year.
Royalty; advance.

Editor's Comments
Study our catalogue to get a feel for our publishing program.
You must be an expert on the topic of the book you are
proposing. While we accept material from many sources, most
of our authors are teachers, researchers, or professors.

Books to Use and Books to Treasure
Heather Gemmen
Faith Kidz, Cook Communications

According to Heather Gemmen, Acquisitions Editor for Faith Kidz, Cook Communications Ministries' history lies in providing quality educational material to churches. Gemmen is an author of both adult and children's books, as well as an editor. She says that Cook is much more than a Christian educational press. "We provide relevant Christian materials also for the home, discipling all ages."

In discussing whether a good manuscript fits with her house or with a secular publisher, Gemmen observes that almost all children's books, no matter who publishes them, are morally sound. But religious publishers have to go beyond that and provide "the reason behind the good morals." Gemmen says that even if she receives a very strong manuscript—but one that doesn't have clear biblical content—she will pass on it. "Sometimes it is very tough to give up an excellent proposal, but I know that my company would not be meeting the very specific needs of our market, if we published it."

Gemmen describes the imprint: "All Faith Kidz books have the purpose of equipping kids for life, using biblical content. The primary focus is one of three things: to teach a lesson on faith, to help kids face a life issue, and to teach kids to read. Books in a series are almost always preferable to standalone items."

Gemmen sorts children's books into two categories, "the kind of books we want our kids to use and the books we want our kids to treasure. The first kind—the read-me books—kids will stuff in their backpacks, take into bed, carry to the blanket in the backyard until they are so tattered Mom will have to buy a new one. The second kind—the treasure books—will stay on display and be read by Grandma to the kids." Gemmen says she loves both kinds, but that Faith Kidz publishes more of the first than the second.

Faith Kidz

4050 Lee Vance View
Colorado Springs, CO 80918

Editorial Assistant

Publisher's Interests
Early- and middle-reader books that have Christian themes
are developed by Faith Kidz. An imprint of Cook Communications Ministries, it offers books about the Bible and Christian
holidays, as well as inspirational fiction. Games, toys, and
other media products are also available from this publisher.
Website: www.cookministries.com

Freelance Potential
Published 20 titles in 2003: 1 was developed from an unsolicited submission. Receives 1,000+ queries yearly.
- **Fiction:** Publishes easy-to-read books, 4–7 years; chapter
  books, 5–10 years; and middle-grade books, 8–12 years.
  Genres include religious and inspirational fiction.
- **Nonfiction:** Publishes easy-to-read books, 4–7 years; chapter
  books, 5–10 years; and middle-grade books, 8-12 years. Topics
  include Christianity, the Bible, and life skills.
- **Representative Titles:** *A Knight in the Forest* is a telling of
  Micah 6:8 about a boy who lives in an enchanted forest and
  who learns what it means to be a true follower of Christ. *All
  About Money* by Larry Burkett uses the wisdom of Scripture
  and money-management experts to help kids become responsible and effective users of money.

Submissions and Payment
Query with writing credits and market analysis of comparative products. Accepts photocopies and computer printouts.
SASE. Response time and publication period vary. All books
are written on a work-for-hire basis.

Editor's Comments
Our primary purpose is to create books and other products
that will promote the spiritual growth and development of children. We place no restrictions on subject matter or style—we're
just looking for top-quality titles that present Christian teachings. We always encourage prospective writers to review our
catalogue, which appears on our website, before contacting us.
Send us a query with a description of the book's competition.

Falcon Publishing

246 Goose Lane
P.O. Box 480
Guilford, CT 06437

Acquisitions Editor

Publisher's Interests

Founded in 1979 and acquired by Globe Pequot Press in 2001, Falcon Publishing specializes in outdoor recreation guides and area-specific titles on hiking, biking, paddling, and wildlife viewing. Its juvenile list includes books on nature, animals, and the environment. It also offers calendars, videos, and gift and photography titles. It publishes no fiction.
Website: www.globepequot.com

Freelance Potential

Published 150 titles in 2003: 3 were developed from unsolicited submissions, 90 were by agented authors, and 6 were reprint/licensed properties. Of the 150 titles, 60 were by authors who were new to the publishing house. Receives 100 queries yearly.

- **Nonfiction:** Publishes chapter books, 5–10 years; middle-grade books, 8–12 years; and young adult books, 12–18 years. Topics include animals, nature, the environment, history, and regional subjects.
- **Representative Titles:** *Family Fun in Florida* by Jan Godown features more than 500 of the best attractions in the Sunshine State and includes information on destinations that encourage appreciation of nature, history, science, art, and culture. *Wild Colorado* by Donna Lynn Ikenberry highlights 51 roadless recreation areas in the state of Colorado.

Submissions and Payment

Guidelines available. Query with synopsis, table of contents, and sample chapter. Accepts photocopies and computer printouts. SASE. Responds in 3 months. Publication in 1 year. Royalty.

Editor's Comments

Log on to our website and review the types of books we publish before querying. You'll see that our focus is on nature, conservation, and how-to and where-to enjoy the outdoors. The best queries include a competitive analysis.

Family Learning Association & ERIC/REC Press

Suite 101
3925 Hagan Street
Bloomington, IN 47401

Director: Carl B. Smith

Publisher's Interests

This publisher provides parents and educators with resource materials, reference books, and research titles that focus on English, reading, and communication. Most of its materials are designed to be used with children in kindergarten through grade eight.
Website: www.kidscanlearn.com

Freelance Potential

Published 20 titles in 2003: 1 was developed from an unsolicited submission and 5 were reprint/licensed properties. Of the 20 titles, 1 was by an unpublished writer. Receives 100 queries yearly.

- **Fiction:** Publishes easy-to-read books, 4–7 years.
- **Nonfiction:** Publishes easy-to-read books, 4–7 years; story picture books, 4–10 years; chapter books, 5–10 years; and middle-grade books, 8–12 years. Also publishes professional development resources, research materials, and reference titles for educators. Features parent meeting leader guides, parent handouts, and Spanish and bilingual material. Topics include reading, writing, English, communications, and family and intergenerational literacy. Also offers interactive books with audio cassettes and turnkey packages for family resource centers.
- **Representative Titles:** *Learning from Heroes* by Vera Frye profiles 75 people from the past and present who make good role models. *How to Talk to Your Children About Books* by Carl B. Smith features five easy techniques to prompt book discussions and offers guidelines for selecting books.

Submissions and Payment

Query with table of contents, sample chapter, and market analysis. Accepts photocopies and computer printouts. SASE. Responds in 1 month. Publication in 1–2 years. Royalty, 6–10%. Flat fee, $250–$1,000.

Editor's Comments

A visit to our website will give you the best sense of the types of materials we're looking for.

Farrar, Straus & Giroux

19 Union Square West
New York, NY 10003

Children's Editorial Department

Publisher's Interests
This publisher primarily offers fiction for readers between the ages of three and eighteen. It also offers some nonfiction picture books and informational titles. Farrar, Straus & Giroux offers original hardcover titles and paperback reprints.
Website: www.fsgkidsbooks.com

Freelance Potential
Published 80 titles in 2003: 5 were developed from unsolicited submissions, 35 were by agented authors, and 5 were reprint/licensed properties. Of the 80 titles, 5 were by unpublished writers. Receives 1,000 queries, 6,000 unsolicited mss yearly.

- **Fiction:** Publishes easy-to-read books, 4–7 years; story picture books, 3–10 years; chapter books, 6–10 years; middle-grade books, 8–12 years; and young adult books, 12–18 years. Genres include fantasy, humor, and contemporary fiction.
- **Nonfiction:** Publishes picture books, 4–10 years; middle-grade books, 8–12 years; and young adult books, 12–18 years. Topics include history, science, and nature.
- **Representative Titles:** *When Catherine the Great and I Were Eight!* by Cari Best (4–8 years) is a picture book about a young girl's adventures with her grandmother as she learns how to swim. *Twists and Turns* by Janet McDonald (12+ years) is a novel about two girls who explore their options after graduating from high school.

Submissions and Payment
Guidelines available. Query for mss longer than 20 pages; send complete ms for shorter works. Accepts photocopies, computer printouts, and simultaneous submissions if identified. SASE. Responds in 2–3 months. Publication in 18 months. Royalty, 3–10% of list price, $3,000–$15,000.

Editor's Comments
Don't submit more than one manuscript at a time, and please don't call about the status of your manuscript. It takes at least two months for us to respond to most submissions.

Frederick Fell Publishers

Suite 305
2131 Hollywood Boulevard
Hollywood, FL 33020

Senior Editor: Linda Parker

Publisher's Interests
Frederick Fell is an independent publisher that has been in business for over 60 years. Its specialty is self-help and how-to books for young adults and adults, as well as religious and inspirational fiction for teens.
Website: www.fellpub.com

Freelance Potential
Published 35 titles in 2003: 17 were developed from unsolicited submissions and 15 were by agented authors. Of the 35 titles, 17 were by unpublished writers and 17 were by authors who were new to the publishing house. Receives 4,000 queries yearly.
- **Fiction:** Publishes young adult books, 12–18 years. Genres include inspirational and religious fiction.
- **Nonfiction:** Features how-to and self-help titles, 12–18 years. Topics include health and spirituality. Also publishes biographies and titles about parenting, child care, business, science, and entertainment.
- **Representative Titles:** *The Greatest Gift in the World* by Og Mandino (YA) is the 2,000-year-old story of a camel boy with a burning desire to improve his position in life. *The Tiniest Acorn* by Marsha T. Danzig (YA) is the tale of an acorn who, after wandering for months, gives birth to an entire forest.

Submissions and Payment
Guidelines available. Query with résumé and marketing plan. Availability of artwork improves chance of acceptance. Accepts photocopies and simultaneous submissions if identified. SASE. Responds in 1 month. Publication in 9–12 months. Royalty.

Editor's Comments
Our mission is to be a real resource teens and young adults can rely on for self-help advice, spiritual guidance, practical how-to information, and just about anything else they need in their lives. Make sure you include your credentials and the way you envision your book being promoted when you query.

The Feminist Press

The Graduate Center
365 Fifth Avenue
New York, NY 10016

Publisher: Jean Casella

Publisher's Interests
Founded in 1970, this non-profit publisher specializes in books by women as well as nonfiction works of women's history, politics, sociology, and educational resources. In the coming year, it will focus on books on women and parenting. It will not consider children's material again until late 2004. **Website:** www.feministpress.org

Freelance Potential
Published 15 titles in 2003: 2 were by agented authors and 2 were reprint/licensed properties. Receives 800 queries yearly.
- **Fiction:** Publishes chapter books, 10+ years; and middle-grade novels, 8–12 years. Genres include multicultural and ethnic fiction featuring strong female characters.
- **Nonfiction:** Publishes middle-grade books, 8–12 years. Features biographies and books on multicultural topics.
- **Representative Titles:** *Families* by Meredith Tax is a story told in picture book format that introduces young readers to the rich variety of families. *Josephina Hates Her Name* by Diana Engel is a picture book that features Josephina, who hated her name until she learned the story of her namesake, Great-Aunt Josephina.

Submissions and Payment
Guidelines available at website. Query via email (200 words or less) with "submissions" in subject line to jcasella@ gc.cuny.edu. Responds in 3–4 months. Publication period varies. Royalty; advance.

Editor's Comments
We are especially interested in titles for our new series, Girls First! The books in this series target middle-grade girls and seek to capture the independent spirit of girls and young women from all over the world. Our books for young people all feature strong, female protagonists and provide positive role models. We are interested in writers who want to join us as we celebrate women from many different cultures, interests, and experiences.

Ferguson Publishing

17th Floor
132 West 31st Street
New York, NY 10001

Editorial Director: Laurie Likoff

Publisher's Interests

An imprint of Facts on File, Inc., Ferguson.Publishing targets elementary school through college students and their guidance counselors. It offers a variety of career and vocational resource materials, including series for kids that explore career possibilities, in addition to books on occupational forecasts and financial aid.
Website: www.fergpubco.com

Freelance Potential

Published 23 titles in 2003. Receives 20–30 queries and unsolicited mss yearly.
- **Nonfiction:** Published 3 middle-grade titles, 8–12 years; and 20 young adult books, 12–18 years. Also publishes chapter books, 5–10 years. Topics include college planning, career awareness, and job training. Also publishes professional development titles and general reference books.
- **Representative Titles:** *Preparing for a Career in Radio & TV* (grades 7–12) takes a proactive, hands-on approach to exploring and preparing for careers in broadcasting; part of the What Can I Do Now? series. *Teamwork Skills* (grades 5–8) discusses the personal skills people need to succeed in the world of work; part of the Career Skills Library series.

Submissions and Payment

Guidelines available at website. Query with table of contents; or send complete ms with proposal. Accepts photocopies, computer printouts, email submissions to editorial@ factsonfile.com, and simultaneous submissions if identified. Publication period varies. Work-for-hire and some royalty assignments.

Editor's Comments

We are always on the lookout for experienced writers to contribute to our career-oriented series. To learn more and to request a free catalogue, visit our website. It includes our submission guidelines; we urge you to review them carefully before sending us a query or manuscript.

Focus on the Family Book Development

8675 Explorer Drive
Colorado Springs, CO 80920

Submissions Editor: Mark Maddox

Publisher's Interests
This non-profit publisher develops both juvenile titles and young adult books that stress family and Christian values. It also offers an extensive list of parenting titles and books about family health.
Website: www.family.org

Freelance Potential
Published 50 titles (15 juvenile) in 2003: 8 were developed from unsolicited submissions and 5 were by agented authors. Of the 50 titles, 1 was by an unpublished writer and 8 were by authors who were new to the publishing house. Receives 100 queries yearly.

- **Fiction:** Published 2 chapter books, 5–10 years; 2 middle-grade novels, 8–12 years; and 2 young adult books, 12–18 years. Genres include religious and inspirational fiction.
- **Nonfiction:** Published 1 easy-to-read book, 4–7 years; 2 story picture books, 4–10 years; and 6 young adult books, 12–18 years. Topics include hobbies, crafts, current events, entertainment, religion, and social issues. Also offers self-help titles.
- **Representative Titles:** *Appleseeds* (9–12 years) is an interactive workbook for girls that answers questions young minds have about God. *God Says I Am* is a keepsake picture book written to help children of all ages grasp the awe and wonder of God.

Submissions and Payment
Guidelines available. Query with outline/synopsis, résumé, and market analysis. Accepts photocopies, disk submissions (Microsoft Word/RTF), and email submissions to maddoxmh@fotf.org. SASE. Responds in 1 month. Publication in 12–14 months. Payment policy varies.

Editor's Comments
This year we're primarily interested in parenting titles, especially titles for young parents and minority or interracial families. Many of our titles are written on a work-for-hire basis, and we have an ongoing need for talented writers.

Forest House Publishing Company

P.O. Box 13350
Chandler, AZ 85248

President: Dianne Spahr

Publisher's Interests

With books for children up to the age of 12, this publisher offers a list that includes both fiction and nonfiction tied to the curriculum. As supplementary materials, these books appeal primarily to the school and library markets. Bilingual Spanish titles are also found in its catalogue.
Website: www.forest-house.com

Freelance Potential

Published 20 titles in 2003. Of the 20 titles, 4 were by unpublished writers and 10 were by authors who were new to the publishing house. Receives 100 unsolicited mss yearly.

- **Fiction:** Publishes concept books, toddler books, and early picture books, 0–4 years; easy-to-read books, 4–7 years; story picture books, 4–10 years; chapter books, 5–10 years; and middle-grade books, 8–12 years. Genres include contemporary and multicultural fiction; fairy tales; and adventure.
- **Nonfiction:** Publishes easy-to-read books, 4–7 years; and chapter books, 5–10 years. Topics include animals, nature, arts and crafts, special education, sign language, history, the environment, and ethnic and multicultural subjects.
- **Representative Titles:** *First Ladies of the White House* (4–6 years) features short biographies of all the first ladies and explores the contributions each one made to history and to the White House. *The Mystery of the Dragon in the Dungeon* by Janet Riehecky (grades 3–6) continues the adventures of a detective team as they try to solve a mystery in their school; part of the Red Door Detective Club mysteries.

Submissions and Payment

Send complete ms. Accepts photocopies and computer print-outs. SASE. Responds in 6 months. Publication in 1 year. Royalty; advance. Flat fee.

Editor's Comments

We have recently added more titles to our section on American history topics and continue to look for ideas that will both engage and educate young readers. Fiction, especially mysteries, is also needed.

Formac Publishing Company Ltd.

5502 Atlantic Street
Halifax, Nova Scotia B3H 1G4
Canada

Senior Editor: Elizabeth Eve

Publisher's Interests

For more than a quarter of a century, Formac Publishing has
offered fiction and nonfiction for beginning readers through
preteens. This Canadian publisher distributes its own titles
as well as those from other publishers. Many of its books
have Canadian themes.

Website: www.formac.ca

Freelance Potential

Published 20 titles (11 juvenile) in 2003: 4 were reprint/
licensed properties. Of the 20 titles, 1 was by an unpublished
writer and 1 was by an author who was new to the publishing house. Receives 80 queries yearly.

- **Fiction:** Published 1 chapter book, 5–10 years; and 2 middle-
  grade novels, 8–12 years. Also publishes easy-to-read books,
  4–7 years; and young adult titles, 12–18 years. Genres include
  mystery, suspense, fantasy, adventure, humor, stories about
  sports, and historical fiction.
- **Nonfiction:** Publishes middle-grade books, 8–12 years. Topics
  include sports, nature, the environment, and regional, multicultural, and ethnic subjects.
- **Representative Titles:** *The Secret Treasures of Oak Island* by
  J. J. Pritchard (YA) follows a girl who accompanies her uncle
  on a dig at a world-renowned treasure site in Nova Scotia. *Danger Zone* by Michele Martin Bossley tells the story of a Calgary
  hockey player who must prove himself after he accidentally
  hurts another player.

Submissions and Payment

Send résumé or query with outline and sample chapters. No
unsolicited mss. Accepts photocopies, computer printouts,
and simultaneous submissions if identified. SAE/IRC.
Responds in 1–12 months. Publication in 1–2 years. Royalty.

Editor's Comments

Chapter books that will appeal to six- to nine-year-old children
are still a top editorial priority. If you have an idea for a fresh,
captivating story, contact us.

Forward Movement Publications

412 Sycamore Street
Cincinnati, OH 45202

Submissions Editor: Edward S. Gleason

Publisher's Interests
As an official agency of the Episcopal church, this publisher offers books and pamphlets that are written "to support persons in lives of prayer and faith." Its children's list includes fiction and nonfiction for 8- to 18-year-old readers.
Website: www.forwardmovement.org

Freelance Potential
Published 30 titles (6 juvenile) in 2003: most were developed from unsolicited submissions. Of the 30 titles, 16 were by unpublished writers and 16 were by authors who were new to the publishing house. Receives 375 queries yearly.
- **Fiction:** Publishes middle-grade books, 8–12 years. Features contemporary fiction with Christian themes.
- **Nonfiction:** Publishes middle-grade books, 8–12 years; and young adult books, 12–18 years. Topics include meditation, spirituality, church history, and contemporary issues such as drug abuse and AIDS.
- **Representative Titles:** *Anglican Learning Centres: The Church Building* by Patricia Bays (teachers) is a Sunday school program that includes information sheets for students and teachers, activity cards, and worksheets. *Best of Blessings: Advent, Christmas, Epiphany* by Ginny Arthur, ed., is a collection of reproducible resource material that provides lively worship programs for children and adults to participate in together.

Submissions and Payment
Guidelines, catalogue, and sample pamphlet available ($1.65 postage; no SASE). Query with sample chapters. Accepts photocopies and computer printouts. SASE. Responds in 1 month. Publication period varies. Flat fee.

Editor's Comments
While we do publish picture books and books for use in Sunday school classrooms, we are primarily interested in material for the 4- to 16-page pamphlets we produce. These focus on spiritual topics and issues of concern to the church, and most are 500 to 1,000 words long.

Frances Foster Books

Farrar, Straus & Giroux
19 Union Square West
New York, NY 10003

Editor: Frances Foster
Assistant Editor: Janine O'Malley

Publisher's Interests

Frances Foster Books offers hardcover works of fiction for children from birth through the young adult years. An imprint of Farrar, Straus & Giroux, it will occasionally publish a nonfiction title related to a historical subject.
Website: www.fsgkidsbooks.com

Freelance Potential

Published 20 titles in 2003: 10 by agented authors. Receives 100 queries, 12,000 unsolicited mss yearly.

- **Fiction:** Publishes early picture books, 0–4 years; story picture books, 4–10 years; chapter books, 5–10 years; middle-grade novels, 8–12 years; and young adult books, 12–18 years. Genres include contemporary, historical, and ethnic fiction; fantasy; adventure; and drama.
- **Nonfiction:** Publishes a few titles on historical subjects.
- **Representative Titles:** *Buddha Boy* by Kathe Koja (YA) is the story of a boy who is different from his peers, and what they learn by accepting him. *Beatrix* by Jeanette Winter is a picture book that tells the story of Beatrix Potter's early childhood, a mixture of privilege and neglect.

Submissions and Payment

Guidelines available. Query with 3 sample chapters and synopsis for novels. Send complete ms for picture books. Do not send original art. Accepts photocopies, computer printouts, and simultaneous submissions if identified. SASE. Responds in 3+ months. Publication in 2+ years. Royalty; advance.

Editor's Comments

All of our books are of the highest quality, and we are looking for works that will become modern-day classics that will survive the test of time for generations. We will consider complete manuscripts for picture books only. All other submissions should be sent as queries with a cover letter and three sample chapters that make it clear why your story will capture a child's imagination. Make sure your characters are unique and memorable, and your writing is lively and age-appropriate.

Free Spirit Publishing

Suite 200
217 Fifth Avenue North
Minneapolis, MN 55401-1299

Acquisitions Assistant: Douglas J. Fehlen

Publisher's Interests
Free Spirit Publishing offers high-quality nonfiction for children, teens, parents, teachers, counselors, and others who live or work with young people. It strives to provide young readers with the tools they need to succeed in life.
Website: www.freespirit.com

Freelance Potential
Published 22 titles (16 juvenile) in 2003: 12 were developed from unsolicited submissions, 3 were by agented authors, and 1 was a reprint/licensed property. Receives 1,800 queries yearly.

- **Nonfiction:** Published 2 toddler books and 6 early picture books, 0–4 years; 2 middle-grade books, 8–12 years; and 6 young adult books, 12–18 years. Topics include family and social issues, character building, relationships, stress management, creativity, self-awareness, and self-esteem. Also publishes titles for parents, teachers, youth workers, and child-care professionals on learning disorders, psychology, and gifted and talented education.
- **Representative Titles:** *Share and Take Turns* by Cheri J. Meiners (4–8 years) helps children understand the benefits of this important social skill, suggests ways they can practice sharing, and explains how and why they should share. *Life Lists for Teens* by Pamela Espeland (YA) features over 200 lists, each one functioning as a mini self-help book for learning, thinking, and making positive choices and decisions.

Submissions and Payment
Guidelines available. Query with résumé, outline, and 2 sample chapters. Accepts photocopies and computer printouts. SASE. Responds in 1–3 months. Publication in 1–3 years. Royalty; advance.

Editor's Comments
We'd like to see queries on diversity, self-esteem, life skills, and media awareness for young adults. Books that deal with character education, bullying, and resilience are also needed.

Front Street Books

Suite 403
20 Battery Park Avenue
Asheville, NC 28801

Submissions Editor: Joy Neaves

Publisher's Interests
This award-winning independent publisher caters to young readers of all ages with both fiction and nonfiction titles. Its list includes picture books, poetry, and titles for middle-grade through young adult readers. At this time, it is not accepting submissions for picture books.
Website: www.frontstreetbooks.com

Freelance Potential
Published 15 titles in 2003: 2 were developed from unsolicited submissions, 1 was by an agented author, and 2 were reprint/licensed properties. Of the 15 titles, 3 were by unpublished writers and 4 were by authors who were new to the publishing house. Receives 2,000 queries, 2,000 unsolicited mss yearly.
- **Fiction:** Published 3 story picture books, 4–10 years; 1 middle-grade book, 8–12 years; and 10 young adult books, 12–18 years. Genres include humor; adventure; fantasy; historical, multicultural and science fiction; and stories about animals.
- **Nonfiction:** Publishes young adult books, 12–18 years. Also publishes novelty books, educational titles, and poetry.
- **Representative Titles:** *A Nice Party* by Elle van Lieshout & Erik van Os (2–6 years) is a story of two bears who spend a birthday in a new way. *Summer of the Skunks* by Wilmoth Foreman (8+ years) tells the story of Jill, who learns to appreciate the value of family.

Submissions and Payment
Guidelines available. Query with sample chapter for nonfiction. Send complete ms for fiction under 100 pages, or 2 sample chapters for fiction over 100 pages. Accepts photocopies, computer printouts, and simultaneous submissions if identified. SASE. Responds in 3 months. Publication in 12–18 months. Royalty; advance.

Editor's Comments
Please visit our website to see what we publish. We often get queries that are totally inappropriate for us.

Fulcrum Publishing

Suite 300
16100 Table Mountain Parkway
Golden, CO 80403-1672

Submissions Editor: T. J. Baker

Publisher's Interests
This publisher offers books for children on a variety of topics including gardening, travel, history, nature, and Native-American culture. Established in 1984, Fulcrum Publishing also offers extensive resources for educators. As of this year, Fulcrum is no longer publishing its fiction line.
Website: www.fulcrum-books.com

Freelance Potential
Published 30 titles (2 juvenile) in 2003: 2 were by agented authors. Receives 250 queries, 1,500 unsolicited mss each year.
- **Nonfiction:** Publishes story picture books, 4–10 years; chapter books, 5–10 years; and middle-grade books, 8–12 years. Also publishes educational activity books and books for parents and educators. Topics include science, nature, animals, geography, and multicultural subjects.
- **Representative Titles:** *Celebrations Around the World* by Carole S. Angell (grades 3–8) follows the calendar to explore the background and context of more than 300 holidays from all over the globe. *Blodin the Beast* by Michael Morpurgo (grades K–6) tells the timeless story of a young boy's quest to save his people from the tyranny of a pitiless beast.

Submissions and Payment
Guidelines available. Query or send complete ms with résumé and competition analysis. Accepts photocopies, computer printouts, and simultaneous submissions if identified. SASE. Responds to queries in 1 month, to unsolicited mss in 2–3 months. Publication in 18–24 months. Royalty; advance.

Editor's Comments
If you are interested in writing for us, it is important that you first review some of the titles on our backlist to get an idea of what appeals to us and what topics we have already covered. We are always open to new, talented writers who can bring a topic to life for children, as long as the subject matter is within our areas of interest.

Gibbs Smith, Publisher

P.O. Box 667
Layton, UT 84040

Children's Book Editor: Jennifer Grillone

Publisher's Interests
Gibbs Smith, Publisher, has a children's line that features
picture and activity books for readers up to the age of 10. It
frequently publishes children's books with Western themes.
Its adult list includes books on art, architecture, gardening,
and cooking.
Website: www.gibbs-smith.com

Freelance Potential
Published 65 titles (10 juvenile) in 2003: 10 were developed
from unsolicited submissions and 8 were reprint/licensed
properties. Of the 65 titles, 8 were by unpublished writers
and 15 were by authors who were new to the publishing
house. Receives 500 queries, 1,500 unsolicited mss yearly.
- **Fiction:** Published 2 easy-to-read books, 4–7 years; and 2
  story picture books, 4–10 years. Genres include Westerns,
  adventure, humor, fantasy, folktales, and stories about animals, nature, and the environment.
- **Nonfiction:** Publishes activity books, 4–10 years. Features
  books about the outdoors.
- **Representative Titles:** *Riding on a Range* by Lawson Drinkard
  (6–12 years) is a book filled with activities with Western
  themes. *Emily Goes Wild* by Betty Lou Phillips (4–8 years)
  depicts the lives of an irresistible, mischievous monkey and the
  refined New Orleans matriarch who cares for her.

Submissions and Payment
Guidelines available. Send complete ms for picture books.
Query with outline and writing samples for nonfiction.
Accepts photocopies, computer printouts, and simultaneous
submissions if identified. SASE. Responds in 10–12 weeks.
Publication in 1–2 years. Royalty; advance.

Editor's Comments
We continue to look for well-written picture books under 1,000
words, especially ones that have cowboy or ranch-lifestyle
themes. We are also interested in reviewing activity books
about the outdoors that have fewer than 15,000 words.

Gifted Education Press

P.O. Box 1586
10201 Yuma Court
Manassas, VA 20108

Publisher: Maurice D. Fisher

Publisher's Interests
Gifted Education Press creates books that assist teachers, homeschoolers, parents, educational administrators, and librarians who work with gifted children. It also publishes a quarterly newsletter that covers topics of interest to professionals in the field, as well as parents of gifted children.
Website: www.giftededpress.com

Freelance Potential
Published 10 titles in 2003. Receives 100 queries, 20 unsolicited mss yearly.
- **Nonfiction:** Publishes concept books, 0–4 years. Also publishes educational resources for teachers and parents working with gifted students, and school administrators running gifted education programs.
- **Representative Titles:** *Essential Mathematics for Gifted Students: Preparation for Algebra, Grades 4–8* by Francis T. Sganga (teachers) is a stimulating and rigorous mathematics program educators can put to use to lay the groundwork gifted students will need to tackle algebra. *Multiple Intelligences in the World* by Maurice D. Fisher (teachers) explains how to apply Gardner's theory of multiple intelligences to educating gifted students.

Submissions and Payment
Submit 1-page query only. No unsolicited mss. SASE. Responds in 3 months. Publication in 3 months. Royalty, 10%.

Editor's Comments
Please review our current list of publications before submitting your query, to be certain you are proposing a new angle or topic not previously covered. Authors who write for Gifted Education Press must be experts on the topic they are writing about, and should have abundant experience working with gifted students. No complete manuscripts will be considered. Submit a one-page query that clearly outlines your topic, source material, and credentials. Books on gifted education advocacy are of particular interest to us at the moment.

The Globe Pequot Press

825 Great Northern Boulevard
Helena, MT 59601

Executive Editor: Erin H. Turner

Publisher's Interests
Western and regional history titles written in a fun, easy-to-read style can be found in The Globe Pequot Press's catalogue. It publishes books for five- to eighteen-year-old readers, as well as a line of travel guides for families.
Website: www.globepequot.com

Freelance Potential
Published 400 titles (12 juvenile) in 2003: 5 were developed from unsolicited submissions and 3 were by agented authors. Of the 400 titles, 6 were by unpublished writers and 3 were by authors who were new to the publishing house. Receives 360–480 unsolicited mss yearly.
- **Nonfiction:** Published 4 chapter books, 5–10 years; 4 middle-grade books, 8–12 years; and 4 young adult books, 12–18 years. Topics include animals, pets, history, nature, the environment, and regional subjects. Also publishes biographies.
- **Representative Titles:** *Safe and Sound* by Marlene M. Coleman (parents) provides a preventative and proactive approach that helps parents ensure that their children return safe and healthy after traveling. *It Happened in Glacier* by Vince Moravek (all ages) presents thrilling episodes from the history of Montana's Glacier National Park; part of the It Happened In series.

Submissions and Payment
Guidelines available on website. Query with clips. Accepts photocopies and disk submissions. Availability of artwork improves chance of acceptance. SASE. Responds in 3 months. Publication in 18 months. Royalty, 8–12%; advance, $500–$1,500.

Editor's Comments
Books about women's history, Western history, and Civil War history will receive special consideration this year. These should all be written for readers between the ages of eight and twelve. Queries that state the author's qualifications and describe the availability of photographs have the best chance of acceptance.

Goodheart-Willcox

18604 West Creek Drive
Tinley Park, IL 60477-6243

Managing Editor: Paul Schreiner

Publisher's Interests
Materials for use in industrial training as well as titles for use in secondary schools fill the catalogue of this educational publisher. In addition to books, Goodheart-Willcox also produces software and resource material.
Website: www.g-w.com

Freelance Potential
Published 50 titles in 2003. Receives 100+ queries yearly.
- **Nonfiction:** Publishes textbooks and how-to titles. Topics include life skills, professional development, family living, career, education, clothing and textiles, and personal development.
- **Representative Titles:** *Child Care Administration: Planning Quality Programs For Young Children* by Linda Nelson & Alan Nelson (adults) features concrete ideas and plans for starting a child-care program. *Parents and Their Children* by Verdene Ryder (parents) covers a wide range of topics related to parenting, including pregnancy, healthy development, family concerns, and family crises.

Submissions and Payment
Guidelines available. Query with résumé, outline, sample chapter, and list of illustrations. SASE. Responds in 2 months. Publication in 2 years. Royalty.

Editor's Comments
We are always interested in innovative textbook proposals devoted to one of our subject areas or a related area. Send us a query that includes your résumé, an analysis for your book's competition, a market analysis, and a description of your book. The description should detail the purpose of your book, the nature of illustrations or artwork available, and explain its place in the curriculum. Your proposal should also tell us about yourself—your writing experience, your professional experience, and your ability to write informatively on your chosen topic. We prefer proposals that include illustrations. We are open to new writers who can deliver innovative ideas for covering topics on our list.

Graphic Arts Center Publishing Co.

P.O. Box 10306
Portland, OR 97296-0306

Submissions Editor: Tricia Brown

Publisher's Interests
This regional publisher develops titles on Pacific Northwest travel, nature, cooking, and history. For children, it features books about animals, the environment, and folklore.
Website: www.gacpc.com

Freelance Potential
Published 20 titles in 2003: 10 were developed from unsolicited submissions, 3 were by agented authors, and 5 were reprint/licensed properties. Of the 20 titles, 5 were by unpublished writers and 10 were by authors who were new to the publishing house. Receives 250 queries, 100 unsolicited mss yearly.

- **Fiction:** Published 2 early picture books, 0–4 years; 2 story picture books, 4–10 years; and 1 chapter book, 5–10 years. Also publishes young adult books, 12–18 years. Genres include historical fiction, folklore, suspense, and stories about animals, nature, and the environment.
- **Nonfiction:** Published 2 early picture books, 0–4 years; and 2 story picture books, 4–10 years. Also publishes middle-grade books, 8–12 years; and young adult books, 12–18 years. Topics include animals, geography, natural history, and humor.
- **Representative Titles:** *Seldovia Sam and the Very Large Clam* by Susan Woodard Springer (6–10 years) follows the misadventures of an 8-year-old boy in Alaska. *Dot to Dot in the Sky* by Joan Marie Galat (7–11 years) combines mythology with astronomy tips to help young astronomers view the night sky.

Submissions and Payment
Guidelines available. Query with clips for fiction; send complete ms for children's books. Accepts photocopies, disk submissions, and simultaneous submissions. SASE. Responds in 2–4 months. Publication in 2 years. Payment policy varies.

Editor's Comments
Remember that our children's books are regionally focused, primarily with Alaskan themes. Out-of-region books must have a demonstrable reader interest and market.

Greene Bark Press

P.O. Box 1108
Bridgeport, CT 06601-1108

Associate Publisher: Michele Hofbauer

Publisher's Interests

This publisher specializes in story picture books for children between the ages of three and nine. It also produces story-based CD-ROMs that come with teachers' guides packed with follow-up activities. Between one and six titles are published each year.
Website: www.greenebarkpress.com

Freelance Potential

Published 1 title in 2003: it was developed from an unsolicited submission. Receives 1,200 unsolicited mss yearly.

- **Fiction:** Publishes story picture books, 3–9 years. Genres include fantasy and mystery. Also offers teachers' guides and titles on CD-ROM.
- **Representative Titles:** *The Magical Trunk* by Gigi Tegge (3–8 years) is the story of a little girl who finds a trunk full of face paints, and as she experiments with color, she is transformed into a clown. *Hey! There's a Goblin Under My Throne!* by Rhett Ransome Pennell is about young King Edwin, who must meet and defeat a different monster each month as he tries to save his kingdom from the wicked witch Slugma.

Submissions and Payment

Guidelines available. Send complete ms with illustrations and story board. Accepts photocopies and simultaneous submissions if identified. SASE. Responds in 2–6 months. Publication in 12–18 months. Royalty, 10–15%.

Editor's Comments

We look for colorful, imaginative stories with a unique story line. Send us something that is truly original; we avoid stories with worn-out plots and classic themes, like an ugly duckling story or a story about the monster in the closet. Color and imagery are important. We prefer to receive one story at a time, ask that manuscripts be well written, and prefer stories submitted with color artwork (no originals please). Please note that we only publish fiction for children between the ages of three and nine.

Greenhaven Press

10911 Technology Place
San Diego, CA 92127

Acquisitions Editor: Chandra Howard

Publisher's Interests

High school students are the intended audience for the educational books offered by Greenhaven Press. It puts a special
emphasis on books about world history, American history,
contemporary social issues, and literary criticism, and it publishes books in series as well as anthologies.
Website: www.gale.com/greenhaven

Freelance Potential

Published 145 titles in 2003: 20 were developed from unsolicited submissions and 2 were by agented authors. Of the
145 titles, 15 were by unpublished writers and 20 were by
authors who were new to the publishing house. Receives 25
queries yearly.
- **Nonfiction:** Publishes educational titles, grades 9–12. Features
  anthologies and books in series about history, contemporary
  social issues, world authors, and literary criticism.
- **Representative Titles:** *Gun Control* (grades 9-12) discusses
  whether private gun ownership poses serious problems and
  examines measures to reduce gun violence; part of the Opposing Viewpoints series. *The Civil Rights Movement* by Nick Tre-
  anor (grades 9–12) portrays the struggle of African Americans
  to obtain basic rights and change resistant attitudes.

Submissions and Payment

Guidelines available. All books written on a work-for-hire
basis by assignment only. Query acquisitions editor for
guidelines and catalogue. SASE. Response time varies. Publication in 1 year. Flat fee, varies.

Editor's Comments

Because all of our titles are written on assignment and on a
work-for-hire basis, we do not accept unsolicited manuscripts.
Prospective authors should study our catalogue and visit our
website. If you feel you are qualified to write for one of our
series, send us a résumé and other appropriate credentials. We
especially encourage graduate students and university professors to contact us.

Greenwood Publishing Group

88 Post Road West
Westport, CT 06881

Editorial Secretary: Celine Reyes

Publisher's Interests
This publisher's mission is to provide high-quality, authoritative reference books on subject areas taught in middle schools, high schools, and colleges. All of Greenwood Publishing Group's materials are marketed directly to schools and libraries.
Website: www.greenwood.com

Freelance Potential
Published 80 titles (40 juvenile) in 2003: 16 were by agented authors. Of the 80 titles, 5 were by unpublished writers and 25 were by authors who were new to the publishing house. Receives 10 queries, 10 unsolicited mss yearly.
- **Nonfiction:** Publishes reference books and high interest/low vocabulary titles, grades 6 and up. Topics include history, geography, mathematics, science, nature, the environment, sports, social issues, health, language arts, and multicultural and ethnic issues.
- **Representative Titles:** *Exploring Animal Rights and Animal Welfare* (grades 6–8) explains the ways in which humans used animals throughout history and the controversies surrounding this use. *The Human Body & the Environment* (grades 6–8) is a four-volume set that examines the human body's inseparable relationship with the environment.

Submissions and Payment
Guidelines and catalogue available at website. Query with clips; or send complete ms with résumé. Accepts photocopies. Availability of artwork improves chance of acceptance. SASE. Responds in 2–4 weeks. Publication in 9 months. Royalty; varies. Flat fee.

Editor's Comments
Your prospectus should indicate the scope and organization of your project and whether a completed manuscript is available. If you would like to be considered for a project and do not have a particular topic in mind, contact the acquisitions editor who develops books in your discipline. See our website for details.

Group Publishing

P.O. Box 481
Loveland, CO 80539

Editorial Assistant: Kerri Loesche

Publisher's Interests
This publisher's mission is to encourage Christian growth in
children, youth, and adults. To that end, it offers resource
titles for Christian educators, including programming materials, nonfiction activity and how-to titles, Bible stories, crafts,
skits, pageants, music, and games. It does not publish children's storybooks or children's fiction.
Website: www.grouppublishing.com

Freelance Potential
Published 15 titles in 2003: 2 were developed from unsolicited submissions. Of the 15 titles, 1 was by an unpublished writer and 4 were by authors who were new to the
publishing house. Receives 500+ queries yearly.
- **Nonfiction:** Publishes activity, how-to, and programming
  books. Features Christian educational titles and books on special education, hobbies, crafts, games, and religion.
- **Representative Titles:** *Wild & Wacky Bible Lessons on Fear,
  Respect, and Helping Others* by Frank Peretti explores essential
  Bible topics using crafts, science experiments, and games;
  includes a teachers' guide, videos, and CDs. *City Lights: Ministry Essentials for Reaching Urban Youth* by Dr. Scott Larson &
  Karen Free is a comprehensive volume on urban youth ministry with practical help and proven practices.

Submissions and Payment
Guidelines available. Query with outline, book introduction,
and 2–3 sample chapters or activities. Accepts photocopies,
computer printouts, and simultaneous submissions if identified. SASE. Responds in 3–6 months. Publication period
varies. Royalty, to 10%. Flat fee, varies.

Editor's Comments
We're constantly working to develop fresh, inspiring tools to
assist Christians in ministering to children and youth. Please
don't send children's fiction—we don't publish that type of
book. Instead, send us material that promotes active learning
and provides lessons that apply the Bible to daily living.

Gryphon House

P.O. Box 207
Beltsville, MD 20704-0207

Editor-in-Chief: Kathy Charner

Publisher's Interests
Gryphon House publishes books of interest to parents and professionals who are dealing with young children every day. From the basics of baby proofing and setting limits, to practical preschool curriculum plans, this publisher covers virtually every topic encountered when dealing with this age group.
Website: www.gryphonhouse.com

Freelance Potential
Published 11 titles in 2003: 1 was developed from an unsolicited submission and 1 was by an agented author. Receives 150 queries yearly.
- **Nonfiction:** Publishes titles for parents and teachers working with children under the age of eight. Topics include art, math, science, language development, teaching strategies, conflict resolution, program development, and bilingual education.
- **Representative Titles:** *The Complete Daily Curriculum for Early Childhood* by Pam Schiller & Pat Phipps (teachers) provides easy activities to support multiple intelligences and learning styles for early childhood. *You Can't Come to My Birthday Party!* by Betsy Evans (adults) offers tips on how to help children resolve disputes successfully and develop the social skills they need to become caring and cooperative people.

Submissions and Payment
Guidelines available. Query with table of contents, introductory material, and 20–30 pages of activities. Accepts photocopies and computer printouts. SASE. Responds in 3–4 months. Publication in 1–2 years. Payment policy varies.

Editor's Comments
We are interested in books that offer actionable, practical advice for teachers and parents of young children. Please send us a detailed query that explains how and why your book will be an excellent resource, and include a substantial selection of activities adults can use with children to put your ideas to work. We do not publish children's books, so activity books without a practical purpose are of no interest.

Gulliver Books

15 East 26th Street
New York, NY 10010

Editorial Director: Elizabeth Van Doren or
Associate Editor: Kate Harrison

Publisher's Interests

Gulliver Books primarily publishes fiction, and its list includes concept books for very young children, books for early and middle-grade readers, and young adult novels. This Harcourt, Inc., imprint accepts submissions from agented authors, previously published authors, or from writers who are members of the Society of Children's Book Writers and Illustrators.
Website: www.harcourtbooks.com

Freelance Potential

Published 23 titles in 2003: 1 was developed from an unsolicited submission and 13 were by agented authors. Of the 23 titles, 1 was by an unpublished writer and 1 was by a new author. Receives 100–200 queries, 500+ mss yearly.

- **Fiction:** Published 2 concept books, 2 toddler books, and 3 early picture books, 0–4 years; 8 story picture books, 4–10 years; 1 chapter book, 5–10 years; 2 middle-grade titles, 8–12 years; and 1 young adult book, 12–18 years. Genres include historical and contemporary fiction and adventure. Also publishes animal stories and poetry.
- **Nonfiction:** Published 2 story picture books, 4–10 years. Topics include sports, history, nature, science, and the environment.
- **Representative Titles:** *B Is For Bulldozer* by June Sobel (2–5 years) is an alphabet book that tells the story of an amusement park's construction over the course of a year. *Mama Played Baseball* by David Adler (5–8 years) is the story of a young girl whose mother has just secured a position in the first professional women's baseball league during World War II.

Submissions and Payment

Accepts submissions from agented and previously published authors or members of SCBWI. SASE. Responds in 6–8 weeks. Publication in 2–4 years. Royalty; advance.

Editor's Comments

We're interested in books about universal childhood experiences such as school anxieties and sibling relationships, or common childhood fascinations such as pirates and dinosaurs.

Hachai Publishing

156 Chester Avenue
Brooklyn, NY 11218

Submissions Editor: D. Rosenfeld

Publisher's Interests
Children's books for the very young that convey the Jewish
experience in modern times or long ago are the specialty of
this publisher. Stories that include the traditional Jewish
observance of holidays and year-round mitzvos such as
mezuzah, tzitzis, and honoring parents, and show positive
character traits such as honesty, charity, respect, and sharing are of particular interest.
Website: www.hachai.com

Freelance Potential
Published 5 titles in 2003: 2 were developed from unsolicited
submissions. Of the 5 titles, 2 were by unpublished writers
and 2 were by authors who were new to the publishing
house. Receives 300+ unsolicited mss yearly.
- **Fiction:** Publishes concept books and early picture books, 0–4
  years; story picture books, 4–10 years; and chapter books,
  7–10 years. Genres include historical and religious fiction;
  adventure; and folktales.
- **Nonfiction:** Publishes concept books, 0–4 years; and story picture books, 4–10 years.
- **Representative Titles:** *Where Does Food Come From?* by Dina
  Rosenfeld (2–5 years) helps toddlers understand that the heart
  of mastering the blessings on food is understanding the origin
  of each type of treat. *The Kingston Castle* by Ruth Abrahamson
  (8+ years) follows a family on an adventurous vacation.

Submissions and Payment
Guidelines available. Send complete ms. Accepts photocopies.
SASE. Responds in 2–6 weeks. Publication in 12–18 months.
Flat fee.

Editor's Comments
We are interested in biographies of spiritually great men and
women in Jewish history, and historical fiction adventure novels for beginning readers that highlight devotion to faith and
the relevance of Torah in making important choices. Please, no
animal stories, romance, violence, or preachy sermonizing.

Hampton-Brown Books

P.O. Box 369
Marina, CA 93933

Submissions Editor

Publisher's Interests

Hampton-Brown Books specializes in quality textbooks and easy-to-read titles for language arts, English-as-a-Second-Language programs, and dual-language educators. Its materials target students in preschool through eighth grade, and include a wide range of high-interest, low-vocabulary books for struggling readers.
Website: www.hampton-brown.com

Freelance Potential

Published 200 titles (150 juvenile) in 2003: 150 were by agented authors. Receives 1,000 queries yearly.

- **Fiction:** Publishes early picture books, 0–4 years; easy-to-read books, 4–7 years; story picture books, 4–10 years; chapter books, 5–10 years; and middle-grade books, 8–12 years. Genres include fairy tales, folklore, drama, and contemporary and multicultural fiction.
- **Nonfiction:** Publishes early picture books, 0–4 years; easy-to-read books, 4–7 years; story picture books, 4–10 years; chapter books, 5–10 years; and middle-grade books, 8–12 years. Also publishes books on phonics, ESL, early literacy, dual-language programs, content-area reading, and homeschooling.
- **Representative Titles:** *My Fish* by Juan Quintana (grade K) teaches phonics with a simple story about a pet fish; part of the Phonics and Friends series. *One Afternoon* by Yumi Heo (grade 1) follows a day in the life of a young child, and uses everyday themes to teach word recognition and reading skills; part of the Into English! series.

Submissions and Payment

Query. No unsolicited mss. SASE. Responds in 3–6 months. Publication period varies. Flat fee.

Editor's Comments

We are very interested in material for at-risk and bilingual children, and struggling readers. The material we publish is for professionals working in those or other language arts programs, so please make sure you are qualified to write for such an audience, and send us a detailed query.

Hampton Roads Publishing

1125 Stoney Ridge Road
Charlottesville, VA 22902

Editor-in-Chief: Frank DeMarco

Publisher's Interests

When Hampton Roads Publishing was founded in 1989, its goal was to publish quality metaphysical fiction and nonfiction that would make a difference in people's lives; books that could help change the world and the people in it. As of 2003, it has discontinued its Young Spirit line and no longer accepts children's book submissions.
Website: www.hrpub.com

Freelance Potential

Published 24 titles (4 juvenile) in 2003. Receives 1,000+ queries yearly.

- **Fiction:** Publishes young adult books, 12–18 years; and adult titles. Genres include inspirational, visionary, and metaphysical fiction.
- **Nonfiction:** Publishes young adult books, 12–18 years; and adult titles. Topics include spirituality, metaphysics, and alternative medicine.
- **Representative Titles:** *The Coyote Bead* by Gerald Hausman (8–13 years) is based on the history of the Navajo and focuses on the coyote beads, symbolic of opposing energies. *Dream House* by Fu-Ding Cheng is about a growing boy who learns that a home is made of the people in one's life. *The Healer of Harrow Point* by Peter Walpole tells how a young boy chose to begin an apprenticeship as a healer.

Submissions and Payment

Guidelines and catalogue available with SASE. Query with synopsis, chapter-by-chapter outline, and 1–2 sample chapters. Accepts photocopies, computer printouts, and simultaneous submissions if identified. SASE. Responds in 6 months. Publication in 18 months. Royalty, 10%–20%; advance, $1,000.

Editor's Comments

Since we have discontinued our Young Spirit line, we are not accepting queries for children's books. However, we continue to seek additions to our list of young adult and adult titles.

Harcourt Children's Books

Harcourt Trade Publishers
15 East 26th Street
New York, NY 10010

Submissions Editor

Publisher's Interests
Harcourt, one of the leading publishers of children's books, accepts submissions from agented authors only. It offers top-quality books for children of all ages, from concept books to young adult novels.
Website: www.harcourtbooks.com

Freelance Potential
Published 185 titles in 2003, all were by agented authors. Receives 2,000 unsolicited mss yearly.
- **Fiction:** Published 2 concept books, 10 toddler books, and 98 early picture books, 0–4 years; 10 easy-to-read books, 4–7 years; 10 story picture books, 4–10 years; 5 chapter books, 5–10 years; 20 middle-grade novels, 8–12 years; and 30 young adult novels, 12–18 years. Genres include mystery, fantasy, suspense, and contemporary, historical, and multicultural fiction. Also publishes poetry and stories about sports, nature, and the environment.
- **Representative Titles:** *How I Became a Pirate* by Melinda Long (3–7 years) is the story of a young boy who joins a pirate crew and looks forward to a life of adventure—but finds he misses bedtime stories and being tucked in at night. *Shining* by Julius Lester (6–9 years) tells the tale of a girl who runs, plays, and smiles like other children, but does not speak until the right moment, when she wins the hearts of her people.

Submissions and Payment
Accepts submissions from agented authors only. No simultaneous submissions. Responds to agented submissions in 1 month. Publication in 2 years. Royalty; advance.

Editor's Comments
We are interested in high-quality fiction for children of all ages. We accept work submitted through literary agents only. Have your agent send us your work if you think it will meet our high standards. Since we receive thousands of submissions every year, do not be discouraged if your work is not accepted.

Harcourt Religion Publishers

6277 Sea Harbor Drive
Orlando, FL 32887

Managing Editor: Sabrina Kersanac

Publisher's Interests

This Catholic publisher features books used in classroom catechism programs and Vacation Bible Schools. It has recently added several new lines to its list: Growing in Love for kindergarten through eighth grade, Living Our Faith, and Journey Through the Old Testament. All focus on some aspect of the ministry of the Catechism.

Website: www.harcourtreligion.com

Freelance Potential

Published 30 titles in 2003: 2 were by unpublished writers and 4 were by authors who were new to the publishing house. Receives 30–35 queries yearly.

- **Nonfiction:** Publishes easy-to-read books, 4–7 years; chapter books, 5–10 years; middle-grade books, 8–12 years; and young adult books, 12–18 years. Topics include faith, catechism, education, Christian lifestyles, contemporary issues, prayer, worship, and family life.
- **Representative Titles:** *On The Day You Were Born* by Debra Frasier (all ages) celebrates the natural miracles of earth. *The Clown of God* by Tomi DePaola (4–8 years) is an original retelling of an old French legend of the juggler who offers the Christ Child the only Christmas gift he has.

Submissions and Payment

Query with outline, résumé, and 3 sample chapters. Accepts photocopies, computer printouts, and simultaneous submissions if identified. SASE. Responds in 2–6 weeks. Publication in 1 year. Royalty. Flat fee.

Editor's Comments

Creative materials that celebrate the Catholic faith and enhance catechetical programs are the foundation of all our books. Please review our new lines, as they provide the best opportunities. We welcome queries for books for children, as well as ideas for books suitable for all ages. If you are new to us, we suggest you visit our website for information on our lines and reviews of some of our titles.

HarperCollins Children's Books

1350 Avenue of the Americas
New York, NY 10019

Executive Editor: Ruth Katcher

Publisher's Interests
Quality fiction and nonfiction titles for toddlers through
young adults appear in the catalogue of this well-known publisher. It currently accepts submissions through agents only.
Website: www.harperchildrens.com

Freelance Potential
Published 525 titles in 2003: 50 were developed from unsolicited submissions, 450 were by agented authors, and 100
were reprint/licensed properties. Of the 500 titles, 25 were by
authors who were new to the publishing house. Receives
15,000 unsolicited mss yearly.
- **Fiction:** Publishes concept books, toddler books, and early picture books, 0–4 years; easy-to-read books, 4–7 years; story picture books, 4–10 years; chapter books, 5–10 years; middle-
grade novels, 8–12 years; and young adult books, 12–18 years.
Genres include historical, multicultural, and contemporary fiction; mystery; fairy tales; adventure; suspense; science fiction;
and humor. Also publishes sports stories.
- **Nonfiction:** Publishes easy-to-read books, 4–7 years; story picture books, 4–10 years; chapter books, 5–10 years; and middle-grade books, 8–12 years. Topics include animals, mathematics, science, history, humor, and entertainment.
- **Representative Titles:** *How They Got Over* by Eloise Greenfield
(grades 3–6) discusses how the connection of African Americans to the sea has influenced them for generations. *Don't
Know Much About the Pioneers* by Kenneth C. Davis (grades
1–4) describes the everyday life of the pioneers who traveled
the Oregon Trail.

Submissions and Payment
Accepts submissions from agented authors only. Responds in
1 month. Publication in 1–2 years. Royalty; advance.

Editor's Comments
Because of the high volume of materials we receive, we can
only consider submissions that come to us through literary
agents. Unless you have an agent, please do not send queries,
proposals, or manuscripts.

HarperCollins Children's Fiction

77-85 Fulham Palace Road
London W6 8JB
England

Submissions Editor

Publisher's Interests
This division of HarperCollins Publishers produces hardcover
and paperback fiction for beginning readers through teens.
Its catalogue showcases a full gamut of fiction genres and a
number of books in series.
Website: www.fireandwater.com

Freelance Potential
Published 100 titles in 2003: 70 were by agented authors. Of
the 100 titles, 4 were by unpublished writers and 12 were by
authors who were new to the publishing house. Receives
1,080 queries, 700 unsolicited mss yearly.
- **Fiction:** Published 10 easy-to-read books, 4–7 years; 40 chapter books, 5–10 years; 30 middle-grade titles, 8–12 years; and
  15 young adult books, 12–18 years. Genres include adventure,
  drama, fantasy, folklore, folktales, horror, humor, mystery,
  suspense; Westerns; stories about sports; and contemporary,
  historical, multicultural, and science fiction.
- **Representative Titles:** *The Wreckers* by Iain Lawrence (10–14
  years) is an adventure story set in 1799 about a boy who finds
  himself shipwrecked on an island full of pirates; part of the
  High Seas Adventures series. *Albie and the Space Rocket* by
  Andy Cutbill features an imaginative six-year-old boy who
  finds moose tangoing in the toilet and zebras asleep in the
  kitchen cupboard.

Submissions and Payment
Catalogue available at website. Query with résumé and clips.
SAE/IRC. Responds in 1 month. Publication in 18 months.
Royalty, varies; advance, varies.

Editor's Comments
Our list features a full spectrum of high-quality fiction for children. Although we will consider books for beginning readers
and young adults, this year we are particularly interested in
reviewing fiction that will appeal to readers between the ages of
nine and twelve. Books of various genres and themes will be
considered for this age group.

Hayes School Publishing Company

321 Pennwood Avenue
Pittsburgh, PA 15221

President: Mr. Clair N. Hayes III

Publisher's Interests
With titles for preschool, elementary, and junior and senior
high school students, this educational publisher features
reproducible books, teacher resources, and classroom workbooks on the subjects of mathematics, social studies, geography, language arts, reading, handwriting, science, and
foreign languages.
Website: www.hayespub.com

Freelance Potential
Published 50–60 titles in 2003: 2–3 were developed from
unsolicited submissions. Of the 60 titles, 2–3 were by
authors who were new to the publishing house. Receives
200–300 queries each year.
- **Nonfiction:** Publishes educational resource materials, grades
  K–12. Topics include reading, vocabulary, language arts, math,
  music, mythology, art, social studies, and creative thinking.
- **Representative Titles:** *Fables, Legends, and Folktales* (grade 6
  and up) introduces students to the major themes, characters,
  and authors of well-known fables, legends, and folktales. *Problem Solving in Mathematics* (grades 1–8) is a series of workbooks with editions for each grade that includes instruction in
  and practice with problem-solving strategies.

Submissions and Payment
Guidelines available. Query with résumé, outline, table of
contents, and sample pages. Accepts photocopies, computer
printouts, and simultaneous submissions if identified. SASE.
Responds in 2–3 weeks. Publication period varies. Flat fee.

Editor's Comments
Our teaching materials have been part of classrooms for
more than 50 years now, and we strive to continue to present
teachers with tools that will help them bring the joy of learning to their students. Each year, we continue to look for fresh
ideas and updated materials to add to our line. Submissions
in all subject areas are welcome from writers who have studied our catalogue and are familiar with our titles.

Hazelden Foundation

P.O. Box 176
Center City, MN 55012-0176

Manuscript Coordinator

Publisher's Interests
This special interest publisher offers titles that deal with
such subjects as substance abuse, recovery, and prevention.
The titles are most often used by educators, counselors,
and doctors to use in treatment as well as parents of kids
in trouble.
Website: www.hazeldenbookplace.org

Freelance Potential
Published 100 titles in 2003: 60 were developed from unsolicited submissions and 5 were by agented authors. Receives
300 queries yearly.
- **Nonfiction:** Publishes middle-grade books, 8–12 years; and
  young adult books, 12–18 years. Topics include alcohol and
  substance abuse, health, fitness, and social issues.
- **Representative Titles:** *A Parent's Guide To Sex, Drugs, and
  Flunking Out* by Joel Epstein (parents) offers advice on issues
  faced by parents of students who are college-bound. *Alateen: A
  Day At a Time* (YA) offers daily meditations for teens whose
  lives are affected by someone else's substance abuse.

Submissions and Payment
Guidelines available. For catalogue, call 1-800-328-0098.
Query with outline/synopsis, 3 sample chapters; and clips or
writing samples. Accepts photocopies. SASE. Responds in 12
weeks. Publication in 12–18 months. Royalty. Flat fee.

Editor's Comments
We are always interested in hearing from experienced writers
who can deliver queries that clearly demonstrate their in-depth
research on a chosen topic. You will see when you review our
catalogue that we are interested in submissions for children in
kindergarten through high school. The topics of drug, alcohol,
and sex abuse and prevention are featured prominently on our
list, but we will also consider books for children that deal with
family and social issues. Remember to include a description of
your book's intended audience and competition as well as your
ideas on how to best market your book.

Heinemann

361 Hanover Street
Portsmouth, NH 03801-3912

Editorial Assistant: Eric Chalek

Publisher's Interests
Heinemann publishes professional resource material for educators working at the elementary, secondary, and college levels. Mathematics, science, social studies, and art education are among the subject areas covered.
Website: www.heinemann.com

Freelance Potential
Published 100 titles in 2003: 70 were developed from unsolicited submissions. Receives 1,000+ queries yearly.
- **Nonfiction:** Publishes educational resource and multi-media materials for teachers and school administrators. Topics include math, science, social studies, art education, reading, writing, ESL, bilingual education, gifted and special education, early childhood, school reform, curriculum development, and the creative arts. Also publishes professional development and assessment materials.
- **Representative Titles:** *The Literature Workshop* by Sheridan Blau (teachers, grades 9–12) provides concrete ideas for workshops that get students excited about reading. *Teaching Struggling Readers* by Carol A. Lyons (teachers, grades K–8) explains how to use brain-based research to maximize the learning potential of children with learning disabilities, language delays, ADD, or other disorders.

Submissions and Payment
Guidelines available. Query with résumé, proposal, outline, table of contents, and chapter summaries. Accepts photocopies, computer printouts, and email submissions to proposals@heinemann.com. SASE. Responds in 6–8 weeks. Publication in 10–12 months. Payment policy varies.

Editor's Comments
We're looking for materials that will help teachers encourage their students to become literate and enthusiastic learners and informed citizens. Most of our authors are outstanding educators who want to give other teachers the benefit of their experience and expertise. Visit our website for additional guidelines.

Hendrick-Long Publishing Company

Suite D
10635 Tower Oaks
Houston, TX 77070

Vice President: Vilma Long

Publisher's Interests

This regional publisher features books about the history and culture of Texas and the Southwest. Its books are used in libraries and classrooms as well as in the home. It would like to expand its list of books for children and young adults.
Website: www.hendricklongpublishing.com

Freelance Potential

Published 4 titles in 2003: 2 were developed from unsolicited submissions and 1 was by an agented author. Of the 4 titles, 1 was by an unpublished writer and 1 was by an author who was new to the publishing house. Receives 200+ queries each year.

- **Fiction:** Publishes story picture books, 4–10 years; middle-grade books, 8–12 years; and young adult books, 12–18 years. Genres include historical and regional fiction.
- **Nonfiction:** Published 2 middle-grade books, 8–12 years; and 2 young adult books, 12–18 years. Topics include geography, animals, nature, and history. Also publishes biographies.
- **Representative Titles:** *Pioneer Children* by Betsy Warren (6+ years) features six stories about children living in Texas during the 1800s. *Life in a Rock Shelter* by G. Elaine Acker (grades 7 and up) explores the lives and culture of the prehistoric Indians of the Lower Pecos.

Submissions and Payment

Guidelines available. Query with outline/synopsis, résumé, table of contents, and 1–2 sample chapters. Accepts photocopies, computer printouts, and simultaneous submissions if identified. SASE. Responds in 1–2 months. Publication in 18 months. Royalty; advance.

Editor's Comments

At this time, we are especially interested in expanding our list of books for children and young adults. If you have a strong background in the culture of Texas and the Southwest and like to write for children, we invite you to review our catalogue and some of our books, and then to send a query.

Heritage House

#6-356 Simcoe Street
Victoria, British Columbia V8V 1L1
Canada

Publisher: Rodger Touchie

Publisher's Interests
Heritage House is a Canadian publisher that specializes in nonfiction books and activity books on Canadian history and nature for middle-grade children in western Canada.
Website: www.heritagehouse.ca

Freelance Potential
Published 24 titles in 2003: 18 were developed from unsolicited submissions and 2 were reprint/licensed properties. Of the 24 titles, 4 were by unpublished writers and 6 were by authors who were new to the publishing house. Receives 100 queries yearly.
- **Nonfiction:** Publishes middle-grade books, 8–12 years. Topics include the environment, history, nature, and wildlife of western Canada; and the Royal Canadian Mounted Police. Also publishes activity books.
- **Representative Titles:** *Blisters and Bliss* by David Foster & Wayne Aitken (8–12 years) is the definitive guide to the 75-kilometer West Coast Trail between Bamfield and Port Renfrew on Vancouver Island. *Fortress of the Grizzlies* by Dan Wakeman & Wendy Shymanski (8–12 years) takes a look inside one of Canada's grizzly strongholds to examine this powerful creature.

Submissions and Payment
Guidelines and catalogue available with 9x12 SAE/IRC. Query with sample illustrations. Accepts photocopies, computer printouts, and disk submissions (Microsoft Word or PageMaker). Availability of artwork improves chance of acceptance. SAE/IRC. Responds in 1 month. Publication in 8–10 months. Royalty.

Editor's Comments
We're looking for books with Canadian themes only, and we're especially interested in original material that focuses on western Canadian native myths, totem poles, animals, and nature. Most of our writers are Canadian, or at least reside in Canada, but we will consider qualified, well-researched material from any writer, as long as it has a Canadian theme and focus.

Heuer Publishing Company

P.O. Box 248
Cedar Rapids, IA 52406

Editor: C. E. McMullen

Publisher's Interests
With the mission of "encouraging creativity through drama,"
Heuer Publishing offers plays and dramatic resource materials for school and community theaters. Full-length and one-
act plays, musicals, melodramas, monologues, and theater-
related texts are found in its catalogue.
Website: www.hitplays.com

Freelance Potential
Published 15 titles in 2003: 14 were developed from unsolicited submissions and 1 was a reprint/licensed property. Of
the 15 titles, 13 were by unpublished writers and 8 were by
authors new to the publishing house. Receives 300 queries,
90+ unsolicited mss yearly.
- **Fiction:** Publishes middle-grade plays, 8–12 years; and young
  adult plays, 12–18 years. Genres include comedy, musicals,
  drama, mystery, suspense, and satire. Also publishes books on
  theater arts, stage production, auditions, sound effects, and
  theater resources.
- **Representative Titles:** *For Whom the Tinkerbell Tolls* by Ray
  Sheers is a play for middle and high school students about the
  ghost of a *Titanic* passenger who haunts a theater and learns
  about the social changes that have happened since 1912. *The
  Bridge Watcher* by Mike Willis is an award-winning one-act
  drama about teen suicide.

Submissions and Payment
Guidelines available. Query or send complete ms with synopsis, cast list, running time, and set requirements. Accepts
photocopies and computer printouts. SASE. Responds in 2
months. Publication period varies. Royalty. Flat fee.

Editor's Comments
We have found that drama directors at school and community theaters want plays that use easy-to-find props and
costumes and simple stage effects. We're still actively seeking plays, musicals, and specialty books for school and
church theater groups.

Holiday House

425 Madison Avenue
New York, NY 10017

Editor: Suzanne Reinoehl

Publisher's Interests
This small publisher specializes in quality hardcovers from picture books to young adult, both fiction and nonfiction, primarily for the school and library market.
Website: www.holidayhouse.com

Freelance Potential
Published 62 titles in 2003: 5 were developed from unsolicited submissions and 57 were by agented authors. Of the 62 titles, 5 were by unpublished writers and 16 were by authors who were new to the publishing house. Receives 8,000 queries yearly.

- **Fiction:** Publishes easy-to-read books, 4–7 years; story picture books, 4–10 years; chapter books, 5–10 years; middle-grade books, 8–12 years; and young adult books, 12–18 years. Genres include mystery, fantasy, humor, and historical and multicultural fiction.
- **Nonfiction:** Publishes easy-to-read books, 4–7 years; story picture books, 4–10 years; chapter books, 5–10 years; middle-grade books, 8–12 years; and young adult books, 12–18 years. Topics include history, social issues, and science. Also publishes biographies.
- **Representative Titles:** *Crandalls' Castle* by Betty Ren Wright follows a 12-year-old girl as she tries to discover why ghosts are haunting the old mansion her uncle hopes to transfrom into an inn. *Bunny Business* by Nancy Poydar (4–8 years) features Harry, a little boy whose poor listening skills threaten the success of the school play.

Submissions and Payment
Guidelines available. Query. Accepts photocopies and computer printouts. SASE. Responds in 2 months. Publication period varies. Royalty; advance.

Editor's Comments
We publish for kindergarten and up, but are now especially interested in acquiring literary middle-grade novels. We do not publish board books, pop-ups, activity books, sticker books, coloring books, series books, or paperback originals.

Henry Holt and Company

115 West 18th Street
New York, NY 10011

Submissions: Books for Young Readers

Publisher's Interests

The Books for Young Readers department of Henry Holt and
Company publishes fiction and nonfiction for toddlers through
young adults.
Website: www.henryholt.com

Freelance Potential

Published 63 titles in 2003: 18 were by agented authors.
Receives 7,000 unsolicited mss yearly.

- **Fiction:** Publishes concept books, toddler books, and early picture books, 0–4 years; story picture books, 4–10 years; chapter
  books, 5–10 years; middle-grade novels, 8–12 years; and young
  adult books, 12–18 years. Genres include adventure, mystery,
  suspense, fantasy, folklore, fairy tales, and contemporary and
  historical fiction. Also publishes poetry.
- **Nonfiction:** Publishes story picture books, 4–10 years; middle-
  grade books, 8–12 years; and young adult books, 12–18 years.
  Topics include multicultural subjects, animals, nature, history,
  mathematics, science, and technology.
- **Representative Titles:** *One Child, One Seed* by Kathryn Cave
  (pre-K–grade 2) is a counting book that focuses on the culture
  of South Africa. *One Shot* by Susan Glick (YA) features a young
  photographer who realizes that great artists need more than
  just technical skills.

Submissions and Payment

Guidelines available with 9x12 SASE ($.55 postage). Send
complete ms. Accepts photocopies. No simultaneous submissions. SASE. Responds in 3–4 months. Publication in 18
months. Royalty, 8–10%; advance, $4,000–$6,000.

Editor's Comments

We are open to receiving the works of new writers for any age
group and in any genre. Although we would like to comment
specifically on each manuscript we do not accept, the large
number of submissions we receive makes this impossible. We
no longer read simultaneous submissions for the same reason.
Please do not submit textbook manuscripts.

Honor Books

Cook Communications Ministries
4050 Lee Vance View
Colorado Springs, CO 80918

Product/Brand Manager

Publisher's Interests

Honor Books publishes devotionals, Bible stories, children's
Bibles, story picture books, board books, and activity books
for readers up to the age of 12. The mission of this Christian
publisher is to inspire, encourage, and motivate readers to
get closer to God and make Him a part of their daily lives.
Website: www.honorbooks.com

Freelance Potential

Published 15 titles in 2003: 1 was developed from an unsolicited submission and 3 were by agented authors. Of the 15
titles, 5 were by unpublished writers and all were by authors
who were new to the publishing house. Receives 120 unsolicited mss yearly.

- **Nonfiction:** Publishes concept books, toddler books, and early
  picture books, 0–4 years; easy-to-read books, 4-7 years; story
  picture books, 4–10 years; and middle-grade books, 8–12
  years. Also offers activity, novelty, and board books, and titles
  in series. Features books about Christianity.
- **Representative Titles:** *The Ultimate Birthday Party Book* by
  Susan Baltrus (parents) gives great ideas for unforgettable
  birthday parties, complete with a variety of theme ideas. *Quiet
  Moments with God* (YA) offers devotional entries that help lead
  teens to a richer spiritual and personal life.

Submissions and Payment

Guidelines available. Send complete ms with interior sample
spreads. Accepts simultaneous submissions if identified.
Availability of artwork improves chance of acceptance. SASE.
Responds in 3 months. Publication in 1–2 years. Royalty;
advance. Flat fee.

Editor's Comments

We're looking for nonfictional devotionals, Bible stories, and
board books that have strong religious themes. Do not send us
proposals for young adult books. We publish for children up to
the age of 12 only. New authors are encouraged to send us
their work for consideration, but having an agent does help.

Horizon Publishers

P.O. Box 490
50 South 500 West
Bountiful, UT 84001-0490

Submissions Editor: Doug Cox

Publisher's Interests
Established in 1971, Horizon Publishers offers a list that includes titles for the general public as well as books for the Mormon market. Books on family life, children, and marriage are featured in its current catalogue.
Website: www.horizonpublishersbooks.com

Freelance Potential
Published 11 titles in 2003: 8 were developed from unsolicited submissions. Receives 100 queries, 200 unsolicited mss yearly.
- **Nonfiction:** Publishes activity and religious teaching books on the Mormon faith for children. Also publishes books about parenting, family life, social issues, crafts, outdoor life, and books of interest to Scouts.
- **Representative Titles:** *Book of Mormon Activity Book* by Sandy Halverson features more than 20 challenging projects that involve children in the Scriptures. *Book of Mormon Stories for Little Children* by Marjorie Johnson features stories from the Book of Mormon, interpreted for young children.

Submissions and Payment
Guidelines available. Query or send complete ms. Accepts photocopies and computer printouts. SASE. Responds to queries in 1–3 months, to mss in 4–5 months. Royalty, 8%; advance, $100–$500. Flat fee.

Editor's Comments
In the coming year we are interested in seeing books of interest to Scouts, books of crafts, family life titles, family promoting short stories, ideas for teaching LDS children and youth, and LDS books for children and youth. Please do not send submissions for secular titles for children or young adults. Because we receive so many submissions yearly, we have to be selective in the books we publish. We look for authors whose writing style demonstrates their knowledge of the given topic; books that have a unique approach; books that are marketable; and books that have potential for profit. We are willing to consider both queries and unsolicited submissions.

Houghton Mifflin Children's Books

222 Berkeley Street
Boston, MA 02116

Submissions Coordinator: Hannah Rodgers

Publisher's Interests

This children's publisher is a leader in the industry and publisher of such well-known award-winning children's authors as Lois Lowry and James Marshall. It receives thousands of submissions each year.
Website: www.houghtonmifflinbooks.com

Freelance Potential

Published 91 titles in 2003: 5 were developed from unsolicited submissions, 25 were by agented authors, and 2 were reprint/licensed properties. Receives 13,000–15,000 unsolicited mss yearly.

- **Fiction:** Publishes concept books, toddler books, and early picture books, 0–4 years; easy-to-read books, 4–7 years; chapter books, 5–10 years; middle-grade novels, 8–12 years; and young adult books, 12–18 years. Genres include historical and multicultural fiction, adventure, and humor.
- **Nonfiction:** Publishes early picture books, 0–4 years; middle-grade books, 8–12 years; and young adult books, 12–18 years. Topics include history and science. Also publishes biographies.
- **Representative Titles:** *Wings: A Tale of Two Chickens* by James Marshall (4–8 years) is the story of two chickens who, though they are close friends, are as opposite as any two can be, and together experience numerous hilarious adventures. *Not as Crazy as I Seem* by George Harrar (11+ years) explores the life of Devon Brown, a teen obsessed with neatness.

Submissions and Payment

Guidelines available with SASE, at website, or by calling 617-351-5959. Send complete ms for fiction. Query with synopsis and sample chapters for nonfiction. Accepts photocopies and computer printouts. SASE. Responds in 3 months. Publication period varies. Royalty; advance.

Editor's Comments

Illustrated books that feature children and animals are always welcome. It is a good idea to review some of our titles before sending a submission. Send only your best work.

Humanics

Suite 200
12 South Dixie Highway
Lake Worth, FL 33460

Acquisitions Editor

Publisher's Interests
Established in 1976, Humanics has always specialized in
materials for children up to age six and their teachers. Most
of the titles found on its list are written by authors who are
authorities in their fields. Resource guides for teachers and
activity books for children make up the bulk of this publisher's list.
Website: www.humanicslearning.com

Freelance Potential
Published 20 titles (10 juvenile) in 2003: 10–15 were developed from unsolicited submissions. Of the 20 titles, 3 were
by unpublished writers and 6 were by authors who were new
to the publishing house. Receives 500 queries yearly.
- **Nonfiction:** Publishes concept and toddler books, 0–4 years.
  Topics include crafts and hobbies. Also publishes titles for parents and educators.
- **Representative Titles:** *Fibber E. Frog* features a story about a
  frog who tells tall tales to make him feel more important and
  learns that to be happy with himself is the most important gift
  he can give himself. *Young Children's Behavior: Developing
  Goals for Young Children* offers a practical approach to teaching
  that encourages students, teachers, and parents to "learn by
  doing" and provides opportunities for setting and achieving
  goals for children's behavior.

Submissions and Payment
Guidelines and catalogue available with 9x12 SASE ($.55
postage). Query with résumé, synopsis, and marketing plan.
A one-time submission fee of $50 is required with all submis-
sions. Accepts photocopies, computer printouts, and disk
submissions (Microsoft Word or WordPerfect). SASE.
Responds in 3 months. Publication in 6 months. Royalty, 8%.

Editor's Comments
Our goal is to better serve the needs of children. We look for
unique, research-based approaches related to this goal from
qualified writers with experience in the education field.

Hunter House Publishers

P.O. Box 2914
Alameda, CA 94501-0914

Acquisitions Editor: Jeanne Brondino

Publisher's Interests

Hunter House publishes books on health, family, and community for therapists, educators, and other professionals who work with children. Topics range from violence and abuse, to cancer and chronic illness.
Website: www.hunterhouse.com

Freelance Potential

Published 18 titles in 2003: 6 were developed from unsolicited submissions, 1 was by an agented author, and 5 were reprint/licensed properties. Of the 18 titles, 2 were by unpublished writers and 5 were by authors new to the publishing house. Receives 1,000 queries yearly.

- **Nonfiction:** Publishes middle-grade books, 8–12 years. Topics include relationships, sexuality, health, fitness, violence prevention, and trauma. Also publishes activity books for children and self-help and psychology books for adults.
- **Representative Titles:** *The Art of Getting Well* by David Spero uses a five-step plan that incorporates medical, psychological, and spiritual aspects for maximizing health in people who have chronic illnesses. *Ditch That Jerk* by Pamela Jayne explains how women can deal with men who try to control and hurt them, exposing the tricks and excuses often used by abusers to keep their victims in line.

Submissions and Payment

Guidelines available. Query with résumé, overview, chapter-by-chapter outline, competitive analysis, and marketing ideas. Accepts photocopies, computer printouts, and simultaneous submissions. SASE. Responds in 3–4 months. Publication in 1–3 years. Royalty.

Editor's Comments

We are always interested in manuscripts from authors whose work would provide our readers with the information necessary to affect personal improvement. It is crucial that authors have credentials and experience in the areas they address. Please do not send fiction or books for children.

John Hunt Publishing

46A West Street
New Alresford, Hants SO24 9AU
United Kingdom

Editor: John Hunt

Publisher's Interests
John Hunt Publishing specializes in religious education materials for Christian classes. In addition to Bible stories for children, it offers nonfiction books on prayer, faith, and family issues for Christians of all ages.
Website: www.johnhunt-publishing.com

Freelance Potential
Published 60 titles (32 juvenile) in 2003: 3 were developed from unsolicited submissions, 20 were by agented authors, and 4 were reprint/licensed properties. Of the 60 titles, 5 were by unpublished writers and 15 were by authors who were new to the publishing house. Receives 600 queries each year.
- **Nonfiction:** Publishes toddler books and early picture books, 0–4 years; chapter books, 5–10 years; middle-grade books, 8–12 years; and young adult books, 12–18 years. Topics include religion, prayer, faith, family issues, and social issues. Also publishes Bible stories and educational titles.
- **Representative Titles:** *Let's Chat About the Bible* by Karen Whiting (families) includes 60 Bible stories and provides a framework for discussing and sharing. *Oaktree Wood* by Alan & Linda Parry is a board book that helps young children discover the delights of the changing seasons through the adventures of a group of animals.

Submissions and Payment
Query with clips. Accepts photocopies. SASE. Responds in 1 week. Publication in 18 months. Royalty. Flat fee.

Editor's Comments
For younger readers, we are looking for board books and novelty titles that talk about Christian holidays, particularly Christmas and Easter. For our older audience, we are interested in titles that provide information about the traditions, culture, beliefs, and history of other faiths. Send queries that show how we can benefit by learning about others. Our market includes Christians of all denominations and viewpoints.

Impact Publishers

P.O. Box 6016
Atascadero, CA 93423

Acquisitions Editor: Freeman Porter

Publisher's Interests
Self-help and psychology books written by human service professionals are the specialty of Impact Publishers. Its books cover topics such as mental health, social issues, and personal growth. Titles for children appear under its Little Imp Books imprint.
Website: www.impactpublishers.com

Freelance Potential
Published 5 titles in 2003. Of the 5 titles, 2 were by authors who were new to the publishing house. Receives 750–1,000 queries yearly.
- **Nonfiction:** Published 2 middle-grade books, 8–12 years; and 1 young adult book, 12–18 years. Also publishes books for adults. Topics include social issues, marriage, parenting, popular psychology, self-esteem, mental health, creativity, relationships, social and emotional growth, and multicultural and ethnic issues.
- **Representative Titles:** *I Wish I Could Hold Your Hand* by Pat Palmer is written to help children deal with grief and loss by showing them how to seek the comfort they need in healthy ways. *The Shelbys Need Help!* by Ken West (parents) is a "choose-your-own-solutions" guidebook that helps parents deal with family battles over bedtimes, baths, eating, homework, and getting dressed.

Submissions and Payment
Guidelines available. Query with résumé and sample chapters. Accepts photocopies, computer printouts, and simultaneous submissions if identified. SASE. Responds in 1–3 months. Publication in 1 year. Royalty; advance.

Editor's Comments
We look for innovative, research-based materials that offer real help for people who need real answers. Our materials are practical and reader-friendly. Virtually all of our titles are written by highly respected psychologists and other human service professionals.

Imperial International

30 Montauk Boulevard
Oakdale, NY 11769

Editor-in-Chief: Laura Solimene

Publisher's Interests
Kindergarten through twelfth-grade classrooms are the target
audience of Imperial International. This division of EDCON
Publishing produces educational resource books, audiocassettes, videos, and CD-ROMs in a wide range of curriculum
areas. Many of its titles are used in remedial programs.
Website: www.edconpublishing.com

Freelance Potential
Published 12 titles in 2003. Of the 12 titles, 6 were by
unpublished writers and 3 were by authors who were new to
the publishing house. Receives 100 unsolicited mss yearly.
- **Fiction:** Publishes easy-to-read books, 4–7 years; chapter
  books, 5–10 years; and middle-grade titles, 8–12 years. Genres
  include multicultural and ethnic fiction, fairy tales, adventure,
  and science fiction. Also publishes hi/lo fiction, 6–18 years;
  and activity books, 6–12 years.
- **Nonfiction:** Publishes chapter books, 5–10 years; and young
  adult books, 12–18 years. Topics include mathematics, science, and technology. Also special education titles.
- **Representative Titles:** *Vowel Tricksters* (grades 2–4) strengthens recognition and usage of vowel diagraphs, r-controlled
  vowels, and y as a vowel. *Sports Math* (12+ years) teaches
  remedial students the four basic math operations and includes
  cassettes, blackline masters, and a teacher's guide.

Submissions and Payment
Guidelines available with 9x12 SASE ($1.35 postage).
Send complete ms. Accepts photocopies and simultaneous
submissions if identified. Submissions are not returned.
Responds in 1–2 weeks. Publication in 6 months. Flat fee,
$300– $1,000.

Editor's Comments
Many of our products are designed for remedial use, and we
offer a variety of high-interest/low-readability books for
students of all ages. We are still interested in reviewing math
concept materials.

Incentive Publications

3835 Cleghorn Avenue
Nashville, TN 37215

Editor: Charlotte Bosarge

Publisher's Interests

Incorporated in 1969 to develop, publish, and disseminate
supplemental education materials, Incentive Publications has
focused on providing creative materials to meet students'
educational needs in a developmentally appropriate manner.
Its catalogue targets children in preschool through middle
school, as well as students enrolled in English-as-a-Second-
Language classes.

Website: www.incentivepublications.com

Freelance Potential

Published 45 titles in 2003: 13 were developed from unsolicited submissions. Of the 45 titles, 12 were by new authors.
Receives 350 queries yearly.

- **Nonfiction:** Publishes early picture books, 0–4 years; chapter
  books, 5–10 years; middle-grade titles, 8–12 years; and young
  adult books, 12–18 years.
- **Representative Titles:** *Science Fair Projects and Research
  Activities* by Leland Graham & Isabelle McCoy offers kids all
  the help they need for creating unique and well-researched science fair projects. *What To Do with the Gifted Child* by Judith
  Cochran (grades 3–8) features an approach that ensures accel-
  erated progress, development of critical thinking skills, and
  student accountability for developing skills.

Submissions and Payment

Guidelines available. Query with table of contents, outline/
synopsis, and 1–3 sample chapters. Accepts photocopies and
simultaneous submissions if identified. SASE. Responds in
4–6 weeks. Publication period varies. Royalty. Flat fee.

Editor's Comments

We continue to look for writers who can bring us queries that
feature cutting-edge research findings that can be used in
classroom settings. Resources to meet national standards,
books for early readers, and titles for middle-grade students
are all of interest. Don't send fiction queries, please! Most of
our writers have extensive teaching experience.

Innovative Kids

18 Ann Street
Norwalk, CT 06854

Editorial Assistant: Rebecca Lehrfeld

Publisher's Interests

This publisher's mission is to create books that offer a multi-sensory experience. All of its titles include an educational component and an interactive activity. It features both fiction and nonfiction for children up to the age of 12.
Website: www.innovativekids.com

Freelance Potential

Published 20 titles in 2003: 12 were by unpublished writers and 12 were by authors who were new to the publishing house. Receives 180 queries, 180 unsolicited mss yearly.

- **Fiction:** Publishes educational books, novelty books, and board books, 1–12 years. Genres include adventure, fairy tales, folklore, folktales, religious fiction, humor, and books about nature, the environment, and sports.
- **Nonfiction:** Publishes concept books and toddler books, 0–4 years; easy-to-read books, 4–7 years; story picture books, 4–7 years; and middle-grade books, 8–12 years. Topics include animals, pets, crafts, hobbies, geography, mathematics, nature, and the environment. Also publishes humor.
- **Representative Titles:** *Where Is My Baby?* by Leslie Bockol is a foam book about baby animals that encourages readers to match patterns, textures, and shapes. *Look Around!* by Nora Gaydos (4–7 years) is a set of read-along books with strong picture clues and predictable patterned text.

Submissions and Payment

Guidelines available at website. Query or send complete ms with dummies and submission agreement. Accepts photocopies. SASE. Responds in 4–6 months. Publication period and response time vary. Flat fee.

Editor's Comments

We offer unique, interactive children's books that present valuable knowledge to children. We strive to create books that are fun as well as educational, because we believe kids are more encouraged to learn when they are having fun. Please note that we don't publish novels.

Interlink Publishing Group

46 Crosby Street
Northampton, MA 01060

Associate Publisher: Pamela Thompson

Publisher's Interests

The juvenile imprint of Interlink Publishing Group, Crocodile Books, specializes in picture books for young readers and chapter books for a slightly older audience. This publisher also offers travel guides, history, literature and ethnic cooking titles for adults.
Website: www.interlinkbooks.com

Freelance Potential

Published 58 titles (8 juvenile) in 2003: 6 were developed from unsolicited submissions, 3 were by agented authors, and 48 were reprint/licensed properties. Of the 58 titles, 2 were by authors who were new to the publishing house. Receives 300+ queries yearly.

- **Fiction:** Published 8 chapter books, 5–10 years. Also publishes story picture books, 3–8 years. Genres include international folklore and folktales.
- **Nonfiction:** Publishes story picture books, 3–8 years. Topics include travel and history. Also publishes travel guides, literature, history, politics, and ethnic cooking titles for adults.
- **Representative Titles:** *The Sea King* by Jane Yolen and Shulamith L. Oppenheim (5–9 years) tells the story of a human king who unwittingly promises his newborn son to the sea king. *My Special Friends* by R. David Stephens (2–5 years) reveals what most young children know—that animals are our special friends.

Submissions and Payment

Query with synopsis. Accepts photocopies and computer printouts. Availability of artwork improves chance of acceptance for picture book submissions. SASE. Responds in 1 month. Publication in 18 months. Royalty; advance.

Editor's Comments

Our children's books are designed for ages three to ten, and we will not consider picture book manuscripts that are not illustrated. We like to think we publish books that change the way our readers think about their world.

International Reading Association

P.O. Box 8139
800 Barksdale Road
Newark, DE 19714-8139

Administrative Assistant: Michele Jester

Publisher's Interests

This nonprofit, global network is committed to literacy and provides professionals with resources on topics from early literacy to adolescent comprehension, as well as information on reading difficulties and different learning styles.
Website: www.reading.org

Freelance Potential

Published 30 titles in 2003. Receives 100 queries yearly.
- **Nonfiction:** Publishes educational titles, research reports, and monographs. Topics include literacy programs, reading research and practice, language comprehension at all levels, and professional development.
- **Representative Titles:** *Kids InSight: Reconsidering How to Meet the Literacy Needs of All Students* by Deborah R. Dillon (teachers) discusses understanding the literacy skills middle school and secondary students need to succeed, and how teachers can help them by improving their instruction. *Guided Comprehension in the Primary Grades* by Maureen McLauglin (teachers, grades 3–8) explains a teaching framework that develops reading comprehension through direct and guided strategy instruction, numerous opportunities for engagement, and a variety of leveled texts and instructional settings.

Submissions and Payment

Guidelines available. Request a Publication Proposal Form before sending ms. Accepts photocopies. No simultaneous submissions. SASE. Responds in 2–3 months. Publication period varies. Payment policy varies.

Editor's Comments

We're interested in material from professionals with knowledge or expertise in selected aspects of reading or literacy education. Prospective authors must be able to communicate effectively, and must be be familiar with our books. Authors should request our Publication Proposal Form before submitting manuscripts. We welcome new authors to the prestigious circle of professionals writing for the International Reading Association.

InterVarsity Press

P.O. Box 1400
Downers Grove, IL 60515

Editor: Elaine Whittenhall

Publisher's Interests

This publisher develops books that are used, and most often written, by professional educators. As a division of InterVarsity Christian Fellowship, a university ministry, it publishes books that are biblically based, including theological, academic, and reference books. It also publishes issue-oriented titles for Christian adults.
Website: www.ivpress.com

Freelance Potential

Published 100 titles (1 juvenile) in 2003: 10 were developed from unsolicited submissions, 5 were by agented authors, and 15 were reprint/licensed properties. Of the 100 titles, 6 were by unpublished writers and 12 were by authors who were new to the publishing house. Receives 700 queries yearly.

- **Nonfiction:** Publishes biblically based, religious titles for educators, parents, and college students. Features informational, educational, how-to, and reference books.
- **Representative Titles:** *Surrender to Love* by David G. Benner explores the themes of love and surrender as the heart of Christian spirituality. *The Making of the New Spirituality* by James A. Herrick looks at the shift away from the Judeo-Christian tradition of Western culture to a new way of viewing spirituality.

Submissions and Payment

Guidelines and catalogue available at website. Query with résumé, chapter-by-chapter summary, and 2 sample chapters. SASE. Responds in 6–10 weeks. Publication in 2 years. Payment policy varies.

Editor's Comments

Most of our authors are professionals in the field of education. If you are associated with a college or seminary and would like to submit an academic manuscript, contact our Academic Editor. Pastors or authors who have had their works published in the past should contact our General Books Editor. Our current interests include survey texts and Bible study series. Please don't send books for children.

Jalmar Press/Innerchoice Publishing

Suite 702
2446 South Main Street
Carson, CA 90745

Submissions Editor: Susanna Palomares

Publisher's Interests

This publisher's books are designed to be used by educators, counselors, and caregivers who work with children from kindergarten through twelfth grade. Jalmar Press specializes in activity books that focus on self-esteem, self-awareness, social skills, character education, and emotional intelligence.
Website: www.jalmarpress.com

Freelance Potential

Published 10 titles in 2003: 5 were developed from unsolicited submissions and 1 was a reprint/licensed property. Of the 10 titles, 2 were by authors who were new to the publishing house. Receives 200 queries yearly.

- **Nonfiction:** Publishes activity-driven educational titles, grades K–12. Topics include self-esteem, emotional intelligence, stress management, social skills, character education, prevention of drug and alcohol abuse, conflict resolution, discipline, and communication.
- **Representative Titles:** *Getting Along* by Dianne Schilling (educators, grades 5–9) features activities, role plays, games, simulations, and worksheets to teach cooperation, responsibility, and respect. *I Can Make My World a Safer Place* by Paul Kivel (6–11 years) is written for adults to read with children and helps children to prevent violence by making positive choices about teasing, anger, and drugs.

Submissions and Payment

Guidelines available. Query with résumé and outline. SASE. Response time varies. Publication in 18 months. Royalty; advance.

Editor's Comments

Most of the books we publish are written for teachers, counselors, or caregivers, rather than the children themselves, and most are nonfiction. We are not publishing storybooks or picture books for children at this time. We are, however, interested in books about study skills, character development, and dealing with divorce.

JayJo Books

Guidance Channel Company
135 Dupont Street
P.O. Box 760
Plainview, NY 11803-0760

Editor-in-Chief: Sally Germain

Publisher's Interests

Established in 1992, JayJo Books is a small publishing house that exclusively features fiction and nonfiction books concerned with children's health issues such as learning disabilities, diabetes, dyslexia, and many others. All of its titles appear as part of one of four established series.
Website: www.jayjo.com

Freelance Potential

Published 6 titles in 2003: 2 were by unpublished writers. Receives 120 queries yearly.

- **Fiction:** Publishes story picture books, 4–10 years. Features stories about children's health issues and special needs.
- **Nonfiction:** Publishes story picture books, 7–12 years. Topics include children's health habits, learning disabilities, ADHD, OCD, and Down Syndrome.
- **Representative Titles:** *Taking Arthritis to School* tells the story of a young boy who shows his schoolmates that his arthritis doesn't keep him from the things he loves, such as biking; part of the Special Kids in School series. *Taking Depression to School* follows the experiences of a young girl suffering from childhood depression and shows how her illness helps schoolmates learn to react in helpful ways; part of the Special Kids in School series.

Submissions and Payment

Guidelines available with #10 SASE ($.55 postage). Query. Accepts photocopies. SASE. Responds in 3 months. Publication in 2 years. Flat fee.

Editor's Comments

Our needs are very specific and we only consider material that fits into one of our established series and meets our other criteria. We strongly recommend that you send for our guidelines and then make sure your idea has not already been covered by one of our books. Writers who can create fun and entertaining stories based on their in-depth knowledge of the illness covered have the best chance of getting noticed here.

Jewish Lights

P.O. Box 237
Sunset Farm Offices
Route 4
Woodstock, VT 05091

Submissions Editor

Publisher's Interests

Based in Vermont, this small publishing house specializes in books for all ages that explore faith and spirituality from a perspective that welcomes people of all faiths and all backgrounds. Its focus is on nonfiction and it rarely publishes fiction. It never publishes biographies or poetry.
Website: www.jewishlights.com

Freelance Potential

Published 30 titles (4 juvenile) in 2003: 10 were developed from unsolicited submissions, 1 was by an agented author, and 5 were reprint/licensed properties. Of the 30 titles, 5 were by unpublished writers and 4 were by authors who were new to the publishing house. Receives 600 queries, 300 unsolicited mss yearly.

- **Nonfiction:** Published 1 toddler book, 0–4 years; 1 easy-to-read book, 4–7 years; 1 story picture book, 4–10 years; and 1 young adult book, 12–18 years. Also publishes religious and inspirational titles, self-help books, and books about recovery for adults.
- **Representative Titles:** *Tough Questions Jews Ask* by Rabbi Edward Feinstein (YA) answers questions young people have about their faith, such as whether the Bible stories are true and why religion has so many rules. *Passover* by Dr. Ron Wolfson is a step-by-step guide to celebrating the holiday of Passover with the whole family.

Submissions and Payment

Guidelines available. Prefers query with résumé, table of contents, and 2 sample chapters. Send complete ms for picture books. Accepts photocopies, computer printouts, and simultaneous submissions if identified. SASE. Responds in 4 months. Publication in 1 year. Payment policy varies.

Editor's Comments

Our authors are at the forefront of spiritual thought. They draw on the Jewish wisdom tradition to deal with the quest for self and for finding the meaning of life.

JIST Publishing

8902 Otis Avenue
Indianapolis, IN 46216-1033

Acquisitions Editor

Publisher's Interests
JIST Publishing is a leading publisher of materials on job search, career exploration, occupational information, life skills, and character development. Through its imprints, it strives to help people help themselves in career and life decisions. Its materials are used by children and students in middle school, high school, and college.
Website: www.jist.com; www.jistlife.com; www.kidsrights.com

Freelance Potential
Published 50+ titles in 2003; several were developed from unsolicited submissions. Receives 250 queries yearly.
- **Nonfiction:** Publishes textbooks, reference books, workbooks, assessment devices, pamphlets, videos, and software products. Topics include job search, career exploration, occupational information, life skills, character education, domestic and family violence, and child abuse.
- **Representative Titles:** *Young Person's Guide to Getting & Keeping a Good Job* by Michael Farr et al. (grades 9–12) is a comprehensive and results-oriented job search course. *Character Education Series* (8–12 years) is a series of pamphlets that teach lessons about everyday life issues such as self-esteem, peer pressure, anger, violence, and conflict resolution.

Submissions and Payment
Guidelines available at www.jist.com. Query with résumé, outline/synopsis, and audience/market analysis. Accepts photocopies and computer printouts. SASE. Responds in 3–4 months. Publication in 1–2 years. Royalty, 8–10%.

Editor's Comments
Our primary focus is on job search, career exploration, and occupational information materials for all ages, and we are always looking for good manuscripts on these topics. We are actively looking for new material for our JIST Life and KIDSRIGHTS imprints for victims of domestic and family violence, abused and neglected children, their families, and the staff who serve them.

Journey Forth

1700 Wade Hampton Boulevard
Greenville, SC 29614-0060

Acquisitions Editor: Nancy Lohr

Publisher's Interests
A division of Bob Jones University Press, Journey Forth features juvenile fiction and biographies with a Christian worldview. It publishes everything from read-aloud books for young children, to adventure stories for young adults.
Website: www.bjup.com

Freelance Potential
Published 10 titles in 2003: 1 was developed from an unsolicited submission and 2 were reprint/licensed properties. Of the 10 titles, 1 was by an unpublished writer and 1 was by an author who was new to the publishing house. Receives 60 queries, 450 unsolicited mss yearly.

- **Fiction:** Published 1 story picture book, 4–10 years; 3 chapter books, 5–10 years; 4 middle-grade books, 8-12 years; and 2 young adult books, 12–18 years. Genres include contemporary and historical fiction and stories about animals.
- **Nonfiction:** Publishes middle-grade books, 8–12 years; and young adult books, 12–18 years. Features biographies of well-known Christians and missionaries.
- **Representative Titles:** *Dust of the Earth* by Donna Lynn Hess (YA) is a biographical fiction book inspired by the life of J. T. Pace, a black sharecropper's son who struggled to be able to read the Word of God for himself. *The Captain's Hat* by Anita Williams (7–9 years) is a story about a boy who dreams of becoming a ship's captain.

Submissions and Payment
Guidelines available. Query with 5 sample chapters; or send complete ms. Accepts photocopies, computer printouts, and simultaneous submissions if identified. SASE. Responds in 3 months. Publication in 18–24 months. Royalty, negotiable. Flat fee.

Editor's Comments
We need mysteries for ages nine to twelve and animal adventure stories for ages seven to twelve. Biographies of Christian heroes of the Faith for ages nine and up are also in demand.

The Judaica Press

123 Ditmas Avenue
Brooklyn, NY 11218

Editor: Norman Shapiro

Publisher's Interests
The Judaica Press publishes books for children and adults
about the history and traditions of the Jewish people. Its
titles cover a range of topics, from Jewish life, to prayers and
the holidays, to Hebrew textbooks and books on the Talmud
and the Torah.
Website: www.judaicapress.com

Freelance Potential
Published 15 titles (7 juvenile) in 2003: 10 were developed
from unsolicited submissions and 3 were reprint/licensed
properties. Of the 15 titles, 4 were by unpublished writers
and 10 were by authors who were new to the publishing
house. Receives 75 queries, 65 unsolicited mss yearly.
- **Fiction:** Publishes early picture books, 0–4 years; easy-to-read
  books, 4–7 years; story picture books, 4–10 years; and young
  adult books, 12–18 years. Genres include inspirational fiction
  and religious mystery and suspense.
- **Nonfiction:** Publishes story picture books, 4–10 years. Topics
  include Jewish traditions, self-help issues, Bible stories, crafts,
  and hobbies.
- **Representative Titles:** *How Mitzvah Giraffe Got His Long, Long
  Neck* by David Sokoloff (4–7 years) conveys the idea to children
  that helping others will improve their own self-image. *Too Big,
  Too Little . . . Just Right!* by Loren Hodes (4–7 years) tells the
  story of a little girl who feels displaced by her baby brother.

Submissions and Payment
Query with outline; or send complete ms. Accepts photocopies and computer printouts. Availability of artwork
improves chance of acceptance. SASE. Responds in 3
months. Publication in 1–2 years. Royalty.

Editor's Comments
We are interested in any book that helps our readers better
understand the Jewish faith and how to incorporate Jewish
traditions into their day-to-day lives. Books for young children
about the Jewish holidays are always welcome.

Just Us Books

356 Glenwood Avenue
East Orange, NJ 07017

Submissions Editor: Katura Hudson

Publisher's Interests
Since its inception in 1988, Just Us Books has established itself as a leading publisher of books for young black people. It features titles on black history, culture, and experiences for readers up to the age of 12. Picture books, biographies, and novels and nonfiction for middle-grade readers can be found in its catalogue.
Website: www.justusbooks.com

Freelance Potential
Published 5 titles in 2003: 1 was by an agented author and 1 was a reprint/licensed property. Receives 1,000 queries yearly.
- **Fiction:** Publishes story picture books, 4–10 years; and middle-grade novels, 8–12 years. Genres include contemporary, multicultural, and historical fiction; adventure; and mystery.
- **Nonfiction:** Publishes middle-grade books, 8–12 years. Features biographies.
- **Representative Titles:** *Scientists, Healers and Inventors* by Wade Hudson (9–12 years) features short biographical sketches of black heroes such as George Washington Carver and Louis Latimer; part of the Book of Black Heroes series. *A Blessing in Disguise* by Eleanora E. Tate (10+ years) tells the story of girl who, facing a boring summer in North Carolina, sets her sights on money, clothes, cars, and parties.

Submissions and Payment
Guidelines available. Query with outline/synopsis. SASE. Responds in 3–4 months. Publication period varies. Royalty.

Editor's Comments
This year we are looking for young adult and middle-reader novels and nonfiction. Material that targets males in the 13- to 16-year-old age group are particularly welcome. Books that include realistic, contemporary characters and have strong and interesting plots that introduce conflict and resolution will get a second look. We look for high-interest readability and authenticity. Please take the time to carefully research publishers' markets.

Kaeden Books

P.O. Box 16190
Rocky River, OH 44116

Submissions Editor: Joan Backus

Publisher's Interests
Kaeden Books publishes supplementary reading and educational materials for early and emergent readers. Its titles feature high story and character interest for the student, as well as instructional suitability.
Website: www.kaeden.com

Freelance Potential
Published 8 titles in 2003: 7 were developed from unsolicited submissions. Of the 8 titles, 6 were by unpublished writers and 2 were by authors who were new to the publishing house. Receives 500 unsolicited mss yearly.
- **Fiction:** Publishes early picture books, easy-to-read books, and story picture books, 5–9 years.
- **Nonfiction:** Publishes easy-to-read books, 5–9 years. Topics include mathematics, history, science, and social studies. Also publishes biographies.
- **Representative Titles:** *The Fishing Contest* by Joe Yukish uses easy vocabulary and modest picture support to tell the story of a family that gets together to see who can catch the biggest fish. *When I Go to Grandma's House* by Brian P. Cleary is a story that touches on the things a child encounters on a visit to grandma's house.

Submissions and Payment
Guidelines available at website. Send complete ms. Accepts photocopies and computer printouts. SASE. Responds only if interested. Publication period varies. Royalty. Flat fee.

Editor's Comments
For the coming year, we need biographies of famous people, science stories that entertain as well as educate, and books on social studies topics—all written for five- to nine-year-old emergent readers. We look for stories with humor, surprise endings, and interesting characters, as well as vocabulary and sentence structure appropriate for beginning readers. Please familiarize yourself with our books. Sending material that does not meet our requirements wastes not only your time, but ours as well.

Kar-Ben Publishing

6800 Tildenwood Lane
Rockville, MD 20852

Submissions Editors: Judye Groner & Madeline Wikler

Publisher's Interests
Books with Jewish themes are produced by this company, a
division of Lerner Publishing Group. Its fiction and nonfiction
titles target preschool children through high school students.
Website: www.karben.com

Freelance Potential
Published 11 titles (9 juvenile) in 2003: 3 were developed
from unsolicited submissions. Of the 11 titles, 3 were by
unpublished writers and 3 were by authors who were new to
the publishing house. Receives 350+ unsolicited mss yearly.
- **Fiction:** Published 3 story picture books, 4–10 years; 1 chapter
  book, 5–10 years; and 1 middle-grade book, 8–12 years. Features Bible stories, holiday stories, life-cycle stories, and folktales. Also publishes concept books, toddler books, and early
  picture books, 0–4 years; activity books; and board books.
- **Nonfiction:** Published 2 toddler books, 0–4 years; and 2 easy-
  to-read books, 4–7 years. Also publishes concept books and
  early picture books, 0–4 years.
- **Representative Titles:** *Hanukkah Cat* by Chaya Burstein (4–8
  years) is the story of a boy who adopts a mischievous stray cat
  on the first night of Hanukkah. *My Jewish Home* by Rabbi
  Andrew Goldstein (1–4 years) is a board book that lets kids
  explore a house room by room to find the objects that make it
  a Jewish home.

Submissions and Payment
Guidelines available. Send complete ms. Accepts photocopies,
computer printouts, and simultaneous submissions if identified. SASE. Responds in 3–5 weeks. Publication period varies.
Royalty, 5–8%; advance $500–$2,000.

Editor's Comments
All of our books for children and their families feature Jewish
themes. For the coming year, stories about the Jewish holidays
are particularly welcome. We would also like to see submissions of stories that focus on Jewish identity and on being a
Jewish kid today.

Key Curriculum Press

1150 65th Street
Emeryville, CA 94608

President and Editorial Director: Steve Rasmussen

Publisher's Interests
Mathematics teachers working in secondary schools turn to
Key Curriculum Press when they are looking for textbooks
and workbooks for use in their classrooms. They also offer
software and manipulatives.
Website: www.keypress.com

Freelance Potential
Published 35 titles in 2003: 2 were developed from unsolicited
submissions. Of the 35 titles, 3 were by authors who were new
to the publishing house. Receives 50 queries yearly.
- **Nonfiction:** Publishes middle-grade books, 8–12 years; and
  young adult books, 12–18 years. Publishes textbooks, workbooks, tools and supplies, grades 9–12. Also publishes professional development titles and books for mathematics educators.
- **Representative Titles:** *A Graphing Matter: Activities for Easing
  into Algebra* by Mark Illingworth (teachers, grades 6–10) shows
  pre-algebra and algebra students real-world applications of
  variables and relationships using comical and sometimes irrev-
  erent activities. *What's Wrong with This Picture?* by Michael
  Serra (teachers, grades 8–10) features 72 pages of blackline
  masters that include problems, one or more of which may contain an error, an optical illusion, or conflicting information.

Submissions and Payment
Guidelines available. Query with résumé, prospectus, table of
contents, and sample chapters. Accepts photocopies, computer printouts, Macintosh disk submissions, and simultaneous submissions if identified. SASE. Responds in 2 months.
Publication period varies. Royalty, 6–10%.

Editor's Comments
Please note that all of the materials we publish conform to the
standards set by NCTM. We continue to look for high-quality,
innovative materials for teaching mathematics in grades nine
through twelve. Don't send queries for books that deal with
other subjects. A review of our catalogue should help you
decide if your book would be appropriate for us.

Key Porter Books

3rd Floor
70 The Esplanade
Toronto, Ontario M5E 1R2
Canada

Editorial Assistant: Janie Yoon

Publisher's Interests
For more than 20 years, this publisher has offered juvenile
books that often focus on the environment, nature, animals,
and history. It offers fiction and nonfiction for children of all
ages, as well as some parenting titles.
Website: www.keyporter.com

Freelance Potential
Published 90 titles (13 juvenile) in 2003: 6 were developed
from unsolicited submissions, 63 were by agented authors,
and 6 were reprint/licensed properties. Receives 200–250
queries yearly.
- **Fiction:** Publishes easy-to-read books, 4–7 years; story picture
  books, 4–10 years; chapter books, 5–10 years; and young adult
  books, 12–18 years. Genres include folklore, fairy tales, and
  stories about animals, nature, and the environment. Also publishes anthologies.
- **Nonfiction:** Publishes story picture books, 4–10 years; middle-
  grade books, 8–12 years; and young adult books, 12–18 years.
  Topics include nature, the environment, natural history,
  health, history, and multicultural and ethnic subjects. Also
  publishes parenting titles.
- **Representative Titles:** *Dancing Elephants and Floating Conti-
  nents: The Story of the Land Beneath Your Feet* by John Wilson
  (8+ years) provides a readily understandable explanation of the
  history of Earth and how it has evolved and changed. *The Mes-
  sengers* by J. C. Mills (9+ years) is a novel that chronicles the
  adventures of a family who, disguised as mice, provide unseen
  inspiration and advice to humans.

Submissions and Payment
Query with résumé, proposal, table of contents, and sample
chapter or 20-page excerpt. SAE/IRC. Response time varies.
Publication period and payment policy vary.

Editor's Comments
Send us innovative, fresh ideas for books about nature, natural history, the environment. We'll also consider stories and
folktales with a multicultural flavor.

Focus on Nonfiction
Erin Clarke
Alfred A. Knopf and Crown Books, Random House

Alfred A. Knopf and Crown Books for Young Readers make up a single imprint of Random House. With its many different imprints, Random House is the largest English-language publisher of children's books today. Titles range from baby books through young adult, from award-winning single titles to franchises, from Golden Books classics to hot new media tie-ins. Random House's catalogues are downloadable online and are divided into sections, so you can download only what you want (a whopping 26 pages for toddler books alone).

Erin Clarke is Associate Editor at Knopf and Crown. Though they are a single imprint, Knopf and Crown offer separate lists. Like her colleagues, Clarke acquires for both.

A major difference between the two is Crown's focus on nonfiction. Nonfiction is often overlooked as a topic for toddler books, and therein lies a big opportunity. "I'd like to see more nonfiction submissions for [toddler books]," Clarke says. "Sam Swope's *Gotta Go! Gotta Go!* features a very simple text about monarch butterflies told in an extremely creative, fun, and informative way."

If nonfiction isn't your interest, how can you make your fiction for the youngest readers stand out from the crowd? "I look for manuscripts featuring simple concepts told in an economy of words in a wholly original way—not an easy task," Clarke says, adding, "I also like submissions with a sense of fun and humor to them."

(See also Crown Books for Young
Readers on page 156)

Alfred A. Knopf Books for Young Readers

1745 Broadway
New York, NY 10019

Submissions Editor

Publisher's Interests
This publisher offers everything from board books, novelty
books, and picture books to novels for teenagers. A division
of Random House Children's Books, it publishes only fiction,
and its list includes classics by such well-known authors as
Leo Lionni and Roald Dahl. You must have an agent to submit to this publisher.
Website: www.randomhouse.com/kids

Freelance Potential
Published 50 titles in 2003: all were by agented authors.
Receives 4,000 unsolicited mss yearly.
- **Fiction:** Publishes picture books, 0–8 years; chapter books,
  5–10 years; middle-grade novels, 8–12 years; and young adult
  books, 12–18 years. Genres include historical, contemporary,
  and multicultural fiction.
- **Representative Titles:** *Hoot* by Carl Hiaasen (10+ years) is a
  story about a boy who moves to Florida and, in his attempt to
  solve a mystery, runs into potty-trained alligators, burrowing
  owls, and several extremely poisonous snakes. *Heaven's All
  Star Jazz Band* by Don Carter (5–8 years) celebrates some of
  jazz's greatest legends and the lasting bond their music creates
  between a boy and his grandfather.

Submissions and Payment
Guidelines available. Accepts submissions through agents
only. Accepts photocopies, computer printouts, and simultaneous submissions if identified. SASE. Responds in 3
months. Publication in 1–2 years. Royalty; advance.

Editor's Comments
Please remember that we only accept fiction submissions, and
we only review material that has been submitted to us by an
agent. Our best recommendation is to visit a local library or
bookstore and take the time to study the types of titles we
publish. You'll see that we publish works of the highest literary
quality. If you think your work can meet our standards, please
submit it through your agent.

Lark Books

67 Broadway
Asheville, NC 28801

Children's Book Editor: Joe Rhatigan

Publisher's Interests

This publisher offers creative books of crafts and craft kits for readers from 8 to 18 years of age. Color illustrations and careful directions make topics such as ceramics, fiber arts, knitting and crocheting easy and fun. Adult craft books and science activity books also appear on its list.
Website: www.larkbooks.com

Freelance Potential

Published 50+ titles (11 juvenile) in 2003: 10 were developed from unsolicited submissions and 5 were reprint/licensed properties. Receives 250+ queries yearly.
- **Nonfiction:** Published 11 middle-grade books, 8–12 years. Also publishes young adult books, 12–18 years. Topics include beading, book making, ceramics, doll making, fiber arts, knitting, crocheting, mosaics, nature crafts, paper, quilting, sewing, theater crafts, and weaving.
- **Representative Titles:** *The Book of Wizard Craft* by Janice Eaton Kilby et al. (8–12 years) offers magical recipes for more than 50 wizardly items, including clothes, tools, potions, party and room decorations, and games. *The Kids' Guide to Nature Adventures* by Joe Rhatigan (8–12 years) features 80 nature-related activities, projects, and games, from making a sleeping bag to constructing an earthworm apartment.

Submissions and Payment

Guidelines available. Prefers query with résumé, table of contents, introduction, 2–3 sample projects, and a description of artwork and illustrations. SASE. Response time varies. Publication period and payment policy vary.

Editor's Comments

We will consider all ideas for books that will inspire young crafters and tap into their creativity. We will also consider clever science activity books for the middle-grade and young adult reader. Please send a one-page query describing the book as specifically as you can, and include information about your background. We give careful consideration to careful queries.

Learning Horizons

One American Road
Cleveland, OH 44144

Editorial Director: Bob Kaminski

Publisher's Interests

A publisher of educational resources, Learning Horizons offers workbooks, activity workbooks, wipe-off activity books and mats, flash cards, science and nature books, and manipulatives. Everything it produces is aimed at children from the toddler years through sixth grade.
Website: www.learninghorizons.com

Freelance Potential

Published 29 titles in 2003: all were assigned. Of the 29 titles, 4 were by authors who were new to the publishing house. Receives 600 queries yearly.

- **Nonfiction:** Publishes toddler books and early picture books, 0–4 years; and story picture books, 4–10 years. Features educational and informational titles. Topics include animals, nature, pets, mathematics, and the environment. Also publishes novelty books and board books.
- **Representative Titles:** *Kittens* (4–8 years) tells how kittens are born, what they eat, how they grow, how they communicate, when they become cats: part of the Know-It-Alls® series. *Volcanoes and Other Earth Wonders* (6–9 years) is a science sticker book that explains how volcanoes form, what happens during an eruption, and how scientists measure their force.

Submissions and Payment

Guidelines available. Query. SASE. Responds in 3–4 months. Publication in 18 months. Payment policy varies.

Editor's Comments

We're always looking for new ideas, especially in the areas of math and science, that will encourage parents to get involved in their child's learning. We know how important it is for children to develop a love of learning, and our hands-on learning materials are designed to excite, stimulate, encourage, and teach children from preschool to grade six. Many of our products have been developed by professional educators and psychologists. Please visit our website or consult our catalogue to see first hand the types of materials we produce.

Learning Resources

380 North Fairway Drive
Vernon Hills, IL 60061

Submissions Editor

Publisher's Interests
Educational resources for early childhood classrooms are
offered by Learning Resources, as well as supplemental materials for teaching language arts, math, science, and geography in kindergarten through sixth grade. Its catalogue also
includes teacher resources, such as overhead materials, magnetic boards, and classroom kits.
Website: www.learningresources.com

Freelance Potential
Published 50 titles in 2003: 2 were developed from unsolicited submissions. Receives 20–30 queries yearly.
- **Nonfiction:** Publishes educational materials, manipulatives,
  workbooks, and activity books, pre-K–grade 6. Topics include
  language arts, phonics, math, science, geography, and nutrition. Also publishes teacher resources.
- **Representative Titles:** *Skill Sharpeners Reading Second Grade*
  provides a variety of enrichment activities that develop students' basic reading skills and includes a bonus worksheet
  generator CD-ROM. *Scrambled Word Building: Cross Curricular*
  (6–8 years) offers a hands-on approach to strengthening reading and spelling skills with 150 word-building lessons and 230
  demonstration cards for classroom use.

Submissions and Payment
Catalogue available with 9x12 SASE ($3 postage). Query with
résumé and writing samples. Accepts photocopies, computer
printouts, and disk submissions. SASE. Responds in 6–12
weeks. Publication in 1–2 years. Flat fee.

Editor's Comments
Please remember that our focus is on supplemental educational materials, such as workbooks and activity books. We
don't publish any fiction for children. Most of the material
we accept is written by professionals in the field of education. We're looking for queries that include an introductory
overview of the subject, a summary of the content, and an
indication of grade level appropriateness.

Lee & Low Books

95 Madison Avenue
New York, NY 10016

Submissions Editor

Publisher's Interests
Lee & Low publishes multicultural literature for children in preschool through the middle grades. Offering picture books primarily, both fiction and nonfiction, it seeks culturally authentic submissions.
Website: www.leeandlow.com

Freelance Potential
Published 20 titles in 2003: 3 were developed from unsolicited submissions and 3 were by agented authors. Of the 20 titles, 3 were by unpublished writers and 4 were by authors who were new to the publishing house. Receives 2,000 unsolicited mss yearly.

- **Fiction:** Published 10 story picture books, 4–10 years; and 1 middle-grade novel, 8–12 years. Genres include realistic, historical, multicultural, contemporary, and ethnic fiction.
- **Nonfiction:** Published 2 story picture books, 4–10 years. Topics include multicultural issues.
- **Representative Titles:** *The Pot That Juan Built* by Nancy Andrews-Goebel (6–10 years) is a picture book biography of Juan Quezada, the Mexican potter. *The Jones Family Express* by Javaka Steptoe (4–8 years) is the story of a young boy who makes a special gift for his aunt.

Submissions and Payment
Guidelines and catalogue available at website or with 9x12 SASE ($1.72 postage). Send complete ms. Accepts photocopies, computer printouts, and simultaneous submissions if identified. SASE. Responds in 2–4 months. Publication in 1–2 years. Royalty; advance.

Editor's Comments
For picture books, we would like to see submissions of realistic fiction set in contemporary America, historical fiction, and nonfiction. We also would like to see fiction and nonfiction manuscripts for middle-grade readers. In nonfiction, we look for a distinct voice or a unique approach to a topic. Do not submit folktales or animal stories; they will be returned unread.

Legacy Press

P.O. Box 261129
San Diego, CA 92196

Editorial Director: Christy Scannell

Publisher's Interests
The books from Legacy Press feature non-denominational,
evangelical Christian themes. Targeting readers ages two
through twelve, it primarily publishes nonfiction titles that are
marketed mostly through Christian bookstores. Devotionals,
journals, and activity books all appear in the catalogue of
Legacy Press.
Website: www.rainbowpublishers.com

Freelance Potential
Published 7 titles in 2003: all were developed from unsolicited submissions. Of the 7 titles, 1 was by an author who
was new to the publishing house. Receives 240 unsolicited
mss each year.
- **Fiction:** Publishes books in series, 2–12 years. All titles include
  activities and devotionals.
- **Nonfiction:** Publishes books based on evangelical Christian
  themes, 2–12 years. Features activity and how-to books. Topics
  include the Bible, religion, crafts, and hobbies.
- **Representative Titles:** *Christian Kids' Gardening Guide* tells
  how to grow all types of gardens and includes a plantable
  bookmark. *Meet the Ponytail Girls* follows the adventures of a
  group of preteen girls as they learn about God and includes
  devotions, activities, and a free hair scrunchie.

Submissions and Payment
Guidelines and catalogue available with 9x12 SASE (2 first-
class stamps). Send complete ms with table of contents and
first 3 chapters. Accepts photocopies. SASE. Responds in
3 months. Publication in 6–36 months. Royalty, 8%+;
advance, $500.

Editor's Comments
At this time, we're interested in reviewing nonfiction additions
to "The Christian Girl's Guide to" series, which targets girls
ages eight to twelve. Devotionals, journals, activity books, and
books that promote Christian values and teach the Bible will
always be considered. We don't accept stand-alone fiction.

Noticing Nonfiction
Marcia Marshall
Lerner Publishing

Lerner Publishing publishes educational books for readers 7 to 18. The company is especially interested in the topics of science, social studies, and history.

Senior Editor Marcia Marshall was with Atheneum Books for Young Readers (a division of Simon & Schuster) for 25 years before retiring as Executive Editor in 2000. She moved to Minneapolis to be closer to family and take the position with Lerner. "It's a different sort of publishing than at Atheneum," she says, "but I'm learning a lot and appreciate a house where nonfiction is so respected. Many houses have cut back on nonfiction. It's time-consuming and doesn't always get the notice fiction does."

Marshall said Lerner's submission policy can make it more difficult for new writers to break in. "It is unlikely Lerner will accept a nonfiction manuscript unless there happens to be a place for that subject in an ongoing series. Of course, there's always the possibility that our readers will be so taken with a submission that the author will be added to the list of people to contact for future projects."

"Enthusiasm for the subject" impresses a Lerner editor, says Marshall. "You can tell when writers are really interested in what they're writing about, and they pass that on to young readers. Accuracy is of utmost importance, and a perspective that places events in the text into a larger context." And Marshall really dislikes seeing submissions with "careless, rote writing. Strings of facts that are not connected into a full and satisfying *story.*"

Marshall invites experienced writers to send a résumé with a list of credits and/or writing samples. "This will help us determine what series might work best for you."

(See listing for Lerner Publishing Group
on following page)

Lerner Publishing Group

241 First Avenue North
Minneapolis, MN 55401

Submissions Editor: Jennifer Zimian

Publisher's Interests
Established in 1959, this educational publisher focuses on
nonfiction targeted to the school library market. It no longer
publishes fiction books. Fiction for all ages now appears
under Lerner Publishing's Carolrhoda imprint.
Website: www.lernerbooks.com

Freelance Potential
Published 240 titles in 2003: 1 was developed from an unsolicited submission, 1–5 were by agented authors, and 27
were reprint/licensed properties. Of the 240 titles, 1–5 were
by authors who were new to the publishing house. Receives
500 queries, 2,000 unsolicited mss yearly.
- **Nonfiction:** Published 40–50 easy-to-read books, 4–7 years;
  50–60 middle-grade books, 8–12 years; and 5–10 young adult
  books, 12–18 years. Also publishes chapter books, 5–10 years.
  Topics include natural and physical science, current events,
  ancient and modern history, world cultures, and sports. Also
  publishes biographies.
- **Representative Titles:** *From Egg to Butterfly* by Shannon Zem-
  licka (grades K–2) shows young children how butterflies grow.
  Jackie Robinson by Sally M. Walker (grades 1–3) tells the story
  of baseball's first black player; part of the On My Own Biographies series.

Submissions and Payment
Guidelines and catalogue available with 9x12 SASE ($3.50
postage). Query with outline and sample chapter; or send
complete ms with résumé. Accepts submissions during
March and October only. Accepts photocopies, computer
printouts, and simultaneous submissions if identified. SASE.
Responds in 4–6 months. Publication period and payment
policy vary.

Editor's Comments
Submissions on the topics of science, history, social studies,
and culture studies, as well as biographies, present the best
opportunity for publication here. No textbooks, please.

Arthur A. Levine Books

Scholastic Press
557 Broadway
New York, NY 10012

Editorial Director: Arthur A. Levine

Publisher's Interests

This publisher, an imprint of Scholastic Press, offers fiction and nonfiction for early readers through young adults. All queries are welcome, but complete manuscripts will be considered from previously published authors only.

Website: www.scholastic.com

Freelance Potential

Published 10 titles in 2003: 1 was developed from an unsolicited submission, 3 were by agented authors, and 5 were reprint/licensed properties. Of the 10 titles, 3 were by unpublished writers and 8 were by authors who were new to the publishing house. Receives 1,000 queries yearly.

- **Fiction:** Publishes story picture books, 4–10 years; middle-grade novels, 8–12 years; and young adult novels, 12–18 years. Genres include fantasy and contemporary fiction. Also publishes multicultural stories and poetry.
- **Nonfiction:** Publishes picture books, 4–10 years; middle-grade books, 8–12 years; and young adult titles, 12–18 years. Also publishes biographies.
- **Representative Titles:** *Plum* by Tony Mitton (all ages) is a poetry collection for fans of Florian. *The Loudest Roar* by Thomas Taylor (0–5 years) features a little tiger with a very loud mouth.

Submissions and Payment

Guidelines available. Query. Accepts complete ms from agented and previously published authors only. Accepts photocopies. SASE. Responds to queries in 2–4 weeks, to mss in 6–8 months. Publication in 18–24 months. Payment policy varies.

Editor's Comments

We are happy to look at your query letter, which provides a general sense of your manuscript, illuminates its strengths, and captures our interest. What is your manuscript about? What makes it original or memorable? Consider your query an opportunity to make an impression; to introduce your work to readers who might enjoy it!

Libraries Unlimited

88 Post Road West
Westport, CT 06881

Acquisitions Editor: Barbara Ittner

Publisher's Interests

Formerly known as Teachers Press/Libraries Unlimited,
this publisher has split the two divisions. Libraries Unlimited
continues to publish bibliographies, library science
books, practical handbooks, and manuals for librarians
and media specialists.
Website: www.lu.com

Freelance Potential

Published 75 titles in 2003: few were developed from unsolicited submissions. Of the 75 titles, 12 were by authors
who were new to the publishing house. Receives 400 queries
each year.

- **Nonfiction:** Publishes curriculum titles. Features bilingual
  books, grades K–6; and activity books, grades K–12. Also
  features biographies, professional reference titles, gifted
  education titles, and regional books. Topics include science,
  mathematics, social studies, whole language, literature, and
  library connections.
- **Representative Titles:** *Best Books for Young Adult Readers* by
  Stephen Calvert (grades 7–12) includes 8,000 listings of fresh,
  contemporary titles that will capture and hold a teen's attention. *Books for Children to Read Alone* by George Wilson &
  Joyce Moss (parents, librarians) is a guide to fostering a love of
  reading in children.

Submissions and Payment

Guidelines available. Query with sample chapters, table of
contents, and résumé; or send complete ms. Accepts photocopies, computer printouts, and simultaneous submissions if
identified. SASE. Responds in 2–3 months. Publication in
10–12 months. Royalty.

Editor's Comments

Before you decide whether or not we are the right place for
your book, please visit our website and review our guidelines.
You will see that we have specific email addresses for different
types of books.

Lightwave Publishing, Inc.

26275-98th Avenue
Maple Ridge, British Columbia V2W 1K3
Canada

Assistant Production Coordinator: Mikal Marrs

Publisher's Interests
This Christian publisher offers religious books for beginning
through middle-grade readers. In addition to Bibles, it develops
titles that explore the basic precepts of Christianity and
explain them in ways that kids find fun and interesting to
read. It also offers resources that help parents guide their
children through their religious development.
Website: www.lightwavepublishing.com

Freelance Potential
Published 18 titles (16 juvenile) in 2003: all were assigned. Of
the 18 titles, 2 were by authors who were new to the publishing house. Receives 100 queries yearly.
- **Nonfiction:** Published 1 story picture book, 4–10 years; and
  12 middle-grade books, 8–12 years. Topics include Christianity
  and religion. Also publishes children's Bibles and resources
  for parents.
- **Representative Titles:** *Teaching Your Child How to Pray* by
  Rick Osborne (parents) offers a simple, step-by-step approach
  that helps parents teach their children the challenging discipline of prayer. *I Want to Know About Jesus* features unusual
  facts and information about archeological discoveries as well as
  activities, cartoons, and puzzles; part of the I Want to Know
  About . . . series.

Submissions and Payment
Guidelines available. Query with clips. All titles are assigned
on work-for-hire basis. Accepts email queries to mikal@
lightwavepublishing.com. SAE/IRC. Responds in 1–2 weeks.
Publication in 8 months. Flat fee.

Editor's Comments
Because we operate on a work-for-hire basis, we ask all interested freelancers to send us a query that includes a résumé,
clips, and a description of the faith you practice. Most of our
writers have a solid understanding of the Bible. Keep in mind
that our purpose is to help children embrace Christianity and
to help parents pass their faith on to their children.

Lillenas Publishing Company

2923 Troost Avenue
Kansas City, MO 64109

Drama Editor: Kimberly R. Messer

Publisher's Interests
Church and school drama programs use the plays and theater resources offered by Lillenas Publishing Company. All of its materials are designed for use in ministry and reflect a Christian point of view.
Website: www.lillenas.com

Freelance Potential
Published 50 titles (7 juvenile) in 2003. Receives 480 unsolicited mss each year.
- **Fiction:** Publishes full-length and one-act plays, monologues, sketches, skits, recitations, puppet plays, and dramatic exercises, 6–18 years. Also publishes dramatic material on Christmas, Easter, Thanksgiving, Mother's Day, Father's Day, and other holiday themes.
- **Nonfiction:** Publishes theater resource materials. Topics include stage design, scenery, production techniques, and drama ministry.
- **Representative Titles:** *United We Stand: A Children's Patriotic Worship Experience* by Pam Andrews is a children's musical that celebrates freedom, religious liberty, and national heritage. *My Almost for His Highest* by Martha Bolton features short sketches that can be used as sermon illustrators, as discussion starters, or at retreats for entertaining and teaching.

Submissions and Payment
Guidelines available. Send complete ms with cast list, scene description, and prop list. Accepts computer printouts. SASE. Responds in 2–3 months. Publication period varies. Flat fee.

Editor's Comments
The dramatic materials you send us shouldn't sermonize; they should provide a strong Christian message that is couched in a highly entertaining script. People involved on both sides of the footlights need to feel that the effort and time spent were worthwhile and that one's spiritual sensibilities are heightened because of the experience. We especially need sketch and monologue collections that include 12 to 15 short scripts.

Linnet Books

The Shoe String Press
2 Linsley Street
New Haven, CT 06473

President: Diantha C. Thorpe

Publisher's Interests
Books for children and teenagers about history and society are featured on Linnet Books' list. It offers curriculum-related biographies, reference books, and multicultural children's programming materials, as well as professional titles for educators and librarians.
Website: www.shoestringpress.com

Freelance Potential
Published 9 titles in 2003. Receives 500 queries yearly.
- **Nonfiction:** Publishes interdisciplinary books, memoirs, biographies, reference books, literary companions, and multicultural children's programming materials. Topics include social studies, natural history, folktales, storytelling, art, archaeology, and anthropology.
- **Representative Titles:** *Theodore Roosevelt: Larger Than Life* by Matt Donnelly (grades 7 and up) is a biography about a president who virtually transformed himself from a sickly boy into a dynamic shaper of American Life. *Photography and the Making of the American West* by Paul Clee (grades 7 an up) shows how the new technology of photography influenced the public perception of the frontier, its landscape, and its inhabitants from the 1840s onward.

Submissions and Payment
Query with 2 sample chapters. Accepts photocopies, computer printouts, and simultaneous submissions if identified. SASE. Responds in 4 months. Publication in 1 year. Royalty; advance.

Editor's Comments
Writers who base their books on primary source research and who can come up with something fresh and different are encouraged to contact us. We are interested in books about Eastern Europe, Africa, and Asia for middle school and high-school students. Of special interest are books that focus on the social history of countries other than the United States. Titles that deal with women's and girls' issues are also needed.

Linworth Publishing

Suite L
480 East Wilson Bridge Road
Worthington, OH 43085

Editorial Director: Carol Simpson

Publisher's Interests
Linworth Publishing offers professional development resources for media specialists and educators who work in kindergarten through high school, with a focus on books about school libraries, literature, and technology. It has been in operation for more than 20 years.
Website: www.linworth.com

Freelance Potential
Published 85 titles in 2003: 10 were developed from unsolicited submissions. Receives 120 queries yearly.
- **Nonfiction:** Publishes books about school libraries, literature, and technology for media specialists and teachers, grades K–12. Also offers professional development books.
- **Representative Titles:** *Information Literacy Search Strategies* by Zorana Ercegovac offers tools and resources to ensure that high school students are competent learners and researchers. *ABCs of an Author/Illustrator Visit* by Sharron L. McElmeel gives ideas on how to promote enhanced literacy by celebrating books and their creators with a number of activities.

Submissions and Payment
Catalogue and guidelines available at website. Query or send complete ms with 2 hard copies and IBM disk. Accepts email queries to linworth@linworthpublishing.com. SASE. Responds in 1 week. Publication in 6 months. Royalty.

Editor's Comments
Our mission is to help enhance the careers of school library media specialists by providing them with excellent resource materials that offer new techniques and insights. We are also interested in materials for those who are considering library science as a first or second career and are looking for titles that provide practical, professional information to help them explore this career option further. Make sure to include your book's target audience, an analysis of competitive works, and your qualifications and background when you submit a proposal. Every book is reviewed by internal and external experts.

Little, Brown and Company

1271 Avenue of the Americas
New York, NY 10020

Assistant, Children's Books: Sara Morling

Publisher's Interests

Fiction and nonfiction by renowned authors and lesser-known writers can be found in Little, Brown and Company's catalogue. It will consider manuscripts for readers of all ages, as long as they come through an agent.
Website: www.lb-kids.com or www.lb-teens.com

Freelance Potential

Published 110 titles in 2003: all were by agented authors and 12 were reprint/licensed properties. Of the 110 titles, 3 were by authors who were new to the publishing house. Receives 1,000 unsolicited mss yearly.

- **Fiction:** Publishes concept books, toddler books, and early picture books, 0–4 years; easy-to-read books, 4–7 years; story picture books, 4–10 years; chapter books, 5–10 years; middle-grade novels, 8–12 years; and young adult books, 12–18 years. Genres include adventure, humor, mystery, suspense, folktales, and multicultural fiction. Also publishes poetry.
- **Nonfiction:** Publishes story picture books, 4–10 years; middle-grade books, 8–12 years; and young adult books, 12–18 years. Topics include nature, the environment, crafts, and social and family issues.
- **Representative Titles:** *Otto Goes to the Beach* by Todd Parr (0–3 years) is a picture book about a dog who faces familiar childhood dilemmas and resolves them in surprising ways. *Almost Home* by Nora Raleigh Baskin (8–12 years) is a novel about a girl with an unstable home life who decides to try acting to express her emotions.

Submissions and Payment

Accepts submissions through literary agents only. Send complete ms with author's qualifications and previous publications. Royalty, 5–10%; advance.

Editor's Comments

Picture books and middle-grade and young adult novels are an ongoing need here, but they must have high literary merit and they must come through an agent.

Novelty Books
Cindy Eng Alvarez
Little Simon

Cindy Eng Alvarez is Vice President and Editorial Director of Little Simon, one of several well-known children's imprints of Simon & Schuster. Little Simon focuses on novelty books, which range from board and cloth books to pop-ups to a wide range of touch-and-feel, pull-the-flap titles. So she's looking for that something *extra* that allows the story or information to be presented in a dynamic or interactive way.

The novelty aspect of Little Simon books makes extra demands on how art and text work together. What doesn't work for Alvarez? "Books that don't integrate the text and art well or those that are too literal. At this age, most kids already know that the pictures relate to the text, and they find reassurances in seeing what's said illustrated on the page." On the other hand, she loves "books that illustrate what's happening in the story but also add another subtext or subplot that only exists in the art or via a novelty element. Toddler books are a stepping stone to picture books, and having another level or offering a more imaginative segment stretches kids as readers."

What does that mean for writers? Manuscripts that suggest or allow different creative interpretations without being too abstract. More specifically, Alvarez is looking for "an entertaining, imaginative story or twist on their everyday experiences; a unique approach to early learning concepts; and or a proposal with an age-appropriate holiday theme."

Little Simon

Simon & Schuster Children's Publishing Division
1230 Avenue of the Americas
New York, NY 10020

Editorial Department

Publisher's Interests
This publisher offers mainly fiction and specializes in novelty
books for children from birth to eight years. Its titles include
interactive books, pop-up books, board books, cloth books,
touch-and-feel books, and lift-the-flap books.
Website: www.simonsayskids.com

Freelance Potential
Published 65 titles in 2003: 20 were by agented authors, and
15 were reprint/licensed properties. Receives 200 queries
each year.
- **Fiction:** Publishes concept, toddler, holiday, and board
  books, 0–4 years; and pull-tab, lift-the-flap, and pop-up
  books, 4–8 years.
- **Representative Titles:** *Sweetheart Fairies* by Cecile Schoberle
  (3–7 years) follows a group of charming fairies who bring fun
  and delight to all whom they touch, building snowmen, baking
  cookies, or reading bedtime stories. *Love Bugs* by David A.
  Carter (all ages) is a funny and ageless mini edition of the
  author's best-selling pop-up book, which looks just like a box
  of valentine chocolates. *Somebunny Loves Me* by Joan Holub
  (2–5 years) is a fuzzy board book that launches a new series
  about adorable animals who cuddle with their parents.

Submissions and Payment
Query only. No unsolicited mss. SASE. Responds in 6
months. Publication in 2 years. Royalty; advance. Flat fee.

Editor's Comments
We are interested in clever, innovative ideas for books that
will appeal to very young readers and their parents. Please do
not send complete projects; they will be returned unread. We
accept queries only. Describe your background and your
experience working on novelty projects in a cover letter, and
explain the format of the book that you are proposing. If we
feel your project is right for us, we will contact you. Standard
picture books, chapter books, and middle-grade or young
adult books are not appropriate for us.

Llewellyn Publications

P.O. Box 64383
St. Paul, MN 55164-0383

Acquisitions Specialist: Megan C. Atwood

Publisher's Interests

This publisher's mission is to develop fiction and nonfiction books that introduce New Age, occult, and metaphysical topics to readers ages eight through eighteen. It publishes fiction in a variety of genres as well as nonfiction about divination, alternative religions, the paranormal, and astrology.
Website: www.llewellyn.com

Freelance Potential

Published 110 titles (12 juvenile) in 2003: 7 were developed from unsolicited submissions and 1 was by an agented author. Of the 110 titles, 6 were by unpublished writers and 9 were by authors who were new to the publishing house. Receives 240 queries, 240 mss yearly.

- **Fiction:** Published 2 middle-grade titles, 8–12 years; and 3 young adult books, 12–18 years. Genres include fairy tales, fantasy, mystery, suspense, and science fiction.
- **Nonfiction:** Published 1 middle-grade book, 8–12 years; and 3 young adult books, 12–18 years. Features self-help and how-to titles. Topics include alternative religions, New Age subjects, astrology, and the paranormal.
- **Representative Titles:** *Teen Goddess: How to Look, Love, and Live Like a Goddess* by Catherine Wishart (12+ years) tells the story of a number of goddesses and offers tips on how to live like one. *Blue Is for Nightmares* by Laurie Stolarz (12+ years) features a girl who dreams about her best friend's murder.

Submissions and Payment

Guidelines available with #10 SASE ($.74 postage) or at website. Catalogue available at website. Send complete ms or query via email to childrensbooks@llewellyn.com. Accepts photocopies. SASE. Responds in 2–6 months. Publication in 1–2 years. Royalty, 10%.

Editor's Comments

We're interested in seeing more middle-grade nonfiction on New Age topics. Good fiction for both middle-grade and young adult readers will also catch our attention.

Lucent Books

10911 Technology Place
San Diego, CA 92127

Senior Acquisitions Editor: Chandra Howard

Publisher's Interests

Books from this publisher cover everything from the indigenous peoples of Africa to great medical discoveries and the history of sports. Lucent Books specializes in nonfiction series for students in middle school and high school. Most of its titles appear in series.
Website: www.gale.com/lucent

Freelance Potential

Published 180 titles in 2003: 60 were developed from unsolicited submissions, 1 was by an agented author, and 5 were reprint/licensed properties. Of the 180 titles, 9 were by unpublished writers and 18 were by authors who were new to the publishing house. Receives 200+ queries yearly.

- **Nonfiction:** Publishes middle-grade books, 8–12 years; and young adult books, 12–18 years. Topics include political, cultural, and social history; science; geo-politics; and current issues. Also publishes biographies.
- **Representative Titles:** *North Korea* by Peggy J. Parks (grades 5 and up) explains how the people of this Communist nation continue to struggle under an oppressive regime; part of the Nations in Conflict series. *Stem Cells* by Keith Greenberg (grades 4–7) discusses the potential medical advances offered by stem cell research and the ethical controversies that surround it; part of the Science on the Edge series.

Submissions and Payment

Guidelines and catalogue available. All books are written on a work-for-hire basis and by assignment only. Query with résumé and writing samples. SASE. Response time varies. Publication in 1 year. Flat fee, $2,500 for first book; $3,000 for subsequent books.

Editor's Comments

Books about geo-political issues and contemporary topics are of special interest this year—particularly if they target readers in the middle grades and junior high. We're looking for ideas for our current series only; don't send single titles.

Magination Press

750 First Street NE
Washington, DC 20002

Project Editor: Cindy Gustafson

Publisher's Interests
An imprint of the American Psychological Association, Magina-
tion Press offers self-help books for children up to the age of
12. Its storybooks and guidebooks are designed to help children understand a variety of personal psychological issues.
Website: www.maginationpress.com

Freelance Potential
Published 8 titles in 2003: 6 were developed from unsolicited
submissions and 1 was by an agented author. Of the 8 titles,
3 were by unpublished writers and 4 were by authors who
were new to the publishing house. Receives 600 unsolicited
mss yearly.
- **Fiction:** Published 3 story picture books, 4–10 years; and 1
  middle-grade book, 8–12 years. Stories address psychological
  concerns and illnesses, family relationships, fears, and learning difficulties.
- **Nonfiction:** Published 1 story picture book, 4–10 years; 1
  middle-grade book, 8–12 years; and 2 workbooks, 5–12 years.
  Topics include grief, divorce, learning disabilities, and family
  issues. Also publishes parenting titles for adults.
- **Representative Titles:** *The Magic Box* by Marty Sederman &
  Seymour Epstein (3–7 years) is the story of a child who learns
  to cope with his father's frequent trips. *The Inside Story on
  Teen Girls* by Karen Zager & Alice Rubenstein (YA–Adult) helps
  teen girls and their parents learn more about themselves and
  each other.

Submissions and Payment
Guidelines and catalogue available with 10x13 SASE (2 first-
class stamps). Send complete ms. Accepts photocopies and
computer printouts. SASE. Responds in 1–6 months. Publication in 18 months. Royalty.

Editor's Comments
We have a current need for submissions addressing Attention
Deficit Disorder. All psychological concerns are of interest, but
we don't need anything dealing with self-esteem at this time.

Master Books

P.O. Box 726
Green Forest, AR 72638

Acquisitions Editor: Roger Howerton

Publisher's Interests
This publisher's goal is to provide books that "bring the lost to Christ and balance the body of Christ." For children, it offers educational, activity, and novelty books that are based on creationism and are free of references to evolution.
Website: www.masterbooks.net

Freelance Potential
Published 23 titles (10 juvenile) in 2003: 3 were developed from unsolicited submissions and 3 were reprint/licensed properties. Of the 23 titles, 4 were by authors who were new to the publishing house. Receives 600 queries yearly.
- **Nonfiction:** Published 5 middle-grade books, 8–12 years; and 5 young adult books, 12–18 years. Also publishes concept books, early picture books, and novelty and board books, 0–4 years; easy-to-read and activity books, 4–7 years; and educational titles, 4–18 years. Topics include religion, science, technology, and animals. Also publishes biographies.
- **Representative Titles:** *Life in the Great Ice Age* by Michael & Beverly Oard and Earl & Bonita Snellenberger (8–12 years) transports readers back to the Ice Age while teaching them the biblical history of the world. *God's Amazing Creatures and Me!* by Helen & Paul Haidle (6–10 years) presents devotionals and pen-and-ink drawings of a number of animals.

Submissions and Payment
Guidelines and catalogue available with 9x12 SASE (5 first-class stamps). Query with clips. SASE. Responds in 3 months. Publication in 1 year. Royalty.

Editor's Comments
We are interested in projects related to creationism, including children's books, scholarly works, and books for the laymen. Children's books should always emphasize the power and majesty of God as Creator. We continue to look for high-quality books about animals as well as educational science books that stress biblical principles. In your cover letter, tell us why you have written your book and why people will read it.

Maval Publishing

567 Harrison Street
Denver, CO 80206

Editor: Mary Hernandez

Publisher's Interests
Maval Publishing offers story picture books published in both Spanish and English for children between the ages of two and ten. Founded in 1994, Maval's children's titles are a more recent offering from this bilingual publisher.
Website: www.maval.com

Freelance Potential
Published 10–15 titles in 2003: all were developed from unsolicited submissions. Of the 10 titles, 5 were by authors who were new to the publishing house. Receives 2,000 unsolicited mss yearly.
- **Fiction:** Publishes story picture books, 2–10 years. Genres include adventure stories, fairy tales, fantasy, folklore, folktales, humor, and mystery. Also offers historical, religious, and Western fiction, multicultural and ethnic fiction, and stories about sports, nature, and the environment.
- **Nonfiction:** Publishes story picture books, 2–10 years. Topics include animals, pets, and multicultural and ethnic issues. Also features humor and biographies.
- **Representative Titles:** *Anything But a Shot* by Sean McKeown (2–8 years) tells the story of a boy who imagines all the things he'd rather do than get a shot. *Jim, the Heavy Cat* by Steve Simsich (2–8 years) is the story of a fat cat who loves himself no matter what other cats might think of him.

Submissions and Payment
Guidelines available with 9x5 SASE ($.80 postage). Send complete ms with artwork (color prints or transparencies). Accepts simultaneous submissions if identified. SASE. Responds in 4–6 months. Publication in 18 months. Royalty.

Editor's Comments
When submitting books for our consideration, please be aware that all of our books are illustrated story picture books for children under the age of ten, and all books are published in 16- to 32-page formats. We are interested in lively, funny, well-conceived books that make the reader want to read!

Mayhaven Publishing

P.O. Box 557
803 Blackburn Circle
Mahomet, IL 61853

Publisher: Doris Wenzel

Publisher's Interests
Easy-to-read books, story picture books, chapter books, and books for middle-grade and young adult readers are all found on this publisher's list. Mayhaven also sponsors an annual fiction award. 20% co-op published material.
Website: www.mayhavenpublishing.com

Freelance Potential
Published 10 titles (6 juvenile) in 2003: all were developed from unsolicited submissions and 3 were by agented authors. Of the 10 titles, 5 were by unpublished writers and 10 were by authors who were new to the publishing house. Receives 3,000+ queries yearly.
- **Fiction:** Published 2 easy-to-read books, 4–7 years; 2 chapter books, 5–10 years; and 2 young adult books, 12–18 years. Also publishes story picture books, 4–10 years; and middle-grade books, 8–12 years. Genres include coming-of-age stories, adventure, humor, and historical fiction.
- **Nonfiction:** Publishes easy-to-read titles, 4–10 years; chapter books, 5–10 years; middle-grade books, 8–12 years; and young adult books, 12–18 years. Topics include nature, travel, cooking, history, and the West.
- **Representative Titles:** *Ten Little Sisters* by Virginia Rackley et al. (4–10 years) is a picture book based on a true story about ten sisters who are separated and eventually reunited. *Kid Posse & the Phantom Robber* by R. Kent Tipton is a chapter book that meshes history from the 1890s and the 1950s.

Submissions and Payment
Guidelines available. Query with 3 sample chapters. Accepts photocopies and computer printouts. SASE. Responds in 9–12 months. Publication in 12–18 months. Royalty; advance, varies.

Editor's Comments
We are always interested in presenting readers with a variety of quality fiction and nonfiction. We welcome submissions from new talent.

Margaret K. McElderry Books

Simon & Schuster Children's Publishing Division
1230 Avenue of the Americas
New York, NY 10009

Vice President & Editorial Director: Emma D. Dryden

Publisher's Interests
Preschool children through young adults read the original
hardcover trade titles published by Margaret K. McElderry
Books. It considers books on a broad spectrum of subjects
and in a variety of styles, and its list includes picture books,
easy-to-read books, fantasy, and young adult fiction.
Website: www.simonsayskids.com

Freelance Potential
Published 30 titles in 2003: 13 were by agented authors and
4 were reprint/licensed properties. Of the 30 titles, 3 were by
unpublished writers and 2 were by authors who were new to
the publishing house. Receives 3,000 queries yearly.
- **Fiction:** Published 2 early picture books, 0–4 years; 15 story
  picture books, 4–10 years; 7 middle-grade novels, 8–12 years;
  and 5 young adult books, 12–18 years. Genres include fantasy,
  folktales, historical fiction, and humor. Also publishes poetry.
- **Nonfiction:** Published 1 story picture book, 4–10 years.
- **Representative Titles:** *Hotshots!* by Chris L. Demarest (5–8
  years) is a nonfiction picture book about men and women who
  fight huge forest and wildland fires. *Alchemy* by Margaret Mahy
  (YA) is an intense supernatural thriller that revolves around
  the ancient study of alchemy.

Submissions and Payment
Guidelines available. Query with résumé, outline/synopsis,
and first three chapters. Accepts queries by email to
childrens.submissions@simonandschuster.com with imprint
indicated in subject line. No unsolicited mss. SASE.
Responds in 1–2 months. Publication in 2–4 years. Royalty;
advance.

Editor's Comments
The style and subject matter of the books we publish is almost
unlimited. Early picture books, humorous middle-grade fiction,
and young adult fiction are still of special interest. Do not send
proposals for textbooks, coloring and activity books, science
fiction books, or religious publications.

McGraw-Hill Children's Publishing

8787 Orion Place
Columbus, OH 43240

Publisher: Tracey Dils

Publisher's Interests

This division of McGraw-Hill Education offers books for all ages—from toddlers to high school students. Its list includes fiction and nonfiction titles used in classrooms and libraries as supplementary material based on curricula. Books for gifted children as well as for children who need extra help are included in the company's publishing program.
Website: www.MHKids.com

Freelance Potential

Published 500 titles in 2003. Of the 500 titles, 10 were by unpublished writers and 5 were by authors who were new to the publishing house. Receives 144 queries yearly.

• **Fiction:** Publishes toddler books, 0–4 years; easy-to-read books, 4–7 years; and story picture books, 4–10 years. Genres include fairy tales, folklore, folktales, and contemporary fiction. Also publishes board books, novelty books, activity books, and books in series.

• **Nonfiction:** Publishes concept and toddler books, 0–4 years; and middle-grade books, 8–12 years. Features reference and education titles, as well as resource materials for teachers and homeschooling materials for parents.

• **Representative Titles:** *The Complete Book of United States History* (grades K–6) teaches youngsters about our nation's history in ways that are fun as well as educational. *Compounds and Contractions* (grade 1) features high-interest activities that can be used with any language program.

Submissions and Payment

Query only. No unsolicited mss. SASE. Response time, publication period, and payment policy vary.

Editor's Comments

We believe that giving children a solid educational foundation has never been so important. Our products are created by authors with strong backgrounds in writing for the educational market. If you're one of these people, send us a detailed query explaining your qualifications and describing your book idea.

Meadowbrook Press

5451 Smetana Drive
Minnetonka, MN 55343

General Submissions Editor

Publisher's Interests
Meadowbrook Press describes itself as one of the leading
Midwest publishers of books sold nationally. Founded in
1975, it offers titles about pregnancy, baby care, child care,
party planning, and children's activities. It is no longer
accepting children's fiction, although it will consider humorous poetry for children.
Website: www.meadowbrookpress.com

Freelance Potential
Published 11 titles (3 juvenile) in 2003: 2 were developed
from unsolicited submissions. Of the 11 titles, 3 were by
unpublished writers. Receives 200+ queries yearly.
- **Nonfiction:** Published 2 concept books, 0–4 years; and 1 middle-grade title, 8–12 years. Features activity, joke, and game
  books for children, as well as books on child care, parenting,
  and family activities for adults.
- **Representative Titles:** *Practical Parenting Tips* by Vicki Lansky
  (parents) is filled with time-tested tips and advice from The
  American Academy of Pediatrics and parents in the trenches.
  Hocus Jokus by Steve Charney is written to help kids become
  confident, funny magicians and includes step-by-step illustrations for 50 funny magic tricks.

Submissions and Payment
Guidelines available. Query. No unsolicited mss. Accepts
photocopies, computer printouts, and simultaneous submissions if identified. SASE. Responds in 4 months. Publication
in 2 years. Royalty; advance.

Editor's Comments
We take great pride in our ability to edit, design, and promote
books to help them achieve their full commercial potential. In
your query, tell us why your book will sell. Why is there a need
for this book? How large is the market? Describe the competition and why your contribution is necessary or better. Also
include information on your credentials. Good books on child
care for parents of infants through preteens are needed.

Meriwether Publishing Ltd.

885 Elkton Drive
Colorado Springs, CO 80907

Submissions Editor

Publisher's Interests
Meriwether Publishing puts out plays, books, and other educational resources with theater-related themes for middle school and high school drama classes. Drama students and teachers, as well as church and community theater groups, use its publications.
Website: www.meriwetherpublishing.com

Freelance Potential
Published 60 titles in 2003: 50 were developed from unsolicited submissions and 9 were by agented authors. Of the 60 titles, 30 were by unpublished writers and 25 were by authors who were new to the publishing house. Receives 1,200 queries, 800 unsolicited mss yearly.
- **Fiction:** Publishes middle-grade titles, 8–12 years. Offers one-act and full-length dramas, musicals, comedies, folktales, and social commentaries, as well as dialogues and monologues.
- **Nonfiction:** Publishes theater reference books and how-to titles, 12–25 years. Topics include stage design, lighting techniques, theatrical makeup, theater games, and improvisation.
- **Representative Titles:** *Teens Have Feelings, Too!* by Deborah Karczewski (YA) offers 100 monologues for young performers. *Self-Supporting Scenery* by James Hull Miller (teachers) presents ideas for the construction of free-standing scenery that creates its own theater in any available space.

Submissions and Payment
Guidelines available. Prefers query with outline, synopsis, and sample chapter. Will accept complete ms. Accepts photocopies and simultaneous submissions if identified. SASE. Responds in 4–6 weeks. Publication in 6 months. Royalty. Flat fee.

Editor's Comments
We're looking for excellent drama materials that will appeal to teens and their teachers, and resource books that will help students and teachers work toward producing the best performance possible. Send a detailed query with a sample chapter.

MightyBook

Suite 225
10924 Grant Road
Houston, TX 77070

Acquisitions Editor: Richard Eaves

Publisher's Interests

An imprint of Guardian Press, this electronic publisher offers
fiction for children up to the age of 10. Games and puzzles as
well as video songbooks are also found at the website. It does
not publish any nonfiction. 20% self-, subsidy-, co-venture,
or co-op published material.
Website: www.mightybook.com

Freelance Potential

Published 30 titles in 2003: 15 were developed from unsolicited submissions and 4 were reprint/licensed properties.
Of the 30 titles, 19 were by unpublished writers and 23 were
by authors who were new to the publishing house. Receives
200+ unsolicited mss yearly.

- **Fiction:** Published 2 toddler books and 10 early picture books,
  0–4 years; 3 easy-to-read books, 4–7 years; 15 story picture
  books, 4–10 years. Genres include fairy tales, fantasy, folktales, humor, multicultural and ethnic fiction, and stories
  about nature and the environment.
- **Representative Titles:** *Abe Lincoln Will You Ever Give Up?* by
  Lloyd Uglow (8+ years) tells a story of President Lincoln. *Barn-
  yard Babies* by Richard Wayne (2–4 years) offers preschoolers a
  chance to explore the many creatures found on a farm.

Submissions and Payment

Guidelines available at website. Send complete ms. Availability
of artwork improves chance of acceptance. Accepts photocopies, disk submissions (Microsoft Word), and email submissions to reaves@houston.rr.com. SASE. Responds in 3–4
weeks. Publication period varies. Royalty, 20%.

Editor's Comments

All children enjoy story time. It's a special time when families
can bond together through the magic of a storybook. This is
the kind of book we strive to offer our readers. Our purpose is
to provide a launching pad for those who seek careers in the
literary arts by providing international exposure to new and
established authors.

Milkweed Editions

Suite 300
1011 Washington Avenue South
Minneapolis, MN 55415

First Reader: Elisabeth Fitz

Publisher's Interests

This publisher's philosophy is that literature is a "transfor-
mative art" that conveys "the essential experiences of the
human heart and spirit." Its children's imprint publishes
middle-grade fiction in a variety of genres.
Website: www.milkweed.org

Freelance Potential

Published 11 titles (3 juvenile) in 2003: 8 were developed
from unsolicited submissions, 3 were by agented authors,
and 1 was a reprint/licensed property. Of the 8 titles, 4 were
by authors who were new to the publishing house. Receives
3,000 queries, 2,000 unsolicited mss yearly.

- **Fiction:** Published 3 middle-grade novels, 8–13 years. Genres
  include multicultural and ethnic fiction, historical fiction, and
  stories about nature.
- **Representative Titles:** *Behind the Bedroom Wall* by Laura E.
  Williams (8–13 years) is a story about a 13-year-old girl in
  Nazi Germany who questions her involvement in her town's
  Nazi youth group when she discovers that her parents are
  sheltering a family of Jewish refugees. *Tides* by V. M. Caldwell
  (8–13 years) follows a girl who spends her summer helping her
  brother grapple with the alcohol-related deaths of his friends
  and working with a woman to find an unknown polluter.

Submissions and Payment

Guidelines available. Query or send complete ms. Accepts
photocopies and simultaneous submissions if identified.
SASE. Responds to queries in 1 month, to mss in 1–6
months. Publication in 1 year. Royalty, 7.5% of list price;
advance, varies.

Editor's Comments

Send us literary fiction for middle readers that explores contemporary or historical issues in a setting that embodies
humane values. Our titles vary widely in subject matter, from
fantasy to books grounded in everyday life. We don't publish
poetry, picture books, or story collections.

The Millbrook Press

2 Old New Milford Road
Brookfield, CT 06804

Editorial Assistant

Publisher's Interests

This publisher specializes in curriculum-oriented nonfiction
books on topics from the arts to social studies, math,
science, and sports. Its imprints, designed to appeal to
schools and public libraries, include Twenty-First Century
Books, Roaring Brook Press, and Copper Beach Books.
Website: www.millbrookpress.com

Freelance Potential

Published 120 titles in 2003: 2 were developed from unsolicited submissions, 25 were by agented authors, and 60
were reprint/licensed properties. Of the 120 titles, 1 was by
an unpublished writer and 2 were by authors who were new
to the publishing house. Receives 520 queries yearly.

- **Nonfiction:** Publishes concept books and toddler books, 0–4
  years; middle-grade books, 8–12 years; and young adult books,
  12–18 years. Topics include the arts, sports, social studies,
  math, science, and crafts. Also publishes biographies.
- **Representative Titles:** *Look Closer: An Introduction to Bug
  Watching* by Gay Holland (grades 2–4) looks at what you'd see
  if you examined bugs through a magnifying glass. *Nature Did
  It First* by Susan Goodman (grades K–3) shows early readers
  how humans and animals solve problems in similar ways.

Submissions and Payment

Guidelines available at website. Accepts agented submissions
only. No unsolicited submissions. Query with résumé, outline, and sample chapter. SASE. Responds in 6–8 weeks.
Publication in 12–18 months. Royalty; advance. Flat fee.

Editor's Comments

We are very interested in material that tackles both contemporary issues and multicultural topics. Books for middle school readers must have strong ties to curriculum
topics such as math, science, American history, or social
studies. We are also interested in historical and sports
biographies that will appeal to younger readers in grades
two through eight.

Mitchell Lane Publishers

34 Decidedly Lane
Bear, DE 19701

President: Barbara Mitchell

Publisher's Interests

Mitchell Lane offers quality nonfiction titles for readers
between the ages of eight and fourteen. Most of its books are
biographies that are published as parts of series, and all are
written on an assignment-only basis.
Website: www.mitchelllane.com

Freelance Potential

Published 45 titles in 2003: 1 was by an agented author. Of
the 45 titles, 1 was by an unpublished writer and 10 were by
authors who were new to the publishing house. Receives 20
queries yearly.
- **Nonfiction:** Publishes chapter books, 5–10 years; middle-grade
  books, 8–12 years; and young adult books, 12–14 years. Publishes biographies of contemporary role models, including
  entertainers, inventors, scientists, sports personalities, political
  leaders, and multicultural figures.
- **Representative Titles:** *Godfrey Hounsfield and the Invention of
  CAT Scans* (grades 4–10) focuses on the scientist who discovered that x-rays could be manipulated by computers and
  invented the diagnostic device known as the CAT scanner; part
  of the Unlocking the Secrets of Science series. *Hernando de
  Soto* (grades 4–8) tells the story of this Spanish explorer who
  discovered the Mississippi River; part of the Latinos in American History series.

Submissions and Payment

Work-for-hire only. Query with writing samples and résumé.
Flat fee.

Editor's Comments

For our middle-grade and young adult readers, we would like
to add to our series of biographies of achievers in science,
medicine, and technology. Our goal is to introduce children to
the people behind familiar discoveries or inventions. We would
also like to add biographies of historical figures to our list. If
you'd like to be considered for an assignment, send us your
résumé and samples of your writing.

Modern Learning Press

P.O. Box 167
Rosemont, NJ 08556

Editor: Robert Low

Publisher's Interests
Modern Learning Press specializes in elementary education by
providing classroom materials that foster the development of
literacy skills. Natural science and social studies are other
focal points of its publishing program. Professional books for
teachers and parenting titles written by authorities in the fields
of education and child development also appear on its list.
Website: www.modlearn.com

Freelance Potential
Published 10 titles in 2003: 1 was developed from an unsolicited submission. Receives 20 queries yearly.
- **Nonfiction:** Publishes classroom materials, grades K–8. Topics
  include reading, language arts, spelling, writing, phonics, handwriting, natural science, and social studies. Also publishes parenting and professional titles about child development, school
  readiness, literacy, and English as a Second Language.
- **Representative Titles:** *Be Your Own Reading Specialist* by
  Carol Einstein (teachers, grades 1–3) explains how teachers
  can work effectively with the full range of students in their
  classes, including ADD, ESL, dyslexic, and other challenging
  students. *"I Hate School!"* by Jim Grant (teachers, parents)
  offers solutions to the readiness dilemma and discusses what
  can happen when children are placed in a grade that does not
  match their stage of development.

Submissions and Payment
Query with overview and short sample chapter. Accepts photocopies and computer printouts. SASE. Response time, publication period, and payment policy vary.

Editor's Comments
Our goal is to provide materials that will assist students in
kindergarten through eighth grade and the teachers who work
with them. Topics related to literacy, natural science, and
social studies are our areas of interest. Our books for teachers
and parents are written by experts, so if you are an authority
on elementary education or child development, contact us.

Modern Publishing

155 East 55th Street
New York, NY 10022

Editorial Director: Kathy O'Hehir

Publisher's Interests

This publisher offers licensed and non-licensed books for children between the ages of two and ten. Its books are sold in outlets for mass market titles and include both fiction and nonfiction titles in a wide array of formats, including novelty and activity titles, coloring books, workbooks, illustrated storybooks, and board books.
Website: www.modernpublishing.com

Freelance Potential

Published 300 titles in 2003: 10–15 were developed from unsolicited submissions. Receives 75 queries and unsolicited mss yearly.

- **Fiction:** Publishes activity books, workbooks, and coloring books; 2–10 years; licensed character books, 4–8 years; beginner novels, 6–8 years; and novelty books. Genres include fairy tales, nursery rhymes, adventure, and books about holidays.
- **Nonfiction:** Publishes picture books, easy-to-read books, and workbooks, 2–10 years. Features books based on licensed characters that are created to develop children's skills in reading, language, and mathematics.
- **Representative Titles:** *Caillou Coloring and Activity Books* (3–8 years) lead children through the early years with puzzles, mazes, and other activities. *Dinosaurs and Prehistoric Creatures* is a large-format hardcover that offers young readers a unique glimpse of the Ages of Dinosaurs.

Submissions and Payment

Guidelines available. Query with outline/synopsis; or send complete ms. Accepts photocopies and simultaneous submissions if identified. Availability of artwork improves chance of acceptance. SASE. Responds in 2 months. Publication period varies. Royalty, by arrangement. Flat fee. Work-for-hire.

Editor's Comments

In general, we look for writers familiar with our licensed characters who can work on assigned projects. Submissions of ideas for series projects are also welcome.

Mondo Publishing

980 Avenue of the Americas
New York, NY 10018

Executive Editor: Don L. Curry

Publisher's Interests
With a mission to help all children become literate, Mondo
Publishing produces quality books on a wide range of topics.
All are written to stimulate the interest of young readers and
to inspire in them the desire to learn to read and write.
Website: www.mondopub.com

Freelance Potential
Published 40 titles in 2003: 15 were developed from unsolicited submissions, 20 were by agented authors, and 5 were
reprint/licensed properties. Of the 40 titles, 9 were by unpublished writers and 12 were by authors who were new to the
publishing house. Receives 500+ unsolicited mss yearly.

- **Fiction:** Published 5 early picture books, 0–4 years; 5 easy-to-
  read books, 4–7 years; 5 story picture books, 4–10 years; 5
  chapter books, 5–10 years; and 2 middle-grade books, 8–12
  years. Genres include fantasy, mystery, folktales, adventure,
  humor, stories about sports and science, and contemporary
  and historical fiction.
- **Nonfiction:** Published 1 early picture book, 0–4 years; 5 easy-
  to-read books, 4–7 years; 5 story picture books, 4–10 years; 2
  chapter books, 5–10 years; and 3 middle-grade books, 8–12
  years. Topics include science, nature, animals, the environment, language arts, history, music, crafts, and hobbies.
- **Representative Titles:** *Buster* by Brent H. Sudduth (4–8 years)
  explores the qualities of uniqueness, individuality, and
  patience through the story of Buster, a firefly. *If Peace Is . . .*
  by Jane Baskwill (6+ years) clarifies the concept of peace for
  young readers.

Submissions and Payment
Send complete ms. SASE. Response time varies. Publication
in 1–3 years. Royalty, varies.

Editor's Comments
We publish books of all genres for children from preschool age
through age 12, but we do not want holiday books relating to
religion. Halloween, witchcraft, and magic are other topics to
avoid if you wish to submit your work to us.

Moody Publishers

Moody Bible Institute
820 North LaSalle Boulevard
Chicago, IL 60610-3284

Acquisitions Coordinator

Publisher's Interests

This Christian publisher seeks timely, life-issue books that are written to educate and inspire readers. Currently, it is only accepting unsolicited fiction manuscripts submitted by literary agents.

Website: www.moodypublishers.org

Freelance Potential

Published 80 titles in 2003: 8 were by agented authors. Of the 80 titles, 1 was by an unpublished writer and 10 were by authors who were new to the publishing house. Receives 1,000+ queries and unsolicited mss yearly.

- **Fiction:** Published 4 middle-grade books, 8–12 years; and 4 young adult books, 12–18 years. Genres include adventure, Western, fantasy, mystery, suspense, and contemporary and historical fiction. Also publishes biblical fiction.
- **Nonfiction:** Published 1 toddler book, 0–4 years; 4 easy-to-read books, 4–7 years; 2 story picture books, 4–10 years; and 2 young adult books, 12–18 years. Topics include religion, social issues, and sports.
- **Representative Titles:** *Totally Free* by Stephanie Perry Moore (YA) tells the story of a high school girl struggling to resist the temptations of drugs and alcohol; part of the Laurel Shadrach series. *The Sweetest Story Ever Told* by Lysa TerKeurst tells about a family whose Christmas sugar cookies spread the miracle of Jesus's birth.

Submissions and Payment

Guidelines available. Query with résumé, outline/synopsis, and 3 sample chapters for fiction. Accepts nonfiction proposals through agents or manuscript services only. SASE. Responds in 2–3 months. Publication in 12–18 months. Payment policy varies.

Editor's Comments

We're currently considering all fiction genres for middle readers and young adults. Send compelling fiction that offers an enjoyable reading experience.

Morehouse Publishing

4475 Linglestown Road
Harrisburg, PA 17112

Editorial Director: Debra Farrington

Publisher's Interests
This religious publisher features fiction and nonfiction titles for young readers from toddlers through middle-grade students. Its books are all written from a Christian point of view and focus on ideas that will help young people understand theological and spiritual concepts.
Website: www.morehousegroup.com

Freelance Potential
Published 4 titles in 2003. Receives 300 mss yearly.
- **Fiction:** Publishes early picture books, 0–4 years; and easy-to-read books, 4–7 years. Genres include inspirational and religious fiction.
- **Nonfiction:** Publishes toddler books, 0–4 years; and easy-to-read books, 4–7 years. Topics include the sacraments, religion, and Christian concepts.
- **Representative Titles:** *Thank God for Rocks* by Esther Bender (3–6 years) is the story of a farmer who, through his faith in God, helps turn a rock-filled farm into the most fertile land in the area. *Bless This Day* by Anne E. Kitch (0–4 years) features short rhyming prayers that capture the Psalms in a language young children will understand.

Submissions and Payment
Guidelines available. Send complete ms with résumé. Accepts photocopies and simultaneous submissions if identified. SASE for US returns only. Responds in 3 months. Publication in 2 years. Royalty; advance.

Editor's Comments
Our goal is to publish the best and most innovative books possible for the mainstream Christian marketplace. Most of our books target children between three and eight. Because our books are written from a Christian point of view, we look for materials that will help children understand the word of God in their faith. We are always interested in writers who can take a fresh look at such topics as faith, prayer, grace, forgiveness, and the church. Seasonal submissions are welcome, too.

Thomas More Publishing

200 East Bethany Drive
Allen, TX 75002

Acquisitions Director: Debra Hampton

Publisher's Interests

Books on contemporary issues for American Catholics are the focus of Thomas More Publishing. It publishes books for parents and teachers as well as a few titles for middle-grade and young adult readers. Its works cover topics such as prayer, Scripture, meditation, personal growth, and inspiration.
Website: www.thomasmore.com

Freelance Potential

Published 20 titles in 2003: 2 were developed from unsolicited submissions and 8 were by agented authors. Receives 240 queries yearly.

- **Nonfiction:** Publishes middle-grade books, 8–12 years. Also offers teacher guides, catechism materials, and educational programs, pre-K–grade 12. Topics include the sacraments, family life, Christian living, leadership, and the lives of the saints.
- **Representative Titles:** *From the Heart of a Father* by William Johnson (parents) is a book of letters, stories, and inspirational words about how a father would like to be remembered by his children. *Creating a Successful Youth Retreat* by Mark J. Furlan takes the reader through the components found in a good retreat and includes ideas for planning prayer services and spiritual exercises.

Submissions and Payment

Query with outline or table of contents, introduction and/or first chapter, and curriculum vitae. Accepts photocopies and computer printouts. No simultaneous submissions. SASE. Responds in 2 months. Publication in 6 months. Payment rate varies.

Editor's Comments

All of the material we publish is grounded in the Catholic faith and is based on Vatican II and the *Catechism of the Catholic Church*. While most of the titles we publish target adult readers, we do offer books for parents and teachers who work with children and young adults.

Morgan Reynolds Publishing

Suite 223
620 South Elm Street
Greensboro, NC 27406

Acquisitions Editor: Elaine Hammer

Publisher's Interests

Morgan Reynolds publishes serious-minded nonfiction titles
for children and young adults that complement the elementary and secondary school curricula. Most of its titles focus
on important events or interesting figures, both contemporary
and historical.
Website: www.morganreynolds.com

Freelance Potential

Published 18 titles in 2003: 8 were developed from unsolicited submissions. Of the 18 titles, 2 were by authors who
were new to the publishing house. Receives 400 queries,
300 unsolicited mss yearly.

- **Nonfiction:** Published 18 young adult books, 10+ years. Topics
  include history, music, science, business, feminism, and world
  events. Also publishes biographies.
- **Representative Titles:** *Nicolaus Copernicus* by William J.
  Boerst (10+ years) profiles the scientist whose sun-centered
  model of the universe started the astronomical achievements of
  the Scientific Revolution; part of the Great Scientists series.
  Gwendolyn Brooks: Poet from Chicago by Martha E. Rhynes
  (10+ years) portrays the life of a writer whose poetry celebrated
  being an African-American woman in a predominantly white
  culture; part of the World Writers series.

Submissions and Payment

Guidelines available. Query with outline and sample chapter;
or send complete ms. Accepts photocopies, computer printouts, and simultaneous submissions if identified. SASE.
Responds to queries in 1 month; to unsolicited mss in 1–2
months. Publication in 6–12 months. Royalty; advance.

Editor's Comments

Biographies of interesting world leaders, writers, and African
Americans are what we're looking for at this time. Do not send
biographies of obscure figures or pop-culture icons such as
rock stars, movie stars, and sports figures. Remember, we do
not publish fiction, memoirs, picture books, or poetry.

National Association for the Education of Young Children

1509 16th Street NW
Washington, DC 20036-1426

Publications Editor: Carol Copple

Publisher's Interests
The target audience of this educational publisher includes caregivers, teachers, and parents who interact on a regular basis with young children up to the age of eight. Nonfiction titles on topics such as nutrition, language, family relationships, and other timely subjects are integral to its list.
Website: www.naeyc.org

Freelance Potential
Published 5 titles in 2003: 3 were developed from unsolicited submissions and 1 was a reprint/licensed property. Of the 5 titles, 3 were by authors who were new to the publishing house. Receives 50 queries yearly.
- **Nonfiction:** Publishes educational materials for adults and parents. Topics include professional development, family relationships, health, nutrition, assessment, language and literacy, social and emotional development, and violence.
- **Representative Titles:** *Changing Kindergartens: Four Success Stories* (educators) presents ideas for making kindergarten programs developmentally appropriate as well as suggestions for making a successful change for a young child. *Teaching in the Key of Life* by Mimi Brodsky Chenfeld (teachers) offers ideas for successful teaching methods that include joy, openness, love, and playfulness.

Submissions and Payment
Guidelines available. Query with outline and 3 sample chapters. Accepts photocopies and computer printouts. No simultaneous submissions. SASE. Responds in 1 month. Publication period varies. No payment.

Editor's Comments
Our books are written for a diverse audience that includes educators, caregivers, and parents, and we tend to favor queries that focus on one of our groups; no title can meet the needs of every reader. Send us a query that demonstrates your ability to bring your audience definitive information and the latest research on a specific topic.

National Council of Teachers of English

1111 West Kenyon Road
Urbana, IL 61801-1096

Director of Book Publications: Zarina Hock

Publisher's Interests

This professional association of English and language arts teachers offers resource books for educators working at the kindergarten through college levels. Its titles cover teaching theory and practice as well as research findings and their classroom applications.
Website: www.ncte.org

Freelance Potential

Published 15 titles in 2003. Receives 150 queries yearly.

- **Nonfiction:** Publishes books for English and language arts educators working with students in grades K–12, as well as with college students. Topics include writing, reading, grammar, literature, diversity and society, poetry, censorship, media studies, technology, research, and teaching ideas.
- **Representative Titles:** *The Writing Workshop* by Katie Wood Ray & Lester L. Laminack (teachers, grades 3–8) addresses the challenges of the writing workshop with chapters on day-to-day instruction, classroom management, and developing writing identities. *Studying Literature* by Brian Moon (teachers, grades 9–12) includes literary texts as well as discussions and exercises to help students investigate the values and practices that underlie literary activity.

Submissions and Payment

Guidelines available. Query with cover letter, formal proposal, chapter summaries, and table of contents. SASE. Responds in 1–2 weeks. Publication in 18 months. Royalty, varies.

Editor's Comments

Even if you have a complete manuscript, we ask you to follow our guidelines and submit only portions of your book. In your cover letter, tell us something about you that will help us distinguish your work from that of others. Use your query as an opportunity to tell us what makes this book valuable and how it compares to others in the field. Current research and issues in language arts education and all types of strategies for teaching English are all acceptable topics.

National Geographic Society

1145 17th Street NW
Washington, DC 20036-4688

Submissions Editor: Nancy Feresten

Publisher's Interests
Books about history and the natural world are the specialty
of this well-known publisher. It offers nonfiction on a variety
of topics for readers through the early teen years, as well as
some fictional picture books and middle-grade mystery and
adventure novels.
Website: www.nationalgeographic.com

Freelance Potential
Published 75 titles (25 juvenile) in 2003. Receives 120–240
queries, 150 unsolicited mss yearly.
- **Fiction:** Publishes story picture books, 4–10 years; and middle-grade novels, 8–12 years. Genres include mystery, adventure, and books about nature and the environment.
- **Nonfiction:** Publishes story picture books, 4–10 years; chapter
books, 5–10 years; and middle-grade books, 8–12 years. Topics
include history, nature, science, technology, animals, pets,
geography, and the environment. Also publishes biographies;
informational books, 3+ years; and reference titles, 10+ years.
- **Representative Titles:** *Servant to Abigail Adams* by Kate Con-
nell (8–12 years) mixes fact and fiction in a story about a
house servant employed by John and Abigail Adams. *An Interview with Harry the Tarantula* by Leigh Ann Tyson (4–8 years)
is a picture book about a talk show host who interviews a
tarantula to teach her audience about the world of spiders.

Submissions and Payment
Query with outline and sample chapter. Send complete ms
for short works. Accepts photocopies and simultaneous submissions if identified. SASE. Responds to queries in 1 month,
to mss in 3+ months. Flat fee.

Editor's Comments
We're looking for high-quality, well-written books that offer a
fresh and unique approach to the subject matter they address.
Most of our books are nonfiction, but we do offer some educational stories that combine fact with fiction. You must be an
expert on the topic you are writing about.

Naturegraph Publishers

P.O. Box 1047
3543 Indian Creek Road
Happy Camp, CA 96039

Managing Editor: Barbara Brown

Publisher's Interests
Naturegraph Publishers has been producing books about
natural history, Native American subjects, and the outdoors
since 1946. Both fiction and nonfiction titles appear in its
catalogue. It primarily targets adults, but some of its titles
are read by preteens and young adults.
Website: www.naturegraph.com

Freelance Potential
Published 2 titles in 2003: both were developed from unsolicited submissions. Of the 2 titles, 1 was by an unpublished
writer and 2 were by authors who were new to the publishing
house. Receives 400 queries yearly.
- **Fiction:** Publishes middle-grade novels, 8–12 years; and young
  adult books, 12–18 years. Genres include mythology, folktales,
  and Native American lore.
- **Nonfiction:** Publishes middle-grade books, 8–12 years; and
  young adult books, 12–18 years. Topics include Native Americans, American wildlife, animals, the environment, crafts, hiking, and backpacking. Also publishes field guides for all ages.
- **Representative Titles:** *The Winds Erase Your Footprints* by
  Shiyowin Miller is the true story of a Navajo family, their rela-
  tives, and their community in the 1930s. *Exploring Pacific
  Coast Tidepools* by Vinson Brown & Ane Rovetta is a field
  guide that describes 341 of the most common species of flora
  and fauna in the intertidal zone of the Pacific Coast.

Submissions and Payment
Guidelines available at website. Query with outline and 1–2
sample chapters. Accepts photocopies and computer printouts.
SASE. Response time and publication period vary. Royalty.

Editor's Comments
This year we're looking for nonfiction Native American titles
dealing with specific tribes and books about natural history
subjects. While many of our books are appropriate for
readers ages 10 and up, we do not accept books written
for young children.

Neal-Schuman Publishers

100 Varick Street
New York, NY 10013

Director of Publishing: Charles Harmon

Publisher's Interests
Professional librarians who work in school and public
libraries turn to books from Neal-Schuman Publishers for
information on library services, management, and funding.
Internet-use guides for teachers, researchers, and information specialists are also included in its catalogue.
Website: www.neal-schuman.com

Freelance Potential
Published 28 titles (4 juvenile) in 2003: 5 were developed
from unsolicited submissions and 1 was a reprint/licensed
property. Of the 28 titles, 26 were by unpublished writers.
Receives 300 queries, 300 unsolicited mss yearly.
• **Nonfiction:** Publishes resource materials for school media specialists and public librarians. Topics include curriculum support, the Internet, technology, literary skills, reading programs,
collection development, reference needs, the first amendment,
staff development, management, and communications.
• **Representative Titles:** *Connecting Fathers, Children, and
Reading* by Sara Willoughby-Herb & Steven Herb (librarians)
focuses on the significant effect fathers have on the language
and literacy development of young children and how libraries
can foster this connection. *Hooking Teens with the Net* by Linda
K. Braun (librarians and teachers) shows educators how to
integrate popular young adult sites into teaching math, science, language arts, and social studies.

Submissions and Payment
Guidelines available. Prefers query with résumé, outline,
table of contents, and sample chapter. Will accept complete
ms. Accepts photocopies and computer printouts. SASE.
Responds to queries in 2 weeks, to mss in 1–2 months. Publication in 10–12 months. Royalty.

Editor's Comments
Currently, we're interested in seeing proposals for books on
information literacy and reading motivation. Internet-use
guides are also still a top editorial priority.

New Canaan Publishing Company

P.O. Box 752
New Canaan, CT 06840

Editor

Publisher's Interests
This publisher offers a variety of titles, from inspirational books on Christian living, theology, and Bible studies for both adults and children, to educational fiction and nonfiction for children from first through ninth grade.
Website: www.newcanaanpublishing.com

Freelance Potential
Published 7 titles (4 juvenile) in 2003.
- **Fiction:** Publishes chapter books, 5–10 years; and middle-grade novels, 8–12 years. Publishes educational stories and stories with strong moral and Christian themes.
- **Nonfiction:** Publishes chapter books, 5–10 years; and middle-grade books, 8–12 years. Publishes supplementary curriculum materials, grades 1–9. Also offers devotionals.
- **Representative Titles:** *My Daddy Is a Guardsman* by Kirk & Sharron Hilbrecht (4–7 years) helps children understand the job of a soldier in the National Guard and why a parent in the Guard may have to be away from home for a long time. *The Grundilini* by Benjamin Doolittle (YA) is a novel that illustrates the power of love over hate, and the ultimate triumph of good over evil.

Submissions and Payment
Guidelines available. Query with synopsis; or send complete ms. Accepts photocopies and computer printouts. SASE. Responds in 10–12 months. Publication period and payment policy vary.

Editor's Comments
The materials and books we produce are designed to complement rather than replace existing curriculum materials. We look for books that will inspire a child to study on his own, and go beyond what he has learned in class. Books on science and history topics, targeted to students in grades one through nine, are always of interest to us. For the general public, we seek innovative books on Christian topics such as the Christian home, pastoral aids, and devotional studies.

The New England Press

P.O. Box 575
Shelburne, VT 05482

Managing Editor: Christopher Bray

Publisher's Interests
Established in 1978, this regional publisher features fiction
and nonfiction titles tied to the heritage and history of northern New England. Its list includes titles for middle-grade and
young adult readers as well as adults. All of its books relate
directly to the region.
Website: www.nepress.com

Freelance Potential
Published 3 titles (1 juvenile) in 2003: all were developed
from unsolicited submissions. Of the 3 titles, 1 was by an
unpublished writer and 2 were by authors who were new to
the publishing house. Receives 300 queries yearly.
- **Fiction:** Published 2 middle-grade novels, 8–12 years. Also
  publishes young adult novels, 12–18 years. Genres include
  regional and historical fiction set in Vermont and northern
  New England.
- **Nonfiction:** Publishes middle-grade books, 8–12 years; and
  young adult books, 12–18 years. Topics include history,
  nature, and subjects related to Vermont. Also publishes
  biographies.
- **Representative Titles:** *Father by Blood* by Louella Bryant (YA)
  is told from the point of view of John Brown's daughter Annie,
  a young woman who finds herself at a crossroads in history.
  Captive of Pittsford Ridge by Janice Ovecka takes place during
  the Revolutionary War and is the story of a young boy who
  comes upon a wounded enemy soldier.

Submissions and Payment
Query with sample chapter. SASE. Responds in 3 months.
Publication in 18 months. Royalty.

Editor's Comments
We are primarily interested in manuscripts related to Vermont
and northern New England, but we will consider submissions
on other areas of the New England region. Our need continues
to be for historical fiction and biographies for young adults
about famous New Englanders.

New Harbinger Publications

5674 Shattuck Avenue
Oakland, CA 94609

Acquisitions Editor: Tesilya Hanauer

Publisher's Interests
Targeting an audience that includes mental health professionals as well as lay persons, New Harbinger Publications'
list includes self-help and health books that teach readers
the skills they need in a given situation. Topics covered
include divorce, coping with grief and self-esteem. Books for
children through adults are found in its catalogue.
Website: www.newharbinger.com

Freelance Potential
Published 43 titles (3 juvenile) in 2003: 10 were developed
from unsolicited submissions and 10 were by agented
authors. Of the 43 titles, 10 were by unpublished writers and
30 were by authors who were new to the publishing house.
Receives 600 queries yearly.
- **Nonfiction:** Publishes self-help psychology and health books
  for lay people as well as professionals.
- **Representative Titles:** *Helping Your Depressed Child* by
  Martha Underwood Barnard (parents) teaches parents how to
  evaluate different therapies, how to find professional help for
  their child, and how to understand the many pharmacological
  treatments available. *Kids Today, Parents Tomorrow* by Kim
  Paleg is a complete research-based student reader that teaches
  parenting and relationship skills to high school students.

Submissions and Payment
Guidelines and catalogue available with 9x12 SASE ($.57
postage). Query. Accepts photocopies and email submissions
to tesilya@newharbinger.com. SASE. Responds in 2–4 weeks.
Publication in 1 year. Royalty, 10%.

Editor's Comments
We look for innovative ideas on helping readers overcome, cope
with, or manage a psychological or health problem. If you're
seeking the right medium for reaching a wider audience with
your treatment strategies, send us a query. Our collaborative,
experienced team will review the viability of your idea and will
work with you throughout the developmental process.

New Hope Publishers

100 Missionary Ridge
Birmingham, AL 35242-5235

Manuscript Submissions

Publisher's Interests
New Hope Publishers is no longer publishing children's books. This publisher offers quality books for women about Christian living, including parenting titles with spiritual themes and nonfiction books that motivate families to share Christ's hope.
Website: www.newhopepubl.com

Freelance Potential
Published 24 titles in 2003: 2 were developed from unsolicited submissions, 4 were by agented authors, and 2 were reprint/licensed properties. Of the 24 titles, 4 were by unpublished writers and 12 were by authors who were new to the publishing house. Receives 40–50 queries, 300 unsolicited mss yearly.
- **Nonfiction:** Publishes inspirational and spiritual books for women and families. Topics include prayer, spirituality, the Bible, and family issues.
- **Representative Titles:** *Traveling Together* by Karla Worley (adults) explores accountability, ministering through struggles, and other issues, always with a focus on helping friends. *Settling for Less Than God's Best?* by Elsa Kok (adults) is full of practical tools to guide women toward God's heart in their search for the right guy.

Submissions and Payment
Guidelines available. Prefers proposal and sample chapter. Will accept query with outline or complete ms. SASE. Response time varies. Royalty. Flat fee.

Editor's Comments
Our mission is to equip our readers to share the hope we profess with families, friends, and the world. We are experiencing unprecedented growth and are open to submissions of books that will help our readers realize their spiritual potential. Please remember that our current focus is on books for women and families. Do not send manuscripts for children's books.

New Leaf Press

P.O. Box 726
Green Forest, AR 72638

Acquisitions Editor: Roger Howerton

Publisher's Interests
The books for young readers on this Christian publisher's list include only nonfiction books that are creation-based. New Leaf Press also offers supplementary materials for home-schooling on all grade levels.
Website: www.newleafpress.com

Freelance Potential
Published 23 titles (6 juvenile) in 2003: 3 were developed from unsolicited submissions and 3 were reprint/licensed properties. Of the 23 titles, 4 were by authors who were new to the publishing house. Receives 600 queries yearly.
- **Nonfiction:** Published 5 middle-grade books, 8–12 years; and 5 young adult books, 12–18 years. Also publishes early picture books, 0–4 years. Topics include current events, history, health and fitness, humor, nature and the environment, social issues, science, technology, and religion.
- **Representative Titles:** *Come Home to Comfort* by Sharon Hoffman (parents) explores how to turn a house into a home where love resides. *G.I. Joe and Lillie* by Joseph S. Bonsall (adults) tells the true-life story of the wartime romance of the author's parents; written by a member of the Oak Ridge Boys. *Eight P.R.O.M.I.S.E.S.* by Dan & Dave Davidson (YA) is a devotional that makes difficult spiritual truths accessible to teens.

Submissions and Payment
Guidelines and catalogue available with 9x12 SASE (5 first-class stamps). Query with cover letter, table of contents, synopsis, and sample chapter. Accepts photocopies and simultaneous submissions. SASE. Responds in 3 months. Publication in 12–18 months. Royalty, 10% of net.

Editor's Comments
All of our titles are written to bring the lost to Christ. We are looking for books that meet the needs of the family, books written especially for women, and books that would fit into a gift line. We do not publish poetry or fiction, and are always interested in projects related to creationism.

Newmarket Press

15th Floor
18 East 48th Street
New York, NY 10017

Executive Editor: Keith Hollaman

Publisher's Interests
Books about parenting and child care are available from
Newmarket Press. It also offers self-help and psychology
titles, as well as books about drama, the performing arts,
health, nutrition, and personal finance. This publisher is no
longer developing titles for children.
Website: www.newmarketpress.com

Freelance Potential
Published 45 titles in 2003: most were by agented authors.
Receives 1,200 queries yearly.
- **Nonfiction:** Publishes parenting and self-help books. Topics
  include child care, health, fitness, nutrition, sports, business,
  history, and multicultural and ethnic issues. Also publishes
  biographies.
- **Representative Titles:** *Baby Massage: Parent-Child Bonding
  Through Touch* by Amelia Auckett (parents) is a fully-illustrated
  book that offers a time-tested approach to the techniques and
  benefits of parent-child touch. *From Diapers to Dating* by Debra
  W. Haffner (parents) is a guide to raising sexually healthy children, from infancy to middle school.

Submissions and Payment
Query with outline, table of contents, marketing information, clips, and detailed author biography. Accepts photocopies. SASE. Responds in 1–3 months. Publication in 1
year. Royalty; advance.

Editor's Comments
We are one of the few mainstream trade publishing houses in
New York City under independent, entrepreneurial ownership.
While we are no longer publishing titles written for children, we
do continue to specialize in books about child care and parenting. If you have a title that might interest us, log on to our
website and follow our guidelines for editorial submissions. In
your query, be sure to include marketing information and
information on competing or similar titles. Tell us what sets
your book apart from existing books.

New Society Publishers

P.O. Box 189
Gabriola Island, British Columbia V0R 1X0
Canada

Publisher: Christopher Plant

Publisher's Interests
The mission of this progressive publisher is to bring readers books that help build ecological sustainability and a just society. It is committed to fundamental social change through nonviolent action.
Website: www.newsociety.com

Freelance Potential
Published 20 titles in 2003: 6–8 were developed from unsolicited submissions, 2 were by agented authors, and 2 were reprint/licensed properties. Of the 20 titles, 8 were by unpublished writers and 16 were by authors who were new to the publishing house. Receives 300 queries yearly.
- **Nonfiction:** Publishes college guides and career resources for young adults. Also publishes titles on education systems, family issues, child development, sustainability, business practices, leadership, feminism, diversity, and community issues for adults.
- **Representative Titles:** *Dumbing Us Down* by John Gatto (educators) explores the tenets of public education and how they fail our children. *Connecting Kids* by Linda Hill explores diversity and helps children celebrate our differences through the use of games and skill-building ideas.

Submissions and Payment
Guidelines available. Query with proposal, table of contents, and sample chapter. SAE/IRC. Responds in 2–3 months. Publication in 1 year. Payment policy varies.

Editor's Comments
While we consider any proposal that fits our broader editorial goals, we are particularly interested in books that fall into these major areas: sustainability, resistance and community, progressive leadership, conscious commerce, educational and parental resources, nonviolence, feminism, and diversity. We cannot give serious consideration to a proposal that does not follow exactly our submission requirements. Please take the time to visit our website before submitting.

NL Associates

P.O. Box 1199
Highstown, NJ 08520

President: Nathan Levy

Publisher's Interests

Titles developed by this publishing house present education
and teaching strategies that encourage a love of learning in
children. Areas typically covered by its books include critical
thinking, special education, classroom management, math,
and language arts.
Website: www.storieswithholes.com

Freelance Potential

Published 5 titles in 2003. Receives 10 queries, 10 unsolicited
mss yearly.

- **Nonfiction:** Publishes educational materials and activity books
  designed to develop critical thinking skills, grades 1–12.
  Features books on special education and titles for parents
  and educators.
- **Representative Titles:** *Artistry for Children* by Kate McSwain
  (6–16 years) introduces famous artists and art to children
  through a written text for teachers and creative projects for
  children. *Teaching Gifted Kids in the Regular Classroom* by
  Susan Winebrenner (teachers) features a definitive guide to
  meet the learning needs of gifted students who have been
  placed in mixed-ability classrooms.

Submissions and Payment

Query or send complete ms. Response time, publication period,
and payment policy vary.

Editor's Comments

Our goal is to offer our audience—which includes parents as
well as professionals in the educational field—thought-provoking, highly interactive, informative research that will help them
raise pupil achievement. We are always interested in hearing
from writers who can demonstrate the in-depth knowledge we
require of all our authors, combined with a talent for making
learning fun. Review our catalogue and you will see that every
title we publish is connected to gifted education or to the nurturing of critical-thinking skills. If you meet our qualifications,
send us a query that offers a fresh approach.

North Country Books

311 Turner Street
Utica, NY 13501

Publisher: Sheila Orlin

Publisher's Interests
For almost 40 years, North Country Books has been publishing and distributing books about New York State. Its titles focus on the Adirondacks, the Finger Lakes, the Hudson Valley, the Catskills, and other regions of the state, as well as on Native-American and nature topics. It offers family guide books and children's storybooks.

Freelance Potential
Published 7 titles (2 juvenile) in 2003. Of the 7 titles, 3 were by unpublished writers and 4 were by authors who were new to the publishing house. Receives 50–100 queries, 20–30 unsolicited mss yearly.
- **Fiction:** Publishes story picture books, 4–10 years. Features folklore about New York State.
- **Nonfiction:** Published 1 easy-to-read book, 4–7 years; and 1 middle-grade book, 8–12 years. Also publishes biographies, field and trail guides, and art and photography books for adults.
- **Representative Titles:** *Winterfest With Abby and Cooper* by Paula Burns is a picture book about the adventures of two retrievers who travel with their family and tour the attractions of Cooperstown, including the annual Winterfest. *The Rascals for the Environment* by Susan O. Steverman is a story about a courageous and fun-loving group of animals from the Adirondack High Peaks that are interested in caring for the planet.

Submissions and Payment
Guidelines and catalogue available with 9x12 SASE ($2 postage). Query or send complete ms. Accepts photocopies. SASE. Responds to queries in 1–2 months, to mss in 6–12 months. Publication in 2–5 years. Royalty.

Editor's Comments
Most of our titles are nonfiction works that focus on the various regions of upstate New York. We occasionally accept children's fiction that is set in the Catskills, the Hudson Valley, the Adirondacks, Central New York, or western New York.

North-South Books

Suite 1901
875 Sixth Avenue
New York, NY 10001

Submissions Editor

Publisher's Interests
The English-language imprint of Swiss publisher Nord-Süd
Verlag, North-South Books publishes fiction and nonfiction
for children from birth to age 10, featuring translations of
books as well as new titles. It began publishing in the United
States in 1985.
Website: www.northsouth.com

Freelance Potential
Published 30 titles in 2003: all were by agented authors.
- **Fiction:** Publishes concept books, toddler books, and early
  picture books, 0–4 years; easy-to-read books, 4–7 years; story
  picture books, 4–10 years; and chapter books, 5–10 years.
  Genres include adventure, drama, fairy tales, folklore, fantasy,
  humor, mystery, nature, the environment, and ethnic, multicultural, and contemporary fiction.
- **Nonfiction:** Publishes early picture books, 0–4 years. Topics
  include animals, hobbies, crafts, humor, nature, religion, science, technology, social issues, sports, and multicultural and
  ethnic issues.
- **Representative Titles:** *Bailey the Bear Cub* by Nannie Kuiper
  (5–8 years) follows a cub as he takes his first steps on his journey to independence and maturity. *Old Beaver* by Udo Weigelt
  (5–8 years) is a story that explores the theme that wisdom and
  experience is just as important as youth and strength.

Submissions and Payment
Accepts mss through literary agents only. Royalty; advance.

Editor's Comments
Our motto is quality over quantity, and we will consider only
the very best new material for publication. Writers familiar with
the works we have published may submit their manuscripts to
us through their agents if they believe their work can meet our
high standards and bring pleasure to children and adults for
many years to come. Our books have been translated into
more than 30 languages, and we enjoy bringing authors and
illustrators from different nations together.

Novalis

Saint Paul University
223 Main Street
Ottawa, Ontario K1S 1C4
Canada

Commissioning Editor: Kevin Burns

Publisher's Interests
Novalis publishes periodicals, books, brochures, and audiovisual resources that help adults and children to explore their religious heritage, to live their faith, and to create a more just world. It is part of St. Paul University, a Roman Catholic center of learning affiliated with the University of Ottawa.
Website: www.novalis.ca

Freelance Potential
Published 60 titles (5 juvenile) in 2003: 5 were developed from unsolicited submissions and 3 were by agented authors. Of the 60 titles, 12 were by unpublished writers and 12 were by authors who were new to the publishing house. Receives 150 queries, 100 unsolicited mss yearly.
- **Nonfiction:** Publishes early picture books, 0–4 years; story picture books, 4–10 years; and young adult books, 12–18 years. Topics include biography, history, and religion. Also publishes reference titles, self-help books, and books in series.
- **Representative Titles:** *Growing Up a Friend of Jesus* by Francoise Darcy-Bérube & John Paul Bérube encourages children to live a life of prayer and integrity. *The Adventures of Fergie* by Nancy Cocks encourages communication within the family.

Submissions and Payment
Guidelines available. Query with clips. Accepts photocopies, disk submissions, and email to kburns@ustpaul.ca. No simultaneous submissions. SAE/IRC. Responds in 2 months. Publication in 12–18 months. Royalty; advance.

Editor's Comments
Our mission at Novalis is to express the Christian faith to contemporary culture in an understandable and accessible manner and in a spirit of ecumenical openness, while remaining faithful to the Scriptures and Tradition. We are looking for books on any topic pertaining to faith and values, particularly submissions of parent and teacher resources that address issues concerning the spiritual lives of children. Check our guidelines for specifics on preparing a proposal.

The Oliver Press

5707 West 36th Street
Minneapolis, MN 55416-2510

Editors: Jenna Anderson & Denise Sterling

Publisher's Interests
This nonfiction publisher covers the fields of business, government, politics, history, medicine, science and technology, and social issues for readers from the elementary grades through high school.
Website: www.oliverpress.com

Freelance Potential
Published 11 titles in 2003: 1 was developed from an unsolicited submission. Of the 11 titles, 1 was by an author who was new to the publishing house. Receives 100 queries yearly.
- **Nonfiction:** Published 4 easy-to-read books, 4–7 years; and 8 young adult books, 12–18 years. Topics include aviation and space flight, business and labor, crime and justice, government and politics, medicine, science and technology, social issues, and prominent women.
- **Representative Titles:** *Business Builders in Fashion* by Jacqueline C. Kent (grades 5 and up) explores the lives and businesses of seven men and women leaders of the fashion industry; part of the Business Builders series. *Meteorology: Predicting the Weather* by Susan & Steven Wills (grades 5 and up) introduces seven scientists whose work advanced weather measurement and prediction; part of the Innovators series.

Submissions and Payment
Guidelines available. Query with résumé, outline, and writing sample. Accepts photocopies, computer printouts, and simultaneous submissions if identified. SASE. Responds in 3–6 months. Publication in 1–2 years. Flat fee, $1,000.

Editor's Comments
We'd like to add to two of our series: Innovators and Business Builders. Innovators introduces readers to scientists who invented technologies that changed the everyday lives of people all over the world. Business Builders spotlights those whose ventures into new fields created jobs, new products, and new technology for others. We invite writers to submit a proposal on a topic that may be a good addition to one of these series.

Orca Book Publishers

P.O. Box 468
Custer, WA 98240-0468

Publisher: Bob Tyrrell

Publisher's Interests

Everything this children's book publisher features, from picture books and chapter books, to middle-grade novels and young adult titles, is written by Canadian authors. Regional and historical fiction are its specialty.
Website: www.orcabook.com

Freelance Potential

Published 60 titles in 2003: 30 were developed from unsolicited submissions, 15 were by agented authors, and 2 were reprint/licensed properties. Receives 1,000 queries, 500 unsolicited mss yearly.

- **Fiction:** Published 5 easy-to-read books, 4–7 years; 10 story picture books, 4–10 years; 10 chapter books, 5–10 years; 15 middle-grade books, 8–12 years; and 15 young adult books, 12–18 years. Genres include contemporary, regional, and historical fiction.
- **Representative Titles:** *Arizona Charlie and the Klondike Kid* by Julie Lawson (4–8 years) is a story about a young boy who longs to become a Wild West star like Arizona Charlie and earn the title of "Klondike Kid." *Marilou Cries Wolf* by Raymond Plante (6–9 years) tells of a girl who uses the telephone to play a prank, but soon gets in over her head.

Submissions and Payment

Canadian authors only. Guidelines available. Query with 2–3 sample chapters for fiction. Send complete ms for picture books. Accepts photocopies and computer printouts. SASE. Responds to queries in 6 weeks, to mss in 2–3 months. Publication in 18–24 months. Royalty, 10% split; advance.

Editor's Comments

We are particularly interested in teen fiction, books for young readers, chapter books, and picture books. We need contemporary stories or fantasy with universal themes, compelling plots, and strong, young protagonists who learn and grow during the course of the story, and who use their own ingenuity to solve the problems in front of them.

Orchard Books

Scholastic, Inc.
555 Broadway
New York, NY 10012-3999

Vice President/Editorial Director: Ken Geist

Publisher's Interests

Orchard Books is an imprint of Scholastic, Inc. Each year it
offers a list that includes hardcover picture books for the very
young, stories for emerging readers, and novels for middle-
graders and young adults. It also publishes some nonfiction.
10% self-, subsidy-, co-venture, or co-op published material.
Website: www.scholastic.com

Freelance Potential

Published 60 titles in 2003: 10 were by agented authors and
12 were reprint/licensed properties. Of the 60 titles, 1 was by
an unpublished writer and 20 were by authors who were new
to the publishing house. Receives 5,000 queries yearly.
- **Fiction:** Publishes concept books, toddler books, and early
  picture books, 0–4 years; story picture books, 4–10 years;
  chapter books, 5–10 years; and middle-grade books, 8–12
  years. Genres include historical, contemporary, and multicultural fiction; fairy tales; folktales; fantasy; humor; and stories
  about sports.
- **Nonfiction:** Publishes story picture books, 4–10 years. Topics
  include history, nature, the environment, and social issues.
- **Representative Titles:** *Miss Hunnicutt's Hat* by Jeff Brumbeau
  (4–8 years) is a picture book about a woman who wants to
  wear a hat with a chicken on the top when the Queen comes to
  town. *Gathering the Dew* by Minfong Ho (11–15 years) is a
  novel written in the first person about a girl whose family is
  forced to evacuate Phnom Penh when the Communists take
  over the city.

Submissions and Payment

Guidelines available. Query only. No unsolicited mss. SASE.

Editor's Comments

Although we receive thousands of queries each year, we do
occasionally choose a title from an unpublished writer, and
many of the books we select are by authors who have never
published with us before. Original picture books always have
the chance of making it out of the slush pile.

Our Sunday Visitor

200 Noll Plaza
Huntington, IN 46750

Acquisitions Editor

Publisher's Interests
The books produced by this Catholic publisher are sold primarily to parishes, schools, and religious bookstores, in addition to the individual consumer. It offers trade titles of a religious nature, religious education materials, magazines, and a weekly newspaper.
Website: www.osv.com

Freelance Potential
Published 51 titles (8 juvenile) in 2003: 1 was developed from an unsolicited submission and 2 were reprint/licensed properties. Receives 1,300 queries yearly.

- **Nonfiction:** Publishes concept books, 0–4 years; story picture books, 4–10 years; chapter books, 5–10 years; middle-grade books, 8–12 years; and young adult books, 12–18 years. Topics include family issues, parish life, church heritage, and the lives of the saints. Also publishes reference titles and prayer books.
- **Representative Titles:** *The Caterpillar That Came to Church* by Irene H. Hooker et al. (4–6 years) introduces children to Holy Communion through the eyes of a curious caterpillar. *Where the Big River Runs* by Carole Therese Plum (3–6 years) follows two squirrels and a sparrow as they search for a new home.

Submissions and Payment
Guidelines available. Query with résumé and sample chapters. Accepts photocopies, computer printouts, and simultaneous submissions if identified. SASE. Responds in 2–3 months. Publication in 1+ years. Royalty; advance. Flat fee.

Editor's Comments
We are dedicated to publishing materials of use to Catholics everywhere. Your query should detail your qualifications for writing your proposed book and include a summary of your personal and professional background. Explain how you plan to research your topic. Compare your proposed book to others on the same subject and tell us what will make yours unique. We always encourage authors to lend their ideas and expertise to the selling of their own books.

The Overmountain Press

P.O. Box 1261
Johnson City, TN 37605

Managing Editor: Daniel Lewis

Publisher's Interests

Southern Appalachia is the subject of the regional children's
books published by The Overmountain Press. Its juvenile list
includes picture books and books about Southern
Appalachia history for students in grades three through ten.
It also offers collections of tall tales and folklore. For adults it
offers cookbooks, guidebooks, and regional history titles.
Website: www.overmountainpress.com

Freelance Potential

Published 32 titles (7 juvenile) in 2003: 3 were developed
from unsolicited submissions, 3 were by agented authors,
and 1 was a reprint/licensed property. Receives 500 queries
each year.

- **Fiction:** Publishes early picture books, 0–4 years; middle-grade
  books, 8–12 years; and young adult books, 12–18 years. Genres include folklore, folktales, mystery, and regional fiction.
- **Nonfiction:** Publishes story picture books, 4–10 years; and
  chapter books, 5–10 years. Topics include Southern
  Appalachia.
- **Representative Titles:** *The Lonely Ameba* by Joshua P. Warren
  tells the story of an ameba named Emo whose soul longs for
  companionship. *Flea Market Fleas from A to Z* by Thelma Kerns
  is an illustrated book about a boy who is disappointed when
  there are no fleas at the flea market.

Submissions and Payment

Guidelines available at website or with 6x9 SASE ($.85
postage). Query with résumé and sample chapters; send
complete ms for the History Series for Young Readers.
Accepts photocopies and computer printouts. SASE.
Responds in 2–3 months. Publication in 1 year. Royalty, 15%.

Editor's Comments

Although we have published a few exceptions, we are now
accepting regional children's titles that focus on Southern
Appalachia only. Illustrated, nonfiction history books for
middle-grade readers are especially welcome.

Richard C. Owen Publishers

P.O. Box 585
Katonah, NY 10536

Director of Children's Books: Janice Boland

Publisher's Interests
The focus of Richard C. Owen Publishers is literacy education with an emphasis on teaching reading and writing from a child-centered, meaning-centered perspective. Its list offers books for readers up to the age of 10. Original fiction and fascinating nonfiction on a wide variety of subjects are all part of the company's publishing program.
Website: www.RCOwen.com

Freelance Potential
Published 15 titles in 2003: all were developed from unsolicited submissions. Of the 15 titles, 10 were by authors new to the publishing house. Receives 1,000 unsolicited mss yearly.
- **Fiction:** Publishes easy-to-read books, 4–7 years; story picture books, 4–10 years; and chapter books, 5–10 years. Genres include mystery; humor; folktales; contemporary fiction; stories about animals and nature; and books about social, ethnic, and multicultural issues.
- **Nonfiction:** Publishes easy-to-read books, 4–7 years; story picture books, 4–10 years; and chapter books, 5–10 years. Topics include current events, geography, music, science, nature, and the environment. Also publishes resource materials, professional development titles, and parenting books.
- **Representative Titles:** *Breakfast with John* (grades K–2) is about a boy who shares his breakfast with a special friend. *Birth of Earth* (grades 5–7) explains the events that occurred in space to form our planet; part of the News Extra series.

Submissions and Payment
Guidelines available. Send complete ms. Accepts photocopies, computer printouts, and simultaneous submissions. SASE. Responds in 3–6 months. Publication period and payment policy vary.

Editor's Comments
We look for fiction that is original, contemporary, and realistic. For older kids, we want to see high-interest, easy-reading manuscripts that are fresh and snappy.

Owl Books

Suite 200
51 Front Street East
Toronto, Ontario M5E 1B3
Canada

Submissions Editor: Anne Shone

Publisher's Interests

For more than 20 years, this Canadian publisher has prided itself on its innovative nonfiction and fact-based fiction. Its titles cover a diverse range of topics, from science and history to crafts and humor. Books for children up to the age of 12 are found in its catalogue.

Freelance Potential

Published 10 titles in 2003. Receives 1,000+ queries yearly.

- **Fiction:** Publishes early picture books, 0–4 years; easy-to-read books, 4–7 years; and middle-grade fiction, 8–12 years. Genres include contemporary fiction.
- **Nonfiction:** Publishes concept and early picture books, 0–4 years; and middle-grade books, 8–12 years. Topics include science, nature, sports, and Canadian history. Also publishes photo essays.
- **Representative Titles:** *Mummies* by Sylvia Funston (8–12 years) introduces readers to some famous and lesser-known mummies and to the techniques that have helped scientists learn about the mummies, including DNA research. *Nose to Toes* by Marilyn Baillie (3–8 years) invites young children to experiment with all the amazing things their bodies can do—everything from flopping feet like a duck to pretending to be a turtle.

Submissions and Payment

Send complete ms for fiction. Query with outline, sample chapter, and clips or writing samples for nonfiction. Accepts photocopies, computer printouts, and simultaneous submissions if identified. SAE/IRC. Responds in 2–3 months. Publication in 2 years. Royalty.

Editor's Comments

A look through our catalogue will show you that our interests include many different kinds of material. We continue to seek queries and manuscripts for both fiction and nonfiction. Keep in mind that we look for authors with a special style who can engage the wonder in children and parents alike.

Pacific Educational Press

6365 Biological Sciences Road
Faculty of Education, University of British Columbia
Vancouver, British Columbia V6T 1Z4
Canada

Director: Catherine Edwards

Publisher's Interests

This publisher's primary audience is educators working in
kindergarten through twelfth-grade classrooms. It specializes
in teacher education programs, resource books, and reference titles. It does, however, offer some juvenile titles, including educational nonfiction, chapter books, and novels for
middle-grade readers.
Website: www.pep.educ.ubc.ca

Freelance Potential

Published 4 titles in 2003. Receives 100–150 queries yearly.
- **Fiction:** Publishes chapter books, 5–10 years; and middle-
  grade books, 8–12 years. Genres include historical and multicultural fiction.
- **Nonfiction:** Publishes middle-grade books, 8–12 years; and
  young adult books, 12–18 years. Also publishes books for
  teachers, grades K–12. Topics include mathematics, science,
  social studies, multicultural education, critical thinking, fine
  arts, and administration.
- **Representative Titles:** *A Sea Lion Called Salena* by Dayle
  Campbell Gaetz (8–11 years) is a novel about a lonely 9-year-
  old girl who tries to befriend and help a wounded sea lion pup
  hiding under a wharf near her home. *Moses, Me & Murder* by
  Ann Walsh (7–11 years) is a story based on an unsolved murder that took place in Barkerville, British Columbia.

Submissions and Payment

Guidelines available. Query with résumé, outline, and 2 sample chapters. Accepts photocopies, computer printouts, and
simultaneous submissions if identified. SAE/IRC. Responds
in 4–6 months. Publication in 10–18 months. Royalty.

Editor's Comments

Send us a proposal that includes a detailed, chapter-by-chapter description along with a description of the book's readership and competition. This year, we're particularly interested in
books on mathematics education and First Nations education,
as well as titles about teaching around the world.

Pacific Press Publishing Association

1350 North Kings Road
Nampa, ID 83687

Acquisitions Editor: Tim Lale

Publisher's Interests

The mission of this Christian publisher is to provide readers
with books that will help them to connect with God and
develop a relationship with Him. It is the publishing arm of
the Seventh-day Adventist Church.
Website: www.pacificpress.com

Freelance Potential

Published 30 titles (6–8 juvenile) in 2003: 3 were reprint/
licensed properties. Of the 30 titles, 1 was by an unpublished
writer and 1 was by an author who was new to the publishing house. Receives 150 queries yearly.
- **Fiction:** Publishes easy-to-read books, 4–7 years, chapter
  books, 5–10 years; and middle-grade books, 8–12 years. Genres include mystery, suspense, and adventure.
- **Nonfiction:** Publishes easy-to-read books, 4–7 years; chapter
  books, 5–10 years; and middle-grade books, 8–12 years. Topics
  include animals and children. Also publishes books in series.
- **Representative Titles:** *Detective Zack and the Mystery on the
  Midway* by Jerry D. Thomas is an adventure set at a country
  fair that leads to the discovery of a truth about angels; part of
  the Detective Zack series. *Tina* by Veralee Wiggins is a story of
  a nearly-dead baby fox who survives and thrives under the
  constant care of the young girl who adopts her.

Submissions and Payment

Guidelines available by mail and at website. Query. Accepts
photocopies, computer printouts, disk submissions, and
email submissions to booksubmissions@pacificpress.com.
SASE. Responds in 3 months. Publication in 6–12 months.
Royalty, 6–12%; advance, to $1,500.

Editor's Comments

For the coming year, we are interested in picture books that
help preschoolers deal with death and scary things through
introducing them to Jesus, heaven, and God's love. For middle-school children, we want chapter books, either single or in
series, that relate to children's interests.

Parenting Press, Inc.

P.O. Box 75267
Seattle, WA 98125-6100

Publisher: Carolyn Threadgill

Publisher's Interests

As its name indicates, this small house is devoted to titles
that help parents and professionals to build self-esteem in
young children and teach them practical life skills. It was
established in 1979.
Website: www.parentingpress.com

Freelance Potential

Published 5 titles (2 juvenile) in 2003: 2 were developed from
unsolicited submissions. Of the 5 titles, 2 were by unpublished writers and 2 were by authors who were new to the
publishing house. Receives 1000+ queries yearly.

- **Nonfiction:** Published 1 concept book, 0–4 years; and 1 easy-
  to-read book, 4–7 years. Topics include self-esteem, problem-
  solving, conflict resolution, safety, values, feelings and emotions, and personal boundaries. Also publishes parenting titles.
- **Representative Titles:** *My Grandma Died* by Lory Britain (3–6
  years) assures children that it is normal to feel emotions when
  a loved one has died and helps them learn how to cope with
  grief and loss. *Dealing with Disappointment* by Elizabeth Crary
  (2–12 years) explains that parents are not obligated to make
  their children happy and gives advice on how to teach children
  to cope with frustrations and disappointments.

Submissions and Payment

Guidelines available. Query with outline and clips or writing
samples. Accepts photocopies, computer printouts, and
simultaneous submissions if identified. SASE. Responds in 2
months. Publication in 18–24 months. Royalty, 4–8% of net.

Editor's Comments

New writers, as well as those who have worked with us before,
are welcome. We are always on the lookout for writers who can
contribute a new idea that fits our list. We are particularly
interested in material that deals in options rather than
"shoulds." Review some of our titles and study our guidelines
to gain an understanding of what works for us. Please do not
send children's fiction.

Paulist Press

997 Macarthur Boulevard
Mahwah, NJ 07430

Children's Editor

Publisher's Interests
This Catholic publisher offers a children's list that includes
picture books, activity books, and guides to Catholic rituals
and traditions. All books have Christian or specifically
Catholic themes. It does not accept Bible retellings or general
interest children's books on angels, adoption, or death.
Website: www.paulistpress.com

Freelance Potential
Published 12 titles in 2003: 6 were developed from unsolicited submissions. Receives 800 queries and mss yearly.
- **Fiction:** Publishes picture books, 2–5 years; and chapter
  books, 8–12 years. Features books with Christian and Catholic
  themes.
- **Nonfiction:** Publishes prayer books and books of blessings,
  5–8 years; chapter books, 8–12 years; biographies of saints and
  modern heroes, 9–14 years; Catholic guidebooks, 5+ years; and
  gift books on saints, favorite Bible stories, and holidays, all
  ages. Also features books on Roman Catholic activities, traditions, and rituals.
- **Representative Titles:** *My Catholic Lent and Easter Activity
  Book* (5–9 years) presents activities for Ash Wednesday through
  Pentecost. *Building a Family* by Marilyn Spaw Krock (parents)
  is a God-centered book of useful, often humorous suggestions
  for nurturing faith-filled families.

Submissions and Payment
Guidelines available at website. Send complete ms for very
short submissions; query with summary and writing sample
for longer works. SASE. Responds to queries in 2 weeks, to
mss in 4 months. Publication in 2–3 years. Royalty, 8%;
advance, $500.

Editor's Comments
We're interested in books that can be used both at home and
in the catechetical market. We no longer consider middle-grade
fiction or young adult biographies of saints. Do not submit
books on general values, such as sharing or self-esteem.

Peachtree Publishers

1700 Chattahoochee Avenue
Atlanta, GA 30318-2112

Submissions Editor: Helen Harriss

Publisher's Interests
An independent house, Peachtree Publishers offers titles of
interest to the general trade, as well as a children's list that
includes fiction and nonfiction picture books, chapter books,
middle-grade books, and young adult titles.
Website: www.peachtree-online.com

Freelance Potential
Published 20 titles in 2003: 2 were developed from unsolicited
submissions, 3 were by agented authors, and 5 were
reprint/licensed properties. Receives 20,000 queries yearly.
- **Fiction:** Publishes early picture books, 0–4 years; story picture
  books, 4–10 years; chapter books, 5–10 years; middle-grade
  books, 8–12 years; and young adult novels, 12–18 years. Genres include regional, historical, and multicultural fiction.
- **Nonfiction:** Publishes early picture books, 0–4 years; story picture books, 4–10 years; middle-grade books, 8–12 years; and
  young adult books, 12–18 years. Topics include nature and
  history. Also publishes parenting and educational titles, self-
  help books, and travel and recreational guides.
- **Representative Titles:** *If You See a Kitten* by John Butler (2–6
  years) offers an interactive look at various animals and the
  responses they evoke. *Aliens from Earth* by Mary Batten (8–12
  years) introduces readers to the serious and ongoing environmental problems caused by invasive plant and animal species.

Submissions and Payment
Guidelines available. Send complete ms for works under
5,000 words. Query with résumé, outline, and 2–3 sample
chapters for longer works. Accepts photocopies and computer
printouts. No queries via email or fax. SASE. Responds in 4–6
months. Publication period varies. Payment policy varies.

Editor's Comments
We do not publish poetry, short stories, plays, science fiction,
fantasy, romance, Westerns, or horror. Please do not submit
work intended to be used as a textbook, or business, scientific,
or technical reference books.

Pearson Education Canada

26 Prince Andrew Place
Don Mills, Ontario M3C 2T8
Canada

Publisher, School Division

Publisher's Interests
Fiction, nonfiction, and learning resources that can be used in educational settings from kindergarten through twelfth grade are offered by Pearson Education Canada. Its materials cover language arts, reading, science, and mathematics. In addition, it produces economics textbooks for college programs, and materials for French-as-a-Second-Language classes.
Website: www.pearsoned.ca

Freelance Potential
Published 50 titles in 2003. Receives 300 queries yearly.
- **Nonfiction:** Publishes language arts, mathematics, science, and French-as-a-Second-Language texts, grades K–12. Also publishes business, economics, and computer education texts, grades K–12 and up, as well as teacher guides and educational resource materials.
- **Representative Titles:** *Write a Story: Open-Ended Activities for Young Children* by Linda Beth Polon (teachers, grades 1–6) features a variety of open-ended story starters that reinforce basic grammar skills while providing creative writing opportunities. *Gift of Literacy in the Multiple Intelligence Classroom* by Evelyn Williams English (teachers, grades K–9) provides lessons and hands-on activities that help educators utilize students' greatest strengths.

Submissions and Payment
Query with 2 sample chapters. Accepts photocopies, computer printouts, and simultaneous submissions if identified. SAE/IRC. Responds in 1 month. Publication in 3–4 years. Royalty. Flat fee.

Editor's Comments
We strive to enrich the learning experiences of students in kindergarten through post-secondary environments while addressing the instructional requirements of teaching professionals and meeting the personal and professional needs of lifelong readers. We're always interested in meeting highly motivated and talented writers.

Pelican Publishing Company

P.O. Box 3110
Gretna, LA 70054-3110

Editorial Department

Publisher's Interests
The list of Pelican Publishers includes hardcover and trade
paperbacks as well as mass market editions. It focuses on
art, architecture, cooking, travel guides, history, children's
books, and textbooks.
Website: www.pelicanpub.com

Freelance Potential
Published 88 titles (22 juvenile) in 2003: 60 were developed
from unsolicited submissions, 10 were by agented authors,
and 20 were reprint/licensed properties. Of the 88 titles, 15
were by unpublished writers and 30 were by authors who
were new to the publishing house. Receives 6,500 queries,
3,500 unsolicited mss yearly.
- **Fiction:** Published 17 easy-to-read books, 4–7 years; and 1
  middle-grade book, 8–12 years. Genres include historical,
  regional, and holiday-related fiction.
- **Nonfiction:** Published 3 easy-to-read books, 4–7 years; and 1
  middle-grade book, 8–12 years. Topics include regional history
  and social commentary. Also publishes travel guides, cookbooks, biographies, and self-help titles for adults.
- **Representative Titles:** *Michael Le Soufflé and the April Fool* by
  Peter J. Welling (5–8 years) is a humorous tale of a somber
  French mayor and how his rival determines to make him
  laugh. *Great Spirit Horse* by Linda Little Wolf (10–14 years) is a
  story based on a Native American legend about a special horse
  with great powers.

Submissions and Payment
Guidelines available. Query with outline and clips or writing
samples. Send complete ms for easy-to-read books only.
Accepts photocopies. No simultaneous submissions. SASE.
Responds in 3 months. Publication in 9–18 months. Royalty.

Editor's Comments
Please review our detailed guidelines and visit our website
before you submit. You should have a solid understanding of
the kinds of subjects that appeal to us.

Pembroke Publishers

538 Hood Road
Markham, Ontario L3R 3K9
Canada

Submissions Editor: Mary Macchiusi

Publisher's Interests
Teachers at all grade levels are the audience for this Canadian publisher. Titles found in its catalogue cover such topics
as assessment, conflict management, science and nature,
reading response, phonics, and grammar.
Website: www.pembrokepublishers.com

Freelance Potential
Published 15 titles in 2003: 2 were developed from unsolicited submissions and 1 was by an agented author. Of the 15
titles, 3 were by unpublished writers and 5 were by authors
who were new to the publishing house. Receives 50 queries
each year.
- **Nonfiction:** Publishes chapter books, 5–10 years; and middle-
grade titles, 8–12 years. Topics include history, science, and
writing. Also publishes titles for educators about literacy,
spelling, grammar, educational assessment, and school safety,
as well as titles on home/school partnerships.
- **Representative Titles:** *High Frequency Words* by Ken Marland
(teachers) focuses on strategies that help build skills in spelling,
vocabulary, and wordplay. *How Do I Teach . . . and Keep My
Sanity?* by Kathy Paterson (teachers) presents simple, common-
sense ideas to help keep classrooms running smoothly.

Submissions and Payment
Guidelines available. Query with résumé, outline, and sample
chapters. Accepts photocopies and simultaneous submissions if identified. SAE/IRC. Responds in 1 month. Publication in 6–24 months. Royalty.

Editor's Comments
Our audience looks to us to bring them the very latest in classroom strategies and practices. We hope to help teachers promote a love of learning in all students. Most of our authors are
educators themselves who can provide stories of real events
and hands-on solutions. We invite writers to send us queries
for all grade levels. Before doing so, please review some of our
recent titles in your area of interest.

A Company with History
Sue Thies
Perfection Learning Corporation

Perfection Learning Corporation is a more than 75-year-old, family-owned publishing company, currently in its third generation leadership. Among Perfection's annual list of 50 to 75 books, 10 to 40 are on history-related topics.

Editorial Director Sue Thies reminds writers that most Perfection titles fall into established series. For history books, she says,"Our on-level social studies books are part of the Reading Essentials program. On the hi/lo side, we have history titles in Cover-to-Cover informational books and Cover-to-Cover chapter books. We also do a lot of historical fiction in the Cover-to-Cover lines." Hi/lo books are high interest, lower reading level books created especially for reluctant readers; while vocabulary and sentence structure are simplified, the subject matter isn't.

Thies says writers must know what a company publishes before they submit, and "don't try to say the submission is something it isn't, just to try and make it fit." Writers can get a good feel for this company by visiting their website.

Perfection accepts queries, proposals, or complete manuscripts, via email or regular mail. Thies says, "Please keep the query or cover letter short and to-the-point, and always include a résumé if you've published for other educational companies."

So how can a writer best capture Thies's attention? "That's a tough one. It just depends on what we're looking for at the time. One thing we're specifically not looking for is picture books."

Perfection Learning Corporation

10520 New York Avenue
Des Moines, IA 50322

Editorial Director, Books: Sue Thies

Publisher's Interests
This educational publisher offers a list that includes fiction
and informational high-interest, low-vocabulary books for
reluctant or below-grade-level readers. Hi/lo books are written
at a reading level that is at least two levels below grade level.
Its list targets preschool through high school students.
Website: www.perfectionlearning.com

Freelance Potential
Published 100+ titles in 2003: 20 were developed from unsolicited submissions and 10 were reprint/licensed properties.
Of the 100+ titles, 15 were by unpublished writers and 20
were by new authors. Receives 500+ queries yearly.
- **Fiction:** Publishes hi/lo chapter books, 7–12 years; middle-
  grade novels, 10–14 years; and 5 young adult books, 12–18
  years. Genres include historical, contemporary, multicultural,
  ethnic, and science fiction; mystery; suspense; humor; folktales; and stories about sports.
- **Nonfiction:** Publishes hi-lo chapter books, 7–12 years; and
  middle-grade books, 10–14 years. Topics include language arts,
  reading skills, literature, drama, history, social studies, math,
  science, sports, and multicultural issues. Also publishes on-
  level science and social studies titles, grades 3–6.
- **Representative Titles:** *Learning to Study* by Charles T. Mag-
  num (grades 3–8) introduces students to important study skills
  and strategies. *One Act* (grades 3–8) introduces students to
  classic literature, folktales, and historical figures through one-
  act plays; includes teacher's guides.

Submissions and Payment
Guidelines available at website or with SASE. Query with
outline and 2–3 sample chapters. Accepts photocopies, computer printouts, and simultaneous submissions. SASE.
Responds in 4 months. Publication in 1 year. Payment varies.

Editor's Comments
If you are interested in working with us, please review some of
our books. Writing hi/lo material is a skill not all writers have.

Perigee Books

Penguin Putnam, Inc.
375 Hudson Street
New York, NY 10014

Publisher: John Duff

Publisher's Interests
Self-help, how-to, and informational books for parents and other adults are the specialty of this imprint of Penguin Putnam. It publishes no books for children and no fiction. It accepts queries, but no unsolicited manuscripts.
Website: www.penguinputnam.com

Freelance Potential
Published 75 titles in 2003: 1 was developed from an unsolicited submission and 74 were by agented authors. Receives 300 queries yearly.
- **Nonfiction:** Publishes reference books for parents.
- **Representative Titles:** *Whose Kids Are These Anyway?* by Ken Swarner takes a humorous look at the daily issues faced by parents—such as understanding the rules of T-ball and operating a homework jail. *Born to be Wild* by Kristi Meisenbach Boylan addresses hyperactive children and provides suggestions for how parents can help free such children from labels and medication.

Submissions and Payment
Query. Accepts photocopies and computer printouts. SASE. Responds in 1–3 weeks. Publication in 18 months. Royalty; advance.

Editor's Comments
Please take the time to review our current list to understand the types of material we publish. We do not publish any books for children or young adults, nor do we publish fiction for any readers. Our goal is to provide the latest ideas and theories in self-help as well as how-to titles related to the topics of social issues, child care, parents and careers, health, fitness, and family. Our primary audience includes both parents and caregivers. We welcome queries from writers with expertise in one of these subject areas. If, after you review our current books in print, you think you can bring us something new or a fresh take on a given topic, we'd like to hear from you. Do not send a complete manuscript.

Philomel Books

Penguin Group (USA)
345 Hudson Street
New York, NY 10014

Editor: Emily Heath

Publisher's Interests

Fiction and nonfiction for the very young through young adults make up Philomel Books' publishing program. This imprint of Penguin Group (USA) offers story picture books, chapter books, novels, biographies, and poetry collections.
Website: www.penguingroup.com

Freelance Potential

Published 30 titles in 2003: 8 were developed from unsolicited submissions, 20 were by agented authors, and 2 were reprint/licensed properties. Receives 1,500 queries yearly.

- **Fiction:** Publishes early picture books, 0–4 years; easy-to-read books, 4–7 years; story picture books, 4–10 years; chapter books, 5–10 years; middle-grade novels, 8–12 years; and young adult books, 12–18 years. Genres include fantasy and contemporary, multicultural, and historical fiction.
- **Nonfiction:** Publishes story picture books, 4–10 years; and young adult books, 12–18 years. Features first-person essays, biographies, and poetry collections.
- **Representative Titles:** *The Big Blue Spot* by Peter Holwitz (0–4 years) is an interactive book that teaches young children about colors as well as friendship. *Skeleton Key* by Anthony Horowitz (10–14 years) features a young James Bond-type character who saves the country from hijackers.

Submissions and Payment

Guidelines available with SASE. Query with outline/synopsis or sample chapters in sequence. Include table of contents for nonfiction. No unsolicited mss. SASE. Responds in 1–2 months. Publication in 1–2 years. Royalty.

Editor's Comments

This year, we're very interested in books that explore contemporary, current issues of interest to teens and young adults. As always, we want to see writing that stretches boundaries artistically and imaginatively and offers new perspectives for our readers. Both fiction and nonfiction should "ring true" and authentically express the author's voice.

Phoenix Learning Resources

2nd Floor
25 Third Street
Stamford, CT 06902

Executive Vice President: John A. Rothermich

Publisher's Interests

Titles from Phoenix Learning Resources are used by educators working in preschools through high schools, and also in adult education and English-as-a-Second Language classrooms. Its catalogue includes books on language skills, reading comprehension, critical thinking, mathematics, and science. It markets its titles to schools and libraries.

Freelance Potential

Published 12 titles in 2003. Of the 12 titles, 3 were by authors who were new to the publishing house. Receives 8–10 queries, 30 unsolicited mss yearly.
- **Nonfiction:** Publishes textbooks and educational materials for pre-K–grade 12 and up. Also publishes biographies, books for gifted and special education students, and titles for use with ESL students. Topics include reading, writing, language arts, mathematics, science, social studies, and life and study skills.
- **Representative Titles:** *Sounds Right, Read, Write* by Elske Brown & Judy Jackson (grades K–3) is a series that helps students learn phonics, practice handwriting, and develop basic literacy skills. *Reading About Science* by Mongillo, et al. (grades 2 and up) teaches reading skills while exposing students to many aspects of the world of science.

Submissions and Payment

Query or send complete ms with résumé. Accepts photocopies, computer printouts, and simultaneous submissions if identified. SASE. Responds in 1–4 weeks. Publication in 1–15 months. Royalty. Flat fee.

Editor's Comments

We're looking for reading and mathematics materials for students between the ages of eight and fourteen. We also want to review programs that will help build vocabulary; these should target students between the ages of eight and eleven. Please note that we are a nonfiction educational publisher that targets schools and libraries. Please don't send us any type of children's fiction.

The Pilgrim Press

700 Prospect Avenue East
Cleveland, OH 44115-1100

Editorial Director: Kim M. Sadler

Publisher's Interests
This religious publisher features books of interest to clergy
and lay people working with children, as well as books targeting religious, trade, and scholarly individuals. Its audience
includes people from many denominations. The Pilgrim Press
is an imprint of the United Church of Christ.
Website: www.pilgrimpress.com

Freelance Potential
Published 54 titles in 2003: 23 were developed from unsolicited submissions and 1 was by an agented author. Of the
54 titles, 1 was by an unpublished writer and 12 were by
authors who were new to the publishing house. Receives
200+ queries and unsolicited mss yearly.
- **Nonfiction:** Publishes educational titles of interest to religious
  educators, clergy, parents, and care givers; and children's sermons. Also publishes informational titles on religion, social
  issues, and multicultural and ethnic issues.
- **Representative Titles:** *Daniel and the Lion* by Sekiya Miyoshi
  is an adaptation of the biblical story of Daniel, whose faith is
  renewed by God. *Loving Changes* by Lynne M. Deming (parents) is a journal with inspirational quotations and photographs for mothers to record their feelings as their children
  grow up.

Submissions and Payment
Guidelines available. Query with table of contents and sample chapters; or send complete ms. Accepts photocopies.
SASE. Responds to queries in 6–8 weeks, to mss in 2–3
months. Publication in 9–12 months. Royalty, 8% paperback,
8% cloth; advance. Flat fee for work for hire.

Editor's Comments
We are especially interested in academic and trade books on
social and religious issues in the areas of ethics, public policy,
gender and sexuality, racial and ethnic issues, and science and
technology. Our mission is to address the complex social
issues in the context of faith.

Piñata Books

Arte Público Press
452 Cullen Performance Hall
University of Houston
Houston, TX 77204-2004

Submissions Department

Publisher's Interests

Hispanic culture in the United States is portrayed in the titles from Piñata Books. As the children's and young adult imprint of Arte Público Press, it features picture books, novels, poetry, drama, biographies, and autobiographies—all with Hispanic themes and subjects.
Website: www.arte.uh.edu

Freelance Potential

Published 30 titles (14 juvenile) in 2003. Of the 30 titles, 2 were by unpublished writers and 2 were by authors who were new to the publishing house. Receives 2,000 queries and unsolicited mss yearly.

- **Fiction:** Published 6 story picture books, 4–10 years; 3 middle-grade books, 8–12 years; and 3 young adult novels, 12–18 years. Features contemporary fiction, anthologies, poetry, and drama.
- **Nonfiction:** Published 2 story picture books, 4–10 years. Also publishes young adult books, 12–18 years. Publishes biographies and autobiographies.
- **Representative Titles:** *Loves Me, Loves Me Not* by Anilú Bernardo (YA) is a novel about a hard-working, responsible Cuban-American teen girl who is facing the challenges of dating. *Uncle Chente's Picnic* by Diane Gonzales Bertrand (3–7 years), published in both Spanish and English, features a family who plans a celebration for their uncle's Fourth of July arrival in Texas.

Submissions and Payment

Guidelines and catalogue available at website. Query with sample chapter. Will accept complete ms for easy-to-read books. Accepts photocopies and computer printouts. SASE. Responds to queries in 2–4 months, to mss in 3–6 months. Publication in 2 years. Royalty.

Editor's Comments

We accept submissions in either English or Spanish, but the majority of our publications are in English. Your book must realistically present themes, characters, and customs that are unique to the US Hispanic culture.

Pineapple Press

P.O. Box 3889
Sarasota, FL 34230

Executive Editor: June Cussen

Publisher's Interests
This regional publisher offers a children's list that includes fiction and nonfiction on topics related to Florida. Its children's books are widely used in Florida's schools.
Website: www.pineapplepress.com

Freelance Potential
Published 22 titles (2 juvenile) in 2003: 14 were developed from unsolicited submissions and 2 were by agented authors. Of the 22 titles, 12 were by unpublished writers and 10 were by authors who were new to the publishing house. Receives 1,500 queries yearly.
- **Fiction:** Publishes young adult novels, 12–18 years. Genres include mystery, folklore, science fiction, mythology, and historical fiction related to Florida. Also publishes titles for adults.
- **Nonfiction:** Published 2 middle-grade books, 8–12 years. Topics include sports and travel related to Florida. Also publishes titles for adults.
- **Representative Titles:** *Florida A to Z* by Susan Jane Ryan (8–12 years) presents numerous facts about Florida's history, personalities, geography, nature, and culture. *Gift of the Unicorn* by Virginia Aronson (9–12 years) relates the story of Lue Gim Gong, who became known as Florida's citrus wizard.

Submissions and Payment
Guidelines available at website. Query with clips, synopsis, and sample chapters for fiction. Query with table of contents and sample chapters for nonfiction. Accepts photocopies and simultaneous submissions if identified. SASE. Responds in 2 months. Publication in 12–18 months. Royalty.

Editor's Comments
For the coming year, we are seeking Florida-related fiction and nonfiction aimed at readers ages eight to fourteen. We do not publish genre fiction—mysteries, romances, science fiction, action-adventure, or Westerns—unless they have a strong tie-in to Florida. Historical fiction, as long as it is Florida-related, is welcome.

Pioneer Drama Service

P.O. Box 4267
Englewood, CO 80155-4267

Assistant Editor: Lori Conary

Publisher's Interests
Theaters at all levels—from community theater to school drama groups—look to Pioneer Drama Service for its wide selection of full-length plays, one-act plays, musicals, and melodramas.
Website: www.pioneerdrama.com

Freelance Potential
Published 25+ titles in 2003: 8–10 were developed from unsolicited submissions and 10+ were by agented authors.
Receives 300+ queries, 300+ unsolicited mss yearly.
- **Fiction:** Publishes plays, 8+ years. Genres include comedy, mystery, fantasy, adventure, folktales, and musicals.
- **Nonfiction:** Publishes books about stage management, scene design, costumes, and acting techniques. Also offers monologue collections and scene books.
- **Representative Titles:** *Just Like Us* by Craig Sodaro is a short play, with sixteen parts, for young children that seeks to teach them about prejudice. *The Elves and the Shoemaker* by Karen Boettcher-Tate is a musical about a kindhearted but poor shoemaker and the elves who come to help him.

Submissions and Payment
Guidelines available. Query with synopsis and clips or writing samples; or send complete ms with résumé and proof of production. Accepts photocopies, computer printouts, and simultaneous submissions if identified. SASE. Responds to queries in 1 month, to mss in 4–6 months. Publication in 3–6 months. Royalty.

Editor's Comments
One-act and full-length plays continue to top our list of needs. Keep in mind that if you choose to send a complete manuscript, you must include proof of production. New writers are always welcome here. If you are a new playwright, review our catalogue to get a sense of what types of work interest us. Remember that many of the plays we publish are used by a variety of groups, so your story should be flexible in its casting.

Pitspopany Press

Suite 16D
40 East 78th Street
New York, NY 10021

Editor: Yaacov Peterseil

Publisher's Interests
Children's books about the Jewish faith are the specialty of
Pitspopany Press. In operation for more than 10 years, it
offers fiction and nonfiction in the form of picture books,
easy-to-read books, chapter books, and titles for middle-
grade and young adult readers.
Website: www.pitspopany.com

Freelance Potential
Published 13 titles (8 juvenile) in 2003: 2 were by agented
authors. Of the 13 titles, 8 were by unpublished writers and
9 were by authors who were new to the publishing house.
Receives 30 unsolicited mss yearly.
- **Fiction:** Publishes early picture books, 0–4 years; easy-to-read
  books, 4–7 years; story picture books, 4–10 years; and middle-
  grade books, 8–12 years. Genres include religious, historical,
  ethnic, multicultural, and science fiction; mystery; adventure;
  fairy tales; and humor.
- **Nonfiction:** Publishes easy-to-read titles, 4–7 years; story picture books, 4–10 years; chapter books, 5–10 years; middle-
  grade books, 8–12 years; and young adult books, 12–18 years.
  Topics include religion, multicultural and ethnic subjects,
  health, fitness, sports, and history.
- **Representative Titles:** *Double Dare of the Gooblyglop* by Tova
  Guttman (9–13 years) is a story about two boys who create a
  machine that will save the world. *Zap It!* by Tamar Peterseil &
  Dana Porath (9–13 years) features fun kosher recipes for kids.

Submissions and Payment
Catalogue and guidelines available at website. Send complete
ms. Accepts photocopies and email submissions to pitspop@
netvision.net.il. SASE. Responds in 3 months. Publication in
4–6 months. Royalty; advance.

Editor's Comments
We usually respond to email from authors who have had work
published by a recognized publishing house within 90 days.
Response to unpublished writers may take longer.

Players Press

P.O. Box 1132
Studio City, CA 91614-0132

Editor: Robert W. Gordon

Publisher's Interests

In addition to plays and musicals, this publisher offers books
on the performing arts, including titles on theater, film, television, music, costume, and fashion. It publishes dramatic
materials for children and teens as well as adults.

Freelance Potential

Published 120 titles (51 juvenile) in 2003: 15 were developed
from unsolicited submissions, 1 was by an agented author,
and 2 were reprint/licensed properties. Of the 120 titles, 13
were by unpublished writers and 15 were by authors who
were new to the publishing house. Receives 1,000–1,200
queries yearly.

- **Fiction:** Published 8 middle-grade plays, 8–12 years; and 23
  young adult plays, 12–18 years. Publishes full-length and one-
  act dramas and musicals.
- **Nonfiction:** Published 4 middle-grade books, 8–12 years; and
  16 young adult books, 12–18 years. Also publishes material for
  drama educators. Topics include stage management, mime,
  makeup, television, film, dance, costumes, clowning, acting
  methods, and directing techniques.
- **Representative Titles:** *Albert the Machine* by Robert Kenney &
  Bryan Williams is a musical for young audiences about a computer that is unhappy with his career and learns to celebrate
  the differences between man and machine. *The Princess, the
  Pickle, and Birdlegs* by Barbara Black Fox (YA) is a comic romp
  about friendship, jealousy, and young love.

Submissions and Payment

Guidelines available. Query with résumé, outline, synopsis,
production flyer, program, and reviews if available. Accepts
photocopies. SASE. Responds in 3–6 weeks. Publication in
3–24 months. Royalty, 10%; advance.

Editor's Comments

It's important to note that dramatic submissions must include
proof of the play's production. Musicals should be accompanied by a tape of the show's music.

Playhouse Publishing

1566 Akron-Peninsula Road
Akron, OH 44313

Submissions Editor

Publisher's Interests

This publisher produces board books for beginning readers
and for parents to read to their children. Books published by
Playhouse Publishing are produced on a work-for-hire basis.
Website: www.playhousepublishing.com

Freelance Potential

Published 15 titles in 2003: all were assigned; 6 were by previously unpublished authors.
- **Fiction:** Publishes concept books, toddler books, and early
  picture books, 0–4 years; and easy-to-read books, 4–7 years.
  Genres include adventure, fairy tales, folktales, humor, and
  religious and inspirational fiction.
- **Nonfiction:** Publishes easy-to-read books, 4–7 years.
- **Representative Titles:** *Picture Me*™ *as a Bunny* (pre-K) is part
  of the rhyming series that allows the reader to become the featured character by inserting his photo inside. *Picture Me*™ *as
  Little Red Riding Hood* (pre-K) allows the reader to become the
  heroine of the popular fairy tale, just by inserting a photo; part
  of the Picture Me™ Books Fairy Tale series.

Submissions and Payment

Query with writing sample or résumé. Email submissions to
webmaster@playhousepublishing.com (no attachments).
Accepts simultaneous submissions if identified. Responds in
2 months. Publication in 1 year. Flat fee.

Editor's Comments

All of the books we publish are assigned. If you think
you have what it takes to write for us, send a query that
includes a writing sample and a résumé. If we think your
style and credentials are right for us and our readers,
we will contact you when we have an appropriate project.
All our books appear under one of our three imprints:
Picture Me™ Books, Nibble Me™ Books, and Little Lucy
and Friends™ Books. Potential writers may want to familiarize themselves with the titles under each imprint before
querying.

Pleasant Company Publications

8400 Fairway Place
Middleton, WI 53562-0998

Submissions Editor

Publisher's Interests

This well-known publisher offers fiction and nonfiction titles for middle-grade girls. It started with the American Girl Collection of dolls accompanied by historical stories and has since expanded to include craft and interactive titles as well as informational titles on social issues. It has recently added the Angelina Ballerina series of books for younger readers.
Website: www.pleasantpublications.com

Freelance Potential

Published 50 titles in 2003: 2 were developed from unsolicited submissions.

- **Fiction:** Publishes middle-grade novels, 10+ years. Genres include mysteries and historical and contemporary fiction.
- **Nonfiction:** Publishes middle-grade books, 8–12 years. Features advice books, activity books, and interactive CD-ROMs. Topics include animals, crafts, hobbies, cooking, games, health, fitness, family relationships, divorce, and sports.
- **Representative Titles:** *Angelina Ballerina's Invitation to the Ballet* by Katharine Holabird (3+ years) is an interactive storybook featuring a colorful poster and special pockets throughout the book. *Amelia's Best Year Ever* by Marissa Moss (8+ years) continues the adventures of this well-loved character.

Submissions and Payment

Guidelines available. Prefers query with first chapter for fiction. Accepts complete ms. Accepts photocopies and simultaneous submissions if identified. SASE. Responds in 3–4 months. Publication period and payment policy vary.

Editor's Comments

We are always willing to consider queries from freelancers who can present an idea that is innovative and fresh and that will excite our readers. Your book ideas must also fall in line with the types of material that fill our catalogue. We strongly urge you to review some of our titles before you consider sending a submission. Most of our books are written by well-known authors, so the competition is very tough.

Polychrome Publishing Corporation

4509 North Francisco Avenue
Chicago, IL 60625-3808

Editorial Department

Publisher's Interests

Multicultural books that deal with the themes of racial,
ethnic, and cultural diversity and tolerance are featured on
this publisher's list. The protagonists in the stories it publishes are usually Asian American, African American, Hispanic, Latino, or Native American.

Website: www.polychromebooks.com

Freelance Potential

Published 3 titles in 2003: 2 were developed from unsolicited
submissions and 1 was by an agented author. Of the 3 titles,
most were by unpublished writers and all were by authors
who were new to the publishing house. Receives 1,000+
unsolicited mss yearly.

- **Fiction:** Published 1 early picture book, 0–4 years; 1 middle-
  grade book, 8–12 years; and 1 young adult book, 12–18 years.
  Also publishes toddler books, 0–4 years; and chapter books,
  5–10 years. Features multicultural stories that promote racial,
  ethnic, cultural, and religious tolerance.
- **Nonfiction:** Publishes books about Asian-American culture for
  families and educators.
- **Representative Titles:** *The Lobster and the Sea* by Esther Chiu
  (7–11 years) is the story of a child who reconciles her American
  values with her grandfather's Asian ones when he returns to
  his roots. *Blue Jay in the Desert* by Marlene Shigekawa (6–11
  years) portrays the life of a Japanese-American boy and his
  family who are interned during World War II.

Submissions and Payment

Send complete ms with résumé. Accepts photocopies, com-
puter printouts, and simultaneous submissions if identified.
SASE. Responds in 3–6 months. Publication in 1–2 years.
Royalty; advance.

Editor's Comments

We welcome submissions for books for preschoolers through
young adults that deal with anti-bias and biracial issues as
well as domestic multiculturalism.

Portage & Main Press

100-318 McDermont Avenue
Winnipeg, Manitoba R3A 0A2
Canada

Marketing Director: Kirsten Phillips

Publisher's Interests

For more than 35 years, Portage & Main Press has been offering educational books and resource materials for kindergarten through college classrooms. In addition to titles about teaching language arts, social studies, and science, it features English-as-a-Second Language materials and assessment tools.

Website: www.portageandmainpress.com

Freelance Potential

Published 10 titles in 2003: 2 were developed from unsolicited submissions and 8 were by agented authors. Of the 10 titles, 6 were by authors who were new to the publishing house. Receives 60 queries, 40–50 unsolicited mss yearly.

- **Nonfiction:** Publishes educational titles and professional development resources for teachers working in grades K–6. Also publishes assessment tools and ESL materials. Topics include writing, spelling, reading, art, poetry, theater, science, and social studies.
- **Representative Titles:** *A Vocal Invitation to Readers Theatre* by Shirley Konrad (teachers, grades 1–8) explores techniques to enhance the expressive quality of the vocal instrument. *Recognition Without Rewards* by Caren Cameron et al. (teachers, grades K–8) argues that rewards interfere with learning and that students need thoughtful, specific recognition instead.

Submissions and Payment

Guidelines available with SAE/IRC ($.50 postage). Query with table of contents and 1 sample chapter; or send complete ms. Accepts photocopies and IBM disk submissions. SAE/IRC. Responds to queries in 1 month, to mss in 1–2 months. Publication in 6 months. Royalty, 8–12%.

Editor's Comments

We're always willing to consider books that offer fresh ideas, new activities, or innovative ways of teaching at all grade levels. This year, we continue to encourage submissions of books about assessment tools and ESL programs.

Pro Lingua Associates

P.O. Box 1348
Brattleboro, VT 05302-1348

Senior Editor: Raymond C. Clark

Publisher's Interests
Pro Lingua Associates has been dedicated to producing superior language teaching materials for over 20 years. Its list includes teacher resources and English-as-a-Second-Language textbooks.
Website: www.ProLinguaAssociates.com

Freelance Potential
Published 4–6 titles in 2003: 2 were developed from unsolicited submissions. Of the 4–6 titles, 1 was by an unpublished writer and 1 was by an author who was new to the publishing house. Receives 40 queries, 10 unsolicited mss yearly.
- **Fiction:** Publishes story picture books, 4–10 years; middle-grade books, 8–12 years; and young adult novels, 12–18 years. Genres include multicultural and contemporary fiction.
- **Nonfiction:** Publishes young adult books, 12–18 years; and ESL materials. Topics include writing, comprehension, and reading. Also publishes card and board games to strengthen literacy skills, as well as teacher resource materials.
- **Representative Titles:** *Heroes from American History* by Anne Siebert and Raymond C. Clark (grades 4–adult) focuses on American heroes while teaching critical thinking and writing skills. *Lexicarry* by Patrick R. Moran (all ages) offers a fun, active, conversational approach to language learning.

Submissions and Payment
Guidelines available. Query with résumé, table of contents, and sample chapters; or send complete ms. Accepts photocopies. Availability of artwork improves chance of acceptance. SASE. Responds to queries in 1 week, to mss in 3–4 weeks. Publication in 1 year. Royalty.

Editor's Comments
Many of the people who write for us are professional ESL teachers. If you feel you have a literacy-related topic that would interest us, we would like to see your proposal. We're always looking for new, original texts and teacher resources. Our materials focus on the basics of teaching language.

Prometheus Books

59 John Glenn Drive
Amherst, NY 14228-2197

Editor-in-Chief: Steven L. Mitchell

Publisher's Interests
Founded in 1969, this nonfiction publisher offers a catalogue
that includes material on such topics as history, religion,
humanism, Jewish studies, health, and psychology. In addition to books, the publisher also offers a selection of audio
tapes and journals.
Website: www.prometheusbooks.com

Freelance Potential
Published 90–105 titles in 2003: 15–20 were developed from
unsolicited submissions. Receives 300 queries, 400 unsolicited mss yearly.
- **Nonfiction:** Publishes easy-to-read books, 4–7 years. Topics
  include social issues, religion, health, sexuality, critical thinking, and decision making.
- **Representative Titles:** *Flat Earth? Round Earth?* by Theresa
  Martin (7+ years) focuses on critical thinking in science as it tells
  the story of a student who realizes that the obvious is not always
  so obvious. *Math Charmers* by Alfred Posamentier is designed to
  help kids learn how exciting the study of math can be.

Submissions and Payment
Guidelines available. Query or send complete ms with
résumé and bibliography. Accepts photocopies, computer
printouts, and simultaneous submissions if identified. Availability of artwork improves chance of acceptance. SASE.
Responds in 2–3 months. Publication in 12–18 months. Payment policy varies.

Editor's Comments
We like submissions that are reader-friendly and written in a
conversational tone. Books that excite young readers about
new worlds and ideas or that discuss a well-known subject in
a new innovative way are the kinds of books that excite us
most. Queries should demonstrate your expertise and ability to
draw research-based conclusions. We strive to help children
develop a curiosity about new ideas as well as ways to learn to
be the best they can be.

Publish America

P.O. Box 151
Frederick, MD 21705

Editorial Director: Miranda N. Prather

Publisher's Interests
Established in 1999, Publish America targets young adults
and adults with a list including both fiction and nonfiction
titles. It publishes no picture books or illustrated books.
Website: www.publishamerica.com

Freelance Potential
Published 800 titles (60 juvenile) in 2003: 450 were developed from unsolicited submissions and 200 were by agented
authors. Of the 800 titles, 500 were by unpublished writers
and 600 were by new authors. Receives 750 mss yearly.
- **Fiction:** Publishes concept books, toddler books, and early
  picture books, 0–4 years; easy-to-read books, 4–7 years; story
  picture books, 4–10 years; middle-grade books, 8–12 years;
  and young adult books, 12–18 years. Genres include adventure; fantasy; humor; mystery; and contemporary, historical,
  and multicultural fiction.
- **Nonfiction:** Published early picture books, 0–4 years; story
  picture books, 4–10 years; middle-grade books, 8–12 years;
  and young adult books, 12–18 years. Topics include current
  events, social concerns, history, ethnic issues, and special education. Also publishes self-help titles and biographies.
- **Representative Titles:** *The Adventures of the Box Canyon
  Gang* by Kammile A. Watt follows a girl from a small town and
  her friends as they challenge their imaginations with stories.
  Cookies at Nana's House by Yvonne Peramaki encourages children to talk about issues that trouble them and ask questions.

Submissions and Payment
Guidelines and catalogue available. Query or send ms with
biography and 9x12 SASE ($.99 postage). Accepts photo-
copies, disk submissions (Microsoft Word or WordPerfect),
and email to writers@publishamerica.com. SASE. Responds
to queries in 1–2 weeks, to mss in 1–2 months. Publication in
10–12 months. Royalty; 8–12%; advance.

Editor's Comments
We're actively seeking new authors and are particularly interested in works about people who overcome life's challenges.

G. P. Putnam's Sons

345 Hudson Street
New York, NY 10014

Manuscript Editor

Publisher's Interests
An imprint of Penguin Group USA (formerly Penguin Put-
nam), G. P. Putnam's Sons develops fiction and nonfiction
titles for children from toddlerhood through the teen years.
Its list includes picture books, chapter books, and novels.
Website: www.penguin.com

Freelance Potential
Published 50 titles in 2003: 2 were developed from unsolicited
submissions. Of the 50 titles, 4 were by unpublished writers
and 10 were by authors who were new to the publishing
house. Receives 1,500 queries, 8,000 unsolicited mss yearly.
- **Fiction:** Publishes toddler books and early picture books, 0–4
  years; story picture books, 4–10 years; chapter books, 5–10
  years; middle-grade novels, 8–12 years; and young adult
  books, 12–18 years. Also publishes novelty books. Genres
  include contemporary and multicultural fiction.
- **Nonfiction:** Publishes early picture books, 0–4 years; story
  picture books, 4–10 years; chapter books, 5–10 years; and
  middle-grade books, 8–12 years.
- **Representative Titles:** *The Sands of Time* by Michael Hoeye
  (all ages) is a story about a mouse whose friend creates a stir
  with his visionary new paintings that are portraits of cats.
  Stand Tall by Joan Bauer (10+ years) is a novel about the challenges faced by an exceptionally tall seventh grader who looks
  much older than he is and is no good at basketball.

Submissions and Payment
Guidelines available. Send complete ms for picture books.
Query with outline/synopsis and 2 sample chapters for chapter books. Accepts photocopies, computer printouts, and
simultaneous submissions if identified. SASE. Responds in 2
months. Publication in 18–36 months. Royalty; advance.

Editor's Comments
We receive thousands of queries and manuscripts each year, so
your book must really stand out. We always need good chapter
books and novels with unusual plotlines and settings.

Quest Books

P.O. Box 270
Wheaton, IL 60189

Editor: Sharron Dorr

Publisher's Interests
Quest Books publishes under the auspices of the Theosophical Society in America, an organization that promotes fellowship among all peoples of the world and encourages the study of religion, philosophy, and science. Although it does not publish children's books, many of its titles are read by young adults.
Website: www.questbooks.net

Freelance Potential
Published 10 titles in 2003: 1 was developed from an unsolicited submission and 3 were by agented authors. Receives 6,000 queries yearly.

- **Nonfiction:** Publishes young adult titles, 12–18 years. Features books about animals, mythology, religion, social issues, and women's studies. Also publishes self-help books.
- **Representative Titles:** *Essential Musical Intelligence: Using Music as Your Path to Healing, Creativity, and Radiant Wholeness* by Louise Montello helps readers cultivate their potential for healing through music. *The Practice of Dream Healing: Bringing Ancient Greek Mysteries into Modern Medicine* by Edward Tick combines elements of mythological study and historical narrative with a personal journey and travelogue.

Submissions and Payment
Guidelines available at website. Query with author biography, table of contents, introduction, and sample chapter. No unsolicited mss. SASE. Responds in 4–6 weeks. Publication period varies. Royalty; advance.

Editor's Comments
We're looking for manuscripts on universal philosophical and religious principles, world religious traditions, Theosophy, meditation, spiritual ecology, transpersonal psychology, new science, men's and women's spirituality, and holistic health and healing. Our books are aimed at educated readers and we demand high-quality writing. Please don't send any fiction, poetry, or books written directly to young children.

Rainbow Publishers

P.O. Box 261129
San Diego, CA 92196

Editorial Director: Christy Scannell

Publisher's Interests

This Christian publisher produces how-to and activity books
as well as "teaching tips" for Sunday school teachers and
Christian homeschoolers. All of its material is based on Bible
stories and lessons.
Website: www.rainbowpublishers.com

Freelance Potential

Published 11 titles (5 juvenile) in 2003: 4 were developed
from unsolicited submissions and 7 were assigned. Of the 11
titles, 1 was by an author who was new to the publishing
house. Receives 1,000 unsolicited mss yearly.

- **Fiction:** Publishes middle-grade titles, 8–12 years. Genres
  include inspirational and religious fiction. Also offers titles in
  series, 8+ years.
- **Nonfiction:** Publishes Christian educational resource materials,
  pre-K–grade 6. Topics include the Bible, religion, crafts, and hobbies. Also publishes activity books, 2–12 years.
- **Representative Titles:** *Hands-on Nature* (2–12 years) is a
  reproducible resource book that helps children experience and
  connect biblical truths to the wonder of God's creation. *More!
  Instant Bible Lessons* (5–10 years) includes puzzles, games,
  and crafts that convey the messages of the Bible.

Submissions and Payment

Guidelines and catalogue available with 9x12 SASE (2 first-
class stamps). Send complete ms with table of contents and
first 3 chapters. Accepts photocopies. SASE. Responds in 3
months. Publication in 1–3 years. Royalty; advance. Flat fee.

Editor's Comments

Generally, our children's ministry products are reproducible
books issued in series for children ages two through twelve. All
are Bible-based and at least 64 pages. Most of our writers have
hands-on experience working with children and are active par-
ticipants in a Bible-believing church. We're always interested in
proposals that would add to our existing series. Check our
website or send for our catalogue for series themes.

Raintree Publishers

Suite 1200
100 North LaSalle
Chicago, IL 60602

Managing Editor: Jamie West

Publisher's Interests
Formerly known as Raintree/Steck-Vaughn Publishers, this company produces nonfiction with a "child-extended" approach that explores new branches of knowledge from a child's perspective. Its books are for children in kindergarten through the eighth grade and all are curriculum-based.
Website: www.raintreelibrary.com

Freelance Potential
Published 255 titles in 2003: 50 were developed from unsolicited submissions. Receives 500 queries yearly.
- **Nonfiction:** Publishes books for grades K–8. Topics include social studies, geography, animals, health, mathematics, science, technology, sports, contemporary issues, and arts and crafts.
- **Representative Titles:** *In The Wild* (grades 2–5) answers children's questions about wild animals, such as chimpanzees, dolphins, and panda bears, while helping them improve their comprehension and reading skills; part of the Animals II series. *Dresses and Skirts* by Helen Reynolds (6–8 years) provides a glimpse of the way we were and are; part of The Fashionable History of Costume series.

Submissions and Payment
Guidelines available. Query with outline, 2 sample chapters, and clips or writing samples. Accepts clear computer printouts and simultaneous submissions if identified. SASE. Responds in 2–4 months. Publication in 12–18 months. Royalty; advance. Flat fee.

Editor's Comments
Our books are for all reading levels and interests. We look for material that will engage a reader through its unique perspective and accompanying photos. This year we are particularly interested in reviewing queries for books that can appear as series, with a minimum of four books. Send us a query that demonstrates the special qualities of your idea, is based on the latest news, and relies on primary-source content.

Rayve Productions Inc.

P.O. Box 726
Windsor, CA 95492

Editor: Barbara Ray

Publisher's Interests

Easy-to-read books, story picture books, and chapter books
with multicultural themes appear on this publisher's list,
along with parenting titles, cookbooks, and books about history for adults. It will not be reviewing children's book submissions again until 2005.
Website: www.rayveproductions.com

Freelance Potential

Published 5 titles in 2003: 2 were developed from unsolicited
submissions. Of the 2 titles, both were by unpublished writers.
Receives 100+ queries and unsolicited mss yearly.

- **Fiction:** Publishes easy-to-read books, 4–7 years; story picture
  books, 4–10 years; and chapter books, 5–10 years. Genres
  include historical, multicultural, and ethnic fiction; folktales;
  and adventure stories.
- **Nonfiction:** Publishes biographies and history books, 5
  years–adult. Also publishes educational titles for teachers and
  parents, as well as cookbooks and how-to books.
- **Representative Titles:** *The Perfect Orange: A Tale from Ethiopia*
  by Frank P. Araujo (3+ years) is a folktale about a girl who
  travels far from her village to take an extraordinary gift to
  Ethiopia's ruler. *Link Across America* by Mary Elizabeth Anderson (8–13 years) tells the story of the historic Lincoln Highway,
  America's first transcontinental highway.

Submissions and Payment

Guidelines available. Query with résumé for adult books.
Send complete ms for children's books. SASE. Responds in 6
weeks. Publication in 1 year. Royalty, 10%; advance, varies.

Editor's Comments

We will begin accepting children's manuscripts again in 2005.
Well-written biographies, sports stories, and ethnic folktales
are most likely to make it out of the slush pile. Send us something unique that is written with energy and insight. Our philosophy is that every project is a team effort in which the publisher, author, and artist work together.

Red Deer Press

MacKimmie Library Tower, Room 813
2500 University Drive NW
Calgary, Alberta T2N 1N4
Canada

Children's Editor: Peter Carver

Publisher's Interests
Children's picture books, chapter books, young adult novels, and family activity books are all available from Red Deer Press. A Canadian publisher, it exclusively publishes books with Canadian themes, written by Canadian authors.
Website: www.reddeerpress.com

Freelance Potential
Published 7 titles in 2003: 1 was developed from an unsolicited submission and 3 were by agented authors. Of the 7 titles, 1 was by an unpublished writer and 1 was by an author who was new to the publishing house. Receives 500 queries, 1,500 unsolicited mss yearly.

- **Fiction:** Published 3 story picture books, 4–10 years; 1 middle-grade book, 8–12 years; and 3 young adult books, 12–18 years. Also publishes chapter books, 5–10 years. Genres include regional and contemporary fiction, adventure, fantasy, mystery, suspense, drama, and multicultural and ethnic fiction.
- **Nonfiction:** Publishes family activity books, 4+ years. Features a nature series as well as field guides, biographies, and anthologies for adults.
- **Representative Titles:** *Amber Waiting* by Nan Gregory (3–6 years) is a picture book about a girl who becomes tired of waiting for her father, so she sends him to the moon. *Why Am I Rare?* by Michelle Gilder (6–10 years) focuses on 10 animals in danger of extinction.

Submissions and Payment
Canadian authors only. Guidelines and catalogue available with 9x12 SASE. Query with outline and 2 sample chapters. Send complete ms for picture books and young adult novels. Accepts photocopies. SASE. Responds in 4–6 months. Publication in 2–3 years. Royalty.

Editor's Comments
We continue to look for early-reader novels, novels for young adults, and picture books for ages four and up. In your cover letter, tell us why your book is unique.

Red Wheel/Weiser/Conari Press

4th Floor
368 Congress Street
Boston, MA 02210

Editorial Acquisitions: Pat Bryce

Publisher's Interests
This publisher offers three imprints: Red Wheel publishes self-help and inspirational books and books about spirituality; Weiser Books publishes books on esoteric topics, such as magic, wicca, tarot, astrology, and kabalah; and Conari Press publishes books on topics such as personal growth, spirituality, and relationships, as well as titles on women's issues and parenting.
Website: www.redwheelweiser.com

Freelance Potential
Published 100 titles in 2003: 20 were developed from unsolicited submissions, 10 were by agented authors, and 1 was a reprint/licensed property. Receives 500 queries yearly.
- **Nonfiction:** Publishes self-help, how-to, and inspirational books. Topics include personal growth, parenting, spirituality, and women's issues. Also publishes titles related to esoteric topics such as magic, wicca, tarot, astrology, and kabalah.
- **Representative Titles:** *Wonderful Ways to Love a Child* by Judy Ford (parents) offers practical suggestions designed to help busy, stressed-out parents engage in positive parenting. *The Naptime Book* by Cynthia MacGregor (parents) presents activities, stories, songs, poems, and creative suggestions for helping children relax.

Submissions and Payment
Guidelines available. Query with outline, résumé, table of contents, and 3 sample chapters. Accepts photocopies and simultaneous submissions if identified. SASE. Responds in 3 months. Publication in 1–3 years. Royalty; advance.

Editor's Comments
The combination of Red Wheel/Weiser and Conari has dramatically increased our presence in the self-help, inspirational, and spiritual-living categories and has broadened the type of book we will consider for publication. We suggest that writers who believe they have an idea for us first visit our websites at www.redwheelweiser.com and www.conari.com to review our mission and selections, and then submit a detailed proposal.

Resource Publications, Inc.

Suite 290
160 East Virginia Street
San Jose, CA 95112

Editor: William Burns

Publisher's Interests
A Christian publisher, Resource Publications, Inc., provides
materials on liturgy, pastoral ministry, catechesis, and service. Its catalogue includes books of interest to those working
with children, as well as some titles written specifically for
young adults.
Website: www.rpinet.com

Freelance Potential
Published 8 titles (4 juvenile) in 2003: 2 were developed
from unsolicited submissions and 1 was a reprint/licensed
property. Of the 8 titles, 1 was by an unpublished writer
and 1 was by an author who was new to the publishing
house. Receives 130–180 queries yearly.
- **Fiction:** Publishes young adult books, 12–18 years. Also publishes activity books and educational fiction for adults.
- **Nonfiction:** Published 1 middle-grade book, 8–12 years; and 1
  young adult book, 12–18 years. Also features educational titles
  and books in series. Topics include religion, catechesis, liturgy,
  pastoral ministry, and books on special education.
- **Representative Titles:** *Praying with Your Children: A Guide for
  Families* by Pat Fosarelli (parents) includes concrete holistic
  strategies that are sensitive to the physical, psychological, and
  spiritual development of children. *30 Celebrations for Youth,
  Families, and Parishes* by Jerry Welte & Marlene Kemper Welte
  includes ritual prayers for the liturgical and school year and
  helps church leaders design services for various occasions and
  communities.

Submissions and Payment
Guidelines and catalogue available with 9x12 SASE ($1.03
postage). Query with clips. SASE. Responds in 6–8 weeks.
Publication in 9–18 months. Royalty, 8% of net.

Editor's Comments
We continue to look for new pastoral ministry programs and
fresh ideas about the current and future trend of catechesis.
Remember, our purpose is to engage people in worship.

Rising Moon

2900 N. Fort Valley Road
Flagstaff, AZ 86001

Children's Editor: Theresa Howell

Publisher's Interests
Dedicated to multiculturalism, Rising Moon offers publications that seek to preserve Latino culture in the US. Its books are written for children between the ages of four and eight.
Website: www.northlandpub.com

Freelance Potential
Published 7 titles in 2003: 3 were developed from unsolicited submissions and most were by agented authors. Of the 7 titles, 2 were by unpublished writers and 2 were by authors who were new to the publishing house. Receives 100 queries, 1,800 unsolicited mss yearly.

- **Fiction:** Published 2 concept books, 0–4 years; and 5 story picture books, 4–8 years. Genres include fairy tales, folklore, folktales, humor, and inspirational and multicultural fiction. Also publishes books about the American Southwest, activity books, novelty and board books, and bilingual Spanish/English books, 4–8 years.
- **Representative Titles:** *Clarence and the Purple Horse Bounce into Town* by Jean Ekman Adams (5–8 years) follows Clarence the pig and Smoky the horse on a visit to the big city. *Do Princesses Wear Hiking Boots?* by Carmela LaVigna Coyle (4–7 years) focuses on the theme of self-acceptance and encourages children to follow their dreams.

Submissions and Payment
Guidelines available. Accepts picture book manuscripts from agented and previously published authors only. Accepts queries and unsolicited mss for books with Southwest themes. SASE. Responds in 3 months. Publication in 1–2 years. Royalty, varies; advance, varies.

Editor's Comments
We're interested in picture book submissions that explore contemporary bicultural experiences of living in the US, stories that feature contemporary Latino role models, and retold Latino stories and folklore. We'll also consider stories with Southwestern themes, and bilingual Spanish/English stories.

River City Publishing

1719 Mulberry Street
Montgomery, AL 36106

Editor: Ashley Gordon

Publisher's Interests
Founded in 1989, River City Publishing offers fiction, nonfiction, poetry, and art books for adults. It publishes a few children's titles each year under its River City Kids imprint. It is interested primarily in picture books and young adult novels. 5% self-, subsidy-, co-venture, or co-op published material.
Website: www.rivercitypublishing.com

Freelance Potential
Published 12 titles (2 juvenile) in 2003: 2 were developed from unsolicited submissions, 1 was by an agented author, and 1 was a reprint/licensed property. Of the 12 titles, 1 was by an unpublished writer and 10 were by authors who were new to the publishing house. Receives 1,000 queries yearly.
- **Fiction:** Published 1 story picture book, 4–10 years; and 1 young adult book, 12–18 years. Genres include regional, historical, and multicultural fiction; humor; and adventure.
- **Representative Titles:** *Jimbo on Board the Nettie Quill* by Henry Ford Harrison is a novel about an African-American boy's adventures on a steamboat. *Little Girls Have to Sleep* by James Muir is an illustrated story about forest creatures that keep quiet so a girl can sleep; includes an audiocassette and sheet music.

Submissions and Payment
Guidelines available. Query with sample chapters. Accepts photocopies, computer printouts, disk submissions, and simultaneous submissions if identified. SASE. Responds in 1–6 months. Publication in 1 year. Royalty; advance, $1,000–$5,000.

Editor's Comments
This year we're looking for illustrated storybooks for children ages four through ten, as well as young adult novels. Titles that focus on Southern literature and history are of special interest, although we will consider all types of high-quality books. We try to keep our list small so that we can give a personal touch to our booksellers and our authors.

Roaring Brook Press

2 Old New Milford Road
Brookfield, CT 06804

Publisher: Simon Boughton

Publisher's Interests
Roaring Brook Press publishes a wide variety of fiction and nonfiction for children four to eighteen years, including humorous middle-grade titles, cutting-edge young adult novels, and early picture books. Roaring Brook Press, an imprint of The Millbrook Press, was established in 2001.
Website: www.millbrookpress.com

Freelance Potential
Published 40 titles in 2003: all were by agented authors. Of the 40 titles, 8 were by unpublished writers and 20 were by authors who were new to the publishing house.
- **Fiction:** Publishes early picture books, 0–4 years; middle-grade books, 8–12 years; and young adult books, 12–18 years. Genres include contemporary and historical fiction, mystery, suspense, adventure, drama, and humorous stories
- **Representative Titles:** *100 Days of School* by Trudy Harris (grades K–3) uses fun and silly objects like centipede's legs and dots on a clown's outfit to show kids the many ways that they can count to 100. *Everybody Works!* by Shelley Rotner (grades K–1) presents a photographic look at the jobs people do for their communities and families.

Submissions and Payment
Catalogue available with 8x10 SASE ($2 postage). Accepts material through literary agents only. All unagented queries and unsolicited mss will be returned unread. Publication in 1 year. Royalty; advance.

Editor's Comments
We accept submissions from agented authors only. Please look at our catalogue to get an idea of the type of material we are interested in, which does not include poetry, science fiction, fantasy, or anything of a religious or didactic nature. We are a small publisher that can give each author and book our focussed attention, and our mission is to bring to our readers top-quality, cutting-edge fiction they will enjoy reading and remember for years to come.

Robins Lane Press

10726 Tucker Street
Beltsville, MD 20704

Acquisitions Editor

Publisher's Interests
This small publisher releases one to two titles each year, and specializes in books that give parents helpful information and guidance on the complex issues and problems they face in the world today.
Website: www.robinslane.com

Freelance Potential
Published 2 titles in 2003: both were developed from unsolicited submissions and 1 was by an agented author. Of the 2 titles, 1 was by an unpublished writer and 1 was by an author who was new to the publishing house. Receives 100+ queries, 20+ unsolicited mss yearly.
• **Nonfiction:** Publishes parenting titles that offer information and guidance for parents confronting complex issues of society, home and self; easy, practical parenting ideas; and activities that engender curiosity and creative play in children.
• **Representative Titles:** *The Busy Family's Guide to Volunteering* by Jenny Friedman (parents) explains how volunteering teaches compassion, gratitude, and empathy to children, and offers ideas for both long-term projects and one-time events. *Covering Home* by Jack Petrash (parents) gives fathers a new perspective on raising children, with lessons learned from the game of baseball.

Submissions and Payment
Guidelines available. Query or send complete ms. SASE. Responds to queries in 4–6 weeks, to mss in 6–8 weeks. Publication in 9–12 months. Royalty; advance.

Editor's Comments
Our goal is to bring parents help and guidance in a world that has new pressures, new technology, new dangers, and new possibilities, all of which drastically affect our children and redefine what it means to be a kid. We would like to see submissions from writers who have thoroughly researched their topic, and who have a fresh perspective that they want to offer to parents.

Ronsdale Press

3350 West 21st Avenue
Vancouver, British Columbia V6S 1G7
Canada

Submissions Editor: Veronica Hatch

Publisher's Interests

Ronsdale Press, a literary publisher, offers novels, poetry collections, and books for children in the middle-grade to young adult range. Historical fiction for young adults is emerging as a major concentration on its children's list. Ronsdale Press will consider submissions from Canadian citizens or landed immigrants only.

Website: www.ronsdalepress.com

Freelance Potential

Published 10 titles (2 juvenile) in 2003: all were developed from unsolicited submissions and all were by agented authors. Of the 10 titles, 1 was by an unpublished writer and 8 were by authors who were new to the publishing house. Receives 2,000 queries, 1,950 unsolicited mss yearly.

- **Fiction:** Published 2 middle-grade novels, 8–12 years. Also publishes young adult books, 12–18 years. Genres include Canadian historical fiction.
- **Nonfiction:** Publishes adult titles about economics, politics, and language, as well as biographies and autobiographies.
- **Representative Titles:** *Shadows of Disaster* by Cathy Beveridge (9+ years) tells the story of Canada's deadliest rockslide through the eyes of a young girl who travels back in time. *Jeannie & the Gentle Giants* by Luanne Armstrong (9+ years) features a young foster child who learns about love and trust through her friendship with two horses.

Submissions and Payment

Canadian authors only. Guidelines available. Query with sample; or send complete ms. Accepts photocopies and computer printouts. SASE. Responds in 1–2 months. Publication in 1 year. Royalty, 10%.

Editor's Comments

For our young readers list, we remain primarily interested in Canadian historical fiction for young adults. Before you mail your manuscript to us, be sure it fits our mandate—consult our catalogue to see the type of book that is important to us.

The Rosen Publishing Group

29 East 21st Street
New York, NY 10010

YA/Rosen Central Submissions: Iris Rosoff
PowerKids Press Submissions: Joanne Randolph

Publisher's Interests
Celebrating more than 50 years of publishing, The Rosen
Publishing Group provides nonfiction guidance- and curriculum-based books for young adults and middle school students on such subjects as science, economics, guidance, and
drug abuse prevention.
Website: www.powerkidspress.com

Freelance Potential
Published 500 titles in 2003: 50 were by authors who were
new to the publishing house. Receives 1,000 queries yearly.
- **Nonfiction:** Publishes chapter books, 5–10 years; middle-grade
  books, 8–12 years; and young adult books, 12–18 years. Topics
  include history, health, science, the arts, animals, sports, safety,
  and guidance.
- **Representative Titles:** *Refuse to Use: A Girl's Guide to Drugs
  and Alcohol* by Ann Kirby-Payne (grades 5–8) helps girls make
  informed decisions about drugs and alcohol by providing them
  with the necessary information and tools. *The Brain and the
  Spinal Cord: Learning How We Move* by Chris Hayhurst (grades
  5–8) looks at the nervous system and how it controls the
  body's muscles.

Submissions and Payment
Query with outline and sample chapter. Accepts photocopies,
computer printouts, and simultaneous submissions if identified. SASE. Responds in 3 months. Publication in 9 months.
Royalty. Flat fee.

Editor's Comments
We are interested in queries for curriculum books that deal
with issues of importance to middle-grade and young adult
students. Titles on academic subjects such as science, economics, and substance abuse prevention are also of interest.
When you send a query, tell us why your idea is unique and
how it will fit in with our publishing program. Then explain
why it is different from other books on the same topic and how
you would market your work.

Running Press Kids

125 South 22nd Street
Philadelphia, PA 19103

Editor: Andra Serlin

Publisher's Interests
Launched in the fall of 2003 as the children's imprint of Running Press, Running Press Kids specializes in innovative, educational nonfiction. It publishes concept, toddler, and preschool books, as well as picture books and titles for the middle grades. Many of its titles are interactive and include discovery kits or learning tools.
Website: www.runningpress.com

Freelance Potential
Published 40 titles in 2003. Receives 800 queries yearly.
- **Nonfiction:** Publishes concept, toddler, and early picture books, 0–4 years; story picture books, 4–10 years; and middle-grade books, 8–12 years. Features discovery, activity, and puzzle books. Topics include science, technology, art, architecture, geography, and animals. Also publishes parenting titles.
- **Representative Titles:** *Trucks: A Magic Wand Adventure Book* encourages children to use their imaginations by reading a story about trucks and then moving five magnetic features and characters from the story over the pages using a special wand. *Hieroglyphics: The Secrets of Ancient Egyptian Writing to Unlock and Discover* is a kit that contains a book, hieroglyphic stamps, inkpad, and papyrus templates.

Submissions and Payment
Catalogue available. Query with outline, table of contents, and synopsis. Send complete ms for picture books. Accepts simultaneous submissions if identified. Availability of artwork improves chance of acceptance. SASE. Responds in 2–3 months. Publication in 1–2 years. Advance, varies.

Editor's Comments
We are looking for innovative products designed to combine learning and fun. We have a new line of "Kinesthetic Learning Tools," which uses movement and activity to help children learn, as in our Magic Wand Adventure Books and our Discovery Kits. Our main interest is in educational nonfiction, but we do have a small picture book program.

St. Anthony Messenger Press

28 W. Liberty Street
Cincinnati, OH 45202

Editorial Director: Lisa Biedenbach

Publisher's Interests
St. Anthony Messenger Press seeks to evangelize, inspire,
and inform those who search for God and who desire a richer
Catholic, Christian, human life. Its catalogue includes books
for children and adults, as well as catechetical materials and
Franciscan resources.
Website: www.americancatholic.org

Freelance Potential
Published 30 titles (2 juvenile) in 2003: 10 were developed from
unsolicited submissions, 1 was by an agented author, and 3
were reprint/licensed properties. Of the 30 titles, 6 were by
unpublished writers and 11 were by authors who were new to
the publishing house. Receives 300 queries yearly.
- **Nonfiction:** Published 1 story picture book, 4–10 years; and 1
  middle-grade book, 8–12 years. Topics include liturgy, the
  sacraments, prayer, spirituality, Scripture, ministry, and religious education. Also offers parenting titles.
- **Representative Titles:** *Seven Lonely Places, Seven Warm
  Places* by April Bolton introduces children to the seven deadly
  sins and the seven virtues. *Everyday Prayers for Children* by
  Lois Rock includes 200 prayers that address the everyday
  aspects of a child's world, including home and school, family
  and friends, personal secrets, and concern for global issues.

Submissions and Payment
Guidelines available. Query with outline/synopsis. Accepts
photocopies. No simultaneous submissions. SASE. Responds
in 6–8 weeks. Publication in 1–2 years. Royalty, 10%;
advance, $1,000.

Editor's Comments
Our books for Catholic Christians are designed to educate and
inspire them, not to challenge church authority. We look for a
writing style that is easy to read and for manuscripts that offer
practical, concrete advice or suggestions and clear examples.
We do not publish fiction, poetry, academic studies, autobiographies, or personal reflections.

Saint Mary's Press

702 Terrace Heights
Winona, MN 55987-1320

Middle School Editor: Steven Roe

Publisher's Interests

Saint Mary's Press publishes books for middle-grade children
and young adults that encourage them in their Christian
spiritual journey. It also offers titles for adults who minister
to youth in parish or school settings.
Website: www.smp.org

Freelance Potential

Published 20 titles (13 juvenile) in 2003: 2 were developed
from unsolicited submissions and 1 was a reprint/licensed
property. Receives 100+ queries, 100+ unsolicited mss yearly.
- **Nonfiction:** Publishes middle-grade books, 8–12 years; and
  young adult books, 12–18 years. Topics include spirituality,
  Christianity, and the Catholic faith. Also publishes titles for
  adults who minister to youth.
- **Representative Titles:** *World Religions: A Voyage of Discovery*
  by Jeffrey Brodd (grades 11 and 12) introduces readers to the
  world's major religions and offers insights into the people who
  embrace these beliefs. *Living the Works of Mercy* by Ellen P.
  Cavanaugh (adults) features strategies for helping young people live the traditional corporal and spiritual works of mercy in
  today's society.

Submissions and Payment

Guidelines available. Query or send complete ms. Accepts
computer printouts, disk submissions (RTF files), and simultaneous submissions if identified. SASE. Responds to queries
in 2 months, to mss in 2–3 months. Publication in 18
months. Royalty, 10%.

Editor's Comments

Please note that we no longer publish fiction. For the coming
year, we're particularly interested in seeing submissions of
works aimed at adults who work with youth in Catholic religious education classes. Please include a cover letter with your
submission that describes your background and related experiences. First impressions are important to us, so be sure to
prepare this introductory letter with care.

Sandcastle Publishing

1723 Hill Drive
P.O. Box 3070
South Pasadena, CA 91301-6070

Acquisitions Editor

Publisher's Interests

Sandcastle Publishing offers read-aloud story picture books
and collections of dramatic scenes and monologues for children and teens. Founded 14 years ago, its mission is to help
young people improve themselves through participation in
the performing arts.
Website: www.childrenactingbooks.com

Freelance Potential

Published 3 titles in 2003. Of the 3 titles, 1 was by an
unpublished writer. Receives 750 queries, 500 unsolicited
mss yearly.
- **Fiction:** Published 2 story picture books, 3–8 years. Features
  32-page read-aloud stories that include parts for children
  to act out. Also publishes collections of monologues and
  dramatic scenes.
- **Nonfiction:** Published 1 young adult title, 12–18 years. Features books about acting and the dramatic arts.
- **Representative Titles:** *The Confetti Company Presents Rumpel-
  stiltskin* is an updated fairy tale with music and acting by children and a celebrity narrator. *Sensational Scenes for Teens* by
  Chambers Stevens (13–18 years) includes more than 30
  comedic and dramatic scenes and interviews with veteran TV
  casting directors.

Submissions and Payment

Guidelines available. Query with résumé. Send complete ms
for early reader fiction. SASE. Responds in 2–3 months. Publication period and payment policy vary.

Editor's Comments

Our goal is to help youth develop their potential by providing
valuable information in a way that motivates them toward
greater possibilities. Send us ideas for books for children and
teens that promote acting and the performing arts. All submissions should include information on the targeted age range.
Please don't send book-length fiction for middle-grade readers
or picture books for the very young.

Scarecrow Press

Suite 200
4501 Forbes Boulevard
Lanham, MD 20706

Acquisitions Editor: Sue Easun

Publisher's Interests

Reference titles, professional texts, and resource materials are the focus of Scarecrow Press. It is a scholarly, academic publisher and specializes in well-researched titles that demonstrate new treatments of traditional topics. Its audience includes educators and librarians.
Website: www.scarecrowpress.com

Freelance Potential

Published 200 titles (15 juvenile) in 2003: 5 were by agented authors and 10 were reprint/licensed properties. Receives 500 queries, 250 unsolicited mss yearly.

- **Nonfiction:** Publishes resource materials and reference works for use in secondary schools. Also publishes lesson plans, project ideas, and books about children's literature.
- **Representative Titles:** *What Do Draculas Do?: Essays on Contemporary Writers of Fiction for Children and Young Adults* by David Rees (educators) critiques the work of such well-known children's authors as Mary Norton, Roald Dahl, Maurice Sendak, and Madeleine L'Engle. *Children's Television: The First Thirty-Five Years, 1946–1981: Part I: Animated Cartoon Series* by George W. Woolery (educators) reviews the material produced for children in the early years of television and what the programs brought to their audience.

Submissions and Payment

Guidelines available. Prefers query with résumé, table of contents, introduction, chapter summaries, and sample chapter. Accepts complete ms with curriculum vitae. Accepts photocopies, computer printouts, and simultaneous submissions. SASE. Responds to queries in 2 months, to mss in 2–4 months. Publication in 6–12 months. Royalty, 8–15%.

Editor's Comments

Our audience comprises professionals and academics who specialize in topics related to children and young adults. Send us a detailed proposal that demonstrates your expertise to write about children's or young adult literature.

Scholastic Canada Ltd.

175 Hillmount Road
Markham, Ontario L6C 1Z7
Canada

The Editors

Publisher's Interests
Scholastic Canada Ltd. publishes fiction as well as nonfiction, written by Canadian authors, for toddlers through young adults.
Website: www.scholastic.ca

Freelance Potential
Published 70 titles (6 juvenile) in 2003: 24 were by agented authors and 11 were reprint/licensed properties. Receives 2,000+ queries yearly.
- **Fiction:** Publishes story picture books, 4–10 years; chapter books, 5–10 years; middle-grade novels, 8–12 years; and young adult books, 12–16 years. Genres include adventure, mystery, suspense, humor, stories about sports, drama, and contemporary and historical fiction.
- **Nonfiction:** Publishes concept books and toddler books, 0–4 years; easy-to-read books, 4–7 years; and middle-grade books, 8–12 years. Topics include Canadian history, regional subjects, animals, technology, and sports. Also publishes activity books and biographies.
- **Representative Titles:** *Zoom!* by Robert Munsch (3–8 years) is the story of Lauretta, who saves the day by speeding her brother to the hospital in her high-speed dirtbike wheelchair. *Made in Canada: 101 Amazing Achievements* by Bev Spencer (8–11 years) details technological as well as cultural achievements by Canadians in fields such as science, medicine, sports, recreation, and entertainment.

Submissions and Payment
Accepts queries from Canadian authors only. Query with outline and table of contents; include résumé for nonfiction. Accepts photocopies and computer printouts. No simultaneous submissions. SASE. Responds in 3 months. Publication in 2 years. Payment policy varies.

Editor's Comments
Our publishing focus is on books written by Canadians. Check our website for up-to-date information on our current submission policy.

Scholastic Inc./Trade Paperback Division

555 Broadway
New York, NY 10012

Editorial Director/Trade Paperbacks: Craig Walker

Publisher's Interests

The trade paperback division of this well-known publisher produces fiction and nonfiction for children of all ages. Its fiction list includes science fiction, adventure stories, and mysteries, while its nonfiction list offers books about science, nature, and world cultures. It accepts queries from agents and authors who have already published through Scholastic. **Website:** www.scholastic.com

Freelance Potential

Published 350–400 titles in 2003: all were by agented authors. Of the 350–400 titles, 52 were by authors who were new to the publishing house. Receives 250 queries, 150 unsolicited mss yearly.

- **Fiction:** Publishes picture books for all ages and middle-grade novels, 8–11 years. Genres include science fiction, fantasy, adventure, mystery, and sports stories.
- **Nonfiction:** Publishes books for all ages. Topics include nature, science, and multicultural issues. Also publishes parenting titles and photo essays.
- **Representative Titles:** *Fall Leaves Fall* by Zoe Hall (4–7 years) is a picture book about two children who try to catch, stomp, and kick leaves as they fall to the ground. *Polar Bears* by Gail Gibbons (7–10 years) is an illustrated book that explains where polar bears live, how they get their food, when they mate, and how they rear their young.

Submissions and Payment

Accepts submissions through agents and queries from authors who have previously published with Scholastic Trade. SASE. Publication period and payment policy vary.

Editor's Comments

Our biggest demand is for original, exceptionally well-written fiction for middle-grade readers. We are especially interested in novels that can be published in series. We're looking for stories that have strong characters that will appeal to eight- to ten-year-old children.

Scholastic Press

557 Broadway
New York, NY 10012

Editorial Director: Elizabeth Szabla

Publisher's Interests
Fiction and nonfiction picture books, middle-grade and young adult fiction, and books that offer unusual approaches to dry subjects are available from Scholastic Press. All submissions must come from previously published authors, through literary agents, or from SCBWI members.
Website: www.scholastic.com

Freelance Potential
Published 40 titles in 2003: all were by agented authors. Of the 40 titles, 1–2 were by unpublished writers and 2–4 were by new authors. Receives 1,200–2,400 queries yearly.
- **Fiction:** Published 1 toddler book and 1 early picture book, 0–4 years; 1 easy-to-read book, 4–7 years; 5 story picture books, 4–10 years; 3 chapter books, 5–10 years; 6 middle-grade novels, 8–12 years; and 6 young adult books, 12–18 years. Genres include adventure, fantasy, humor, and historical, multicultural and ethnic fiction. Also publishes poetry.
- **Nonfiction:** Published 1 early picture book, 0–4 years; 1 easy-to-read book, 4–7 years; 4 story picture books, 4–10 years; 1 chapter book, 5–10 years; 4 middle-grade books, 8–12 years; and 2 young adult books, 12–18 years. Topics include nature, the environment, history, biography, and multicultural issues.
- **Representative Titles:** *A Time to Love* by Walter Dean Myers (12+ years) features Old Testament stories that explore human relationships. *Mama Will Be Home Soon* by Nancy Minchella (2–5 years) is a picture book about separation anxiety.

Submissions and Payment
Guidelines available. Query or send complete ms. Accepts submissions from agents, previously published authors, or SCBWI members only. Accepts photocopies. SASE. Responds to queries in 2–3 weeks, to mss in 6–8 months. Publication in 2–3 years. Royalty, varies; advance, varies.

Editor's Comments
Books that offer subtly handled treatments of the key relationships in children's lives are welcome.

Scholastic Professional Books

557 Broadway
New York, NY 10012-3999

Editorial/Production Coordinator: Adriane Rozier

Publisher's Interests
This division of Scholastic Inc. develops books on teaching
language arts and reading, science, mathematics, social
studies, and art. Its materials are used by language arts
specialists, curriculum specialists, and teacher trainers
working at the preschool through eighth-grade level. Children's titles do not appear on its list.
Website: www.scholastic.com/professional

Freelance Potential
Published 120 titles in 2003: 8–10 were developed from
unsolicited submissions. Receives 300–400 queries, 150–200
unsolicited mss yearly.
- **Nonfiction:** Publishes titles for educators working with students in pre-K–grade 8. Also offers literature-based and cross-
  curriculum materials for teaching reading, language arts,
  mathematics, science, social studies, and art, as well as books
  on assessment, evaluation, cooperative learning, and classroom management.
- **Representative Titles:** *My First Library Board Books* (grades
  pre-K–K) features four board books about babies, movement,
  feelings, and big and little. *Teaching Reading in the Middle
  School* by Laura Robb (teachers, grades 5–8) offers a strategic
  approach to teaching reading that improves comprehension
  and thinking.

Submissions and Payment
Guidelines available. Query with outline and 2 sample
chapters; or send complete ms. Accepts photocopies, com-
puter printouts, and simultaneous submissions if identified.
SASE. Responds in 4 months. Publication in 12–14 months.
Royalty; advance. Flat fee.

Editor's Comments
We are eager to help teachers communicate their most exciting
projects, activities, and specific teaching approaches and
strategies. We're also interested in the results of research con-
ducted in classrooms.

Scorpius Digital Publishing

Box 19423
Queen Anne Station
Seattle, WA 98109

Publisher: Marti McKenna

Publisher's Interests
Science fiction, fantasy, horror, and mystery are all covered in books found at this electronic publisher's website. Its non-fiction offerings include self-help books, biographies, and photo essays. It does not publish any titles in print form.
Website: www.scorpiusdigital.com

Freelance Potential
Published 20 titles (4 juvenile) in 2003: 5 were developed from unsolicited submissions and all were by agented authors. Of the 20 titles, 2 were by unpublished writers and 5 were by new authors. Receives 60+ queries yearly.
- **Fiction:** Publishes story picture books, 4–10 years; middle-grade novels, 8–12 years; and young adult books, 12–18 years. Genres include fantasy, folklore, folktales, horror, mystery, suspense, science fiction, historical fiction, and fairy tales. Also publishes books in series, 12–18 years.
- **Nonfiction:** Publishes multicultural and ethnic titles, regional and historical titles, self-help books, biographies, and photo essays, 4–10 years.
- **Representative Titles:** *Hong on the Range* by William F. Wu is a CyberWestern story about coming of age in a strange and dangerous land. *The Hedge, the Ribbon* by Carol Orlock is a magical tale about the inhabitants of a town named Millford who have extraordinary powers.

Submissions and Payment
Guidelines and catalogue available at website. Query. Accepts email submissions to submissions@scorpiusdigital.com. Responds in 1 month. Publication in 6 months. Royalty.

Editor's Comments
Our mission at Scorpius Digital Publishing is to bring readers of all ages the very best fiction and nonfiction—all in electronic format. We don't see electronic books as a replacement for print books, but rather as an addition with their own special qualities. We welcome writers with good stories who are interested in exploring this new, exciting publishing format.

Scott Foresman

1900 East Lake Avenue
Glenview, IL 60025

Administrative Assistant: Maria Sandoval

Publisher's Interests

Scott Foresman offers books, software, and resource materials for teaching language arts, reading, mathematics, social studies, science, and music to kindergarten through sixth-grade students. Its imprints include Scott Foresman-Addison Wesley and Silver Burdett Ginn.
Website: www.scottforesman.com

Freelance Potential

Published 1,000 titles in 2003. Of the 1,000 titles, 50 were by authors who were new to the publishing house. Receives 350 queries yearly.

- **Nonfiction:** Publishes textbook-based curriculum programs and teacher resources for grades K–6. Subjects include reading, language arts, science, social studies, mathematics, music, spelling, handwriting, technology, early learning, and bilingual education. Also offers educational software, audio and visual materials, and online resources.
- **Representative Titles:** *The Time Machine* by Fay Robinson (grades K–1) is an adventure story; part of the Independent Reader Package. *AstroWord*™ (grades K–6) is a series of CD-ROMS with an intergalactic theme and exciting graphics and animation to teach phonics and word skills.

Submissions and Payment

Query with résumé, outline, and sample chapters. Accepts photocopies and computer printouts. SASE. Responds in 2 months. Publication in 1–3 years. Royalty. Flat fee.

Editor's Comments

We're looking for books and resource materials for all curriculum areas. It is essential that everything we publish be well-written, and present information in a clear, easy-to-implement manner. Potential authors must have the proper credentials to tackle the topic they wish to write about, so be sure to include a detailed résumé with your query. One area of particular interest to us is material that explores ways to include Spanish in reading, mathematics, science, and social studies programs.

Seedling Publications

4522 Indianola Avenue
Columbus, OH 43214-2246

Submissions Editor: Lynn Salem

Publisher's Interests
Seedling Publications specializes in books for the emergent
reader. It offers high-quality books that feature strong,
unique story lines or surprise endings. Each book is designed
to ensure success for young readers.
Website: www.seedlingpub.com

Freelance Potential
Published 45 titles in 2003: 5 were developed from unsolicited submissions. Of the 45 titles, 3 were by unpublished
writers and 5 were by authors who were new to the publishing house. Receives 300 unsolicited mss yearly.

- **Fiction:** Published 25 easy-to-read books, 4–7 years. Genres
  include adventure, fairy tales, stories about sports and nature,
  and humor.
- **Nonfiction:** Published 20 easy-to-read books, 4–7 years. Topics
  include science, nature, animals, multicultural events, mathematics, and technology.
- **Representative Titles:** *Charlie's Black Hen* by Bonnie High-
  smith Taylor (4–7 years) allows readers to practice color words
  as the story moves from a green meadow, to a blue pond, to a
  red coop. *Molly Makes a Graph* by Lynn Salem & Josie Stewart
  (4–7 years) shows how Molly makes a graph of her friends'
  favorite shoes.

Submissions and Payment
Send complete ms. Accepts photocopies, computer printouts,
and simultaneous submissions if identified. SASE. Responds
in 6 months. Publication in 1 year. Payment policy varies.

Editor's Comments
We review manuscripts up to 150–200 words that are written
in an 8-, 12-, or 16-page format. Our products have the appeal
of literature in both story and art, but it is not necessary for
you to include illustrations with your manuscript. Do not send
us rhyming stories, full-length picture books, poetry books, or
chapter books. We could use books on math, nature, and multicultural themes this year. Visit our website before submitting.

Silver Dolphin Books

5880 Oberlin Drive
San Diego, CA 92121

Submissions Editor

Publisher's Interests
Silver Dolphin Books is an imprint of Advantage Publishers Group, founded in 1990. It publishes nonfiction only, and its catalogue includes novelty, activity, and educational material for readers up to the age of 12.
Website: www.silverdolphinbooks.com

Freelance Potential
Published 55 titles in 2003: most were reprint/licensed properties. Receives 50+ unsolicited mss yearly.
- **Nonfiction:** Publishes concept books, toddler books, and early picture books, 0–4 years; easy-to-read books, 4–7 years; story picture books, 4–10 years; and middle-grade titles, 8–12 years. Topics include the alphabet, animals, numbers, magic, science, and history.
- **Representative Titles:** *When I'm Big* by Christine Tagg (3–5 years) is a pop-up book that follows the adventures of one lovable bee named Zed; part of the BusyBugz series. *Be a Star Magician!* by Cheryll Charming is an all-inclusive kit that introduces young children to the world of magic and illusion.

Submissions and Payment
Guidelines available. Send complete ms. Availability of artwork improves chance of acceptance. SASE. Responds in 1 month. Publication period and payment policy vary.

Editor's Comments
We are very specific about what we expect from writers who want us to review their submissions. You must include: your biography and publishing credits; an outline and table of contents; sample chapters; an estimation of your book's length; and a market analysis. The more concise and detailed your query is, the better your chance of getting our attention. We are currently accepting work in the following subject areas: children's nonfiction; games; crafts and hobbies; family; child care; and relationships. Books that feature a highly interactive format and lovable characters, as well as series for older readers, are always of interest.

Crown Jewels
Hope Killcoyne
Silver Moon Press

Silver Moon Press publishes fiction and nonfiction for middle-grade readers. The company's focus is history and curriculum materials. Of special interest in history are stories about the American Revolution, the Colonial time period, and New York State history.

"We are a New York company, and many of our books find their way into school curriculums. Here, they teach New York history in grades seven and eight," explains Managing Editor Hope Killcoyne. "Our list does have notable exceptions. For instance, we've published some California history, and we've also done a few picture books. But the crown jewel of our publishing program is historical fiction."

Killcoyne knows what it's like to be on the "flip side of the coin," having written children's books. "I understand the feelings of writers, waiting to hear about their beloved manuscripts, often for months at a time. Unfortunately, we have a small staff here at Silver Moon. Sometimes it takes a while for us to get to the slush pile."

Killcoyne says writers shouldn't submit blindly. "For example, we only publish children's books, but we've received adult submissions. It can be frustrating, because it's really such a waste of time." Writers should include a brief cover letter with their submissions. "Tell me what the story is about, what resources you used, and the approximate word count. Also, tell me if you've published in the past."

Killcoyne can usually tell by the first page or two if a manuscript is worth pursuing. "I want to be engaged right from the start. When you write historical fiction, you're serving two masters. You have to get the history right, but you also need to tell a good story, with great characters and a solid plot. And because our books are only about 15,000 words, they must move along quickly."

(See listing for Silver Moon Press
on following page)

Silver Moon Press

Suite 622
160 Fifth Avenue
New York, NY 10010

Managing Editor: Hope Killcoyne

Publisher's Interests

American historical fiction is a specialty of the Silver Moon Press, with a particular interest in the Revolutionary War, colonial times, and history of New York State. It also features nonfiction biographies and English language arts titles.
Website: www.silvermoonpress.com

Freelance Potential

Published 4 titles in 2003: 3 were developed from unsolicited submissions. Of the 4 titles, 2 were by unpublished writers and 3 were by new authors. Receives 500 queries yearly.

- **Fiction:** Published 4 middle-grade books, 8–12 years. Genres include historical, multicultural, and ethnic fiction; adventure; mystery; folktales; and books about family issues.
- **Nonfiction:** Publishes chapter books, 8–12 years. Topics include history, politics, geography, civil rights, ecology, nature, the environment, science, and technology. Also publishes biographies and test preparation materials for language arts and social studies.
- **Representative Titles:** *A Silent Witness in Harlem* by Eve Creary (8–12 years), set in the Harlem Renaissance, is the story of a girl who witnesses a kidnapping; part of the Mysteries in Time series. *Ride for Freedom* by Judy Hominick & Jeanne Spreier (8–12 years) is the story of a 16-year-old girl who takes part in the Revolution; part of the Heroes to Remember series.

Submissions and Payment

Guidelines available. Query with sample chapters for stand-alone titles. Query with outline, synopsis of each book, and sample chapter of first book for series. Accepts computer printouts and simultaneous submissions. SASE. Responds in 6–12 months. Publication period and payment policy vary.

Editor's Comments

We accept historical fiction with protagonists between ages 11 and 14. We're particularly interested in submissions for our new nonfiction series, Heroes to Remember.

Silver Whistle

Harcourt, Inc.
15 East 26th Street
New York, NY 10010

Submissions Editor

Publisher's Interests
This publisher, an imprint of Harcourt, offers a wide range
of material, from picture books for early readers, to fiction
for middle-grade and young adult readers, to biographies for
all ages.
Website: www.harcourtbooks.com

Freelance Potential
Published 12 titles in 2003: 1 was developed from an unsolicited submission and 11 were by agented authors. Of the 12
titles, 1 was by an unpublished writer and 1 was by an
author who was new to the publishing house. Receives
100–200 queries yearly.

- **Fiction:** Published 6 early picture books, 0–4 years; and 6
  story picture books, 4–10 years. Also publishes easy-to-read
  books, 4–7 years; chapter books, 5–10 years; middle-grade
  books, 8–12 years; and young adult books, 12–18 years.
  Genres include inspirational and contemporary fiction and
  adventure stories.
- **Nonfiction:** Publishes early picture books, 0–4 years; and story
  picture books, 4–10 years. Also publishes biographies and
  books about history.
- **Representative Titles:** *Hoptoad* by Jane Yolen (2–5 years) tells
  what happens when a boy, his dog, and his dad go out for a
  drive and unexpectedly meet a toad on the road. *Beverly
  Billingsly Takes a Bow* by Alexander Stadler (3–7 years) is the
  story of a young girl whose love of dress-up leads to a first
  experience with theater, and a lesson that no role is too small.

Submissions and Payment
Not currently accepting unsolicited manuscripts. Query for
nonfiction, biographies, and collections. SASE. Responds in
1 month. Payment policy varies.

Editor's Comments
We look for strong voices and characters in stories that touch
the heart and involve the reader. We are interested in picture
books and biographies as well as longer fiction.

Simon & Schuster Books for Young Readers

1230 Avenue of the Americas
New York, NY 10020

Submissions Editor

Publisher's Interests
This large, well-known publishing house offers nonfiction and fiction books for children of all ages under its many imprints, which include Aladdin Paperbacks, Margaret K. McElderry, Simon Pulse, Little Simon, Simon Spotlight, and Atheneum Books.
Website: www.simonsayskids.com

Freelance Potential
Published 75 titles in 2003: 60 were by agented authors. Receives 2,500 queries yearly.
- **Fiction:** Publishes toddler books and early picture books, 0–4 years; easy-to-read books, 4–7 years; story picture books, 4–10 years; chapter books, 5–10 years; middle-grade novels, 8–12 years; and 5 young adult books, 12–18 years. Genres include historical, contemporary, and multicultural fiction, mystery, fantasy, folklore, and fairy tales.
- **Nonfiction:** Publishes story picture books, 4–10 years; and middle-grade books, 8–12 years. Topics include mathematics, science, nature, history, and social issues. Also publishes biographies and anthologies.
- **Representative Titles:** *A Solitary Blue* by Cynthia Voigt (12+ years) is a novel about a boy whose mother re-enters his life after abandoning him. *Clorinda* by Robert Kinerk (4–8 years) is a picture book about a bold and imaginative cow who fulfills her dream of dancing in the ballet.

Submissions and Payment
Guidelines available. Query. Accepts email queries with outline/synopsis and sample chapter to childrens.submissions@simonandschuster.com (include imprint name in subject line). No unsolicited mss. SASE. Responds in 2 months. Publication in 2–4 years. Royalty; advance.

Editor's Comments
Please don't send us a finished manuscript. Send us a query only. We will consider queries sent by email, and we are again accepting them through the regular mail as well.

Simon Pulse

Simon & Schuster
1230 Avenue of the Americas
New York, NY 10020

Submissions Editor

Publisher's Interests
Contemporary writing on topics that appeal to teens is the
focus of this publisher's list. Both fiction and nonfiction
appear in Simon Pulse's catalogue, but most of the books it
publishes are from agented authors. Many titles appear as
part of series.
Website: www.simonsays.com

Freelance Potential
Published 50 titles in 2003: 40 were by agented authors. Of
the 50 titles, 1 was by an unpublished writer and 3 were by
authors who were new to the publishing house. Receives
1,000+ queries and unsolicited mss yearly.
- **Fiction:** Publishes middle-grade novels, 8–12 years; and
  young adult novels, 12–18 years. Genres include adventure,
  mystery, suspense, romance, fantasy, folktales, drama, horror, humor, and contemporary, inspirational, and ethnic and
  multicultural fiction.
- **Nonfiction:** Publishes middle-grade books, 8–12 years; and
  young adult books, 12–18 years. Topics include animals, pets,
  current events, entertainment, multicultural and ethnic subjects, science, technology, sports, and social issues. Also publishes biographies and self-help books.
- **Representative Titles:** *The Book of the Shadow* by Carrie Asai
  (YA) follows the adventures of a teenage Japanese mystery girl
  who survived a plane crash at age two, but has never been
  claimed by a family. *Rainbow Boys* by Alex Sanchez (12+ years)
  chronicles the ups and downs in the lives of three boys whose
  friendship helps them survive high school.

Submissions and Payment
Guidelines available. Query. SASE. Response time varies.
Publication in 6–24 months. Payment policy varies.

Editor's Comments
We are now willing to review unsolicited queries, but most of
the material we accept is submitted through literary agents.
Working on an established series offers the best chance for
new writers who want to break in with a major publisher.

Smith and Kraus

P.O. Box 127
Lyme, NH 03768

Submissions

Publisher's Interests
Dramatic materials for amateur and professional theater groups are the specialty of Smith and Kraus. It targets drama teachers, directors, and actors with its monologues, plays, and books about theater arts. Its Young Actors series features books designed for performers between the ages of seven and twenty-two.
Website: www.smithkraus.com

Freelance Potential
Published 30 titles in 2003: 4 were developed from unsolicited submissions. Receives 240 queries yearly.
- **Nonfiction:** Publishes collections of plays, scenes, and monologues, grades K–12. Also offers instructional books for teachers; anthologies; collections of work by contemporary playwrights; translations; books on career development; and period and special interest monologues.
- **Representative Titles:** *Hooves and Horns, Fins and Feathers* by Helen Landalf & Pamela Gerke (teachers, grades K–1) features dramatic exercises that revolve around students "in role" as nature photographers who are preparing to study wild animals. *Now I Get It!* by L. E. McCullough (teachers, grades K–3) features 36 ten-minute skits about science, math, language, and social studies for fun and learning.

Submissions and Payment
Catalogue available. Query with résumé. Accepts photocopies, computer printouts, and simultaneous submissions if identified. SASE. Responds in 1 month. Publication in 1 year. Royalty; advance. Flat fee.

Editor's Comments
Please note that we no longer publish single plays. We accept submissions for two anthologies each year: *New Playwrights: The Best New Plays* and *Women Playwrights: The Best New Plays.* We also accept submissions for our annual scene and monologue books. All submitted plays, scenes, and monologues must have been produced.

Soundprints

353 Main Avenue
Norwalk, CT 06851-1552

Assistant Editor: Chelsea Shriver

Publisher's Interests
Books about nature and wildlife that are created to
educate and entertain young readers are the specialty of
Soundprints. All of its titles are published in series and
adhere to strict specifications. Most are fictional stories
that are based on facts, and many are packaged with a
companion toy or audiotape.
Website: www.soundprints.com

Freelance Potential
Published 30 titles in 2003. Of the 30 titles, 1 was by an
author who was new to the publishing house. Receives 200
queries yearly.
- **Fiction:** Published 18 story picture books, 4–10 years; and
  12 chapter books, 5–10 years. Publishes books in series
  about nature, the environment, and animals. Also offers multicultural and adventure stories.
- **Representative Titles:** *Wake Up, Black Bear!* by Dawn Bentley
  (pre-K–grade 1) shows how a black bear teaches her cubs to
  catch trout, climb trees, and lick honey out of the comb; part
  of the Atlantic Wilderness series. *River Otter at Autumn Lane* by
  Laura Gates Galvin (pre-K–grade 2) features a river otter who
  nurses her three newborn cubs and then has to teach them to
  swim in the river; part of the Smithsonian's Backyard series.

Submissions and Payment
Query with clips or writing samples. Accepts photocopies and
computer printouts. SASE. Responds in 1 month. Publication
period varies. Flat fee.

Editor's Comments
Most of the titles we publish appear as part of a series; to
become a part of a series, a manuscript must adhere to strict
guidelines. For that reason, most of our authors are contracted
on a work-for-hire basis to create stories that follow certain
specifications, depending on our needs. The best advice we can
give prospective authors is to send us writing samples or samples of your published work.

Sourcebooks

Suite 139
1935 Brookdale Road
Naperville, IL 60563

Submissions: Peter Lynch

Publisher's Interests

Although Sourcebooks is not a children's publisher, it develops a number of titles on parenting, child development, childbirth, and family issues. Its list also includes books for adults on entertainment, history, and sports. It distributes its titles through the retail market, including bookstores, gift stores, and specialty shops.
Website: www.sourcebooks.com

Freelance Potential

Published 120 titles in 2003: 5 were developed from unsolicited submissions. Receives 500 queries, 1,500 unsolicited mss yearly.

- **Nonfiction:** Publishes self-help books. Topics include parenting, single parenting, family issues, childbirth, multicultural issues, and lifestyle issues.
- **Representative Titles:** *101 Things Every Kid Should Do Growing Up* by Alecia Devantier describes hands-on, creative experiences every child should have as he or she grows into adulthood. *Deadbeats: What Responsible Parents Need to Know About Collecting Child Support* by Simone Spence (parents) offers tips on modifying and enforcing child support orders, finding an attorney, and tracking down absent parents.

Submissions and Payment

Guidelines and catalogue available. Query with résumé, synopsis, table of contents, 2 sample chapters, and market analysis. Accepts photocopies, computer printouts, and simultaneous submissions if identified. SASE. Responds in 4–6 weeks. Publication in 1 year. Royalty, 6–15%.

Editor's Comments

Successful queries provide information about a well-defined target market for the proposed book. We also want to see a list of competing or comparable titles and a discussion of how your book differs. We always try to work with our authors to develop books that will find and inspire a wide audience, and we seek writers who are as committed to success as we are.

The Speech Bin, Inc.

1965 25th Avenue
Vero Beach, FL 32960

Senior Editor: Jan J. Binney

Publisher's Interests
The Speech Bin caters to professionals who work with children and adults who have communication disorders. Its customers include speech-language pathologists, audiologists, and occupational therapists. Its picture books, concept books, and middle-grade titles are all designed for use by these professionals.
Website: www.speechbin.com

Freelance Potential
Published 10 titles in 2003: 5 were developed from unsolicited submissions. Receives 500+ queries yearly.
- **Fiction:** Publishes picture books, 4–10 years. Features stories that deal with stuttering, conversation, phonology, articulation, communication, and language skills.
- **Nonfiction:** Publishes concept books and early picture books, 0–4 years; story picture books, 4–10 years; and middle-grade books, 8–12 years. Topics include stuttering, phonology, articulation, and language skills. Also features textbooks and how-to titles for parents, speech pathologists, and occupational therapists.
- **Representative Titles:** *I Love Phonics* uses entertaining activities, animated characters, and sticker rewards to teach children the phonics skills they need to learn to read fluently and spell. *Expression Connection* is an instructional program that moves elementary school children from simple narratives to complex stories.

Submissions and Payment
Guidelines available with #10 SASE ($.37 postage); catalogue available with 9x12 SASE ($1.47 postage). Query with résumé and outline/synopsis. Accepts photocopies. SASE. Responds in 1–2 months. Publication in 1 year. Royalty.

Editor's Comments
Include information on your book's goals, objectives, and audience. In what setting will it be used? For what purpose? Provide information on your education and experience.

Sports Publishing Inc.

804 North Neil
Champaign, IL 61820

Acquisitions Editor: Mike Pearson

Publisher's Interests
Sports Publishing offers a range of books on the topic of sports, from biographies of athletes, to histories of specific sports, to comprehensive encyclopedias of sports. This publisher was established in 1989, and its offerings include Kids Superstars, a series for children in grades three through five. **Website:** www.sportspublishing.com

Freelance Potential
Published 150 titles (10 juvenile) in 2003. Receives 50 queries yearly.
- **Fiction:** Publishes middle-grade novels, 8–14 years. Features stories about sports and athletes.
- **Nonfiction:** Publishes middle-grade titles, 8–14 years. Topics include auto racing, baseball, basketball, football, golf, and hockey. Also publishes biographies.
- **Representative Titles:** *Charlie Ward: Winning by His Grace* by Charlie Ward with Joe Cooney (7–11 years) tells the story of Ward, the reserved, unassuming Heisman Trophy winner who relied on faith to give him focus and determination. *Mark McGwire: Slugger!* by Rob Rains (6–11 years) is a biography of one of baseball's most popular and prolific home run hitters.

Submissions and Payment
Guidelines available. Query with outline, synopsis, 2–3 sample chapters, competition analysis, and résumé. Accepts photocopies, computer printouts, and email queries to mpearson @sagamore.com. SASE. Response time varies. Publication period and payment policy vary.

Editor's Comments
We urge writers to visit our website to see the type of titles we publish, and to make sure that their query suggests a new angle or topic not covered previously. We insist on accuracy, and are eager to hear from authors who can write authoritatively and enthusiastically about sports figures and personalities. Please be sure to tell us what distinguishes your book from other titles, and include your credentials.

Standard Publishing

8121 Hamilton Avenue
Cincinnati, OH 45231

Managing Director, Consumer Products: Diane Stortz
Executive Director, Church Resources: Paul Learned

Publisher's Interests
Standard Publishing serves the Christian community with
children's products and church resources. Its catalogue
includes Bible curriculum materials and resources as well as
picture and board books, devotions, and novelty items for
children from birth through age twelve.
Website: www.standardpub.com

Freelance Potential
Published 60 titles (50 juvenile) in 2003. Of the 60 titles, 4
were by authors who were new to the publishing house.
Receives 500 queries, 1,500 unsolicited mss yearly.
- **Fiction:** Publishes concept books, 0–4 years; and story picture
  books, 4–10 years. Genres include religious fiction.
- **Nonfiction:** Publishes early picture, concept, and toddler
  books, 0–4 years; story picture books, 4–10 years; and young
  adult books, 12–18 years. Features activity books, coloring
  books, religious education titles, devotionals, and reference
  books, as well as Bible study guides.
- **Representative Titles:** *Hi God, Let's Talk About My Life* by
  Karen Ann Moore (8–12 years) talks about situations found in
  day-to-day life that are addressed with devotions and biblical
  advice. *A Child's Book of Parables* by Lori Froeb (3–8 years)
  retells seven of Jesus's parables for young readers and
  includes illustrations.

Submissions and Payment
Guidelines available. Query with outline/synopsis and 1–2
sample chapters. Send complete ms for picture books only.
Accepts photocopies, computer printouts, and simultaneous
submissions if identified. SASE. Responds in 2–3 months.
Publication in 18 months. Royalty. Flat fee.

Editor's Comments
While we don't usually use freelancers, you are welcome to
review our guidelines. Most of the books we publish are either
done on assignment, or by book packagers. If you do decide to
submit, please review our materials and books first.

Star Bright Books

42-26 28th Street
Long Island City, NY 11101

Director of Marketing: Katie Sudol

Publisher's Interests

An independent publishing house, Star Bright Books is dedicated to producing high-quality books for children. Its founding in 1994 was based on a belief in the importance of teaching children to read at an early age. Over half of the books on its current list are designed for pre-readers and beginning readers. Its inclusion books, such as beginning-reader books on sign language for toddlers, are aimed at children of all abilities. Many of its titles are published in Spanish, with more languages to follow shortly.
Website: www.starbrightbooks.com

Freelance Potential

Published 15–20 titles (13 juvenile) in 2003: 2 were developed from unsolicited submissions and 1 was by an agented author. Receives 360–480 queries, 240–360 unsolicited mss yearly.
- **Fiction:** Publishes concept books, toddler books, and early picture books, 0–4 years; easy-to-read books, 4–7 years; story picture books, 4–10 years; chapter books, 5–10 years; and middle-grade books, 8–12 years. Features multicultural and educational books. Also publishes board books.
- **Representative Titles:** *Alicia's Happy Day* by Meg Starr (3–8 years) follows Alicia on a journey through her urban neighborhood as her family, friends, and neighbors help her celebrate her birthday. *Prince Zucchini* by Neil Philip (4–8 years) features a prince with a large nose who rescues a princess and discovers that looks are not important.

Submissions and Payment

Guidelines available. Query or send complete ms. SASE. Response time and publication period vary. Royalty; advance.

Editor's Comments

It is important that children learn to love to read books at an early age, and we make this easier for them through our Books Kids Love™ line. To appeal to older readers, we select books for their outstanding illustrations and writing.

Starseed Press

P.O. Box 1082
Tiburon, CA 94920

Acquisitions: Jan Phillips

Publisher's Interests

The editors at Starseed Press look for juvenile titles that encourage positive values in young readers while also building self-esteem and promoting nonviolence. It primarily publishes children's picture books for readers under the age of 12. An imprint of H J Kramer, its books are found in the catalogue of New World Library, a publisher that has been offering adult inspirational and New Age books for more than 25 years.
Website: www.nwlib.com

Freelance Potential

Published 2 titles in 2003. Receives 1,500 queries yearly.
- **Fiction:** Published 2 story picture books, 4–10 years. Also publishes toddler books and early picture books, 0–4 years. Genres include inspirational fiction and books about nature, personal growth, and self-esteem.
- **Nonfiction:** Publishes parenting titles.
- **Representative Titles:** *Today I Am Lovable* by Diane Loomans (7–11 years) gives young people 365 ways to think positively and build self-esteem and includes inspirational activities such as fun facts, word games, and riddles. *Quest for the Crystal Castle* by Dan Millman (4–10 years) is a story about a boy who goes on an unexpected summer adventure and learns about confidence, kindness, and the power within all children to overcome obstacles.

Submissions and Payment

Query. No unsolicited mss. No submissions via fax or email. SASE. Responds in 8–10 weeks. Publication in 6–18 months.

Editor's Comments

This year, we're primarily interested in picture books for children between the ages of two and ten. The books must encourage nonviolence, build self-esteem, and honor human relationships to the natural world. While our titles are often inspirational and spiritual in nature, we do not accept titles that have strong Christian themes.

Stemmer House Publishers

2627 Caves Road
Owings Mills, MD 21117

President: Barbara Holdridge

Publisher's Interests

Stemmer House, dedicated to excellence in text, design, illustration, and production, offers a selection of nonfiction children's literature in addition to adult titles that encompass the humanities, art and design, crafts, and cooking.
Website: www.stemmer.com

Freelance Potential

Published 3 titles (1 juvenile) in 2003: all were developed from unsolicited submissions. Of the 3 titles, 1 was by an author who was new to the publishing house. Receives 1,000 queries, 800 unsolicited mss yearly.

- **Nonfiction:** Published 1 story picture book, 4–10 years. Also publishes easy-to-read books, 4–7 years; chapter books, 5–10 years; and middle-grade books, 8–12 years. Topics include natural history, art, music, and geography. Also publishes biographies and titles for adults.
- **Representative Titles:** *The Insectalphabet Encyclopedia* by Julia Pinkham presents an insect for each letter of the alphabet and includes descriptions, habits, colorations, and geographical locations. *Runaway Molly Midnight, the Artist's Cat* by Nadja Maril (5+ years) follows a cat who, while exploring the sand dunes of Provincetown, discovers the secret ingredient of her artist's paintings.

Submissions and Payment

Guidelines and catalogue available with 9x12 SASE ($.77 postage). Send complete ms for picture books. Query with outline/synopsis and 2 sample chapters for longer works. Accepts photocopies, computer printouts, and simultaneous submissions if identified. SASE. Responds in 2 weeks. Publication in 1–3 years. Royalty; advance.

Editor's Comments

Please do not send fiction picture book manuscripts, as our focus is on nonfiction. We welcome freelance submissions and will care for them as if they were our own children if they include a cover letter and a self-addressed, stamped envelope.

Sterling Publishing Company

387 Park Avenue South
New York, NY 10016-8810

Editorial Director: Frances Gilbert

Publisher's Interests

Established in 1959, this publisher is known for its nonfiction titles and excels in books for children as well as titles on the topics of science, puzzles, games, crafts, gardening, woodworking, and health. It publishes no fiction.
Website: www.sterlingpub.com

Freelance Potential

Published 250 titles in 2003: 25 were developed from unsolicited submissions, 10 were by agented authors, and 50 were reprint/licensed properties. Of the 250 titles, 20 were by unpublished writers. Receives 500 queries yearly.

- **Nonfiction:** Publishes how-to, activity, craft, and reference books, 0–14 years. Topics include science, math, games, optical illusions, origami, mazes, and magic.
- **Representative Titles:** *Come to Tea* by Stephanie Dunnewind et al. is written for young girls who delight in hosting tea parties for friends; includes party themes for birthdays, holidays, and other special events. *100 Award-Winning Science Fair Projects* by Glen Vecchione brings students a wealth of fresh ideas for science projects, including many that make use of common household materials and objects.

Submissions and Payment

Guidelines available. Query with outline. Accepts photocopies, computer printouts, and simultaneous submissions if identified. SASE. Response time varies. Publication in 1 year. Royalty; advance.

Editor's Comments

Our main need continues to be for ideas for books covering science and math. We'd also like to see ideas for puzzles, activities, and crafts. New writers should review our newest line of books for preschoolers, and picture books. The best way to get a feel for what our editors like is to visit our website and review some titles. Pick a few books that focus on your area of interest and visit the library or bookstore to read them. Our titles always stress a "hands-on" approach.

Storytellers Ink Publishing Co.

P.O. Box 33398
Seattle, WA 98133-0398

Editor-in-Chief: Quinn Currie

Publisher's Interests

This publisher targets readers between the ages of two and twelve with its fiction and nonfiction books about nature, the environment, animals, and wildlife. Its purpose is to foster a sense of responsibility and compassion toward living creatures, and all of its titles are distributed free as part of a national literacy program.
Website: www.storytellers-ink.com

Freelance Potential

Published 1–3 titles in 2003. Receives 120 queries yearly.
- **Fiction:** Publishes adventure, folktales, fantasy, and multicultural and ethnic fiction, 2–12 years. Features stories about animals, nature, and the environment.
- **Nonfiction:** Publishes biographies and books about animals, nature, the environment, and social issues. Features bilingual, multicultural, and ethnic titles.
- **Representative Titles:** *Sadie Learns a Lesson* by Jane Matthews (kindergarten) is a story about a cat that teaches children about safety issues for themselves and their pets. *Beautiful Joe* by Marshall Saunders (grade 4) is the true tale of an abused dog who displays courage in repaying his kind rescuers under unusual circumstances.

Submissions and Payment

Send complete ms. Accepts photocopies and simultaneous submissions if identified. SASE. Response time, publication period, and payment policy vary.

Editor's Comments

Our mission is straightforward: to help teach children to love reading through exciting books about animals and the environment. We want to provide literature that instills compassion and a love of all living things as well as a sense of justice and responsibility. We're always interested in reviewing stories and informational books that will help us achieve that goal while educating and entertaining our readers. Send us your complete book rather than a query.

Teacher Created Materials

6421 Industry Way
Westminster, CA 92683

Editor-in-Chief: Sharon Coan

Publisher's Interests

Teacher Created Materials is an educational publishing company founded in 1982 by two classroom teachers. It publishes quality resource books at the early childhood, elementary, middle school, and high school levels that cover all aspects of the curriculum, from language arts and social studies, to math, science, technology, and the arts.
Website: www.teachercreated.com

Freelance Potential

Published 200 titles in 2003. Receives 500 queries yearly.

- **Nonfiction:** Publishes workbooks and activity books, pre-K–grade 12. Topics include art, geography, history, social studies, science, mathematics, reading, phonics, spelling, writing, language arts, and technology. Also publishes teacher resource materials on student testing, gifted education, multiple intelligences, reading plans, assessment techniques, classroom management, and professional development.
- **Representative Titles:** *Nonfiction Readers* by Timothy Rasinski, ed. helps teach reading skills by utilizing the writing and photographs from *TIME For Kids* and *Write Time For Kids*. *Science Fair Projects* (8–12 years) provides plenty of activities and project ideas to help young scientists plan, complete, and present their projects with confidence and enthusiasm.

Submissions and Payment

Guidelines available. Query with outline or table of contents, summary, and 10–12 sample pages. Accepts photocopies, computer printouts, and simultaneous submissions if identified. SASE. Responds in 1 year. Publication in 6–12 months. Flat fee.

Editor's Comments

Our mission is to provide educators around the world with quality educational materials that have been successfully used in classrooms. All our products are "created by teachers for teachers and parents," so firsthand experience is a must. We look for books that address new techniques or trends.

Teaching & Learning Company

P.O. Box 10
1204 Buchanan Street
Carthage, IL 62321

Vice President of Production: Jill Day

Publisher's Interests

Supplementary educational materials are the specialty of
Teaching & Learning Company. It offers materials for teachers
and parents working with children in preschool through middle school on subjects such as science, social studies, mathematics, and arts and crafts. It also publishes books on
responsibility education, as well as decorations and banners.
Website: www.TeachingLearning.com

Freelance Potential

Published 40 titles in 2003: 5 were developed from unsolicited
submissions and 1 was by an agented author. Of the 40
titles, 6 were by authors who were new to the publishing
house. Receives 350 unsolicited mss yearly.

- **Nonfiction:** Publishes educational resource materials for
  pre-K–grade 8. Topics include language arts, social studies,
  current events, biography, mathematics, computers, science,
  nature, the environment, animals, pets, holidays, arts and
  crafts, hobbies, multicultural and ethnic issues, and responsibility education. Also offers materials for gifted and special
  education classrooms.
- **Representative Titles:** *Mayans & Aztecs* by Mary Tucker
  (grades 3–6) teaches students to write number glyphs using the
  code of the Maya, design battle uniforms using ideas from the
  Aztecs, and learn about the forerunners of modern Mexico;
  part of the Exploring Ancient Civilizations series. *Manners,
  Please!* (grades K–3) discusses table manners, telephone manners, and manners in conversation.

Submissions and Payment

Guidelines available. Send complete ms. Accepts photocopies
and computer printouts. SASE. Responds in 6–9 months.
Publication in 1–3 years. Payment policy varies.

Editor's Comments

Authors should note that we serve a diverse and culturally rich
audience; please keep this in mind when preparing your materials—especially holiday and seasonal items.

TEACH Services, Inc.

254 Donovan Road
Brushton, NY 12916

Editor: Wayne Reid

Publisher's Interests
This publisher offers a children's list that includes easy-to-read books, picture books, and middle-grade and young adult nonfiction. It follows the teachings of the Seventh-day Adventist church, and it therefore publishes no fiction. TEACH Services also offers adult titles on religion, health, and education, as well as biographies and cookbooks.
Website: www.teachservicesinc.com

Freelance Potential
Published 45 titles (25 juvenile) in 2003: 10 were developed from unsolicited submissions and 35 were reprint/licensed properties. Of the 45 titles, 7 were by unpublished writers and 8 were by authors who were new to the publishing house. Receives 200 queries yearly.

• **Nonfiction:** Published 3 easy-to-read books, 4–7 years; 4 story picture books, 4–10 years; 6 chapter books, 5–10 years; 8 middle-grade books, 8–12 years; and 4 young adult books, 12–18 years. Topics include history, health, fitness, nature, and religion. Also publishes biographies, self-help titles, and poetry.

• **Representative Titles:** *Choice Readings for Children* by Ellen G. White is a collection of scrapbook stories that are helpful to boys and girls. *Children's Bible Lessons #2* by Bessie White includes seven illustrated lessons that cover the Holy Bible, conversion, faith, prayer, and angels.

Submissions and Payment
Guidelines and catalogue available at website or with 9x12 SASE ($2 postage). Query. Accepts photocopies, IBM disk submissions, and simultaneous submissions if identified. SASE. Responds in 1 week. Publication in 6 months. Royalty, 10%.

Editor's Comments
For a book to succeed, it must be timely, it must be well-written, and it must appeal to a clearly defined market. Please remember that the biblical injunction found in Philippians 4:8 prevents us from publishing fiction or fantasy.

Texas Tech University Press

P.O. Box 41037
Lubbock, TX 79409-1037

Acquiring Editor: Judith Keeling

Publisher's Interests
Since 1971, Texas Tech University Press has offered titles
relating to the American West, including books on history
and natural history, memoirs, and travel titles. While most of
its books are written for adults, it does offer some fiction and
nonfiction for readers ages eight and up.
Website: www.ttup.ttu.edu

Freelance Potential
Published 20 titles (3 juvenile) in 2003: 18 were developed
from unsolicited submissions and 1 was by an agented
author. Of the 20 titles, 18 were by authors who were new to
the publishing house. Receives 300 queries yearly.
- **Fiction:** Publishes middle-grade novels, 8–12 years. Genres
  include contemporary fiction, mystery, and suspense.
  Also publishes stories about nature and the environment,
  and poetry.
- **Nonfiction:** Published 2 middle-grade books, 8–12 years. Topics include regional history, Texana, sports, Southwest literature, American history, Vietnam studies, science, and nature.
  Also publishes literary criticism.
- **Representative Titles:** *The Fowler Family Celebrates Statehood
  and a Wedding* by Mary K. Inman & Louise F. Pence is an illustrated history book with paper dolls about a family living on
  the East Fork of Ohio's Little Miami River in 1789. *Remember
  the Alamo!* by Lisa Waller Rogers (8–12 years) is the fictional
  diary of a girl whose family was part of a mass exodus in Texas
  known as the Runaway Scrape.

Submissions and Payment
Guidelines available at website. Query with clips. Accepts
photocopies. SASE. Responds in 1–2 months. Publication in
1 year. Royalty; 10%.

Editor's Comments
Biographies, memoirs, and travel titles about the American
West are always needed here. You can also send queries for
titles on the eighteenth century and textile history.

Third World Press

P.O. Box 19730
7822 South Dobson
Chicago, IL 60619

Assistant to the Publisher

Publisher's Interests
Third World Press features fiction and nonfiction for children of all ages that focus on black and African-centered material. Its mission is to provide information that is inspirational and life-affirming for the African-American community and other African communities in the diaspora.
Website: www.thirdworldpressinc.com

Freelance Potential
Published 12 titles (2 juvenile) in 2003: 2 were developed from unsolicited submissions and 2 were by agented authors. Of the 12 titles, 4 were by unpublished writers and 5 were by authors who were new to the publishing house. Receives 200 queries, 400 unsolicited mss yearly.
- **Fiction:** Publishes concept, toddler, and early picture books, 0–4 years; easy-to-read books, 4–7 years; story picture books, 4–10 years; chapter books, 5–10 years; middle-grade novels, 8–12 years; and young adult books, 12–18 years. Features books about African, African-American, and Caribbean life.
- **Nonfiction:** Publishes easy-to-read books, 4–7 years; story picture books, 4–10 years; chapter books, 5–10 years; middle-grade books, 8–12 years; and young adult books, 12–18 years. Topics include ethnic and multicultural issues.
- **Representative Titles:** *I Look at Me* by Mari Evans (2–4 years) teaches children self-love and introduces African-centered concepts. *The Story of Kwanzaa* by Safisha Madhubuti (5–7 years) visually presents the origin and rich tradition of Kwanzaa.

Submissions and Payment
Guidelines available. Prefers query with synopsis. Accepts unsolicited mss in July only. Accepts photocopies, computer printouts, and simultaneous submissions. SASE. Response time varies. Publication in 1 year. Royalty.

Editor's Comments
We are dedicated to publishing progressive, culturally enlightening material that is both life-giving and life-saving to the African communities in the diaspora.

Charles C. Thomas Publishers Ltd.

2600 South First Street
Springfield, IL 62704

Editor: Michael P. Thomas

Publisher's Interests

Educators in the fields of physical education, special education, child psychology, and administration, as well as concerned parents, are the target audience of this publisher. Its list concentrates on bringing new, definitive texts to the education market.

Website: www.ccthomas.com

Freelance Potential

Published 800 titles in 2003: 600 were developed from unsolicited submissions. Receives 600 queries and unsolicited mss yearly.

- **Nonfiction:** Publishes titles for educators, pre-K–grade 12. Topics include early childhood, elementary, secondary, and higher education; reading research and statistics; physical education and sports; special education; the learning disabled; teaching the blind and visually impaired; gifted and talented education; and speech and language pathology. Also offers some parenting titles.
- **Representative Titles:** *Read This Book Before Your Child Starts School* by Miriam W. Lukken (parents) helps families to ready their children for the school experience and informs them on how to choose the right school. *Play with Them—Theraplay Group in the Classroom* by Phyllis B. Rubin & Jeanine Tregay brings teachers tips and techniques for developing self-confidence in children.

Submissions and Payment

Guidelines and catalogue available at website. Query or send complete ms. Accepts disk submissions. SASE. Responds in 1 week. Publication in 6–8 months. Royalty.

Editor's Comments

Our list features books on education, special education, social science, and behavioral science. We look for writers with the appropriate educational backgrounds who can bring us ideas as well as the latest research that will help us meet the needs of our readers.

Thompson Educational Publishing

Suite 200
6 Ripley Avenue
Toronto, Ontario M6S 3N9
Canada

Submissions Editor: Keith Thompson

Publisher's Interests

Thompson Educational Publishing targets the Canadian and international markets with textbooks, supplementary texts, and edited readers written for use at colleges and universities. Most of its titles deal with social sciences and the humanities, and it offers textbooks.
Website: www.thompsonbooks.com

Freelance Potential

Published 6 titles in 2003: 1 was developed from an unsolicited submission. Of the 6 titles, 1 was by an unpublished writer and 2 were by authors who were new to the publishing house. Receives 20 queries yearly.

- **Nonfiction:** Publishes undergraduate textbooks and single-author monographs for use in undergraduate education. Topics include social studies, sociology, social work, economics, communications, native studies, labor studies, and sports.
- **Representative Titles:** *The Art of Evaluation: A Handbook for Educators and Trainers* by Tara Fenwick & Jim Parsons (educators) offers practical ways to plan evaluation and develop tools to record and report learner growth. *Exercise Science* by Ted Temertzoglou & Paul Challen (grade 12) is prepared for use with the new Canadian Grade 12 Health and Physical Education curriculum.

Submissions and Payment

Guidelines available. Query with curriculum vitae and market analysis. Accepts email submissions to publisher@ thompsonbooks.com. SAE/IRC. Response time, publication period, and payment policy vary.

Editor's Comments

If you are sending us a proposal for a new textbook, you should clearly indicate the specific course for which the book is intended. It must be developed essentially as a pedagogical tool to facilitate the delivery of that course. We also encourage authors to indicate the kinds of supplementary materials that would accompany the book.

Tilbury House, Publishers

2 Mechanic Street
Gardiner, ME 04345

Publisher: Jennifer Bunting

Publisher's Interests
Tilbury House now concentrates its publishing efforts on
picture books for readers ages seven to twelve. It specializes
in books that deal with issues of cultural diversity, nature,
and the environment. Marketed nationally, the books often
include teacher's guides. For adults, this publisher offers
nonfiction about Maine and the Northeast.
Website: www.tilburyhouse.com

Freelance Potential
Published 9 titles (3 juvenile) in 2003: 5 were developed from
unsolicited submissions and 1 was a reprint/licensed property.
Of the 9 titles, 1 was by an unpublished writer and 6 were by
authors who were new to the publishing house. Receives
300–400 queries and unsolicited mss yearly.
- **Fiction:** Publishes story picture books, 7–12 years. Genres
  include multicultural and ethnic fiction and stories about
  nature and the environment.
- **Nonfiction:** Publishes story picture books, 7–12 years. Topics
  include nature, the environment, history, social studies, and
  multicultural subjects.
- **Representative Titles:** *The Carpet Boy's Gift* by Pegi Deitz
  Shea (grades 3–6) tells the story of a boy who is a bonded
  laborer in a rug factory in Pakistan. *Everybody's Somebody's
  Lunch* by Cherie Mason (grades 3–6) is a fiction book that
  teaches children about the roles of predator and prey.

Submissions and Payment
Guidelines available. Prefers query with outline/synopsis and
sample chapters. Accepts partial ms with outline, or complete
ms. Accepts photocopies and computer printouts. SASE.
Responds in 1 month. Publication in 1 year. Royalty;
advance, negotiable.

Editor's Comments
Please note that we publish children's books about global
diversity, nature, and the environment only. We don't offer
general children's titles about animals, fables, or fantasy.

Megan Tingley Books

Little, Brown and Company
1271 Avenue of the Americas
New York, NY 10020

Editor: Sara Morling

Publisher's Interests
Megan Tingley Books, an imprint of Little, Brown and Company, publishes a range of books for children from toddlers through the middle grades.
Website: www.lb-kids.com

Freelance Potential
Published 20 titles in 2003: 17 were by agented authors and 1 was a reprint/licensed property. Receives 600+ queries each year.
- **Fiction:** Publishes concept books, toddler books, and early picture books, 0–4 years; and story picture books, 4–10 years. Also publishes lift-the-flap books. Genres include contemporary and multicultural fiction and stories about music and holidays.
- **Nonfiction:** Publishes middle-grade books, 8–12 years. Also publishes story picture books, 4–10 years; and self-help titles. Topics include crafts, hobbies, and multicultural and ethnic issues.
- **Representative Titles:** *The Girls' Book of Success* by Catherine Dee, ed. (10+ years) is a collection of quotes, poems, true stories, and celebrity advice selected to inspire girls to achieve success in all areas of life. *Harlem Stomp* by Laban Carrick Hill (12+ years) brings the Harlem Renaissance alive for young adult readers.

Submissions and Payment
Reviews materials submitted by literary agents or sent at the direct solicitation of the editors only. No unsolicited mss or queries. Accepts photocopies. SASE. Responds in 2 months. Publication period varies. Royalty; advance.

Editor's Comments
The only manuscripts we will consider at this time include those submitted through literary agents and those that have been solicited by one of our editors. Our current interest is primarily picture books of fewer than 1,000 words for very young children. Stories with strong female characters continue to appeal to us.

Torah Aura Productions

4423 Fruitland Avenue
Los Angeles, CA 90058

Submissions Editor: Jane Golub

Publisher's Interests
In addition to textbooks for use in Jewish schools, Torah
Aura Productions develops fiction titles for readers up to the
age of 18. Its titles cover subjects such as Hebrew, prayer,
Jewish values, the Bible, Jewish celebrations and history,
and Israel.
Website: www.torahaura.com

Freelance Potential
Published 15 titles (10 juvenile) in 2003: 4 were developed
from unsolicited submissions. Of the 15 titles, 2 were by
unpublished writers and 1 was by an author who was new to
the publishing house. Receives 36 unsolicited mss yearly.
- **Fiction:** Publishes chapter books, 5–10 years; middle-grade
  novels, 8–12 years; and young adult books, 12–18 years.
  Genres include religious and inspirational fiction with Jewish
  themes.
- **Nonfiction:** Publishes story picture books, 4–10 years; chapter
  books, 5–10 years; middle-grade books, 8–12 years; and young
  adult books, 12–18 years. Topics include religion, history, current events, and family issues—all as they relate to Judaism.
  Also publishes books on Jewish law, prayer, and the Bible.
- **Representative Titles:** *Jewish Values from Alef to Tav* by Joel
  Lurie Grishaver (grades 2–4) teaches students the important
  values that influence their religious and secular lives through
  biblical, rabbinic, hasidic, and folk stories. *Where God Dwells*
  by Dr. Steven Fine & Leah Bierman Fine (grades 3–7) describes
  the evolution of Jewish worship spaces.

Submissions and Payment
Send complete ms. Accepts photocopies. SASE. Responds in
6 months. Publication in 18 months. Royalty, 10%.

Editor's Comments
We're looking for authors who understand that we want books
that are appropriate for classroom use while also being entertaining and fulfilling. Our purpose is to get Jewish kids reading
about Judaism and Jewish life.

Tor Books

175 Fifth Avenue
New York, NY 10010

Children's/Young Adult Editor: Jonathan Schmidt

Publisher's Interests

Tor Books specializes in hardcover and softcover science fiction and fantasy books for middle-grade, young adult, and adult readers. It is an imprint of Tom Doherty Associates, founded in 1980. Limited general interest and how-to titles about science and crafts are also published.
Website: www.tor.com

Freelance Potential

Published 25 titles in 2003: 22 were by agented authors. Of the 25 titles, 3 were by unpublished writers. Receives 1,200 unsolicited mss yearly.
- **Fiction:** Publishes middle-grade books, 8–12 years; and young adult books, 12–18 years. Genres include fantasy and science fiction.
- **Nonfiction:** Publishes middle-grade books, 8–12 years; and young adult books, 12–18 years. Features general interest and how-to titles, as well as books about science and crafts.
- **Representative Titles:** *The Giant Leap: Mankind Heads for the Stars* by Adrian Berry (YA) is a book by a veteran British science writer that advocates interstellar travel as the key to man's survival. *The Dragon Reborn* by Robert Jordan (YA) presents the third book in the exciting Wheel of Time fantasy series.

Submissions and Payment

Guidelines available at website. Query with synopsis and first 3 chapters. Accepts photocopies, computer printouts, and email to torquery@panix.com. Availability of artwork improves chance of acceptance. SASE. Responds in 4–6 months. Publication in 18–24 months. Royalty; advance.

Editor's Comments

We will take a look at query letters, but we prefer to receive a synopsis of your book with the first three chapters included. We can't tell whether we'll like the book until we see a chunk of the manuscript. If your book is very good, it has an excellent chance of publication. It may take us a while to get back to you, but every submission is carefully reviewed.

Toy Box Productions

7532 Hickory Hills Court
Whites Creek, TN 37189

Submissions Editor

Publisher's Interests
This publisher occupies a special niche in children's publish-ing, offering a line of read-along, audio-interactive story-books. All its titles feature creative illustrations as well as sound effects and music. It is known for its Time Traveler Adventure series and also offers Bible stories for children. **Website:** www.crttoybox.com

Freelance Potential
Published 6 titles in 2003: all were assigned. Of the 6 titles, one was by an unpublished writer.
- **Fiction:** Publishes story picture books, 4–10 years; chapter books, 5–10 years; and middle-grade novels, 8–12 years. Also publishes educational titles, 4–8 years. Genres include West-ern, historical, and religious fiction.
- **Nonfiction:** Publishes story picture books, 4–10 years; and chapter books, 5–10 years. Also publishes biographies and history-related audio sets for adults. Topics include history and religion.
- **Representative Titles:** *He Is Risen* features Don the donkey and Carol and Clara cats who tell the story of Jesus' miracles. *A Whale of a Tale* features God's animals as narrators of the story of Jonah and how God showed him mercy.

Submissions and Payment
Query with résumé and clips. All work is done on assign-ment. Accepts photocopies. SASE. Response time, publication period, and payment policy vary.

Editor's Comments
We are always looking for quality ideas for our very special line of books. Our concept books are designed to help strengthen children's reading skills; Edu-tainment features easy-to-read illustrated titles that are perfect for family trips; Our Time Traveler Adventures are a wonderful way to introduce children to influential historical figures from American history. Because our products are so unique and specifically formatted, we strongly encourage prospective writers to review our titles.

Tricycle Press

P.O. Box 7123
Berkeley, CA 94707

Assistant Editor: Abigail Samoun

Publisher's Interests
Books for children from preschool age through the middle
grades, including activity books, picture books, and novels,
appear in the catalogue from Tricycle Press.
Website: www.tenspeed.com

Freelance Potential
Published 20 titles in 2003: 4 were developed from unsolicited
submissions, 4 were by agented authors, and 3 were
reprint/licensed properties. Of the 20 titles, 5 were by unpublished writers and 3 were by authors who were new to the
publishing house. Receives 15,000 unsolicited mss yearly.
- **Fiction:** Published 2 toddler books, 0–4 years; 8 story picture
  books, 4–10 years; and 1 middle-grade novel, 8–12 years. Also
  publishes concept books, 0–4 years; board books; and activity
  books. Topics include nature, tolerance, and contemporary
  issues.
- **Nonfiction:** Published 2 toddler books, 0–4 years. Also publishes story picture books, 4–10 years; middle-grade books,
  8–12 years; and board books. Topics include real-life issues,
  mathematics, gardening, and cooking.
- **Representative Titles:** *The Young Adventurer's Guide to Everest*
  by Jonathan Chester (8–11 years) offers information on the
  world's tallest mountain along with advice on how to prepare for
  a climb. *The Sea House* by Deborah Turney Zagwÿn (5–8 years)
  follows two children on a visit to their uncle's floating home.

Submissions and Payment
Guidelines and catalogue available with 9x12 SASE ($1.02
postage). Send complete ms for picture books. Send 2–3 sample chapters for chapter books, or one-half of the manuscript
for activity books. No queries. Accepts photocopies, computer
printouts, and simultaneous submissions. SASE. Responds
in 2–6 months. Publication period varies. Royalty.

Editor's Comments
We carefully consider each manuscript we receive. Submit
something that will distinguish itself from the rest of the slush.

Turtle Press

P.O. Box 290206
Wethersfield, CT 06129-0206

Editor: Cynthia Kim

Publisher's Interests
Turtle Press is a leader in the publication of books, videos, and DVDs related to the martial arts industry. Its children's list offers fiction and nonfiction titles that cover weight training, speed training, and adventures focused on the martial arts. Books for parents are also found in its catalogue.
Website: www.turtlepress.com

Freelance Potential
Published 8 titles in 2003: 3 were developed from unsolicited submissions. Of the 8 titles, 1 was by an unpublished writer and 2 were by authors who were new to the publishing house. Receives 400–500 queries yearly.
- **Fiction:** Publishes chapter books, 5–10 years. Features stories about the martial arts, including adventure stories.
- **Nonfiction:** Publishes chapter books, 5–10 years. Topics include martial arts, self-improvement, fitness, health, sports, and Eastern philosophy.
- **Representative Titles:** *A Part of the Ribbon* is an action adventure story that introduces readers to the world of Korean martial arts as told through the eyes of two children. *Martial Arts Training Diary for Kids* by Dr. Art Brisacher is an interactive book designed to help children get the most out of their martial arts training.

Submissions and Payment
Guidelines available. Query. SASE. Responds in 2–3 weeks. Publication period and payment policy vary.

Editor's Comments
We have a small children's list at this time, but are always interested in expanding it with books that will complement our existing titles and bring a fresh approach to some aspect of martial arts. Writers with a background in martial arts or other fitness techniques related to the martial arts are invited to send us a query. Make sure to include a brief, in-depth summary of your idea and list your qualifications. Tell us what makes your idea right for us.

Twenty-First Century Books

2 Old New Milford Road
Brookfield, CT 06804

Editorial Assistant

Publisher's Interests
This imprint from Millbrook Press publishes nonfiction titles
for young adults for the school and library market. All of its
titles are meant to be used as supplementary texts and all
are curriculum-based. It considers submissions from agented
authors only.
Website: www.millbrookpress.com

Freelance Potential
Published 45 titles in 2003: all were by agented authors.
Receives 100 queries yearly.
- **Nonfiction:** Publishes young adult books, 12–18 years. Topics include science, technology, health, medicine, history,
  social studies, contemporary issues, language arts, government, politics, and sports. Also publishes biographies and
  multicultural titles.
- **Representative Titles:** *The Universe* by Alvin Silverstein
  (grades 5–8) offers clear explanations of topics related to the
  study of the universe; part of the Science Concepts series.
  Earth and the Moon by Ron Miller (grades 7 and up) is designed
  to make the complex subject of planets accessible; part of the
  Worlds Beyond series.

Submissions and Payment
Agented submissions only. Query with outline, sample chapters, and publishing history. Accepts simultaneous submissions if identified. SASE. Responds in 2 months. Publication
in 1–2 years. Royalty; advance.

Editor's Comments
We cannot stress enough that we accept submissions from
agented authors only, and accept no unsolicited manuscripts.
We are interested in works that have a strong, relevant tie to
the school curriculum. Topics of interest include math, science, social studies, biography, and American history. Do not
send proposals of books for teachers and please remember
that we do not publish fiction, activity books, novelty titles, or
picture books.

Tyndale House Publishers

351 Executive Drive
Carol Stream, IL 60188

Manuscript Review Committee

Publisher's Interests
The children's imprint of this publishing house, Tyndale Kids,
produces Bibles, Bible storybooks, devotional books, music,
games, and videos. Its mission is to communicate with children and to meet their spiritual needs.
Website: www.tyndale.com

Freelance Potential
Published 300 titles (75 juvenile) in 2003: 2 were developed
from unsolicited submissions and 75 were by agented
authors. Receives 500 queries yearly.
- **Nonfiction:** Publishes concept and toddler books, 0–4 years;
  easy-to-read titles, 4–7 years; story picture books, 4–10 years;
  middle-grade books, 8–12 years; and young adult books, 12–18
  years. Features books about Christian faith. Also publishes
  parenting books.
- **Representative Titles:** *Actual Factuals for Kids* by Nancy S.
  Hill (8–12 years) brings readers 100 devotionals that educate
  and entertain with informative and intriguing facts. *Almost 12*
  by Kenneth Taylor (10–12 years) teaches children about
  human reproduction in an easy-to-read format that includes
  art, photography, and a question-and-answer section.

Submissions and Payment
Guidelines available. Accepts work from agented authors,
Tyndale authors, and authors introduced through other publishers only. Accepts email submissions to manuscripts@
tyndale.com. SASE. Responds in 3 months. Publication period
varies. Royalty; advance. Flat fee.

Editor's Comments
We continue to look for material that will help us to minister to
children. Submissions are accepted only from agented authors,
or authors with whom we have worked previously. Devotionals,
Bible stories, and nonfiction that bring the Scriptures to young
people in ways that entertain are always on our list of needs.
Remember who your audience is: material for kids must be fun
as well as educational.

UAHC Press

633 Third Avenue
New York, NY 10017

Editorial Director: Rabbi Hara Person

Publisher's Interests
UAHC Press, the publishing division of the Union of American Hebrew Congregations, offers a variety of religious educational titles on Judaism for readers of all ages.
Website: www.uahcpress.com

Freelance Potential
Published 25 titles (15 juvenile) in 2003: 10 were developed from unsolicited submissions, 1 was by an agented author, and 1 was a reprint/licensed property. Of the 25 titles, 2 were by unpublished writers and 7 were by authors who were new to the publishing house. Receives 200 queries, 600 unsolicited mss yearly.

- **Fiction:** Publishes story picture books, 4–10 years. Also publishes early picture books, 0–4 years. Genres include Judaism, Bible stories, and religious and historical fiction.
- **Nonfiction:** Publishes toddler books and early picture books, 0–4 years; chapter books, 5–10 years; and young adult books, 12–18 years. Topics include Jewish history, holidays, the Holocaust, and Hebrew. Also publishes bar and bat mitzvah study guides.
- **Representative Titles:** *The Book of Miracles* by Lawrence Kushner explores the connections between God and the Torah and every element of creation. *A Candle for Grandpa* by David Techner & Judith Hirt-Manheimer (families) explains the Jewish view of death.

Submissions and Payment
Guidelines available. Query with résumé, outline, and 2 sample chapters. Send complete ms for picture books. Proposals may be submitted through website. Accepts photocopies and computer printouts. SASE. Response time and publication period vary. Royalty; advance.

Editor's Comments
We continue to be most interested in receiving proposals for textbooks, as well as nonfiction and picture books that deal with important topics in Jewish history and heritage.

Upstart Books

P.O. Box 800
Fort Atkinson, WI 53538-0800

Publications Director: Matt Mulder

Publisher's Interests

Upstart Books is an educational publisher that focuses on producing titles for the school and library markets. Its list includes material covering the topics of library skills, reading, and storytelling. Programming and Internet activities are also found in its catalogue.
Website: www.highsmith.com

Freelance Potential

Published 15 titles in 2003: 5 were developed from unsolicited submissions. Of the 15 titles, 5 were by unpublished writers and 5 were by authors who were new to the publishing house. Receives 150 queries, 75 unsolicited mss yearly.

- **Nonfiction:** Publishes elementary and middle-grade books, 6–12 years. Also publishes educational resource materials for teachers and librarians, pre-K–grade 12. Topics include storytelling, study skills, and literature activities.
- **Representative Titles:** *Dewey & the Decimals* by Paige Taylor & Kent and Susan Brinkmeyer (pre-K–grade 6) features learning games and activities to introduce students to using a library. *Booktalks and Beyond* by Nancy J. Keane (grades K–6) features thematic learning activities that grab students' attention and interest to make them want to read a book.

Submissions and Payment

Prefers query with outline or sample chapters for manuscripts longer than 100 pages. Prefers complete ms for shorter works. Accepts photocopies and computer printouts. SASE. Responds in 2 months. Publication period varies. Royalty, 10–12%; advance.

Editor's Comments

Our goal is to provide our audience with the latest innovations and techniques for teaching students about library and Internet tools, and storytelling. We welcome writers with a background in library science or teaching who can bring fresh ideas to our existing list of materials. Send us your ideas for books that will stimulate a love of learning.

UXL

27500 Drake Road
Farmington Hills, MI 48331-3535

Editorial Coordinator: Carol Nagel

Publisher's Interests

UXL offers online and print reference books for middle school children on topics from history and social studies, to science and technology, sports, literature, careers, and the arts. It is an imprint of the Gale Group.
Website: www.gale.com

Freelance Potential

Published 24 titles in 2003.

- **Nonfiction:** Published 24 young adult books, 12–18 years. Topics include science, health, nutrition, history, social studies, current events, multicultural subjects, and careers. Features curriculum-based reference books and encyclopedias.
- **Representative Titles:** *Cold War: Biographies* (12–18 years) presents 25 intriguing stories of the lives and actions of world leaders like Harry Truman, Winston Churchill, Joseph Stalin, Mao Zedong, and others. *French and Indian War* (12–18 years) offers historical overviews, biographical entries, and primary source material on the period and its most famous people.

Submissions and Payment

Catalogue available at website. Query with résumé and writing samples. Accepts photocopies and computer printouts. No simultaneous submissions. SASE. Response time varies. Publication period varies. Flat fee.

Editor's Comments

We are interested in hearing from writers experienced in educational writing. Send us your résumé and a description of your credentials, plus writing samples. We'll contact you if we feel we have a project that's appropriate for someone with your background and experience. If you log on to our website, you can see that we look for ideas for easy-to-read reference materials that get middle school students excited about their topic, materials that encourage them to approach their assignments with a positive attitude of fun and discovery. We are mostly interested in titles that will work with our existing series, so we discourage the submission of complete manuscripts.

J. Weston Walch, Publisher

P.O. Box 658
321 Valley Street
Portland, ME 04104-0658

Editor-in-Chief: Susan Blair

Publisher's Interests
Founded in 1926, this educational publisher produces supplementary teaching aids for students in grades six through adults in the United States and Canada. Its books cover the subjects of science, special needs, social studies, and English. Books on issues related to the transition from school to career are also found on its list.
Website: www.walch.com

Freelance Potential
Published 55 titles in 2003. Receives 400 queries yearly.
- **Nonfiction:** Publishes young adult books, 12–18 years. Topics include science, social studies, mathematics, language arts, and art. Also offers books about careers, special education titles, and books for teachers and guidance counselors.
- **Representative Titles:** *How to Care for Your Musical Instrument* (grade 5–Adult) teaches students how to handle and care for their own musical instruments. *Multicultural Science and Math Connections* (grades 5–9) gives students the opportunity to explore the discoveries and contributions of 14 cultures through hands-on activities.

Submissions and Payment
Guidelines available. Query with résumé, outline, table of contents, and sample chapter. Accepts photocopies and simultaneous submissions if identified. SASE. Responds in 2–4 months. Publication period varies. Royalty. Flat fee.

Editor's Comments
Our goal is to continue to produce innovative educational books for use as supplementary texts by teachers and students. If, after reviewing some of our titles, you think your book is right for us, send us a query that will indicate why your book is unique and why it should be on our list. We continue to seek titles related to the topics of language arts, mathematics, science, and social studies. For the coming year, we are focusing on publishing more material for middle-grade and high school students.

Books
Timothy Travaglini
Walker Books for Young Readers

Walker Books for Young Readers has published such distinguished authors as Isaac Asimov, Barbara Cooney, Michael McCurdy, and Anne Rockwell. The children's division focuses on picture books and middle-grade fiction and nonfiction.

Editor Timothy Travaglini says good writing is always the most important quality in any submission. "It's also important that a manuscript's format and length are right for our publishing house. For instance, we don't do series."

Travaglini says about a third of Walker's picture books are straightforward nonfiction, a third are historical fiction or curriculum-related, and the rest are straightforward storybooks. Their middle-grade books are half fiction, and half nonfiction, with a heavy lean toward history and biography. As for subjects, he's open. "Primary curriculum topics—Abraham Lincoln or the Revolutionary War, for example—are double-edged swords. There are a lot of books on such perennial favorites, but there always will be a demand for them. A quirky topic might get a lot of rejections. But that doesn't mean a writer shouldn't pursue such topics. Write about something you love, something that fascinates you. Be passionate about the subject matter and convey that passion."

An extensive bibliography of sources is also important. "A surprising number of manuscripts come in based on one or two books. Thin research is a bad first step. Research as thoroughly as humanly possible. Award winners (in addition to being the best writers) do the most research, going back to primary sources." New writers should be hopeful, however. "The truth is we read all submissions enough to make a fair assessment," Travaglini says. "If something is compelling enough, it doesn't matter if the writer is brand new or well published."

(See listing for Walker & Company
on following page)

Walker & Company

435 Hudson Street
New York, NY 10014

Submissions Editor

Publisher's Interests
Children's fiction and nonfiction appear in the catalogue
of Walker & Company. It features picture books as well as
middle-grade and young adult titles.
Website: www.walkeryoungreaders.com

Freelance Potential
Published 37 titles in 2003: 3 were developed from unsolicited
submissions, 14 were by agented authors, and 2 were
reprint/licensed properties. Of the 37 titles, 1 was by an
unpublished writer and 6 were by authors who were new to
the publishing house. Receives 600 queries, 2,200 unsolicited
mss yearly.
- **Fiction:** Published 3 early picture books, 0–4 years; 13 story
  picture books, 4–10 years; 1 middle-grade book, 8–12 years;
  and 3 young adult novels, 12–18 years. Genres include contemporary and historical fiction.
- **Nonfiction:** Published 10 story picture books, 4–10 years; and
  7 middle-grade books, 8–12 years. Topics include nature, history, and social issues. Also publishes biographies and books
  in Spanish.
- **Representative Titles:** *The Giant* by Claire Ewart (4–8 years) is
  the story of a young girl, grieving the loss of her mother, who
  seeks the guardian her mother promised would look after her.
  Fabulous Fluttering Tropical Butterflies by Dorothy Hinshaw
  Patent (6–10 years) showcases the butterflies that live in the
  world's tropical rain forests.

Submissions and Payment
Guidelines available. Query with outline and 3–5 sample
chapters. Send complete ms for picture books. Accepts photocopies, computer printouts, and simultaneous submissions
if identified. SASE. Responds in 3–4 months. Publication in
18–24 months. Royalty; advance.

Editor's Comments
We're extremely particular about the projects we take on.
Check our website for more specific submission guidelines.

Warner Press

P.O. Box 2499
1200 East Fifth Street
Anderson, IN 46018-9988

Senior Editor: Karen Rhodes

Publisher's Interests
This Christian publisher produces a wide range of material for people of all ages and strives to bring its audience inspiration and education. Its children's line includes storybooks, coloring and activity books, puzzlers, memory guides, Bible foldoramas, and trivia games. Its line of books includes both fiction and nonfiction.
Website: www.warnerpress.com

Freelance Potential
Published 14 titles in 2003: 5 were developed from unsolicited submissions. Receives 20 queries yearly.
- **Fiction:** Publishes story picture books, 4–10 years. Also publishes novelty and board books. Features religious fiction.
- **Nonfiction:** Publishes resource materials for religious educators, 3–12 years. Offers workbooks, classroom resources, devotionals, and activity and coloring books.
- **Representative Titles:** *Easter "Do"- votionals* is one of a series of lessons centering on a common subject, Easter, combined with a visual aid to remind children of God. *Bible Trivia Challenge* offers children a fun way to learn God's Word through cards that present questions from the Old Testament, New Testament, and the life of Jesus.

Submissions and Payment
Guidelines available. Query. Accepts photocopies. SASE. Responds in 10–12 weeks. Publication in 12–18 months. Flat fee.

Editor's Comments
We have been in business since 1906 and have always maintained the same goal: to create a variety of products that serve the specific needs of Christians everywhere. You will see when you review our catalogue that everything we publish for children successfully combines learning with fun. We are looking for fiction and nonfiction for children between the ages of three and twelve. If you think your idea is right for us, send us a detailed query to convince us to publish your work.

WaterBrook Press

Suite 160
2375 Telstar Drive
Colorado Springs, CO 80920

Senior Editor: Ron Lee

Publisher's Interests

This publisher was launched in 1996 as an autonomous
evangelical religious publishing division of Random House,
Inc. All of its titles focus on Christian living and spiritual
growth, and its children's list includes fiction for readers ages
four through twelve.
Website: www.waterbrookpress.com

Freelance Potential

Published 76 titles (9 juvenile) in 2003: 1 was developed from
an unsolicited submission and 55 were by agented authors.
Of the 76 titles, 6 were by unpublished writers and 27 were
by authors who were new to the publishing house. Receives
1,000+ queries yearly.
- **Fiction:** Published 2 easy-to-read books, 4–7 years; 2 story
  picture books, 4–10 years; and 4 middle-grade books, 8–12
  years. Genres include inspirational and religious fiction.
- **Nonfiction:** Published 1 young adult book, 12–18 years. Topics
  include Christianity and religion.
- **Representative Titles:** *God Gave Us You* by Lisa Tawn Bergren
  is a book for bedtime, naptime, or storytime about a young
  polar bear cub who learns that he is a welcomed, treasured gift
  from the Lord. *God Gave Us Two* by Lisa Tawn Bergren is a
  sequel that affirms the cub's place in the family when a new
  cub comes along.

Submissions and Payment

Catalogue available with 9x12 SASE. Accepts queries submitted through literary agents only. No unsolicited mss. SASE.
Responds in 4–6 weeks. Publication in 1 year. Payment policy
varies.

Editor's Comments

We're always looking for authors who will challenge and pro-
voke thought among our readers, ultimately leading them to
renewed hope and redemption. If you have a title that will help
children develop a deeper relationship with God, have your
agent contact us.

Wayne State University Press

The Leonard N. Simons Building
4809 Woodward Avenue
Detroit, MI 48201-1309

Acquisitions Assistant: Annie Martin

Publisher's Interests
Wayne State University Press publishes books on a wide range
of topics for a diverse audience, including scholars, librarians,
and the general public. Subject areas covered in its current
catalogue include African studies, economics, Jewish studies,
literature, architecture, political satire, automotive history, and
regional studies. It does not publish fiction.
Website: http://wsupress.wayne.edu/

Freelance Potential
Published 50 titles (2 juvenile) in 2003: 10 were developed from
unsolicited submissions, 1 was by an agented author, and 10
were reprint/licensed properties. Receives 180 queries yearly.
- **Nonfiction:** Publishes middle-grade books, 8–12 years. Topics
  include Michigan history, the Upper Peninsula, and the Great
  Lakes. Also publishes titles on Jewish folklore and anthropology,
  labor history, urban studies, German theory, speech and language pathology, contemporary film, and television.
- **Representative Titles:** *Willie Horton* by Grant Eldridge &
  Karen Elizabeth Bush (10+ years) tells the life story of this
  major league baseball player from Detroit. *First Lady of Detroit*
  by Karen Elizabeth Bush (10+ years) profiles the wife of the
  founder of Detroit.

Submissions and Payment
Guidelines available. Query with résumé, clips, table of con-
tents, and chapter-by-chapter outline. Accepts photocopies,
computer printouts, and email to annie.martin@wayne.edu.
SASE. Responds in 2–3 weeks. Publication in 15 months.
Royalty, 7.5–10%.

Editor's Comments
We welcome new authors who can contribute fresh ideas or
innovative approaches to the topics we cover on our list.
Review our catalogue and some of our titles to get a sense of
what we publish. If your work fits our needs, please send a
brief summary of your idea, describing its scope, length, and
intended audience.

Weigl Educational Publishers Limited

6325 10th Street SE
Calgary, Alberta T2H 2Z9
Canada

Series Editor: Jennifer Nault

Publisher's Interests

Based in Canada, Weigl Educational Publishers produces books for use in both Canadian and American classrooms, as well as distance-learning materials. It does not publish poetry or fiction.
Website: www.weigl.com

Freelance Potential

Published 105 titles in 2003: 8–10 were reprint/licensed properties. Of the 105 titles, 1 was by an unpublished writer and 3–4 were by authors who were new to the publishing house. Receives 500 queries yearly.

- **Nonfiction:** Published 47 chapter books, 5–10 years; 50 middle-grade books, 8–12 years; and 8 young adult books, 12–18 years. Topics include social studies, history, science, nature, art, career guidance, and multicultural, ethnic, and global issues.
- **Representative Titles:** *A Guide to American States Fact Book* (grades 4–6) offers lists, maps, and charts that take readers on a journey through the US; part of the American States series. *Roald Dahl* by Rennay Craats (grades 4–6) profiles the much-loved children's writer; part of the My Favorite Writer series.

Submissions and Payment

Send résumé only. No queries or unsolicited mss. Accepts photocopies, computer printouts, and email to kara@ weigl.com. SAE/IRC. Responds in 6 months. Publication in 2 years. Work-for-hire fee paid on acceptance of ms.

Editor's Comments

Our mission is to bring our readers the best in teaching and library resources. To meet that goal, we are interested in hearing from writers with a background in education, and strong writing skills, who can write for both the Canadian and US markets. All of our titles and textbooks conform to national curricula, and our list of classroom and library resources has increased dramatically in the past couple of years. Please send a résumé if you wish to be considered for work.

Whitecap Books Ltd.

351 Lynn Avenue
North Vancouver, British Columbia V7J 2C4
Canada

Publisher: Robert McCullough

Publisher's Interests
Fiction and nonfiction books for early and middle-grade
readers are available from Whitecap Books. It offers juvenile
titles on Canadian regional topics and natural history, as
well as picture books and chapter books. It also publishes
books on parenting and family issues for adults.
Website: www.whitecap.ca

Freelance Potential
Published 65 titles (10–15 juvenile) in 2003: 6 were developed
from unsolicited submissions, 4 were by agented authors,
and 17 were reprint/licensed properties. Of the 65 titles, 8
were by unpublished writers and 17 were by new authors.
Receives 1,000 queries yearly.
- **Fiction:** Publishes story picture books, 4–10 years; and chapter books, 5–10 years. Genres include adventure; fantasy; books about sports and nature; and contemporary fiction.
- **Nonfiction:** Publishes easy-to-read books, 4–7 years. Topics include natural history, regional subjects, Canadian history, nature, the environment, and science. Also publishes parenting, history, and nature books for adults.
- **Representative Titles:** *Dot to Dot in the Sky: Stories in the Stars* by Joan Marie Galat (7–11 years) is a fun guide to astronomy that portrays 15 constellations. *In Disguise! Stories of Real Women Spies* by Ryan Ann Hunter (8+ years) is a collection of biographies about women who fought secretly and heroically for their countries.

Submissions and Payment
Guidelines available. Query with outline/synopsis, table of
contents, and sample chapter. Accepts photocopies, computer
printouts, and simultaneous submissions if identified.
SAE/IRC. Responds in 2–3 months. Publication in 1 year.
Royalty, negotiable; advance.

Editor's Comments
We still need high-quality nonfiction for children under the age
of thirteen. Books on natural history are especially needed.

White Mane Publishing Company

P.O. Box 708
63 West Burd Street
Shippensburg, PA 17257

Acquisitions Department

Publisher's Interests

White Mane Kids, an imprint of White Mane Publishing Company, features historical fiction for middle-grade and young adult readers based on accurate historical information and details. Most of the books found in its catalogue relate to the Civil War. It publishes no picture books. 10% self-, subsidy-, or co-op published material.

Freelance Potential

Published 14 titles in 2003: all were developed from unsolicited submissions. Receives 360 queries each year.

- **Fiction:** Publishes middle-grade books, 8–12 years; and young adult books, 12–18 years. Genres include historical fiction. Features books about the Civil War.
- **Nonfiction:** Publishes young adult books, 12–18 years. Topics include history and the American Civil War.
- **Representative Titles:** *Lottie's Courage: A Contraband Slave's Story* by Phyllis Hall Haislip is a historical novel based on memoirs and other records describing the experiences of runaway slaves who found refuge at Fortress Monroe in Virginia during the Civil War. *Nowhere to Turn* by Alan Kay is set at the Civil War battle of Antietam; part of the Young Heroes of History series.

Submissions and Payment

Guidelines available. Query. Accepts photocopies. SASE. Responds in 2–3 months. Publication in 12–18 months. Payment policy varies.

Editor's Comments

We're interested in writers who can create engrossing and captivating stories that will educate young readers while entertaining them. A good story for us is one based on accurate historical information, presented in such a way that kids will want to pick up that story and not put it down. We welcome authors who can present us with stories based solidly on fact. In addition, explain why your topic is important, what new insights you can present, and how you would market the book.

Albert Whitman & Company

6340 Oakton Street
Morton Grove, IL 60053-2723

Editor-in-Chief: Kathleen Tucker

Publisher's Interests

Albert Whitman & Company was founded in 1919 with a
mission to provide good books for children. The publisher's
list includes nonfiction titles on timely topics, as well as fiction for beginners in the form of concept and picture books,
and novels for middle-grade readers.
Website: www.albertwhitman.com

Freelance Potential

Published 30 titles in 2003: 5 were by agented authors and 2
were reprint/licensed properties. Of the 30 titles, 2 were by
unpublished writers and 8 were by authors who were new to
the publishing house. Receives 300 queries, 4,500 unsolicited
mss yearly.

- **Fiction:** Publishes early picture books, 0–4 years; chapter
  books, 5–10 years; and middle-grade novels, 8–12 years.
  Genres include mystery, humor, and historical fiction.
- **Nonfiction:** Publishes early picture books, 0–4 years. Topics
  include family issues, social issues, and ethnic and multicultural issues.
- **Representative Titles:** *Haunting at Home Plate* by David Pat-
  neaude (9–13 years) is the story of a baseball team and the
  young ghost who keeps trying to tell them what to do; part of
  the Boxcar Mysteries series. *Shelter Dogs* by Peg Kehret (8–13
  years) features true stories of dogs sent to the pound because
  of medical conditions that have triumphed in amazing ways.

Submissions and Payment

Guidelines available. Send complete ms for picture books.
Query with 3 sample chapters for novels and nonfiction. Indicate if package is a query or ms. Accepts simultaneous submissions. SASE. Responds to queries in 6 weeks, to mss in
3–4 months. Publication in 18–24 months. Royalty; advance.

Editor's Comments

We are best known as the original publisher of the Boxcar
series of books and continue to publish books under the name.
We are interested in mysteries as well as timely nonfiction.

Wiley Children's Books

John Wiley
111 River Street
Hoboken, NJ 07030

Editor: Kate Bradford

Publisher's Interests

Wiley Children's Books publishes books about science, mathematics, and history, as well as biographies, for middle-grade and young adult readers. Parenting and education titles are also available from this publisher, which is the children's imprint of a well-known nonfiction publisher.
Website: www.wiley.com/children

Freelance Potential

Published 20 titles (19 juvenile) in 2003: 2 were developed from unsolicited submissions and 3 were by agented authors. Receives 300 queries yearly.

- **Nonfiction:** Publishes middle-grade books, 8–12 years; and young adult books, 12–18 years. Topics include history, mathematics, science, nature, arts and crafts, multicultural issues, and sports. Also offers biographies, activity books, books about parenting, and books for teachers.
- **Representative Titles:** *Outrageous Women of Civil War Times* by Mary Rodd Furbee (10–14 years) focuses on the amazing pioneers and trailblazers of the time; part of the Outrageous Women series. *The Maya* by Arlette N. Braman (8–12 years) provides activities that bring Mayan culture to life for kids.

Submissions and Payment

Guidelines available. Query with résumé, outline, sample chapter, artwork if applicable, and summary of primary market and competition. Accepts photocopies, computer printouts, and simultaneous submissions if identified. SASE. Responds in 1–3 months. Publication in 18 months. Royalty; advance.

Editor's Comments

We are looking for innovative, educational materials that will appeal to our audience of children from eight to eighteen. Books that make math, science, and history interesting, and biographies of intriguing people are always at the top of our list. Queries should explain why your approach is different or unique, and give a detailed description of your target audience.

Williamson Publishing

1355 Church Hill Road
Charlotte, VT 05445

Editorial Director: Susan Williamson

Publisher's Interests
Children's interactive and how-to paperback books are the
specialty of Williamson Publishing. These books are published in four series: Little Hands, Kaleidoscope Kids, Quick
Start for Kids, and Kids Can. It also offers titles on parenting,
educational trends, and child psychology.
Website: www.williamsonbooks.com

Freelance Potential
Published 20 titles in 2003: 10 were developed from unsolicited submissions. Of the 20 titles, 8 were by unpublished
writers and 10 were by authors who were new to the publishing house. Receives 1,500 queries yearly.
- **Nonfiction:** Publishes easy-to-read books, 4–7 years; and
  middle-grade books, 8–12 years. Features interactive and how-
  to titles. Topics include science, history, math, arts and crafts,
  and multicultural subjects. Also publishes parenting books
  and books on child psychology and educational issues.
- **Representative Titles:** *Awesome Ocean Science!* by Cindy A.
  Littlefield (7–14+ years) provides hands-on projects for investi-
  gating the secrets of the underwater world; part of the Kids
  Can! series. *Early Learning Skill-Builders* by Mary Tomczyk
  (2–6 years) includes developmentally appropriate activities to
  introduce colors, shapes, numbers, and letters; part of the
  Little Hands series.

Submissions and Payment
Query with outline and sample chapters. Accepts photocopies
and computer printouts. SASE. Responds in 3–4 months.
Publication in 12–18 months. Royalty; advance. Flat fee.

Editor's Comments
We are dedicated to providing well-written, high-quality, original trade paperbacks that offer interactive learning experiences
for kids. We do not publish children's fiction. We are still interested in series ideas for books about insects, global warming,
and the human genome for readers between the ages of eight
and fourteen. History books are also of interest.

Windward Publishing

3943 Meadowbrook Road
Minneapolis, MN 55426-4505

President: Alan E. Krysan

Publisher's Interests

Windward Publishing offers educational titles for readers age
four through adult. Marketed primarily in the southeast US
and the Caribbean, they focus on natural history, science,
and outdoor recreation.
Website: www.finney-hobar.com

Freelance Potential

Published 12 titles in 2003: 8–10 were developed from unsolicited submissions. Of the 12 titles, 6 were by unpublished
writers and 8 were by authors who were new to the publishing house. Receives 120+ queries, 90+ unsolicited mss yearly.

- **Nonfiction:** Published 1 easy-to-read book, 4–7 years; 1 story
  picture book, 4–10 years; 2 chapter books, 5–10 years; 6
  middle-grade books, 8–12 years; and 2 young adult books,
  12–18 years. Topics include animals, nature, gardening, horti-
  culture, agriculture, recreation, science, and sports.
- **Representative Titles:** *Sea Turtles Hatching* by Katherine Orr
  follows Loggerhead sea turtles as they hatch in their nest and
  head for the sea. *Billy's Search for Florida Undersea Treasure*
  by Minerva J. Smiley takes readers on an underwater sea journey to explore marine life.

Submissions and Payment

Query with publishing credits, synopsis, table of contents,
introduction, and up to 3 chapters; or send complete ms with
artwork. Accepts photocopies, computer printouts, and
simultaneous submissions if identified. No electronic submissions. Availability of artwork improves chance of acceptance.
Accepts 8x10 or 35mm B/W or color prints or transparen-
cies, line art, and drawings. SASE. Responds in 4–6 weeks.
Publication in 6–8 months. Royalty, 10% of net.

Editor's Comments

We will consider submissions on almost any topic that
has educational value. Do not send mysteries, romances,
science fiction, poems, short story collections, or anything
of a religious nature.

Wizards of the Coast

P.O. Box 707
Renton, WA 98057-0707

Submissions Editor

Publisher's Interests
Role-playing and "shared world" series are the focus of this publisher. Its titles are read by young adults and adults. The list includes epic high fantasy, sword and sorcery, and science fiction books.
Website: www.wizards.com

Freelance Potential
Published 50+ titles in 2003. Receives 1,200 queries yearly.
- **Fiction:** Publishes young adult novels, 12–18 years. Genres include adventure, science fiction, and medieval, heroic, and epic fantasy.
- **Representative Titles:** *A Rumor of Dragons* by Margaret Weis & Tracy Hickman is an adaptation of the Dragonlance novel, created for younger readers. *The Bloody Eye* by T. H. Lain (YA–adult) is a new title in the Dungeons & Dragons series featuring the iconic character of the paladin.

Submissions and Payment
Guidelines available. Query with 10-page writing sample. All work is assigned. Accepts photocopies and simultaneous submissions if identified. SASE. Responds in 4 months. Publication in 1 year. Payment policy varies.

Editor's Comments
We started this company in 1997 because of our love for adventure games and stories. We have grown tremendously since then to include card games, magazines, board games, and electronic media products, but novels remain the core of our publishing program. We are always interested in writers who have as much passion for fantasy worlds as we do, and we welcome hearing from you. If this describes your interests, we suggest you begin your journey by studying the information found at our website. At this time we are in need of authors for our Magic: The Gathering and Dungeons & Dragons series. Remember that all of our authors work on existing series. Send us a writing sample in the appropriate genre and we will contact you if we feel your talent meets our needs.

Woodbine House

6510 Bells Mill Road
Bethesda, MD 20817

Acquisitions Editor: Nancy Gray Paul

Publisher's Interests
Woodbine House publishes books for children with special
needs and for parents, teachers, and other professionals who
work with them.
Website: www.woodbinehouse.com

Freelance Potential
Published 12 titles (2 juvenile) in 2003: 6 were developed
from unsolicited submissions and 4 were by agented authors.
Of the 12 titles, 5 were by unpublished writers and 4 were by
authors who were new to the publishing house. Receives
1,000 queries, 600 unsolicited mss yearly.
- **Fiction:** Published 1 story picture book, 4–10 years; and 1
  chapter book, 5–10 years. Also publishes middle-grade fiction,
  8–12 years. All stories feature children with disabilities.
- **Nonfiction:** Publishes educational titles and parent guides.
  Topics include developmental disabilities such as autism, cere-
  bral palsy, Down Syndrome, and others.
- **Representative Titles:** *Early Communication Skills for Children
  with Down Syndrome* by Libby Kumin (parents, professionals)
  offers information on speech and language development from
  birth through the stage of making three-word phrases. *All Kinds
  of Friends, Even Green!* by Ellen B. Senisi (grades K–4) shows
  how living with a disability can be a positive experience.

Submissions and Payment
Guidelines available. Query with outline, 3 sample chapters,
and clips. Accepts complete ms for picture books only.
Accepts photocopies, computer printouts, and simultaneous
submissions if identified. SASE. Responds to queries in 1
month, to mss in 3 months. Publication in 1–2 years.

Editor's Comments
In addition to books about children with physical and developmental disabilities, we seek submissions that cover mental
health issues such as depression, obsessive-compulsive disorder, and bipolar disorder. We also need young adult fiction and
high-interest/low-level nonfiction about popular culture.

Workman Publishing Company

708 Broadway
New York, NY 10003-9555

Submissions Editor

Publisher's Interests
Books for adults and children may be found in this publisher's
catalogue. It offers nonfiction titles for toddlers, early readers,
middle-grade students, and young adults. Its list also
includes board books, game books, and activity books. It
does not publish fiction.
Website: www.workman.com

Freelance Potential
Published 50 titles (10 juvenile) in 2003: most were by agented
authors. Of the 50 titles, 3 were by unpublished writers and
6 were by authors who were new to the publishing house.
Receives 1,000 queries, 2,000 unsolicited mss yearly.
- **Fiction:** Publishes toddler books, 0–4 years; story picture
  books, 4–10 years; and board and novelty books. Features
  humor and books about nature.
- **Nonfiction:** Publishes concept and early picture books, 0–4
  years; story picture books, 4–10 years; middle-grade books,
  8–12 years; and young adult books, 12–18 years.
- **Representative Titles:** *What to Expect: The Toddler Years* by
  Arlene Eisenberg et al. (parents) is the third in a line of books
  by the same authors and offers month-by-month growth and
  development phases of babies. *1,000 Play Thinks* by Ivan
  Moscovich is a puzzle book that features games of science, art,
  and mathematics.

Submissions and Payment
Guidelines available. Query with clips or send complete ms
with illustrations for fiction. Query with table of contents,
outline/synopsis, sample chapters, and clips for nonfiction.
Accepts photocopies and computer printouts. SASE.
Responds in 6 weeks. Publication period varies. Royalty;
advance.

Editor's Comments
We take the time to review each submission very carefully and
ask that you extend the same respect to us by doing your
homework first to determine whether your book is right for us.

World Book

Suite 2000
233 North Michigan Avenue
Chicago, IL 60601

Product Development Director: Paul A. Kobasa

Publisher's Interests
This well-known publisher of encyclopedias and reference materials offers nonfiction titles for beginning readers through young adults. It also publishes biographies, activity books, and how-to titles. World Book has been in operation for more than 80 years.
Website: www.worldbook.com

Freelance Potential
Published 30 titles (15 juvenile) in 2003.
- **Nonfiction:** Publishes easy-to-read books, 4–7 years; middle-grade books, 8–12 years; and young adult books, 12–18 years. Topics include social studies, cultural studies, science, nature, history, geography, hobbies, careers, the environment, and arts and crafts. Also publishes biographies, activity books, reference books, and how-to titles.
- **Representative Titles:** *I Can Do It! Gardening* explains to kids how to garden indoors and outdoors and with a variety of plants, and includes advice on growing flowers, bulbs, herbs, and vegetables. *Arithmetricks* teaches children how to think by sorting out clues as they solve number games; part of the Mind Benders series.

Submissions and Payment
Catalogue available with 9x12 SASE. Query with outline or synopsis. No unsolicited mss. Accepts simultaneous submissions if identified. SASE. Responds in 1–2 months. Publication in 18 months. Payment rate and policy vary.

Editor's Comments
Since 1917, we have set the standard for accuracy, objectivity, and reliability in research materials, and we are committed to publishing reference books that meet the highest standards of editorial excellence while keeping pace with the technological developments that define the computer age. We'll consider ideas that fit in with *TutorLink*, our innovative peer-tutoring program. Prospective writers may also want to look at our *Student Discovery Encyclopedia*.

Wright Group/McGraw-Hill

Suite 400
1 Prudential Plaza
130 East Randolph Street
Chicago, IL 60601

Editor: Thomas Schiele

Publisher's Interests

Curriculum materials and supplementary resources are the core of this educational publisher's list. It strives to provide teachers with captivating, research-based strategies and ideas to make teaching more effective. With materials for use in preschool through grade six, it covers the topics of language arts, mathematics, and guided reading, and it also offers high-interest/low-reading-level titles.
Website: www.wrightgroup.com

Freelance Potential

Published 225 titles in 2003: 30 were developed from unsolicited submissions, 30 were by agented authors, and 16 were reprint/licensed properties. Of the 225 titles, 35 were by authors who were new to the publishing house. Receives 300 queries, 200 unsolicited mss yearly.

- **Fiction:** Publishes easy-to-read books, 4–7 years; story picture books, 4–10 years; chapter books, 5–10 years; and middle-grade books, 8–12 years. Genres include Western, contemporary, ethnic, and multicultural fiction; adventure; fantasy; folklore; mystery; and science fiction.
- **Nonfiction:** Publishes easy-to-read titles, 4–7 years. Topics include animals, crafts, history, and multicultural and ethnic subjects. Also offers biographies.
- **Representative Titles:** *'Round the Rug Math: Adventures in Problem Solving* (pre-K–grade 2) is used to supplement existing core mathematics programs. *Sunshine* (ages 6–12) is a set that includes stories for shared reading with older students.

Submissions and Payment

Query or send complete mss. Publication period and payment policy vary.

Editor's Comments

At the Wright Group, our mission is to help teachers make the learning experience more engaging with titles that take new and different approaches. We would like to see more submissions on mathematics at this time.

XC Publishing

16006 19th Avenue CT E
Tacoma, WA 98445

Editor: Cheryl Dyson

Publisher's Interests
This electronic publisher offers fiction for adults and young adults in a number of genres, including science fiction, horror, romance, and mystery. It is also interested in receiving fiction of all types for children of all ages. In addition to electronic books, it plans to offer audio books and paperbacks. It does not accept nonfiction.
Website: www.xcpublishing.com

Freelance Potential
Published 6 titles in 2003: all were developed from unsolicited submissions. Of the 6 titles, 5 were by unpublished writers and all were by authors who were new to the publishing house. Receives 50 queries yearly.
- **Fiction:** Publishes young adult books, 12–18 years. Genres include fantasy, horror, mystery, suspense, romance, and science fiction. Also publishes adult titles.
- **Representative Titles:** *Intimate Shadows* by Linda Chapman is a novel about a woman who falls from a mountain ledge and is rescued by an alien scientist on a routine expedition to Earth. *Queen of Diamonds* by Richard L. Graves is a book about a "consultant" for a top secret government agency who gets into trouble with a diamond cartel and the mob.

Submissions and Payment
Guidelines available. Query with clips or writing samples. Accepts photocopies, disk submissions, and email submissions to editor@xcpublishing.com. Availability of artwork improves chance of acceptance. SASE. Responds in 1 week. Publication in 4–6 months. Royalty, 40%.

Editor's Comments
Please note that we only publish fiction—no nonfiction, please! This year, we are very interested in reviewing children's books. The books can be on any topic, and we will consider titles for all age ranges. For older readers, we are particularly interested in cross-genre novels. Our standards are high—send us only your best work.

Zephyr Press

3316 North Kapok Lane
Tucson, AZ 85716

Managing/Acquisitions Editor: Veronica Durie

Publisher's Interests

This publisher offers titles on all curriculum subjects for teachers who work with children in kindergarten through high school. It also features books on brain-compatible learning, multiple intelligences, and gifted education.
Website: www.zephyrpress.com

Freelance Potential

Published 8–10 titles in 2003: 4 were developed from unsolicited submissions and 3 were reprint/licensed properties. Of the 8–10 titles, 4 were by unpublished writers. Receives 250 queries yearly.

- **Nonfiction:** Publishes educational titles for use in grades K–12. Topics include gifted education, multiple intelligences, brain-based learning, thinking skills, science, technology, history, mathematics, social studies, literacy, and character education.
- **Representative Titles:** *Higher-Order Thinking the Multiple Intelligences Way* by David Lazear (teachers) explores ways of teaching that promote deep understanding of subjects by raising students' thinking to higher-order realms. *Creating the Peaceable Classroom* by Sandy Bothmer (teachers) explores the use of techniques such as movement, music, yoga, Feng Shui, and Reiki to calm, uplift, and focus teachers and students.

Submissions and Payment

Guidelines and submission packet available. Send completed submission packet, detailed outline, and sample chapter. Accepts photocopies and computer printouts. Availability of artwork improves chance of acceptance. SASE. Responds in 3–6 months. Publication in 1–2 years. Royalty varies.

Editor's Comments

We're interested in publishing unique, teacher-friendly materials that have been tested in the classroom and that offer innovative approaches to teaching children at all grade levels. We consider submissions for all subjects. Visit our website if you have an idea for a poster set or educational comic book, to get an idea of what we already offer.

Innovative & Vigorous
Gwen Ellis,
Zonderkidz

Zonderkidz, the children's division of Zondervan Publishing, is "the leading publisher of biblical, innovative, and imaginative products that meet the spiritual and developmental needs of children ages 12 and under," according to Editor Gwen Ellis.

The publishing house relies largely on a stable of writers for its children's fiction, but they are not closed to new authors. The ultimate criteria about whether to purchase a book are whether it's "a great story" and it fits the company's mission statement.

Ellis says that a manuscript has to be very well written to be considered, but that any story can be helped by an editor's work. "We work with authors in making revisions. Each editor has his or her own style for this process."

Zonderkidz has a vigorous marketing program. Ellis assesses it as one of their best strengths. "There are contests—both online and through bookstores, there are features at trade shows, and there is a strong publicity factor."

Several Zonderkidz books have sold upwards of 75,000 copies. An average seller is around 20,000. "One thing to remember," Ellis explains, "is that our books have a longer shelf life than a book from a general trade publisher. We keep them around for several years." There are always at least two Zonderkidz books on the Christian best-seller list.

The Academy Award for the kind of books Zonderkidz publishes is the Christian industry's Gold Medallion Award, which was won by the company's *Toddler's Rhyme Bible.*

Zonderkidz

5300 Patterson Avenue SE
Grand Rapids, MI 49530

Senior Acquisitions Editor: Amy DeVries

Publisher's Interests
Zonderkidz strives to create imaginative books that are written from a Christian, biblical perspective. It publishes both fiction and nonfiction written for toddlers, preschoolers, young readers, and "tweens." Its list also includes full-text Bibles and Bible storybooks. Zonderkidz is a division of Zondervan Publishing.
Website: www.zonderkidz.com

Freelance Potential
Published 46 titles in 2003. Receives 500 queries yearly.
- **Fiction:** Publishes concept books, toddler books, and early picture books, 0–4 years; easy-to-read titles, 4–7 years; story picture books, 4–10 years; chapter books, 5–10 years; and middle-grade novels, 8–12 years. Genres include adventure and contemporary, historical, inspirational, religious, and multicultural fiction—all written from a biblical perspective.
- **Nonfiction:** Publishes concept books, toddler books, and early picture books, 0–4 years; easy-to-read titles, 4–7 years; story picture books, 4–10 years; chapter books, 5–10 years; and middle-grade titles, 8–12 years. Also offers Bibles, biographies, and devotionals. Topics include religion and social issues.
- **Representative Titles:** *The Parable of Two Builders* by Melody Carlson (4–6 years) is a humorous retelling of Jesus's parable about the wise man and the foolish man. *The Amazing Beginning of You* by Matt & Lisa Jacobson (8–12 years) teaches kids about the beginnings of life in utero and how the Creator makes each person unique.

Submissions and Payment
Guidelines available at website. Query with clips or writing samples. Accepts photocopies. SASE. Responds in 2–3 weeks. Publication in 18 months. Royalty; advance. Flat fee.

Editor's Comments
We're actively seeking adventure series for boys and stories that express multicultural themes. Our goal is to meet the spiritual and developmental needs of children. Please don't send material that is not written from a biblical perspective.

Additional Listings

We have selected the following publishers to offer you additional marketing opportunities. Most of these publishers have special submissions requirements or they purchase a limited number of juvenile titles each year.

For published authors, we include information about houses that produce reprints of previously published works. For writers who are proficient in foreign languages, we list publishers of foreign-language material. You will also find publishers who accept résumés only; who work with agented authors; or who usually accept unsolicited submissions, but due to a backlog, are not accepting material at this time.

As you survey these listings, you may find that a small regional press is a more appropriate market for your submission than a larger publisher. Also, if you are involved in education or are a specialist in a certain field, consider sending your résumé to one of the educational publishers— you may have the qualifications they are looking for.

Publishers who usually accept unsolicited submissions but were not accepting unsolicited material at our press time are designated with an ⊗. *Be sure to contact the publisher before submitting material to determine the current submissions policy.*

As you review the listings that follow, use the Publisher's Interests section as your guide to the particular focus of each house.

A & B Publishers Group

100 Atlantic Avenue
Brooklyn, NY 11238

Managing Editor: Maxwell Taylor

Publisher's Interests
Fiction and nonfiction that encourage self-esteem and explore cultural diversity appear on this publisher's list. Its titles target children of all ages, from toddlers through young adults.
Website: www.anbdonline.com

Freelance Potential
Published 18 titles (14 juvenile) in 2003: 6 were developed from unsolicited submissions. Of the 18 titles, 12 were by unpublished writers and 6 were by authors who were new to the publishing house. Receives 110 queries yearly.
Submissions and Payment: Query with sample chapters and table of contents. Accepts photocopies, computer printouts, and simultaneous submissions if identified. SASE. Responds in 2–3 months. Publication period varies. Royalty, 4–5%; advance, $500.

Abbeville Kids

Suite 500
116 West 23rd Street
New York, NY 10011

Editor: Susan Costello

Publisher's Interests
Abbeville Kids is a division of Abbeville Press, a publisher of art and illustrated books. Its children's line features both illustrated fiction and nonfiction titles for readers up to the age of 12, including books about famous artists and writers. 50% self-, subsidy-, co-venture, or co-op published material.
Website: www.abbeville.com

Freelance Potential
Published 40 titles (1–3 juvenile) in 2003. Receives 120 unsolicited mss yearly.
Submissions and Payment: Send complete ms with illustrations. Prefers agented authors. Accepts photocopies and computer printouts. SASE. Responds in 5 weeks. Publication in 18–24 months. Royalty; advance. Flat fee.

Abingdon Press

P.O. Box 801
201 Eighth Avenue South
Nashville, TN 37203

Editor: Peg Augustine

Publisher's Interests
Abingdon Press provides books and nonprint media such as
audio and video cassettes and computer software. The curriculum resources it offers are written on assignment by active members of the United Methodist Church who are involved with the
age level for which they write. 50% co-op published material.
Website: www.abingdonpress.com

Freelance Potential
Published 20 titles (4 juvenile) in 2003: 10 were developed from
unsolicited submissions. Receives 600 queries yearly.
Submissions and Payment: Guidelines available. Query with
outline and 1–2 chapters. Accepts photocopies and email submissions to paugustine@umpublishing.org. SASE. Responds in 3
months. Publication in 2 years. Royalty, 5–10%. Flat fee, $1,000+.

Accord Publishing

Suite 202
1732 Wazee Street
Denver, CO 80202

Editor: Ken Fleck

Publisher's Interests
Accord Publishing offers fiction for young readers up to the age
of nine, including activity books, novelty books, and board
books. Adventure fiction, fantasy, and humor are all found in its
current catalogue. New writers will find guidelines at the website
and are encouraged to review some of the publisher's titles.
Website: www.accordpublishing.com

Freelance Potential
Published 18 titles in 2003: 2 were developed from unsolicited
submissions and 6 were by agented authors. Receives 360
queries, 192 unsolicited mss yearly.
Submissions and Payment: Guidelines available at website.
Query or send complete ms. SASE. Response time varies.
Publication period varies. Payment policy varies.

ACTA Publications

4848 North Clark Street
Chicago, IL 60640

Editor: Gregory Pierce

Publisher's Interests
This small publishing house features books, films, and audio
resources for young adult and adult Christians interested in
enhancing their faith. It does not publish fiction. For the coming
year, its editors would like to see queries on the subjects of spirituality and grief. Writers may review its catalogue at the website.
Website: www.actapublications.com

Freelance Potential
Published 17 titles (3 juvenile) in 2003: 3 were by authors who
were new to the publishing house and all were assigned.
Receives 360 queries yearly.
Submissions and Payment: Query with clips. Accepts photocopies. SASE. Responds in 1–3 weeks. Publication in 9–12
months. Royalty, 10%.

Activity Resources Company

20655 Hathaway Avenue
Hayward, CA 94541

Editor: Mary Laycock

Publisher's Interests
Teachers in kindergarten through ninth-grade classrooms come
to this publisher for books and materials related to teaching
mathematics. Its products help teachers assess students' skill
levels. Manipulatives, games, and investigations are found in the
current catalogue alongside books on traditional math subjects
such as algebra, statistics, geometry, and measurement.
Website: www.activityresources.com

Freelance Potential
Published 4 titles in 2003. Receives 25–30 queries yearly.
Submissions and Payment: Query with résumé, sample chapter, and bibliography. Accepts photocopies, computer printouts,
and simultaneous submissions if identified. SASE. Responds in
2–4 weeks. Publication in 1 year. Royalty, varies.

Advocacy Press

402 E. Carillo
Santa Barbara, CA 93102

Curriculum Specialist: Luke Besner

Publisher's Interests
Established in 1983, Advocacy Press is committed to publishing
and distributing books for elementary children through young
adults that promote self-reliance and gender equality, and
encourage realistic life and career planning. It is currently interested in submissions for children's books, as well as titles on
personal development.
Website: www.advocacypress.com

Freelance Potential
Published 2 titles in 2003: both were assigned. Receives 500
unsolicited mss yearly.
Submissions and Payment: Guidelines available with SASE or
at website. Send complete ms. Accepts photocopies. SASE.
Responds in 1 month. Publication in 1 year. Royalty.

Alpha Publishing

P.O. Box 53788
Lafayette, LA 70505

Publisher: Mark Anthony

Publisher's Interests
Alpha Publishing produces a wide variety of adult nonfiction
titles, and is currently looking for material on topics such as
family issues, social issues, women's issues, education, and current events. It also publishes some inspirational fiction targeted
to young adults.
Website: www.alphapublishingonline.com

Freelance Potential
Published 10–20 titles in 2003. Receives 2,000 queries yearly.
Submissions and Payment: Guidelines available. Query with
200- to 300-word proposal. No unsolicited mss. Accepts photocopies, computer printouts, and simultaneous submissions if
identified. SASE. Responds in 3–4 months. Publication in 6–8
months. Royalty.

Alyson Wonderland

Suite 1000
6922 Hollywood Boulevard
Los Angeles, CA 90028

Editor

Publisher's Interests
Alyson Wonderland specializes in books by, for, and about lesbians, gay men, and bisexuals of all ages and from all walks of life. Its catalogue includes several parenting and family titles, all as they relate to the publisher's targeted audience.
Website: www.alyson.com

Freelance Potential
Published 50 titles (3 juvenile) in 2003: 30 were developed from unsolicited submissions and 3 were reprint/licensed properties. Receives 1,000 queries yearly.
Submissions and Payment: Guidelines available. Query with 1-page synopsis and available artwork. No unsolicited mss. Accepts photocopies and computer printouts. SASE. Responds in 10–12 weeks. Publication in 2 years. Payment policy varies.

Ambassador Books

91 Prescott Street
Worcester, MA 01605

Submissions: Kathryn Conlan

Publisher's Interests
Established in 1996, Ambassador Books publishes children's and adult books that have a spiritual or inspirational element and that have a positive impact on people's lives.
Website: www.ambassadorbooks.com

Freelance Potential
Published 7 titles (3 juvenile) in 2003: 1 was developed from an unsolicited submission and 1 was assigned. Of the 7 titles, 1 was by an unpublished writer and 2 were by authors new to the publishing house. Receives 1,800 queries yearly.
Submissions and Payment: Guidelines and catalogue available at website. Query. Accepts photocopies. Availability of artwork improves chance of acceptance. SASE. Responds in 4 months. Publication in 1 year. Royalty, 10%.

AMG Publishers

6815 Shallowford Road
Chattanooga, TN 37421

Editor: Dan Penwell

Publisher's Interests
With a focus on books that promote personal devotion and that
make the Bible more accessible, AMG Publishers offers Christian
nonfiction, Bible study guides, and Christian reference books.
Family and parenting titles also appear on its list.
Website: www.amgpublishers.com

Freelance Potential
Published 35 titles (2 juvenile) in 2003: 3–4 were developed
from unsolicited submissions, 6 were by agented authors, and
2 were assigned. Receives 900–1,200 queries yearly.
Submissions and Payment: Guidelines available at website.
Query. Accepts email queries to danp@amginternational.org.
SASE. Response time and publication period vary. Royalty;
advance.

Amirah Publishing

P.O. Box 541146
Flushing, NY 11354

Submissions Editor: Adam Emerick

Publisher's Interests
All of the books from Amirah Publishing focus on Middle Eastern
and Muslim culture. Fiction and nonfiction for preschool children through young adults appear on its list, along with educational resources related to the study of Islam.
Website: www.amirahpublishing.com

Freelance Potential
Published 6 titles in 2003: 2 were by agented authors. Of the
6 titles, 2 were by unpublished writers. Receives 30 queries
each year.
Submissions and Payment: Query. Accepts email submissions
to amirahpbco@aol.com and simultaneous submissions if identified. SASE. Responds in 4–6 weeks. Publication in 4–6 months.
Flat fee.

Aquila Communications Ltd.

2642 Diab Street
St. Laurent, Quebec H4S 1E8
Canada

President: Sami Kelada

Publisher's Interests
Since 1970, this publisher has produced French-as-a-Second-Language reading materials for students in fourth grade through college. Its titles reflect a variety of themes and styles and are grade-level and age appropriate. Most books feature end-of-book exercises and lexica and some also include audiocassettes. Teachers' guides are sold separately.
Website: www.aquilacommunications.com

Freelance Potential
Published 14 titles in 2003: 1 was by an unpublished writer. Receives 500 queries yearly.
Submissions and Payment: Guidelines available. Query with synopsis. Accepts photocopies. SAE/IRC. Responds in 1 month. Publication in 2–6 months. Royalty, 5%. Flat fee, $50–$500+.

Association for Childhood Education International

Suite 215, 17904 Georgia Avenue
Olney, MD 20832-2277

Director, Editorial Department: Anne Bauer

Publisher's Interests
This international publisher strives to promote and support optimal education and development of children in the global community. Its materials are used with children from birth through adolescence and are read by educators as well as child development specialists and parents. Videotapes and audiocassettes are also found in its catalogue.
Website: www.acei.org

Freelance Potential
Published 5 titles in 2003. Receives 120 mss yearly.
Submissions and Payment: Guidelines available. Send complete ms. Accepts photocopies, computer printouts, and disk submissions (ASCII or Microsoft Word 5.0). SASE. Responds in 2 weeks. Publication in 1–3 years. No payment. Provides author's copies.

ATL Press

P.O. Box 4563 T Station
Shrewsbury, MA 01545

Submissions Editor

Publisher's Interests
Fiction and nonfiction books on science, especially earth science, biochemistry, and astronomy are the focus of this publisher.
Website: www.atlpress.com

Freelance Potential
Published 10–15 titles in 2003: 2 were developed from unsolicited submissions and 1 was by an agented author. Of the 12 titles, 2 were by authors who were new to the publishing house. Receives 100–150 queries yearly.
Submissions and Payment: Guidelines available at website. Query with sample chapters and résumé; or send complete ms with résumé. Accepts photocopies, computer printouts, and IBM disk submissions. SASE. Responds in 3–4 weeks. Publication in 2–4 months. Royalty.

Avocet Press

19 Paul Court
Pearl River, NY 10965

Editor: Cynthia Webb

Publisher's Interests
Avocet Press offers a catalogue of books for young adult and adult readers—everything from poetry, to mysteries, to historical fiction. It prides itself on the high quality of all the books on its list. Queries for books that will bring readers fresh ideas are welcome, especially if they are written in a style that represents the best in quality literature.
Website: www.avocetpress.com

Freelance Potential
Published 8 titles in 2003: 4 were developed from unsolicited submissions. Receives 2,400 queries yearly.
Submissions and Payment: Guidelines available at website. Query. SASE. Response time and publication period vary. Royalty; advance.

Avocus Publishing

4 White Brook Road
Gilsum, NH 03448

Editor: Craig Thorn

Publisher's Interests
This publisher offers chapter books, middle-grade books, and young adult titles along with parenting and educational titles for adults. Many of its books are used by homeschooling parents. Books that deal with gifted and special education target parents of special needs children and the professionals who work with them.
Website: www.avocus.com

Freelance Potential
Published 4 titles (2 juvenile) in 2003: 1 was developed from an unsolicited submission and 3 were assigned. Receives 144 queries, 72 unsolicited mss yearly.
Submissions and Payment: Guidelines and catalogue available at website. Query or send complete ms. SASE. Response time and publication period vary. Royalty; advance.

Azro Press

PMB 342
1704 Llano St B
Sante Fe, NM 87505

Submissions Editor

Publisher's Interests
This publisher offers fiction for two- to ten-year-old children that focuses on the American Southwest. It will not be reviewing queries or unsolicited manuscripts until late 2004.
Website: www.azropress.com

Freelance Potential
Published 5 titles in 2003: all were developed from unsolicited submissions. Of the 5 titles, all were by unpublished writers. Receives 1,000+ queries and unsolicited mss yearly.
Submissions and Payment: Guidelines available. Query with clips for nonfiction; send complete ms for fiction. Accepts photocopies and simultaneous submissions if identified. SASE. Responds to queries in 1 week, to mss in 3–4 months. Publication in 2 years. Royalty, 5%.

Ballyhoo Books

P.O. Box 534
Shoreham, NY 11786

Executive Editor: Liam Gerrity

Publisher's Interests

Ballyhoo Books offers activity-oriented nonfiction titles that teachers or parents can use with young children, or that middle-grade children can read and learn from on their own.

Freelance Potential

Published 2 titles in 2003: both were developed from unsolicited submissions. Receives 300 queries, 100 unsolicited mss yearly.

Submissions and Payment: Guidelines available. Query with outline and 3 sample chapters for long works. Send complete ms for shorter works. Accepts photocopies, computer printouts, and simultaneous submissions if identified. SASE. Responds to queries in 2 weeks, to mss in 1–2 months. Publication in 6–12 months. Royalty; advance. Flat fee.

Barefoot Books Ltd.

124 Walcot Street
Bath BA1 5BG
United Kingdom

Submissions Editor

Publisher's Interests

Barefoot Books publishes children's picture books and anthologies for readers from birth to 12 years of age. Its mission is to encourage children to read deeper and to explore their own creativity by offering inspiring stories that capture the imagination. It is interested in material that deals with personal independence, love of learning, and acceptance of other traditions.

Website: www.barefoot-books.com

Freelance Potential

Published 11 titles in 2003.

Submissions and Payment: Guidelines available at website. Send complete ms with artwork. Accepts photocopies and computer printouts. SAE/IRC. Responds only if interested. Publication period and payment policy vary.

Barron's Educational Series

250 Wireless Boulevard
Hauppauge, NY 11788

Acquisitions Editor: Wayne Barr

Publisher's Interests
Children of all ages find books of fiction and nonfiction on the
list of this well-known educational publisher. It targets the
school and library markets with curriculum-based material.
50% self-, subsidy-, co-venture, or co-op published material.
Website: www.barronseduc.com

Freelance Potential
Published 400 titles (100 juvenile) in 2003. Receives 1,000
queries, 600 unsolicited mss yearly.
Submissions and Payment: Guidelines available. Send ms with
résumé for fiction. Query with résumé, table of contents, out-
line/synopsis, 2 sample chapters, and description of audience
for nonfiction. SASE. Responds to queries in 1–3 months, to mss
in 6–8 months. Publication in 2 years. Royalty; advance. Flat fee.

Bay Light Publishing, Inc.

P.O. Box 3032
Mooresville, NC 28117

Publisher: Charlotte Soutullo

Publisher's Interests
A Christian publisher, Bay Light Publishing offers easy-to-read
books and story picture books with religious or inspirational
themes. It seeks to help children discover a Christ-centered life
through the books it publishes, and to teach them values and
morals. Many of the titles that appear on its list are published as
series. At this time, it is not accepting unsolicited manuscripts.
Please send queries only.
Website: www.baylightpub.com

Freelance Potential
Published 3 titles in 2003. Receives 25 queries yearly.
Submissions and Payment: Query. No unsolicited mss. Accepts
photocopies and simultaneous submissions if identified. SASE.
Responds in 3–6 weeks. Publication in 1 year. Flat fee.

Baylor University Press

P.O. Box 97363
Waco, TX 76798-7363

Director: Carey C. Newman

Publisher's Interests
An academic publisher, Baylor University Press offers titles for
college students and young adults on religion, ethics, church-
state issues, oral history, and the arts.
Website: www1.baylor.edu/BUPress/

Freelance Potential
Published 6 titles in 2003: 2 were developed from unsolicited
submissions. Of the 6 titles, 3 were by unpublished writers
and 3 were by authors who were new to the publishing house.
Receives 120–180 queries yearly.
Submissions and Payment: Guidelines and catalogue available
with 9x14 SASE or at website. Query. Accepts photocopies and
IBM disk submissions. SASE. Responds in 3–30 days.
Publication in 9 months. Royalty, 10%.

Alexander Graham Bell Association for the Deaf and Hard of Hearing

3417 Volta Place NW
Washington, DC 20007-2778

Director of Publications: Elizabeth Quigley

Publisher's Interests
The Alexander Graham Bell Association for the Deaf and Hard of
Hearing offers nonfiction books that focus on issues related to
children and deafness, including books on cochlear implants
and the use of hearing aids to promote speech. It also publishes
fiction titles and inspirational biographies for children with hearing loss, and is interested in books on all topics in Spanish.
Website: www.agbell.org

Freelance Potential
Published 8 titles in 2003. Receives 10–15 unsolicited mss
each year.
Submissions and Payment: Guidelines available. Send up to 15
ms pages. Accepts computer printouts. SASE. Responds in 3
months. Publication in 9–16 months. Royalty, to 10%.

The Benefactory

P.O. Box 128
Cohasset, MA 02025

Creative Director: Cynthia Germain

Publisher's Interests
With a list that offers books for children between seven and nine, this small house specializes in stories about animals. Each book is accompanied by an audiotape, toy, or videotape. The publisher is licensed with a number of nonprofit groups devoted to animal protection. Its goal is to encourage children to learn to love reading and to become proactive citizens.
Website: www.readplay.com

Freelance Potential
Published 6 titles in 2003. Receives 200 queries yearly.
Submissions and Payment: Guidelines available. Most work is done on assignment. Query only. No unsolicited mss. SASE. Responds in 6–8 weeks. Publication in 2 years. Royalty; advance, 5%.

BePuzzled

University Games Corporation
2030 Harrison Street
San Francisco, CA 94110

General Manager: Steve Peek

Publisher's Interests
This publisher specializes in thrillers and mysteries that appeal to seven- to nine-year-old readers. Stories must not include sex, drugs, profanity, violence, or terrorism, and each story should be paired with a jigsaw puzzle that will give the reader clues to help solve the mystery.
Website: www.areyougame.com

Freelance Potential
Published 15 titles (10 juvenile) in 2003: all were developed from unsolicited submissions. Receives 500 queries yearly.
Submissions and Payment: Guidelines available. Query with short mystery story sample. Accepts computer printouts. SASE. Responds in 2 weeks. Publication in 1 year. Buys world rights. Flat fee.

Bick Publishing House

307 Neck Road
Madison, CT 06443

President: Dale Carlson

Publisher's Interests
This publisher's list includes books written specifically for teens on topics such as psychology, science, life planning, and pain management. It also offer books for adults on similar topics.
Website: www.bickpubhouse.com

Freelance Potential
Published 2 titles in 2003: 1 was by an agented author. Of the 2 titles, 1 was by an unpublished writer and 1 was by a new author. Receives 50–100 queries yearly.
Submissions and Payment: Guidelines and catalogue available with 9x12 SASE ($1 postage). Query with 3 chapters, outline/synopsis, table of contents, and author biography. Accepts photocopies. SASE. Responds in 2 weeks. Publication in 1 year. Royalty, 10% net; advance.

A & C Black

37 Soho Square
London W1D 3QZ
United Kingdom

Submissions Editor: Claire Weatherhead

Publisher's Interests
High-quality educational titles that tie in with the curriculum are the focus of this publisher. Fiction titles include many books for readers from age eight, as well as books for reluctant readers. Nonfiction titles include books on topics such as literacy, numeracy, and other cross-curriculum subjects.
Website: www.acblack.com

Freelance Potential
Published 70 titles (20 juvenile) in 2003: 40 were by agented authors. Receives 600 queries yearly.
Submissions and Payment: Guidelines available. Query with résumé. Accepts photocopies and email queries to childrens@acblack.com. SAE/IRC. Responds in 1 week. Publication period and payment policy vary.

Blue Marlin Publications

823 Aberdeen Road
West Bay Shore, NY 11706

Publisher: Francine Poppo Rich

Publisher's Interests
This independent publishing house, family-owned and operated,
was established in 1999. Each year it produces a small list of
quality books for young children through young adults.
Website: www.bluemarlinpubs.com

Freelance Potential
Published 2 titles in 2003: 1 was developed from an unsolicited
submission. Of the 2 titles, 1 was by an unpublished writer
and 2 were by authors who were new to the publishing house.
Receives 250 unsolicited mss yearly.
Submissions and Payment: Send complete ms. Accepts photocopies and simultaneous submissions if identified. Availability of
artwork may improve chance of acceptance. SASE. Responds in
6 weeks. Publication in 12–18 months. Royalty; advance.

Blushing Rose Publishing

P.O. Box 2238
San Anselmo, CA 94979

Publisher: Nancy Cogan Akmon

Publisher's Interests
In operation for more than 10 years, Blushing Rose Publishing
offers a small number of children's books. Its product line consists primarily of gift books, wedding and baby photo albums,
friends and family albums and books, and flower books. It also
produces baby and wedding announcements, invitations, and
fine stationery items, and it markets its products to customers
around the world. Writers are welcome to submit queries, but it
will not review unsolicited manuscripts.
Website: www.blushingrose.com

Freelance Potential
Published 5 titles in 2003.
Submissions and Payment: Query. No unsolicited mss. SASE.
Response time, publication period, and payment policy vary.

Books of Wonder

Room 806
16 West 18th Street
New York, NY 10011

Editor: Peter Glassman

Publisher's Interests
For more than twenty years, this highly specialized publisher has offered a catalogue of books written in the style and tradition of L. Frank Baum, creator of the *Wizard of Oz*, and books by the author himself. Gift books of classic children's stories are also found on its list. Interested authors may find information at the Books of Wonder website and should also send for guidelines.
Website: www.booksofwonder.com

Freelance Potential
Published several titles in 2003. Receives 30 unsolicited mss each year.
Submissions and Payment: Guidelines available. Send ms. Accepts photocopies and computer printouts. SASE. Responds in 6 months. Publication period varies. Royalty; advance.

The Boxwood Press

138 Ocean View Boulevard
Pacific Grove, CA 93950

Editorial Assistant: Patricia Kelly

Publisher's Interests
Established in 1952 as a publisher of lab materials, The Boxwood Press later expanded its line to include a variety of mainly biological titles. Its catalogue now includes books on natural history, regional titles, and biographies. It recently added a line of books for children, offering fiction as well as nonfiction.
Website: www.boxwoodpress.com

Freelance Potential
Published 8 titles in 2003: 2 were assigned.
Submissions and Payment: Guidelines and catalogue available at website. Query with clips or send complete ms. Accepts photocopies and simultaneous submissions if identified. SASE. Availability of artwork improves chance of acceptance. Response time, publication period, and payment policy vary.

Caddo Gap Press

PMB 275
3145 Geary Boulevard
San Francisco, CA 94118

Executive Editor: Alan H. Jones

Publisher's Interests
Established in 1987, Caddo Gap Press specializes in books for teachers and educators. Topics covered by titles on its current list include women in education, multicultural education, curriculum, judicious learning and teaching, science and museum education, and international education. This publisher occasionally offers parenting titles as well. Its list is small and usually includes only two to three new titles each year.
Website: www.caddogroup.com

Freelance Potential
Published 2–3 titles in 2003. Receives 12 queries, 12 unsolicited mss yearly.
Submissions and Payment: Query or send complete ms. SASE. Response time varies. Publication period varies. Royalty, 10%.

Camex Books

535 Fifth Avenue
New York, NY 10017

Submissions Editor: Victor Benedetto

Publisher's Interests
This publisher's list includes children's books as well as how-to and self-help titles, art and photography books, and cookbooks for adults. For young readers, it offers novelty books, picture books, middle-grade mysteries and adventure stories, folktales, fairy tales, and young adult romance novels. It also produces promotional titles and celebrity biographies. Writers who wish to contact Camex Books about their work are invited to telephone the editors instead of mailing a query or manuscript.

Freelance Potential
Published 12 titles in 2003: 8 were by agented authors.
Submissions and Payment: No queries or unsolicited mss. Editors prefer writers to call 212-682-8400 before submitting work. Publication in 6 months. Royalty; advance. Flat fee.

Carousel Press

P.O. Box 6038
Berkeley, CA 94706-0038

Publisher: Carole T. Myers

Publisher's Interests
For more than twenty years, this California publisher has offered a list of travel guides. It caters to all ages and includes material for families and young travelers. Its catalogue features titles on camping in Europe, European castles and palace hotels, week-end adventures, activity books for car trips, and family guides for travel to national monuments.
Website: www.carousel-press.com

Freelance Potential
Published 1 title in 2003. Receives 50 queries yearly.
Submissions and Payment: Query with table of contents and sample chapter. Accepts photocopies and computer printouts. SASE. Responds in 1 month. Publication in 1 year. Royalty; advance.

Cavendish Children's Books

99 White Plains Road
Tarrytown, NY 10591

Editorial Director: Margery Cuyler

Publisher's Interests
This imprint of Marshall Cavendish is again reviewing unsolicited manuscripts for picture books, middle-grade fiction and nonfic-tion, and young adult titles. It publishes historical and contempo-rary fiction, mysteries, humorous stories, and folklore. For the coming year, it is particularly interested in submissions of young adult novels. Send complete manuscripts rather than queries.
Website: www.marshallcavendish.com

Freelance Potential
Published 40 titles in 2003: 2 were developed from unsolicited submissions and 10 were by agented authors.
Submissions and Payment: Send complete ms. Accepts photo-copies and computer printouts. SASE. Responds in 3–6 months. Publication period and payment policy vary.

Chaosium

895 B Street #423
Hayward, CA 94541

Editor-in-Chief: Lynn Willis

Publisher's Interests
Role-playing games, horror anthologies, adventure stories, and classic works of fiction are found in Chaosium's catalogue. It has been publishing for more than 27 years.
Website: www.chaosium.com

Freelance Potential
Published 14 titles (8 juvenile) in 2003: 6 were developed from unsolicited submissions and 4 were reprint/licensed proper-ties. Of the 14 titles, 2 were by unpublished writers and 4 were by new authors. Receives 40 queries yearly.
Submissions and Payment: Guidelines available. Query with summary and writing samples. Accepts photocopies and Macintosh disk submissions. SASE. Responds in 1–2 weeks. Publication in 1–2 years. Flat fee, $.03–$.05 per word.

Children's Press

Scholastic Inc.
90 Sherman Turnpike
Danbury, CT 06816

Editor-in-Chief: Kate Nunn

Publisher's Interests
Known for its high quality books, this venerable publisher specializes in nonfiction for use in libraries and schools. It publishes nonfiction only, and most of its titles target middle-grade to high school students. Most of its books appear as part of series. Writers may submit queries, not unsolicited manuscripts.
Website: www.scholastic.com

Freelance Potential
Published 300 titles in 2003: 50 were by agented authors. Of the 300 titles, 15 were by authors who were new to the publishing house. Receives 2,000 queries yearly.
Submissions and Payment: Query with outline/synopsis and sample chapters. No unsolicited mss. SASE. Responds in 2–6 months. Publication in 1–2 years. Royalty. Flat fee.

Children's Story Scripts

2219 West Olive Avenue
PMB 130
Burbank, CA 91506

Editor: Deedra Bébout

Publisher's Interests
This publisher offers scripts for teachers to use with children in kindergarten through eighth grade. All of the scripts it publishes are linked to the core curriculum and include numerous parts to be read aloud by the students. The objective of this publishing house is "to nurture the minds and souls of kids without their even noticing."

Freelance Potential
Published 4 titles in 2003: all were developed from unsolicited submissions. Receives 500 unsolicited mss yearly.
Submissions and Payment: Guidelines available. Send complete ms. Accepts computer printouts and simultaneous submissions if identified. SASE. Responds in 2–4 weeks. Publication period varies. Royalty, 10–15%.

Chrysalis Children's Books

64 Brewery Road
London N7 9NT
England

Marketing Manager: Ben Cameron

Publisher's Interests
Readers up to the age of 14 enjoy the educational titles, picture books, and novelty and board books offered by this British publisher. It is primarily interested in nonfiction at this time.
Website: www.chrysalisbooks.co.uk

Freelance Potential
Published 550 titles in 2003: 25 were by agented authors and 20 were reprint/licensed properties. Of the 550 titles, 3 were by unpublished writers and 7 were by authors new to the publishing house. Receives 100 unsolicited mss yearly.
Submissions and Payment: Catalogue available at website. Send complete ms. Availability of artwork improves chance of acceptance. Accepts photocopies. SAE/IRC. Responds in 1 month. Publication period and payment policy vary.

Clark City Press

P.O. Box 1358
Livingston, MT 59047

Submissions Editor

Publisher's Interests
This publisher launched its first line in 1988 but ceased production in 1993. Now back in operation, it is committed to publishing titles of high quality in writing, design, and production. It offers fiction, nonfiction, books on art and nature, and a few children's titles.
Website: www.clarkcitypress.com

Freelance Potential
Published 4–6 titles in 2003: 1 was by an unpublished writer and 3 were by authors who were new to the publishing house. Receives 24 queries, 10 unsolicited mss yearly.
Submissions and Payment: All work is assigned. Query. No unsolicited mss. SASE. Responds in 2–3 weeks. Publication in 6 months. Payment rates and policy vary.

The Colonial Williamsburg Foundation

Publications Department
P.O. Box 1776
Williamsburg, VA 23187-1776

Editor

Publisher's Interests
This publisher went through major structural changes in 2003 and will not be accepting manuscripts for the present time. Writers are invited to check with the company in 2004 for changes to this policy, and are strongly advised to become familiar with the material The Colonial Williamsburg Foundation publishes.
Website: www.history.org

Freelance Potential
Published 3 titles in 2003: each was developed from an unsolicited submission and each was by an agented author.
Receives 25 queries yearly.
Submissions and Payment: Not accepting queries or unsolicited mss at this time. Check for updates to this submission policy in 2004.

Consortium Publishing

640 Weaver Hill Road
West Greenwich, RI 02817-2261

Chief of Publications: John M. Carlevale

Publisher's Interests
Books on early education, counseling, child abuse, and child
development are the focus of this special interest publisher. Its
books are written primarily for educators. 5% self-, subsidy-, co-
venture, or co-op published material.

Freelance Potential
Published 20 titles in 2003: 2 were developed from unsolicited
submissions and 1 was by an agented author. Of the 20 titles,
2 were by unpublished writers and 1 was by an author who
was new to the publishing house. Receives 150 queries yearly.
Submissions and Payment: Guidelines available. Query or send
complete ms with résumé. Accepts photocopies, computer printouts, and Macintosh disk submissions (Microsoft Word). SASE.
Responds in 1–2 months. Publication in 3 months. Royalty.

Contemporary Books

Suite 900
130 East Randolph Street
Chicago, IL 60601

Submissions Editor: Betsy Lane

Publisher's Interests
Contemporary Books specializes in educational products for use
in adult education programs, including titles for English-as-a-
Second-Language and GED classes. A division of McGraw-Hill,
the company publishes no fiction. Interested writers may submit
a prospectus, market analysis, outline, and table of contents.
Website: www.contemporarybooks.com

Freelance Potential
Published several titles in 2003. Receives 500 queries yearly.
Submissions and Payment: Guidelines available. Query with
résumé, prospectus, table of contents, sample chapters, and
market analysis. Accepts photocopies and disk submissions.
SASE. Response time varies. Publication period and payment
policy vary.

Continental Press

520 East Bainbridge Street
Elizabethtown, PA 17022

Vice President, Publications: Beth Spencer

Publisher's Interests
An educational publisher, Continental Press provide textbooks
and resource materials for use in kindergarten through twelfth
grade, as well as for adult education programs. It looks for high-
quality, classroom-tested materials in the areas of reading, language arts, social studies, and mathematics. It publishes single
titles and titles in series.
Website: www.continentalpress.com

Freelance Potential
Published 50 titles in 2003: 2 were by authors who were new
to the publishing house. Receives 50 unsolicited mss yearly.
Submissions and Payment: Guidelines available. Query or send
complete ms. Accepts computer printouts. SASE. Responds in 2
months. Publication period and payment policy vary.

Cornell Maritime Press

P.O. Box 456
Centreville, MD 21617

Managing Editor: Charlotte Kurst

Publisher's Interests
As a specialty publisher, this company accepts three types of
material: works for the merchant marine, practical books about
boating, and regional works on Maryland, the Delmarva
Peninsula, and the Chesapeake Bay. Its companion company,
Tidewater Publishers, offers fiction and nonfiction for children.
Website: www.cornellmaritimepress.com

Freelance Potential
Published 12 titles (3 juvenile) in 2003: all were developed from
unsolicited submissions. Receives 500 queries yearly.
Submissions and Payment: Guidelines available. Query with
synopsis and sample chapters. Accepts photocopies and computer
printouts. SASE. Responds in 1 month. Publication in 7 months.
Royalty.

Cornerstone Press Chicago

939 West Wilson Avenue
Chicago, IL 60640

Fiction Editor: Libby Kahler
Nonfiction Editor: Chris Rice

Publisher's Interests
This publisher offers books with a Christian world view and markets its titles to a general interest audience. It needs proposals for books with Christian themes for pre-teens and teens.
Website: www.cornerstonepress.com

Freelance Potential
Published 1 title in 2003: it was developed from an unsolicited submission and it was by an author who was new to the publishing house. Receives 100+ mss yearly.
Submissions and Payment: Guidelines available at website. Send ms with author biography, synopsis, 3–5 sample chapters, description of book's audience, and estimated length. Accepts disk submissions and email to cspress@jpusa.org. SASE. Responds in 2 weeks. Publication period varies. Royalty, 10%.

Cottonwood Press

107 Cameron Drive
Fort Collins, CO 80525

President: Cheryl Thurston

Publisher's Interests
Cottonwood Press is a publisher of activity books and other classroom materials designed to be used by English and language arts teachers working with students in grades five through twelve.
Website: www.cottonwoodpress.com

Freelance Potential
Published 3 titles in 2003: 3 were developed from unsolicited submissions. Of the 3 titles, 1 was by an unpublished writer and 3 were by authors who were new to the publishing house. Receives 50–60 queries, 100 unsolicited mss yearly.
Submissions and Payment: Guidelines available. Query with sample pages; or send complete ms. Accepts computer printouts and simultaneous submissions if identified. SASE. Responds in 1–4 weeks. Publication in 6–12 months. Royalty, 10%.

Course Crafters

44 Merimac Street
Newburyport, MA 01950

Editor

Publisher's Interests
This educational publisher specializes in materials for students in kindergarten through high school who are in English-as-a-Second-Language classes. Course Crafters, a book packager and developer, has plans to publish its own titles in the near future. Freelance writers will find numerous opportunities at this company.
Website: www.coursecrafters.com

Freelance Potential
Published 12 titles in 2003. Of the 12 titles, 3 were by authors who were new to the publishing house.
Submissions and Payment: Guidelines available. Query with clips. Accepts photocopies. SASE. Responds in 1 month. Publication in 1–2 years. Flat fee.

Creative Paperbacks

123 South Broad Street
Mankato, MN 56001

Managing Editor: Aaron Frisch

Publisher's Interests
Readers in kindergarten through grade six are the target audience of Creative Paperbacks, a new imprint of Creative Company. It publishes fiction, including adventure, fantasy, and contemporary and historical fiction. It also publishes nonfiction about animals, science, technology, history, geography, and entertainment. Biographies also appear on its list.

Freelance Potential
Published 30 titles in 2003: 20 were reprint/licensed properties. Receives 1,200–1,800 queries yearly.
Submissions and Payment: Guidelines available. Query with manuscript sample. Accepts photocopies and computer printouts. SASE. Responds in 4–6 months. Publication in 2–4 years. Payment rate varies.

Delmar Learning

Executive Woods
5 Maxwell Drive
Clifton Park, NY 12065

Acquisitions Editor: Erin O'Connor

Publisher's Interests
Educators, students, professionals, and parents interested in
early childhood development are among the readers of the books
found on this publisher's list.
Website: www.earlychilded.delmar.com

Freelance Potential
Published 30 titles in 2003: 5 were developed from unsolicited
submissions. Of the 30 titles, 4 were by unpublished writers.
Receives 120 queries yearly.
Submissions and Payment: Guidelines available. Query with
résumé, description of project, detailed outline, and sample
chapters. Accepts photocopies, computer printouts, and simultaneous submissions if identified. SASE. Responds in 1 month.
Publication in 2 years. Royalty; advance; grant.

Different Books

3900 Glenwood Avenue
Golden Valley, MN 55422

Editor: Roger Hammer

Publisher's Interests
An imprint of The Place In The Woods, this publisher specializes
in stories about individuals who succeed despite adversity. It
welcomes the works of new authors, but does charge a $10 fee
to read and critique manuscripts submitted.

Freelance Potential
Published 3 titles in 2003: each was developed from an unsolicited submission. Of the 3 titles, each was by an unpublished
writer. Receives 1,000 queries, 300 unsolicited mss yearly.
Submissions and Payment: Guidelines available. Query or send
complete ms. Accepts photocopies and computer printouts. No
simultaneous submissions. SASE. Responds to queries in 1
week, to mss in 2 months. Publication in 1 year. Royalty. Flat fee
for each new printing.

Displays for Schools, Inc.

1825 NW 22nd Terrace
Gainesville, FL 32605

Manager: Sherry DuPree

Publisher's Interests
The nonfiction list of this publisher targets teachers of kindergarten through twelfth-grade students, as well as educators working in churches, museums, libraries, and community centers. Its goal is to bring them classroom-tested material on a wide range of topics including history, religion, writing, reading, and special education.
Website: www.displaysforschools.com

Freelance Potential
Published 2 titles (1 juvenile) in 2003. Receives 180 queries each year.
Submissions and Payment: Guidelines available. Query with outline/synopsis, sample chapters, and a brief biography. SASE. Responds in 2 months. Publication in 4–24 months. Royalty, 10%.

Dog-Eared Publications

P.O. Box 620863
Middleton, WI 53562-0863

Publisher: Nancy Field

Publisher's Interests
This nature publisher offers books for children in the middle grades. Its catalogue includes nonfiction, activity books, interactive titles, and mysteries on subjects related to nature and science. The company's mission is to encourage children to read, explore, and experiment, and to develop a love for wild things and wild places.
Website: www.dog-eared.com

Freelance Potential
Published 2 titles in 2003. Receives 120 queries yearly.
Submissions and Payment: Query with outline/synopsis. Prefers email queries to field@dog-eared.com. Accepts photocopies and computer printouts. SASE. Response time varies. Publication period varies. Royalty; advance.

Eastgate Systems

134 Main Street
Watertown, MA 02472

Acquisitions Editor: Diane Greco

Publisher's Interests
Eastgate Systems publishes books for all ages, working in hyper-test form, with linked texts, pictures, sound, and video. It offers juvenile fiction and nonfiction, but does not consider ebooks or downloadable manuscripts.
Website: www.eastgate.com

Freelance Potential
Published 10 titles in 2003: all were developed from unsolicited submissions. Receives 25 unsolicited mss yearly.
Submissions and Payment: Guidelines available at website. Send complete ms. Accepts disk submissions, CD-ROMS, email submissions to dgreco@eastgate.com, and simultaneous submissions if identified. SASE. Responds in 4–6 weeks. Publication in 1 year. Royalty, 15%; advance.

Encounter Books

Suite 330
665 Third Street
San Francisco, CA 94107-1951

Acquisitions Editor: Steve Wiley

Publisher's Interests
Encounter Books publishes serious nonfiction books in the areas of history, religion, biography, education, public policy, and social sciences. Its books are read by young adults and adults. It does not publish fiction.
Website: www.encounterbooks.com

Freelance Potential
Published 20 titles (2 juvenile) in 2003: 1 was developed from an unsolicited submission and 15 were by agented authors. Receives 2,400 queries, 600 unsolicited mss each year.
Submissions and Payment: Guidelines available at website. Query or send complete ms. No email submissions. SASE. Response time varies. Publication period varies. Advance: one-third at signing, one-third when received, one-third at publication.

ESP Publishers, Inc.

Suite 444
1212 North 39th Street
Tampa, FL 33605

Editor: Dan Brooks

Publisher's Interests
Workbooks that correlate with the kindergarten through twelfth-grade curricula are produced by ESP Publishers, Inc. Writers with teaching backgrounds may submit queries or manuscripts on subjects such as mathematics, reading and phonics, health, nutrition, art, vocabulary, handwriting, and science.
Website: www.espbooks.com

Freelance Potential
Published 100–150 titles in 2003: all were by agented authors. Receives 24 queries, 4 unsolicited mss yearly.
Submissions and Payment: Query or send complete ms. Accepts photocopies, computer printouts, and simultaneous submissions if identified. SASE. Responds in 1 week. Publication period and payment policy vary.

Excelsior Cee Publishing

P.O. Box 5861
Norman, OK 73070

Publisher: J. C. Marshall

Publisher's Interests
A publisher of nonfiction, Excelsior Cee offers books for young adults and adults. Biographies appear on its list, along with inspirational books, humor, books on personal philosophy and family history, and how-to and self-help titles. It also publishes books of poetry.
Website: www.excelsiorcee.com

Freelance Potential
Published 10 titles in 2003: 6 were developed from unsolicited submissions. Receives 700–1,000 queries yearly.
Submissions and Payment: Query with synopsis; include sample chapter for longer works. Accepts photocopies, computer print-outs, and simultaneous submissions if identified. SASE. Responds in 6 weeks. Publication in 6 months. Payment policy varies.

Fiesta City Publishers

P.O. Box 5861
Santa Barbara, CA 93150-5861

Submissions: Ann Cooke

Publisher's Interests
This small house offers musical plays and books for use by middle-grade and young adult students. Its material focuses on cooking, musical instruction, instruments, and songwriting. Musical plays, children's books, and biographical books top its list of current needs. Writers with unique, fresh, contemporary writing styles are encouraged to submit their queries.

Freelance Potential
Published 3 titles (2 juvenile) in 2003. Receives 100 queries each year.

Submissions and Payment: Query with clips or writing samples. Accepts photocopies and simultaneous submissions if identified. SASE. Responds in 1–2 months. Publication period varies. Royalty.

Finney Company

3943 Meadowbrook Road
Minneapolis, MN 55426

Editor: Alan E. Krysan

Publisher's Interests
Established in the late 1940s, this publisher specializes in career and technical education books. Its readers include young adults and adults. It believes that career development is a lifelong process. Its Hobart imprint specializes in books on technical subjects and agricultural topics.
Website: www.finney-hobar.com

Freelance Potential
Published 4–6 titles (4 juvenile) in 2003: 1 was developed from an unsolicited submission. Receives 240 queries, 240 unsolicited mss yearly.

Submissions and Payment: Guidelines available at website. Query or send complete ms. SASE. Response time varies. Publication period varies. Royalty, 10% of net.

Focus Publishing

502 Third Street
Bemidji, MN 56601

President: Jan Haley

Publisher's Interests
This publisher's philosophy is that "Christian effectiveness is based on faithfulness." Founded in 1992, its books offer guidance on living a Christian life. While it publishes no titles for children, it occasionally accepts real-life stories for young adults.
Website: www.focuspublishing.com

Freelance Potential
Published 2 titles in 2003: both were developed from unsolicited submissions. Receives 800 queries yearly.
Submissions and Payment: Guidelines available. Query with synopsis; include market description for fiction. Availability of artwork improves chance of acceptance. Accepts photocopies and computer printouts. SASE. Responds in 1 week. Publication in 6 months. Royalty, 7.5–10%.

Fondo de Cultura Economica USA

2293 Verus Street
San Diego, CA 92154

Submissions Editor: B. Mireles

Publisher's Interests
Fondo de Cultura Economica USA publishes books for Spanish-speaking Latin Americans who reside in the US. It offers fiction and nonfiction books for all ages, including picture books, middle-grade books, and young adult titles.
Website: www.fceusa.com

Freelance Potential
Published 40 titles in 2003: 5 were developed from unsolicited submissions and 35 were by agented authors. Receives 300 queries yearly.
Submissions and Payment: Query with résumé. Accepts photocopies, computer printouts, and disk submissions. Availability of artwork improves chance of acceptance. SASE. Responds in 6 months. Publication in 6 months. Royalty; advance. Flat fee.

Franklin Watts

Scholastic Inc.
90 Sherman Turnpike
Danbury, CT 06816

Editor-in-Chief: Kate Nunn

Publisher's Interests
This well-known children's publisher, now a part of the Scholastic family, specializes in nonfiction books for middle-grade through high school students. All of its titles are curriculum-based, and designed for use in the classroom and library.
Website: www.scholastic.com

Freelance Potential
Published 100 titles in 2003: 5 were developed from unsolicited submissions and 20 were by agented authors. Of the 100 titles, 8 were by unpublished writers and 13 were by new authors. Receives 1,000+ queries yearly.
Submissions and Payment: Query with résumé, outline, and sample chapters. No unsolicited mss. SASE. Responds in 3–5 weeks. Publication period and payment policy vary.

Samuel French, Inc.

45 West 25th Street
New York, NY 10010

Editor: Lawrence Harbison

Publisher's Interests
The catalogue of this specialty publisher includes plays, monologues, audition material, classic works, and classroom guides for use by theatrical groups around the world. It does not plan to publish any titles in 2003. The company has been in business since 1830.
Website: www.samuelfrench.com

Freelance Potential
Published no titles in 2003. Receives many queries and unsolicited mss yearly.
Submissions and Payment: Guidelines available. Query or send complete ms. Accepts photocopies. SASE. Responds to queries in 1 week, to mss in 2–3 months. Publication in 1 year. Payment policy varies.

Gefen Publishing House

12 New Street
Hewlett, NY 11557-2012

Editor: Ilan Greenfield, Jr.

Publisher's Interests
This Jewish publisher offers children's titles about Israel, Jewish
folklore and folktales, and religious titles. Based in Jerusalem, it
also distributes books by other Israeli publishers.
Website: www.israelbooks.com

Freelance Potential
Published 30 titles (5 juvenile) in 2003: most were developed
from unsolicited submissions. Of the 30 titles, 20 were by
authors who were new to the publishing house. Receives 240
queries, 100+ unsolicited mss yearly.
Submissions and Payment: Guidelines available. Query or send
complete ms. Accepts photocopies, computer printouts, and
simultaneous submissions if identified. SASE. Response time,
publication period, and payment policy vary.

David R. Godine, Publisher

9 Hamilton Place
Boston, MA 02108

Editorial Department

Publisher's Interests
This publisher's juvenile list includes toddler books, easy-to-
read books, story picture books, chapter books, and young
adult novels. It is primarily a publisher of fiction, and it tries to
offer an "eclectic list" that includes works that won't necessarily
become bestsellers but still merit publication.
Website: www.godine.com

Freelance Potential
Published 30 titles (2 juvenile) in 2003: 10 were by agented
authors, and 20 were reprint/licensed properties. Receives
1,000 queries yearly.
Submissions and Payment: Guidelines available at website.
Query. No unsolicited mss. Publication period and payment
policy vary.

Good Year Books

299 Jefferson Road
Parsippany, NJ 07054

Editorial Director

Publisher's Interests
Good Year Books offers titles for teachers, parents, and children
and strives to meet the educational needs of students at school
as well as those who are homeschooled. It did not accept manuscripts in the last year, but will do so again beginning in 2004.
Website: www.pearsonlearning.com

Freelance Potential
Plans to resume publishing (1 or more titles) in 2004. Receives
200 unsolicited mss yearly.
Submissions and Payment: Guidelines available. Prefers complete ms; will accept query with 1–2 sample chapters and out-
line/synopsis. Accepts photocopies, computer printouts, disk
submissions, and simultaneous submissions if identified. SASE.
Responds in 3 months. Publication in 18 months. Flat fee.

Greenwillow Books

HarperCollins Children's Books
1350 Avenue of the Americas
New York, NY 10019

Editorial Department

Publisher's Interests
This imprint of HarperCollins Children's Books offers books for
children of all ages. Nature and family life are among the topics
covered by its nonfiction titles. Its fiction list includes contemporary fiction, poetry, and stories about animals. Due to the overwhelming number of submissions it receives, Greenwillow Books
is currently not accepting unsolicited manuscripts or queries.
Website: www.harperchildrens.com

Freelance Potential
Published 43 titles 2003: 11 were by agented authors. Of the
43 titles, 7 were by authors who were new to the publishing
house. Receives 5,500 queries, 8,000+ unsolicited mss yearly.
Submissions and Payment: Not accepting queries or unsolicited
mss at this time.

Halstead Press

9A Boundary Street
Rushcutters Bay, New South Wales 2065
Australia

Children's Book Editor

Publisher's Interests
This small Australian publisher offers nonfiction for children between the ages of four and twelve, parenting titles, and books on reading that target educational programs. It does not publish fiction. Topics covered include animals, pets, history, nature, the environment, self-help, and sports. Agented authors have a better chance of acceptance.

Freelance Potential
Published 24 titles (4 juvenile) in 2003: 14 were developed from unsolicited submissions and 10 were by agented authors. Of the 24 titles, all were by authors new to the publishing house. Receives 60 queries yearly.
Submissions and Payment: Query. Accepts photocopies. SASE. Responds in 1 month. Publication in 1 year. Royalty.

Harcourt Canada Ltd.

55 Horner Avenue
Toronto, Ontario M8Z 4X6
Canada

Publisher: Nancy Reilly

Publisher's Interests
Educational curriculum and resource materials are published by Harcourt Canada. Its textbooks and supplements cover science, social studies, music, language arts, mathematics, and media education for kindergarten through grade 12 classrooms.
Website: www.harcourtcanada.com

Freelance Potential
Published 60 titles (40 juvenile) in 2003: all were by agented authors and 10 were reprint/licensed properties. Of the 60 titles, 8 were by authors new to the publishing house. Receives 100 queries yearly.
Submissions and Payment: Query. No unsolicited mss. SAE/IRC. Responds in 6–12 months. Publication period and payment policy vary.

Harvard Common Press

535 Albany Street
Boston, MA 02118

Executive Editor: Pamela Hoenig

Publisher's Interests
Parenting titles and books on pregnancy, childbirth, and child care are featured in the catalogue of this nonfiction publisher.
Website: www.harvardcommonpress.com

Freelance Potential
Published 13 titles in 2003: 12 were by agented authors. Of the 13 titles, 2 were by unpublished writers and 9 were by authors who were new to the publishing house. Receives 1,200 queries yearly.
Submissions and Payment: Guidelines available. Query with résumé, outline, 1–2 sample chapters, and market analysis. Accepts photocopies, computer printouts, and simultaneous submissions if identified. SASE. Responds in 1–3 months. Publication period varies. Royalty, 5%; advance, $1,500+.

Health Press

P.O. Box 37470
Albuquerque, NM 87176

Editor: Kathleen Frazier

Publisher's Interests
Health Press publishes books on a wide variety of health topics, written by health care professionals for the layperson. All of its writers are experts in the field about which they choose to write. Some of the topics covered include pediatrics, women's health, psychology, and diet and nutrition.
Website: www.healthpress.com

Freelance Potential
Published 6 titles (2 juvenile) in 2003: 4 were developed from unsolicited submissions and 1 was by an agented author. Receives 120 queries yearly.
Submissions and Payment: Guidelines available at website. Query with brief synopsis, résumé, and 3 sample chapters. SASE. Response time varies. Publication period varies. Royalty.

Hodder Children's Books

338 Euston Road
London NW1 3BH
United Kingdom

The Reader

Publisher's Interests
Fiction and nonfiction for children under the age of twelve are
available from this British publisher. It features picture books,
beginning readers, chapter books, and story books.
Website: www.hodderheadline.co.uk

Freelance Potential
Published 500 titles in 2003: 10 were developed from unsolicited submissions, 200 were by agented authors, and 20
were reprint/licensed properties. Receives 3,000 queries, 2,000
unsolicited mss yearly.
Submissions and Payment: Query with synopsis; or send complete ms. Accepts photocopies and computer printouts.
SAE/IRC. Responds in 3–6 months. Publication in 12–18
months. Royalty; advance. Flat fee.

Holloway House Publishing Group

8060 Melrose Avenue
Los Angeles, CA 90046

Submissions Editor: Neal Colgrass

Publisher's Interests
Offering books that focus on the black experience, Holloway
House features a line of biographies of outstanding African-
American achievers for young adults.
Website: www.hollowayhousebooks.com

Freelance Potential
Published 12 titles in 2003: 2 were developed from unsolicited
submissions. Of the 12 titles, 10 were by unpublished writers
and all were by authors who were new to the publishing
house. Receives 500+ queries, 100 unsolicited mss yearly.
Submissions and Payment: Guidelines available. Query with
résumé; or send ms. Accepts photocopies, computer printouts,
and disk submissions. SASE. Responds to queries in 3 weeks, to
mss in 3 months. Publication period and payment policy vary.

Hyperion Books for Children

114 Fifth Avenue
New York, NY 10011

Editor-in-Chief: Liza Baker

Publisher's Interests
This well-known publisher is part of the Walt Disney Company. It does not currently accept unsolicited queries or manuscripts unless they are submitted through a literary agent. Its list offers books for all ages, from kindergarten through young adult readers. Since this company is so well-known, it receives far more submissions than it can publish. Agented authors who are new to publishing should consider other houses that are smaller.
Website: www.disney.com

Freelance Potential
Published 197 titles (183 juvenile) in 2003: all were by agented authors.
Submissions and Payment: Accepts manuscripts through literary agents only.

I B Publications Pty Ltd

P.O. Box 5123
South Murwillumbah 2484
Australia

Director: David Vickers-Shand

Publisher's Interests
This Australian publisher specializes in books for Christian children and families involved in the Rudolph Steiner educational movement. It needs fantasy novels for ages eight to eighteen. 25% self-, subsidy-, co-venture, or co-op published material.
Website: www.immortalbooks.com.au

Freelance Potential
Published 5 titles (4 juvenile) in 2003: 1 was developed from an unsolicited submission and 4 were assigned. Of the 5 titles, 2 were by unpublished writers. Receives 8–10 mss yearly.
Submissions and Payment: Send ms with illustrations if available. Accepts email submissions to info@immortalbooks.com.au. Artwork improves chance of acceptance. SASE. Responds in 3–4 weeks. Publication in 3–6 months. Payment policy varies.

Illumination Arts

P.O. Box 1865
Bellevue, WA 98009

Editorial Director: Ruth Thompson

Publisher's Interests
Picture books for children ages four through eight are the main-stay of Illumination Arts' publishing program. It specializes in books with inspirational and spiritual (but not religious) themes.
Website: www.illumin.com

Freelance Potential
Published 3 titles in 2003: all were developed from unsolicited submissions. Of the 3 titles, 1 was by an unpublished writer and 3 were by authors who were new to the publishing house. Receives 2,000 queries and unsolicited mss yearly.
Submissions and Payment: Guidelines available. Query or send complete ms with sample illustrations. Accepts simultaneous submissions if identified. SASE. Response time, publication period, and payment policy vary.

ImaJinn Books

P.O. Box 162
Hickory Corners, MI 49060-0162

Senior Editor: Linda Kichline

Publisher's Interests
This publisher focuses exclusively on science fiction and fantasy. It offers a small number of titles for middle-grade readers—uplift-ing stories full of action and adventure. The company is currently undergoing changes and will not accept submissions until 2004, unless otherwise noted on their website.
Website: www.imajinnbooks.com

Freelance Potential
Published 30 titles (2 juvenile) in 2003: all were developed from unsolicited submissions. Of the 30 titles, 1 was by an author who was new to the publishing house. Receives 180–240 queries yearly.
Submissions and Payment: Visit the website for changes in submission policy.

InQ Publishing Co.

P.O. Box 10
North Aurora, IL 60542

Publisher: Jana Fitting

Publisher's Interests
Established in 1988, this publisher's mission is to produce quality books and associated products that educate and inform its readers in a fun and interesting way. It features material on safety education, genealogy, and child care. One series is written specifically for young babysitters.
Website: www.inqbooks.com

Freelance Potential
Published 2–3 titles (1 juvenile) in 2003. Receives 50 queries each year.
Submissions and Payment: Catalogue available at website. Query with writing samples. No unsolicited mss. Accepts photocopies. SASE. Responds in 6 weeks. Publication in 18 months. Payment policy varies.

Iron Crown Enterprises

112 Goodman Street
Charlottesville, VA 22902

Managing Editor

Publisher's Interests
Board games, card games, puzzles, and fantasy role-playing games are the specialty of this publisher. Its materials target a young adult and adult audience. Because of the stylistic requirements for these products, new writers are encouraged to review detailed guidelines found at the publisher's website.
Website: www.ironcrown.com

Freelance Potential
Published 6 titles in 2003. Receives 10–20 queries yearly.
Submissions and Payment: Guidelines available. Query with outline/synopsis and writing sample. Accepts computer printouts, disk submissions, and email queries to ozmar_ice@ yahoo.com. SASE. Responds in 6 months. Publication in 6–12 months. Royalty, 2–6%; advance, $100. Flat fee, $500–$1,500.

January Productions

116 Washington Avenue
Hawthorne, NJ 07507

Creative Director: Barbara Peller

Publisher's Interests
Multi-media materials for use with students in kindergarten through grade eight appear in the catalogue of January Productions. It offers videos, CD-ROMs, filmstrips, kits, games, posters, and read-along titles. Many of its publications target high-interest/low-reading-level students. Submissions of curriculum-related, nonfiction materials are welcome.
Website: www.awpeller.com

Freelance Potential
Receives 100 queries, 50 unsolicited mss yearly.
Submissions and Payment: Catalogue available at website. Prefers query with outline/synopsis. Accepts complete ms with résumé. Accepts photocopies. SASE. Response time and publication period vary. Flat fee, $325–$375.

Jump at the Sun

114 Fifth Avenue
New York, NY 10011

Submissions Editor

Publisher's Interests
Owned by Disney Enterprises and launched in 1998, Jump at the Sun features books that celebrate the black cultural experience. Its list includes interactive novelty books, picture books by award-winning authors, photo essays, poetry, historical fiction, and middle-grade series. Toddlers through young adults read this publisher's titles.
Website: www.hyperionbooksforchildren.com

Freelance Potential
Published 20 titles in 2003: most were by agented authors. Receives 240 queries yearly.
Submissions and Payment: Query. Accepts photocopies. SASE. Responds in 1–3 months. Publication in 2 years. Royalty; advance.

Kidszip Ltd

Boite Postale 30
Barbizon 77630
France

Editor

Publisher's Interests
This website is devoted entirely to children's literature and offers
books in seven different languages. Its list features books for
children between the ages of three and thirteen. The fiction and
nonfiction titles cover such topics as animals, pets, crafts, science, sports, entertainment, and history.
Website: www.kidszip.com

Freelance Potential
Published 150 titles (20 juvenile) in 2003: most were developed
from unsolicited submissions. Receives 4,800 mss yearly.
Submissions and Payment: Guidelines and catalogue available
at website. Send complete ms. Accepts email submissions
through website. Does not accept mss sent by mail. SASE.
Responds in 2 months. Publication in 3 months. Royalty, to 8%.

Kingfisher

215 Park Avenue South
New York, NY 10003

Submissions Editor

Publisher's Interests
This imprint of Houghton Mifflin Company specializes in illustrated nonfiction for children ages two and up. Kingfisher also
offers series titles, anthologies, Spanish language titles, and a
very select number of picture books. Its list includes books
about science, nature, the environment, animals, geography,
history, myths and legends, holidays, and food. It does not
accept fiction, and all of its titles are written on assignment.
Website: www.houghtonmifflinbooks.com/kingfisher

Freelance Potential
Published 60 titles in 2003: all were by agented authors.
Submissions and Payment: Catalogue available with 9x12
SASE (5 first-class stamps). All work is assigned by publisher.
No unsolicited mss.

Kodiak Media Group

P.O. Box 1029-A
Wilsonville, OR 97070

Marketing Director: Rhonda Grabenhorst-Pachl

Publisher's Interests
This publisher targets teachers, parents, administrators, special
education professionals, and others who work with hearing-
impaired and deaf children. Although most of its titles are developed in-house, it will consider queries from experts working in
this field.

Freelance Potential
Published 2 titles in 2003. Receives 10 queries, 10 unsolicited
mss yearly.
Submissions and Payment: Query or send complete ms.
Accepts photocopies, computer printouts, and simultaneous
submissions if identified. Accepts camera-ready artwork and
B/W prints. SASE. Responds in 1 month. Publication period
varies. Royalty, negotiable.

LangMarc Publishing

P.O. Box 90488
Austin, TX 78709

Submissions Editor

Publisher's Interests
LangMarc Publishing specializes in fiction and nonfiction books
that inspire and motivate adolescents, teens, and young adults.
Its offerings include well-written, practical nonfiction on a variety
of topics of interest to teens, thought-provoking fictional stories,
and books that focus on the difficult issues faced by adolescents,
offering positive options and attitudes for readers to consider. It
also offers science and technology titles, as well as humor, and
inspirational and religious fiction.
Website: www.langmarc.com

Freelance Potential
Published 4–5 titles (1 juvenile) in 2003.
Submissions and Payment: Query. Response time varies.
Publication in 9 months. Payment policy varies.

Leadership Publishers Inc.

P.O. Box 8358
Des Moines, IA 50301-8358

Editor/Owner: Dr. Lois F. Roets

Publisher's Interests
Leadership Publishers is a small publisher that does not expect to publish any new titles in 2004. It specializes in teacher reference books and material for gifted students.

Freelance Potential
Published 1–3 titles in 2003. 1 was by an unpublished writer and 1 was by an author who was new to the publishing house. Receives 15 queries yearly.
Submissions and Payment: Send for guidelines and catalogue before submitting (SASE with 2 first-class stamps). Then query with table of contents, outline, and 2 sample chapters. Accepts photocopies and computer printouts. No simultaneous submissions. SASE. Responds in 2 months. Publication in 6–12 months. Royalty, 10%. Flat fee.

Learning Links Inc.

2300 Marcus Avenue
New Hyde Park, NY 11042

Chairman: Joyce Friedland

Publisher's Interests
This publisher specializes in study guides to classic literature for students in kindergarten through high school. Query only if you are a writer who has worked on teacher's manuals, or if you have experience in writing study guides. We have a specific format and we will work only with writers who have this type of experience.
Website: www.learninglink.com

Freelance Potential
Published 25 titles in 2003: 6 were developed from unsolicited submissions and 19 were assigned. Of the 25 titles, 4 were by unpublished writers and 3 were by authors who were new to the publishing house. Receives 24 queries yearly.
Submissions and Payment: Guidelines available. Query. Responds in 1 week. Publication in 3 months. Flat fee.

LifeSong Publishers

P.O. Box 183
Somis, CA 93066

Editor: Laurie Donahue

Publisher's Interests
This Christian publisher produces books for readers of all ages.
Many of its titles are written for parents. While it does not publish writers' guidelines, new writers are encouraged to visit its
website and review current titles. LifeSong Publishers will consider subsidy publishing in certain cases. Because its list is so
small, writers are encouraged to send only their best work.
Website: www.lifesongpublishers.com

Freelance Potential
Published 4 titles in 2003. Receives 48 queries, 24 unsolicited
mss yearly.
Submissions and Payment: Query or send complete ms. SASE.
Response time varies. Publication period varies. Royalty, 10%
of net.

Lion Books

Suite B
210 Nelson Road
Scarsdale, NY 10583

Editor: Harriet Ross

Publisher's Interests
Founded in 1966, this publisher offers books for children and
young adults, craft activity books, and biographies. Books about
politics written in an easy-to-understand style also appear on its
list, along with books about how to play various sports. Many of
the juvenile titles published by Lion Books are marketed to
libraries and schools.

Freelance Potential
Published 8 titles (6 juvenile) in 2003: 5 were developed from
unsolicited submissions. Of the 8 titles, 2 were by unpublished
writers. Receives 50–70 queries yearly.
Submissions and Payment: Query with outline. No unsolicited
mss. Accepts photocopies. SASE. Responds in 1 month.
Publication in 6 months. Royalty; advance. Flat fee.

Little Blue Works

P.O. Box 28
Port Orchard, WA 98366

Editor: Cris DiMarco

Publisher's Interests
This publisher of children's and young adult titles focuses on
books that entertain and captivate as well as teach. Its goal is to
show the world as it is seen through the eyes of children and
teens, not the way others think they should see it. Visit its website for details about its five-step submission process.
Website: www.windstormcreative.com

Freelance Potential
Published 25 titles in 2003: most were developed from unsolicited submissions. Receives 10,000+ queries yearly.
Submissions and Payment: Guidelines available at website.
Query with 1-page synopsis. Submissions that do not indicate a
website visit will be returned. SASE. Response time and publication period vary. Royalty, 10–15%.

Living the Good News

Suite 400
600 Grant Street
Denver, CO 80203

Editorial Management Team

Publisher's Interests
This small publishing house concentrates on books with a spiritual center. It offers titles for children and families, as well as
titles developed for religious education. It continues to seek submissions of children's fiction, poetry, and nonfiction.
Website: www.livingthegoodnews.com

Freelance Potential
Published 30 titles in 2003: 5 were developed from unsolicited
submissions. Of the 30 titles, 1 was by an unpublished writer.
Receives 150 queries yearly.
Submissions and Payment: Query with sample chapter. Accepts
photocopies, computer printouts, Macintosh disk submissions,
and simultaneous submissions if identified. SASE. Responds in
2 months. Publication in 2 years. Royalty.

Lobster Press

1620 Sherbrooke Street West, Suites C & D
Montreal, Quebec H3H 1C9
Canada

Submissions Editor

Publisher's Interests
Lobster Press offers picture books for young children, as well as
fiction and nonfiction titles for older children and young adults.
It is not accepting queries or manuscripts at this time; check its
website for up-to-date submission information.
Website: www.lobsterpress.com

Freelance Potential
Published 11 titles in 2003: 8 were developed from unsolicited submissions, 2 were by agented authors, and 2 were
reprint/licensed properties. Of the 11 titles, 3 were by
unpublished writers and 3 were by authors who were new
to the publishing house.
Submissions and Payment: Guidelines available at website. Not
accepting queries or unsolicited mss at this time.

James Lorimer & Company

35 Britain Street
Toronto, Ontario M5A 1R7
Canada

Children's Book Editor: Hadley Dyer

Publisher's Interests
James Lorimer & Company publishes the work of Canadian
authors only. Its list offers books for seven- to ten-year-old
readers. All of its titles feature realistic storylines with
Canadian characters and settings.
Website: www.lorimer.ca

Freelance Potential
Published 20 titles (8 juvenile) in 2003: 2 were developed from
unsolicited submissions and 2 were reprint/licensed properties. Of the 20 titles, 2 were by unpublished writers. Receives
96 queries yearly.
Submissions and Payment: Canadian authors only. Query with
outline/synopsis and 2 sample chapters. SASE. Responds in 4–6
months. Publication period varies. Royalty; advance.

The Love and Logic Press

2207 Jackson Street
Golden, CO 80401-2300

Publisher

Publisher's Interests
This publisher provides training materials that are used to teach
the "Love and Logic" approach to raising children. The approach
puts teachers and parents in control while helping children to be
responsible and preparing them for the real world. Its product
line includes books, audio cassettes, compact discs, and training
programs, as well as quarterly newsletters.
Website: www.loveandlogic.com

Freelance Potential
Published 10 titles in 2003. Receives 300 queries yearly.
Submissions and Payment: Query with proposal or outline.
Accepts photocopies, computer printouts, and simultaneous
submissions if identified. SASE. Responds in 1 month.
Publication in 18 months. Royalty, 5–7%.

LTDBooks

200 North Service Road West, Unit 1, Suite 301
Oakville, Ontario L6M 2Y1
Canada

Editors: Dee Lloyd & T. K. Sheils

Publisher's Interests
This electronic publisher offers young adult titles for readers
ages 10 to 13 as well as genre romance, fantasy, mystery, and
science fiction for adult readers. LTDBooks is not accepting submissions at this time.
Website: www.ltdbooks.com

Freelance Potential
Published 25 titles (4 juvenile) in 2003: 5 were developed from
unsolicited submissions. Of the 25 titles, 10 were by unpublished writers and 12 were by authors new to the publishing
house. Receives 200 queries, 100 unsolicited mss yearly.
Submissions and Payment: Guidelines and sample contracts
available at website. When reopen to submissions, will accept
email submissions only to editor@ltdbooks.com.

The Lutterworth Press

P.O. Box 60
Cambridge CB1 2NT
United Kingdom

Managing Editor: Adrian Brink

Publisher's Interests
The children's books that appear on this publisher's list include
fiction and nonfiction for young readers of all ages. Originally
founded as the Religious Tract Society, Lutterworth features books
that stress moral values. Nature stories, animal stories, mysteries,
fantasies, Christian novels, and stories of different times and cultures are featured in its current catalogue.
Website: www.lutterworth.com

Freelance Potential
Published 10 titles in 2003.
Submissions and Payment: Guidelines available at website.
Query with outline/synopsis and 1–2 sample chapters.
Availability of artwork improves chance of acceptance. SAE/IRC.
Responds in 2 months. Royalty.

MacAdam/Cage ☆

Suite 550
155 Sansome Street
San Francisco, CA 94104

Editor: Pat Walsh

Publisher's Interests
This publisher of literary fiction and narrative nonfiction for
adult readers was established in 1998. While many of its titles
appeal to teen readers, it does not accept manuscripts written
specifically for young adults or for children.
Website: www.macadamcage.com

Freelance Potential
Published 30 titles in 2003: 15 were developed from unso-
licited submissions and 15 were by agented authors.
Receives 6,000 queries yearly.
Submissions and Payment: Guidelines and catalogue available
at website or with SASE ($2.21 postage). Query with clips.
Accepts photocopies. SASE. Responds in 4–5 months.
Publication period and payment policy vary.

Mage Publishers

1032 29th Street NW
Washington, DC 20007

Submissions Editor: Amin Sepehri

Publisher's Interests
This publisher is dedicated to producing books about Persian
culture and history. Its list includes children's tales and legends,
as well as biographies, cookbooks, and translations of literature.
Website: www.mage.com

Freelance Potential
Published 4 titles in 2003: 1 was developed from an unsolicited
submission. Of the 4 titles, 1 was by an author who was new
to the publishing house. Receives 50 queries, 25 mss yearly.
Submissions and Payment: Guidelines available at website.
Query or send complete ms. Accepts photocopies and computer
printouts. Availability of artwork improves chance of acceptance.
SASE. Responds in 1–3 months. Publication in 9–15 months.
Royalty; advance.

Marlor Press

4304 Brigadoon Drive
St. Paul, MN 55126

Editorial Director: Marlin Bree

Publisher's Interests
This small house is primarily a publisher of titles on boating and
travel. It offers books for travel and travel journals designed for
family trips, as well as activity books for children between four
and twelve. In the coming year, it is interested in queries for
activity books. Queries should include marketing information.

Freelance Potential
Published 1 title in 2003: it was developed from an unsolicited
submission and was by an unpublished writer. Receives 100+
queries yearly.
Submissions and Payment: Query with market analysis. No
unsolicited mss. Accepts photocopies and computer printouts.
SASE. Response time varies. Publication in 1 year. Royalty,
8–10% of net sales.

Marsh Media

8025 Ward Parkway Plaza
Kansas City, MO 64112

Submissions Editor: Joan K. Marsh

Publisher's Interests
This publisher of character-education materials targets children
in kindergarten through fourth grade. Most of its products are
sold as multi-media sets that include storybooks, videos, and
teacher guides. Marsh Media specializes in titles that focus on
issues of self-control, personal development, respect, courtesy,
trust, friendship, creative thinking, responsibility, personal
power, risk taking, and ecology. It has been in operation for
more than 30 years.
Website: www.marshmedia.com

Freelance Potential
Published 1 title in 2003. Receives 12 queries yearly.
Submissions and Payment: Query with résumé. SASE.
Response time, publication period, and payment policy vary.

McGraw-Hill School Division

21st Floor
2 Penn Plaza
New York, NY 10121

Editor: Andre Mattis

Publisher's Interests
The McGraw-Hill School Division offers a wide variety of classroom materials, activity books, series titles, and educational
titles for students in kindergarten through grade six. The topics
covered include bilingual education, language arts, science,
math, reading, and social studies, and every product is designed
to help educational professionals by providing the highest-quality
material and services available.
Website: www.mhschool.com

Freelance Potential
Published 50 titles in 2003.
Submissions and Payment: Query with résumé. SASE. All
materials are written on assignment. No unsolicited mss.
Response time and publication period vary. Flat fee.

Miles Kelly Publishing

Bardfield Centre, Great Bardfield
Braintree CM6 4SL
United Kingdom

Submissions Editor

Publisher's Interests
Children's encyclopedias, atlases, quiz books, and posters are available from Miles Kelly. This British publisher also offers illustrated nonfiction for young readers on topics such as animals, geography, nature, mathematics, science, technology, and history. It publishes some novelty books, poetry, and juvenile fiction as well. It continues to seek ideas for innovative reference titles and quiz books.
Website: www.mileskelly.net

Freelance Potential
Published 100 titles (90 juvenile) in 2003.
Submissions and Payment: Guidelines available at website. Query with clips. SAE/IRC. Response time varies. Publication period varies. Flat fee.

Morning Glory Press

6595 San Haroldo Way
Buena Park, CA 90620-3748

President: Jeanne Lindsay

Publisher's Interests
Morning Glory Press publishes books for parents and professionals who work with teens. This specialty publisher offers a wide range of fiction and nonfiction titles on an extensive variety of contemporary topics, including dealing with teen pregnancy, teen fathers, abuse, parenting, child development, life skills, and personal relationships.
Website: www.morningglorypress.com

Freelance Potential
Published 2 titles in 2003: 1 was developed from an unsolicited submission. Receives 20 queries yearly.
Submissions and Payment: Query. Accepts photocopies. SASE. Responds in 1–3 months. Publication in 6–8 months. Royalty; advance, $500.

Mountain Meadow Press

P.O. Box 447
Kooskia, ID 83539

Submissions Editor

Publisher's Interests
Homeschooling and topics related to the history of the Pacific
Northwest and travel to the region fill the catalogue of this
regional publisher. Mountain Meadow Press has been in business for twenty years. While it is not accepting unsolicited manuscripts at this time, writers interested in the house are welcome
to send queries. The publisher no longer has a website.

Freelance Potential
Published 1 title in 2003. Receives 6 queries and unsolicited
mss yearly.
Submissions and Payment: Catalogue available. Query only.
No unsolicited mss. Accepts photocopies and computer print-
outs. SASE. Responds in 3 months. Publication period varies.
Royalty.

Mount Olive College Press

634 Henderson Street
Mount Olive, NC 28365

Acquisitions Editor: Pepper Worthington

Publisher's Interests
This regional press seeks to advance the experiences, scholar-
ship, and thoughts of individuals living in North Carolina. It is
interested in work that relates to some aspect of the culture,
wildlife, or history of North Carolina.

Freelance Potential
Published 3 titles (1 juvenile) in 2003: 1 was developed from an
unsolicited submission. Of the 3 titles, 2 were by authors who
were new to the publishing house. Receives 500+ queries, 400
unsolicited mss yearly.
Submissions and Payment: Guidelines available. Query with
outline/synopsis and 3 sample chapters; or send complete ms.
Accepts photocopies and computer printouts. SASE. Responds in
6–12 months. Publication in 1 year. Payment policy varies.

Munchweiler Press

P.O. Box 2529
Victorville, CA 92393-2529

Publisher: Ted Lish

Publisher's Interests
Munchweiler Press publishes picture books for children ages
four to eight. It prefers humorous stories, but is open to anything of quality. It will not consider middle-grade titles, chapter
books, or books for adults or young adults. Send queries only.
Website: www.munchweilerpress.com

Freelance Potential
Published 2 titles in 2003: each was developed from an unso-
licited submission and each was by an unpublished writer.
Receives 20–30 queries yearly.
Submissions and Payment: Guidelines available. Query. No
unsolicited mss. Accepts email queries to publisher@
munchweilerpress.com. SASE. Responds in 2 months.
Publication in 1 year. Royalty, 5%. Flat fee.

National Geographic Children's Books ☆

1145 17th Street NW
Washington, DC 20036-4688

⊗

Editorial Assistant: Susan Donnelly

Publisher's Interests
This imprint of the National Geographic Society is designed for
readers age four through young adult. Its current catalogue
includes books on science, technology, history, sports, biography, geography, technology, and multicultural subjects. It is not
accepting unsolicited submissions at this time.
Website: www.nationalgeographic.com/books/kids.splash

Freelance Potential
Published 25 titles in 2003: 3 were developed from unsolicited
submissions, 2 were by agented authors, and 12 were
assigned. Of the 25 titles, 3 were by unpublished writers and
15 were by authors new to the publishing house.
Submissions and Payment: Not accepting queries or unsolicited
manuscripts at this time.

Can we trade?

...sy times, we've found that it's sometimes more effective and convenient to reach many of our
...ds via email. It gives us one more option when we can't reach a busy person by telephone.
...ts are providing us with an email address when they enroll … but we may not have one for you.

...rade?

...each us anytime at: **StudentServices@InstituteChildrensLit.com**

...ess, would you please provide it: _____

_____ State/Province: _____

...er: _____

...is information to us in the enclosed postage-paid envelope,
...ove, or fax to 203-792-8406.

106
129
165

...of Student Services

...tly provided your email address, thanks—and please ignore this request.)

National Resource Center for Youth Services

College of Continuing Education, University of Oklahoma
4502 East 41st Street
Tulsa, OK 74135
Marketing Manager: Rhoda Baker

Publisher's Interests
This publisher produces reference titles and curricula for social service professionals who work with at-risk teenagers. Topics covered include self-esteem, sex, drugs, and depression.
Website: www.nrcys.ou.edu

Freelance Potential
Published 2 titles (1 juvenile) in 2003: 1 was developed from an unsolicited submission. Of the 2 titles, 1 was by an unpublished writer and 1 was by an author who was new to the publishing house. Receives 50 queries yearly.
Submissions and Payment: Guidelines available. Query with outline and 1–3 sample chapters. Accepts computer printouts and disk submissions. SASE. Responds in 1–3 months. Publication in 8–18 months. Royalty.

Natural Heritage Books

P.O. Box 95, Station O
Toronto, Ontario M4A 2M8
Canada

Editor: Jane Gibson

Publisher's Interests
Natural Heritage Books specializes in titles on Canadian history, heritage, and culture. It is currently interested in fiction and nonfiction for readers ages eight and up.
Website: www.naturalheritagebooks.com

Freelance Potential
Published 14 titles (2 juvenile) in 2003: 7 were developed from unsolicited submissions, 2 were by agented authors, and 1 was a reprint/licensed property. Of the 14 titles, 5 were by unpublished writers and 6 were by authors new to the publishing house. Receives 100+ queries yearly.
Submissions and Payment: Guidelines available. Query with clips or writing samples. Accepts photocopies. SAE/IRC. Responds in 2–3 months. Publication in 1–2 years. Royalty; advance.

New World Library

14 Pamaron Way
Novato, CA 94949

Submissions Editor

Publisher's Interests
This publisher targets a general interest audience and specializes
in books on spiritual growth, health and wellness, and parenting.
Website: www.nwlib.com

Freelance Potential
Published 35 titles (2 juvenile) in 2003: 2 were developed from
unsolicited submissions and 33 were by agented authors. Of
the 35 titles, 1 was by an unpublished writer and 2 were by
new authors. Receives 600 queries, 1,400 mss yearly.
Submissions and Payment: Guidelines available at website.
Query with 2–3 sample chapters, outline or table of contents,
market assessment, and biographical information; or send complete ms. SASE. Responds in 3 months. Publication period and
payment policy vary.

Nomad Press

P.O. Box 875
Route 5 South
Norwich, VT 05055

Acquisitions Editor: Lauri Berkenkamp

Publisher's Interests
Nomad Press is a nonfiction publisher. For adults, it offers parenting titles, and for children it seeks picture books on topics such as
science, math, and physics. Do not submit fiction or poetry.
Website: www.nomadpress.net

Freelance Potential
Published 8 titles in 2003: 1 was developed from an unsolicited
submission. Of the 8 titles, 2 were by unpublished writers and
2 were by authors who were new to the publishing house.
Receives 100+ unsolicited mss yearly.
Submissions and Payment: Guidelines available at website.
Send complete ms. Accepts photocopies and disk submissions.
SASE. Responds in 1–3 months. Publication in 6–18 months.
Royalty. Flat fee.

NorthWord Books for Young Readers

18705 Lake Drive East
Chanhassen, MN 55317

Acquisitions Editor

Publisher's Interests
This publisher's list includes fiction and nonfiction books for
readers up to the age of 12. Founded in 1989, this imprint of
Creative Publishing International specializes in titles that deal
with animals, natural history, nature, and environmental
themes. Its publishing program includes trade picture books as
well as nonfiction series and stand-alone titles in interactive and
fun-to-read formats. NorthWord Books for Young Readers is not
accepting submissions at this time.
Website: www.northwordpress.com

Freelance Potential
Published 20 titles in 2002. Receives 500 queries yearly.
Submissions and Payment: Not accepting queries or mss at
this time. Check website for up-to-date submission information.

OnStage Publishing

214 East Moulton Street NE
Decatur, AL 35601

Senior Editor: Dianne Hamilton

Publisher's Interests
Books for beginning readers, middle-grade children, and young
adults are featured in the catalogue of OnStage Publishing. Its
titles include fiction as well as nonfiction, and it is open to all
genres and subject areas with the exception of religious or spiritual material. Do not submit poetry.
Website: www.onstagebooks.com

Freelance Potential
Published 5 titles in 2003: all were developed from unsolicited
submissions. Receives 1,000 unsolicited mss yearly.
Submissions and Payment: Guidelines available with 9x12
SASE (3 first-class stamps). Send complete ms; include outline
for nonfiction. Accepts photocopies. SASE. Responds in 2–4
weeks. Publication in 1–2 years. Royalty, varies; advance, varies.

Our Child Press

79 Woodbine Avenue
Paoli, PA 19301

President: Carol Hallenbeck

Publisher's Interests
Our Child Press offers a small list of titles that focus on parenting issues and adoption. 50% self-, subsidy-, co-venture, or co-op published material.
Website: www.ourchildpress.com

Freelance Potential
Published 2 titles in 2003: 1 was developed from an unsolicited submission and 1 was a reprint/licensed property. Of the 2 titles, 1 was by an unpublished writer. Receives 50 queries, 35 unsolicited mss yearly.
Submissions and Payment: Guidelines available. Query with outline/synopsis; or send complete ms. Accepts photocopies and computer printouts. SASE. Responds to queries in 1 month, to mss in 3 months. Publication in 1 year. Royalty.

Pacific View Press

P.O. Box 2657
Berkeley, CA 94702

Acquisitions Editor: Pam Zumwalt

Publisher's Interests
This publisher focuses on the Pacific Rim, with a children's imprint that features nonfiction about Asia for readers ages eight to twelve. It currently needs biographies of Chinese women and Chinese Americans.
Website: www.pacificviewpress.com

Freelance Potential
Published 3 titles in 2003: 1 was developed from an unsolicited submission. Of the 3 titles, 1 was by an unpublished writer and 1 was by a new author. Receives many queries yearly.
Submissions and Payment: Guidelines available. Query with outline and sample chapter. Accepts photocopies. SASE. Responds in 1 month. Publication period varies. Royalty, 8–10%; advance, $500–$1,000.

Parachute Press

Suite 302
156 Fifth Avenue
New York, NY 10010

Submissions Editor

Publisher's Interests
Parachute Press, a book packager, offers fiction and nonfiction titles for children of all ages, from toddlers to teens.
Website: www.parachuteproperties.com

Freelance Potential
Published 100 titles in 2003: 10 were developed from unsolicited submissions, 50 were by agented authors, and many were reprint/licensed properties. Of the 100 titles, 1 was by an unpublished writer and 20 were by new authors.
Submissions and Payment: Guidelines available for work-for-hire with SASE. Send résumé and writing sample no longer than 5 pages. No unsolicited mss. Accepts mss from agented authors only. Accepts photocopies. No simultaneous submissions. SASE. Publication in 9 months. Flat fee, $3,000–$4,000.

Parkway Publishers

P.O. Box 3678
Boone, NC 28607

President: Rao Aluri

Publisher's Interests
This regional publisher focuses on the history, culture, and nature of western North Carolina. Its children's list includes retold legends and folktales.
Website: www.parkwaypublishers.com

Freelance Potential
Published 12 titles (2 juvenile) in 2003: all were developed from unsolicited submissions. Of the 12 titles, 9 were by unpublished writers and 9 were by authors who were new to the publishing house. Receives 10–15 unsolicited mss yearly.
Submissions and Payment: Send complete ms. Accepts photocopies, computer printouts, and IBM disk submissions (Microsoft Word or WordPerfect). SASE. Responds in 2–6 weeks. Publication in 6–12 months. Royalty, 10%.

Paws IV Books

Suite 400
119 South Main Street
Seattle, WA 98104

Editor

Publisher's Interests
A regional publisher, Paws IV Books has created a line of books about the history, culture, and lifestyle of the West Coast of the US. It targets 4- to 10-year-old readers with its line of easy-to-read and early picture books. Titles that portray the Alaskan wilderness and Alaskan nature remain a special interest of this publisher.
Website: www.SasquatchBooks.com

Freelance Potential
Published 19 titles in 2003: 8 were developed from unsolicited submissions. Receives 200 unsolicited mss yearly.
Submissions and Payment: Send complete ms with résumé and clips. SASE. Responds in 4 months. Publication period varies. Royalty; advance.

Pearson Learning Group

135 South Mount Zion Road
P.O. Box 2500
Lebanon, IN 46052

V. P. Publisher: Celia Argiriou

Publisher's Interests
The Pearson Learning Group publishes books that cover all curriculum areas, and produces a range of educational materials for teachers to use in kindergarten through grade 12 classrooms. Most of its books are published as part of a series.
Website: www.pearsonlearning.com

Freelance Potential
Published 50 titles in 2003: 1 was developed from an unsolicited submission and 1 was a reprint/licensed property. Of the 50 titles, 1 was by an unpublished writer. Receives 30 queries each year.
Submissions and Payment: Query with résumé and writing sample. SASE. Response time, publication period, and payment policy vary.

Peartree

P.O. Box 14533
Clearwater, FL 33766

Publisher: Barbara Birenbaum

Publisher's Interests
This small publishing house seeks titles written by teachers
working in elementary and middle-school classrooms. It is especially interested in original stories that blend fact and fiction.
50% subsidy-published material.

Freelance Potential
Published 5 titles in 2003: 4 were developed from unsolicited
submissions. Of the 5 titles, 4 were by unpublished writers
and 3 were by authors new to the publishing house. Receives
100 queries, 100 unsolicited mss yearly.
Submissions and Payment: Query or send complete ms.
Accepts photocopies and computer printouts. Availability of artwork improves chance of acceptance. SASE. Responds in 6–8
weeks. Publication in 1 year. Payment policy varies.

Peel Productions

P.O. Box 546
Columbus, NC 28722-0546

Editor: Susan DuBosque

Publisher's Interests
With a list for children between the ages of eight and fourteen,
this small house publishes series titles only. Its list includes several series, including ABC Nature Riddles and Alphabet Riddles,
designed to encourage young children to explore words and to
develop their reading and writing skills.
Website: www.peelbooks.com

Freelance Potential
Published 6 titles in 2003. Of the 6 titles, 1 was by an unpublished writer. Receives 1,500 queries and unsolicited mss
each year.
Submissions and Payment: Query or send complete ms.
Accepts photocopies. SASE. Response time varies. Publication
period varies. Royalty, 11% of net sales.

Penguin Books Canada Limited

Suite 300, 10 Alcorn Avenue
Toronto, Ontario M4V 3B2
Canada

Submissions Editor

Publisher's Interests
Primarily a publisher of fiction, Penguin Books Canada Limited
offers titles for middle-grade through young adult readers. Some
historical nonfiction also appears on its list. It will consider submissions that are sent by literary agents only, and only those
that are written by Canadian authors.
Website: www.penguin.ca

Freelance Potential
Published 88 titles (14 juvenile) in 2003: all were by agented
authors.
Submissions and Payment: Canadian authors only. No unsolicited manuscripts. Accepts submissions from literary agents
only. SASE. Responds in 1 month. Publication in 1–2 years.
Royalty, 8–10%.

Perspectives Press, Inc.

P.O. Box 90318
Indianapolis, IN 46290-0318

Editor: Pat Johnston

Publisher's Interests
This small company publishes books that focus on infertility
issues, adoption, and closely related child welfare issues such as
foster care and psychological services. Its purpose is to promote
a greater understanding of these issues.
Website: www.perspectivespress.com

Freelance Potential
Published 2 titles in 2003: both were developed from unso-
licited submissions and both were by agented authors.
Receives 300 queries yearly.
Submissions and Payment: Guidelines available at website.
Query with résumé and outline. No unsolicited mss. Accepts
photocopies and computer printouts. Responds in 1 month.
Publication in 9–18 months. Royalty, 5–15%.

Peter Pauper Press

Suite 400
202 Mamaroneck Avenue
White Plains, NY 10601

Editorial Director: Nick Beilenson

Publisher's Interests
This specialty publisher focuses on upbeat works for women that focus on a single theme or relationship, such as friendship, sisters, mothers, and teachers, as well as special occasions. It publishes no poetry, fiction, or children's books. It does offer activity journals for tweens and teens.
Website: www.peterpauper.com

Freelance Potential
Published 46 titles (3 juvenile) in 2003: all were assigned. Of the 46 titles, 7 were by authors new to the publishing house. Receives 120 queries yearly.
Submissions and Payment: Guidelines available. Query with clips. Accepts photocopies. SASE. Responds in 2 weeks. Publication period varies. Flat fee.

Piano Press

P.O. Box 85
Del Mar, CA 92014-0085

Editor: Elizabeth C. Axford

Publisher's Interests
Music-related educational materials and poetry for preschool through elementary school children appear on this publisher's list.
Website: www.pianopress.com

Freelance Potential
Published 8 titles in 2003: 4 were developed from unsolicited submissions. Of the 8 titles, 2 were by unpublished writers and all were by authors who were new to the publishing house. Receives 250+ queries and unsolicited mss yearly.
Submissions and Payment: Guidelines available. Query for fiction and nonfiction. Send complete ms for poetry. Accepts photocopies, computer printouts, and disk submissions (Microsoft Word). SASE. Responds in 2–4 months. Publication in 1 year. Royalty.

Pippin Press

Gracie Station, Box 1347
229 East 85th Street
New York, NY 10028

Publisher: Barbara Francis

Publisher's Interests
Pippin Press publishes a small list of titles for young readers. For the coming year, it seeks historical fiction for ages seven to eleven, humor for ages four through twelve, nonfiction on unusual but interesting subjects, and childhood memoirs. It is not interested in rhyming picture books, plays, or riddles. Send queries only.

Freelance Potential
Published 5 titles in 2003: 3 were developed from unsolicited submissions and 2 were by agented authors. Of the 5 titles, 2 were by unpublished writers and 3 were by authors who were new to the publishing house. Receives 1,000 queries yearly.
Submissions and Payment: Guidelines available. Query. No unsolicited mss. SASE. Responds in 3 months. Publication in 1–2 years. Royalty; advance.

The Place in the Woods

3900 Glenwood Avenue
Golden Valley, MN 55422-5302

Editor & Publisher: Roger Hammer

Publisher's Interests
This small publisher of multicultural titles for children ages four and up features adventure stories and uplifting stories of triumph over adversity. It welcomes the work of first-time authors, but charges a $10 fee to review and critique manuscripts submitted. 10% self-, subsidy, co-venture, or co-op published material.

Freelance Potential
Published 2 titles in 2003: both were developed from unsolicited submissions and both were by unpublished writers. Receives 1,000 queries, 300 unsolicited mss yearly.
Submissions and Payment: Guidelines available. Query or send complete ms. Accepts computer printouts. No simultaneous submissions. SASE. Responds in 1–4 weeks. Publication in 18 months. Royalty. Flat fee.

Playwrights Canada Press

54 Wolseley Street
Toronto, Ontario M5T 1A5
Canada

Publisher: Angela Rebeiro

Publisher's Interests
This Canadian publisher offers plays for all ages as well as
monologues and texts on drama. It accepts contemporary drama
and mystery plays from writers who can include proof of production by an Equity theater company. You must be Canadian to
submit your work.
Website: www.playwrightscanada.com

Freelance Potential
Published 20 titles (2 juvenile) in 2003: 1 was developed from
an unsolicited submission. Receives 10–15 queries yearly.
Submissions and Payment: Canadian authors only. Query with
synopsis. Accepts computer printouts and simultaneous submissions. SASE. Responds in 6–12 months. Publication in 5
months. Royalty.

Polar Bear & Company

Brook Street
P.O. Box 311
Solon, ME 04979

Submissions Editor: Alex duHoux

Publisher's Interests
Folktales, mythology, and books that celebrate cultural diversity
appear on this publisher's list. 50% co-venture published material.
Website: www.polarbearandco.com

Freelance Potential
Published 6 titles (2 juvenile) in 2003: all were developed from
unsolicited submissions. Of the 6 titles, 5 were by unpublished
writers and all were by authors who were new to the publishing house. Receives 50 queries yearly.
Submissions and Payment: Guidelines available. Query;
include outline/synopsis and sample chapter for fiction.
Accepts photocopies, computer printouts, and simultaneous
submissions if identified. SASE. Responds in 2–4 weeks.
Publication in 1 year. Royalty.

Prep Publishing

1110½ Hay Street
Fayetteville, NC 28305

Submissions Editor: Frances Sweeney

Publisher's Interests
Prep Publishing has been in business for more than twenty
years and continues to offer both fiction and nonfiction on a list
that includes Judeo-Christian titles as well as Christian books
for young readers and titles for a general interest audience.
Website: www.prep-pub.com

Freelance Potential
Published 25 titles in 2003: all were developed from unsolicited
submissions. Of the 25 titles, 5 were by authors new to the
publishing house. Receives 5,000 queries, 1,000 mss yearly.
Submissions and Payment: Guidelines and catalogue available.
Query with synopsis; or send complete ms with $225 reading
fee. Accepts photocopies. SASE. Responds in 3 months.
Publication in 18 months. Royalty; 15%.

Prima Publishing

3000 Lava Ridge Court
Roseville, CA 95661

Submissions Editor

Publisher's Interests
The focus of Prima Publishing has recently shifted. It may be
closing its lifestyle division, but its gaming division will continue
to seek proposals. Visit its website for up-to-date information.
Website: www.primapublishing.com

Freelance Potential
Published 200+ titles in 2003: 100 were developed from unsolicited submissions, 100 were by agented authors, and 70 were
reprint/licensed properties. Of the 200+ titles, 10 were by
unpublished writers. Receives 1,200 queries yearly.
Submissions and Payment: Guidelines available. Query with
table of contents, outline, and sample chapter. Accepts photocopies and computer printouts. SASE. Responds in 1 month.
Publication in 6–12 months. Royalty; advance.

Pruett Publishing Company

Suite A-9
7464 Arapahoe Road
Boulder, CO 80303-1500

Editor: Jim Pruett

Publisher's Interests
Pruett Publishing offers nonfiction titles and guidebooks that focus on aspects of the American West, such as recreation, history, and the environment. Its list includes titles for young readers.
Website: www.pruettpublishing.com

Freelance Potential
Published 8 titles in 2003. Of the 8 titles, all were by unpublished writers and 4 were by authors new to the publishing house. Receives 300 queries, 300 unsolicited mss yearly.
Submissions and Payment: Guidelines available. Query or send complete ms. Accepts photocopies, computer printouts, and simultaneous submissions if identified. SASE. Responds to queries in 2 weeks, to mss in 1–2 months. Publication period varies. Royalty, 10–12%; advance, to $1,000.

Puffin Books

Penguin Putnam Books for Young Readers
345 Hudson Street
New York, NY 10014

Manuscript Submissions

Publisher's Interests
Puffin Books is primarily a publisher of reprint paperback editions of popular hardcover titles. Its list includes picture books, lift-the-flap books, easy-to-read titles, story picture books, chapter books, middle-grade series, and young adult novels. The imprint publishes few original titles and does not publish original picture books.
Website: www.penguinputnam.com

Freelance Potential
Published 210 titles in 2003. Of the 210 titles, 189 were reprint/licensed properties. Receives 100+ queries yearly.
Submissions and Payment: Guidelines available. Query with outline/synopsis. Accepts computer printouts. SASE. Responds in 4–5 months. Publication in 12–18 months. Royalty, 2–6%.

Quixote Press

1834 345th Street
Wever, IA 52658

President: Bruce Carlson

Publisher's Interests
Books for young readers up to the age of 10 are found in the catalogue of this small publishing house, along with titles targeting a general interest audience. Its children's line includes both fiction and nonfiction. 50% self-, subsidy-, co-venture, or co-op published material.

Freelance Potential
Published 50 titles in 2003: 9 were developed from unsolicited submissions. Of the 50 titles, 21 were by unpublished writers. Receives 50 unsolicited mss yearly.
Submissions and Payment: Guidelines available. Send complete ms. Accepts photocopies, computer printouts, and simultaneous submissions if identified. SASE. Responds in 1 week. Publication in 6 months. Royalty.

Rainbow Books, Inc.

P.O. Box 430
Highland City, FL 33846-0430

Editorial Director: Betsy Lampe

Publisher's Interests
Self-help and how-to titles for middle-grade students are among the books for young readers on this publisher's list. Its How to Handle series deals with issues important to middle-graders.

Freelance Potential
Published 20 titles in 2003: 16 were developed from unsolicited submissions and 2 were by agented authors. Of the 20 titles, 13 were by unpublished writers. Receives 20 mss yearly.
Submissions and Payment: Guidelines available. Prefers complete ms with author biography. Accepts query with word count, table of contents, and author biography. Accepts photocopies, computer printouts, and simultaneous submissions if identified. SASE. Responds in 6 weeks. Publication in 1 year. Royalty, 6%+; advance.

Rand McNally

8255 North Central Park
Skokie, IL 60076

Editorial Director: Laurie Borman

Publisher's Interests
Rand McNally publishes a small number of children's books
each year. Activity books, maps for home and school, travel
games, atlases, and reference books are among the types of
material it produces for children ages three to twelve. This publishing house accepts no queries or unsolicited manuscripts
from freelancers. All writing is done on a work-for-hire basis.
Interested writers may submit a résumé for possible future
consideration by Rand McNally.
Website: www.randmcnally.com

Freelance Potential
Published 4 titles in 2003: all were written by in-house staff.
Submissions and Payment: Send résumé only. All work is done
on assignment.

Random House Children's Books

61-63 Uxbridge Road
Ealing, London W5 5SA
United Kingdom

Editorial Assistant: Lucy Walker

Publisher's Interests
This juvenile division of Random House UK includes the Bodley
Head, Jonathan Cape, Hutchinson, and Red Fox imprints as well
as the former Transworld Children's imprints of Doubleday and
Corgi. Children of all ages read its fiction and nonfiction, which
includes picture books, chapter books, middle-grade titles, and
young adult novels in a variety of genres. You must have an
agent to submit your work to this publisher.
Website: www.kidsatrandomhouse.co.uk

Freelance Potential
Published 200 titles in 2003. Receives 2,000–3,000 queries
each year.
Submissions and Payment: Accepts submissions from agented
authors only. Publication in 1–2 years. Royalty; advance.

Random House Children's Publishing

1745 Broadway
New York, NY 10019

Submissions Editor

Publisher's Interests
Random House Children's Publishing targets young readers of all ages with its fiction and nonfiction titles. Mystery, fantasy, adventure, and contemporary and historical fiction appear in its catalogue, along with nonfiction on animals, nature, sports, hobbies, science, current events, and history. It will consider queries for fiction, nonfiction, and poetry.
Website: www.randomhouse.com

Freelance Potential
Published 10–12 titles in 2003. Receives 2,000 queries yearly.
Submissions and Payment: Guidelines available. Query with writing sample or partial ms. Accepts photocopies, disk submissions, and simultaneous submissions if identified. SASE.
Responds in 1 month. Publication in 1 year. Royalty; advance.

Redbird Press

P.O. Box 11441
Memphis, TN 38111

Editor: Virginia McLean

Publisher's Interests
The books produced by Redbird Press explore foreign countries and cultures by combining text, photographs, and children's drawings. They include audio components that allow kids to hear the language of the spotlighted country. With this combination, Redbird Press strives to provide readers age six to twelve with a sense of seeing and exploring the culture for themselves.

Freelance Potential
Plans to resume publishing (1 or more titles) in 2004. Receives 30 queries yearly.
Submissions and Payment: Query with outline/synopsis and clips or writing samples. Accepts photocopies, computer printouts, and simultaneous submissions if identified. SASE.
Response time, publication period, and payment policy vary.

Redleaf Press

450 North Syndicate #5
St. Paul, MN 55104

Submissions Editor: Kathy Kolb

Publisher's Interests
Redleaf Press is a nonprofit organization specializing in issues
related to child care, and its mission is to advance quality early
care and education. Its catalogue offers curriculum-management
books and business resource materials for professionals in the
field of child care.
Website: www.redleafpress.org

Freelance Potential
Published 10 titles in 2003: 5 were developed from unsolicited
submissions. Receives 24 queries yearly.
Submissions and Payment: Guidelines available. Query with
résumé, outline, table of contents, and writing sample. SASE.
Responds in 3 months. Publication in 6–9 months. Payment
policy varies.

Renaissance House Publishers

9400 Lloydcrest Drive
Beverly Hills, CA 90210

Editor

Publisher's Interests
This publisher of bilingual Spanish/English books offers picture
books for preschool children, middle-grade titles, and books for
young adult readers. Its fiction list features folklore, folktales,
and stories with multicultural themes. Animals, pets, and multicultural topics are the subjects of many of its nonfiction titles.
Website: www.renaissancehouse.net

Freelance Potential
Published 20 titles (10 juvenile) in 2003. Of the 20 titles, 5
were by authors who were new to the publishing house.
Submissions and Payment: Guidelines and catalogue available
at website. Query or send complete ms. Prefers email submissions to submissions@laredopub.com. SASE. Response time and
publication period vary. Royalty.

Rocky River Publishers

P.O. Box 1679
Shepherdstown, WV 25443

Acquisitions Editor

Publisher's Interests
This publisher targets an audience of parents, teachers, counselors, and child-care professionals. Its mission is to help children learn to cope with life as they mature. Topics covered in recent titles include self-esteem, drug education, and stress.
Website: www.rockyriver.com

Freelance Potential
Published 10 titles in 2003. Receives 240 queries, 720 unsolicited mss yearly.
Submissions and Payment: Guidelines available. Query or send complete ms. Accepts photocopies. Availability of artwork improves chance of acceptance. SASE. Response time varies. Publication in 9–18 months. Royalty; 8–12% of net (softcover), 10–15% of net (hardcover); advance, $500.

Salina Bookshelf

Suite 130
1254 West University Avenue
Flagstaff, AZ 86001

Publisher: Eric Lockard

Publisher's Interests
Salina Bookshelf features textbooks, children's picture books, reference books, and electronic media that authentically depict traditional and contemporary Navajo life. Everything on its list is published in English and Navajo.
Website: www.salinabookshelf.com

Freelance Potential
Published 12 titles in 2003: 10 were developed from unsolicited submissions. Of the 12 titles, 6 were by authors who were new to the publishing house. Receives 150–200 mss yearly.
Submissions and Payment: Send complete ms. Accepts photocopies, computer printouts, and disk submissions (Adobe Acrobat). SASE. Responds in 3 weeks. Publication in 4–6 months. Royalty, 5–25%; advance, $200.

Sandlapper Publishing

1281 Amelia Street
Orangeburg, SC 29115

Managing Editor: Amanda Gallman

Publisher's Interests
Sandlapper Publishing offers nonfiction about the history, nature,
culture, literature, cuisine, and lifestyle of South Carolina.
Photography titles, books on regional travel, and biographies of
area personalities also appear on its list. For young readers, it features chapter books and middle-grade titles on regional historical
topics and the natural history of the area.
Website: www.sandlapperpublishing.com

Freelance Potential
Published 6 titles in 2003. Receives 150 queries yearly.
Submissions and Payment: Guidelines available. Query with
résumé, outline/synopsis, 3 sample chapters, and bibliography.
Accepts photocopies and computer printouts. SASE. Responds in
2 months. Publication in 2 years. Royalty.

Sandpiper Paperbacks

222 Berkeley Street
Boston, MA 02116

Editor: Eden Edwards

Publisher's Interests
Sandpiper Paperbacks' list comprises mainly reprints of fiction
and nonfiction for early and middle-grade readers. It does, however, accept original, innovative fiction for teens that deals with
contemporary issues. It is an imprint of Houghton Mifflin.
Website: www.hmco.com

Freelance Potential
Published 35 titles in 2003: all were reprint/licensed properties. Receives 100 queries, 200 unsolicited mss yearly.
Submissions and Payment: Guidelines available with SASE.
Query with sample chapter; or send complete ms. Accepts photocopies, computer printouts, and simultaneous submissions if
identified. SASE. Responds to queries in 3–8 weeks, to mss in
3–5 months. Publication period and payment policy vary.

Sasquatch Books

Suite 400
119 South Main Street
Seattle, WA 98104

The Editors

Publisher's Interests
A publisher of regional books about the Pacific Northwest,
Sasquatch Books offers adult titles on travel, the environment,
gardening, literature, and natural history. It is currently seeking
32-page picture books for children ages three to five that feature
regional or national themes.
Website: www.sasquatchbooks.com

Freelance Potential
Published 32 titles (4 juvenile) in 2003: all were by agented
authors. Receives 200+ unsolicited mss yearly.
Submissions and Payment: Guidelines available at website.
Send complete ms. Accepts photocopies and computer printouts.
No electronic submissions. SASE. Responds in 1–3 months.
Publication period and payment policy vary.

Scholastic Book Group

Scholastic Inc.
557 Broadway
New York, NY 10012

Book Group Editorial Department

Publisher's Interests
This well-known publisher offers books for children of all ages,
from preschoolers to young adults. Due to the enormous volume
of submissions it receives, however, Scholastic is not reviewing
unsolicited manuscripts or queries unless they are submitted
through literary agents. It will also consider submissions from
previously published book authors.
Website: www.scholastic.com

Freelance Potential
Published 500 titles in 2003.
Submissions and Payment: Guidelines available. Accepts
queries and unsolicited mss from agented or previously published book authors only. Responds in 4–6 months. Publication
period and payment policy vary.

School Zone Publishing

P.O. Box 777
1819 Industrial Drive
Grand Haven, MI 49417

Editor

Publisher's Interests
The catalogue of School Zone Publishing features educational
materials for use with children in preschool through the elementary grades. This publisher occasionally uses freelancers, but usually chooses professionals who have previously worked on School
Zone materials. Freelancers with an education background may
send résumés and writing samples for future consideration.
Website: www.schoolzone.com

Freelance Potential
Published 5 titles in 2003: 4 were by agented authors. Receives
100 queries yearly.
Submissions and Payment: Query with résumé and writing
samples. No unsolicited mss. Response time and publication
period vary. Flat fee.

Seaburn Publishing

P.O. Box 2085
Astoria, NY 11103

President: Tyra Mason

Publisher's Interests
Books for a general interest audience are found in the catalogue
of this publisher. Its list includes fiction and nonfiction for children from infancy through young adult. Some of the topics covered by its books include humor, history, and health. The publisher also features a line of inspirational literature.
Website: www.seaburn.com

Freelance Potential
Published 20 titles (6 juvenile) in 2003: 2 were developed from
unsolicited submissions and 1 was by an agented author.
Receives 120 queries yearly.
Submissions and Payment: Guidelines available. Query.
Accepts photocopies and computer printouts. SASE. Responds in
1 month. Publication in 4 months. Royalty.

Seal Press

Suite 375
300 Queen Anne Avenue North
Seattle, WA 98109

Editorial Department

Publisher's Interests
Seal Press publishes nonfiction for an audience of women. It
focuses on memoir, women's studies, travel, outdoor adventure,
and parenting issues. Interested writers may submit to one of its
in-progress literary anthologies; see its website for specific guidelines. Writers who wish to query the editors about individual projects are asked to carefully review the website of Seal Press first,
to determine whether their projects would be appropriate for this
publisher's list.
Website: www.sealpress.com

Freelance Potential
Published 22 titles in 2003. Receives 1,000 queries yearly.
Submissions and Payment: Query. SASE. Responds in 6–8
weeks. Publication period and payment policy vary.

Shen's Books

40951 Fremont Boulevard
Fremont, CA 94538

Owner: Renee Ting

Publisher's Interests
This publisher offers culturally-diverse books written to inspire
children of all backgrounds to look beyond the classroom and
see what it is like to live in distant places and times. Its books
target children ages five to twelve and carry universal messages.
Website: www.shens.com

Freelance Potential
Published 2 titles in 2003: 1 was by an unpublished writer and
both were by authors who were new to the publishing house.
Receives 50 unsolicited mss yearly.
Submissions and Payment: Send complete ms. Accepts computer printouts, disk submissions (Microsoft Word), and simultaneous submissions if identified. SASE. Responds in 6–12
months. Publication in 18 months. Payment policy varies.

Shining Star Publications

3195 Wilson Drive NW
Grand Rapids, MI 49544

Publisher: Carol Marcotte

Publisher's Interests
Shining Star Publications, a division of McGraw-Hill Children's
Books, offers a wealth of religious education materials for use
with students in preschool through grade eight. Its catalogue
includes resources for Sunday school and Vacation Bible School
teachers, as well as for homeschooling parents. Bible story
books, songbooks, activity books, puzzles, and games appear
along with teacher aids such as stickers and bulletin board sets.
Website: www.mhkids.com

Freelance Potential
Published several titles in 2003. Receives 50 queries yearly.
Submissions and Payment: Guidelines available. Query with
clips and sample pages. SASE. Responds in 2–6 weeks.
Publication in 1 year. Flat fee.

Siphano Picture Books

Regent's Place, 338 Euston Road
London NW1 3BT
England

Editor

Publisher's Interests
Toddler books, easy-to-read books, and story picture books for
children between the ages of three and seven appear on this
publisher's list. It currently seeks humorous picture books and
animal stories written in a contemporary style.
Website: www.siphano.com

Freelance Potential
Published 10 titles in 2003. Of the 10 titles, 2 were by unpublished writers and 2 were by authors who were new to the
publishing house. Receives 100 queries yearly.
Submissions and Payment: Guidelines available at website.
Query with clips. Accepts email to info@siphano.com and simultaneous submissions if identified. SASE. Responds in 2–3
months. Publication in 6 months. Payment policy varies.

Sleeping Bear Press

Suite 300
310 North Main Street
Chelsea, MI 48118

Acquiring Editor

Publisher's Interests
This small publisher, established in 1997, offers story picture
books for children ages four to ten. Many of its titles are pub-
lished as nonfiction series, such as its Discover America State by
State series. Legends also appear on its list.
Website: www.sleepingbearpress.com

Freelance Potential
Published 31 titles in 2003. Of the 31 titles, 12 were by
unpublished writers and 15 were by authors who were new to
the publishing house. Receives 1,500–2,000 unsolicited mss
each year.
Submissions and Payment: Guidelines available at website.
Send complete ms. SASE. Response time, publication period,
and payment policy vary.

Small Horizons

P.O. Box 669
Far Hills, NJ 07931

Publisher: Dr. Joan S. Dunphy

Publisher's Interests
An imprint of New Horizon Press, Small Horizons features a line of
self-help books for mental health professionals to use to help children deal with issues such as tolerance, self-esteem, and divorce.
Website: www.newhorizonpressbooks.com

Freelance Potential
Published 3 titles in 2003: 1 was developed from an unsolicited
submission and all were by unpublished writers. Receives 100
queries yearly.
Submissions and Payment: Guidelines available. Query with
résumé, outline, 2 sample chapters, and market comparison.
Accepts photocopies and computer printouts. Availability of artwork improves chance of acceptance. SASE. Responds in 3
months. Publication period varies. Royalty, 7.5% of net; advance.

Smith and Kraus Books for Kids

P.O. Box 127
Lyme, NH 03768

Publisher: Marisa Smith

Publisher's Interests
Smith and Kraus Books for Kids offers a wide variety of plays, acting guides, monologues, anthologies, and theater arts books for students from kindergarten to grade 12. Picture books for four- to eight-year-old readers and chapter books for 10- to 14-year-old readers that focus on topics related to the theater are some of the titles offered by this publisher.
Website: www.SmithKraus.com

Freelance Potential
Published 2 titles in 2003.
Submissions and Payment: Query with résumé for fiction. Query with outline for nonfiction. Accepts photocopies, computer printouts, and simultaneous submissions. SASE. Responds in 2 months. Publication in 1 year. Royalty; advance. Flat fee.

Soho Press

853 Broadway
New York, NY 10003

Submissions Editor: Laura Hruska

Publisher's Interests
Soho Press primarily publishes fiction, with the occasional auto-biography or cultural historical account. The publisher is particularly interested in showcasing new writers on its list.
Website: www.sohopress.com

Freelance Potential
Published 35 titles in 2003: 8 were developed from unsolicited submissions, 6 were by agented authors, and 19 were reprint/licensed properties. Of the 35 titles, 5 were by unpublished writers and 12 were by authors who were new to the publishing house. Receives 2,400 queries yearly.
Submissions and Payment: Guidelines available. Query with 3 sample chapters. Accepts photocopies. SASE. Responds in 6 weeks. Publication in 12–15 months. Royalty; advance.

Southern Early Childhood Association

P.O. Box 55930
Little Rock, AR 72215-5930

Executive Director: Glenda Bean

Publisher's Interests
The Southern Early Childhood Association publishes material on literacy development, arts and movement, teacher instruction, and other topics of interest to early childhood professionals and parents. 50% self-, subsidy-, co-venture, or co-op published material.
Website: www.southernearlychildhood.org

Freelance Potential
Published 2 titles in 2003: 1 was developed from an unsolicited submission and both were by unpublished writers. Receives 4 unsolicited mss yearly.
Submissions and Payment: Guidelines available. Send 4 copies of complete ms. Accepts disk submissions (WordPerfect or Microsoft Word). SASE. Responds in 4 months. Publication in 9–12 months. No payment.

Starry Puddle Publishing

1923 North Gramercy Place
Los Angeles, CA 90068

Publisher: Anthony Boyd

Publisher's Interests
Established in 1998, this publisher is interested in receiving submissions of humorous stories only. Its easy-to-read books, early picture books, and story picture books target children ages four to eight.
Website: www.starrypuddle.com

Freelance Potential
Published 2 titles in 2003: 1 was by an agented author and 1 was a reprint/licensed property.
Submissions and Payment: Guidelines available at website or with SASE ($1.50 postage). Send complete ms with artwork if applicable. Accepts simultaneous submissions and email submissions to publisher@starrypuddle.com. SASE. Responds in 2–3 months. Publication in 6–12 months. Royalty; advance.

Stiles-Bishop Productions Inc.

12652 Killion
Valley Village, CA 91607

Editor: Kathryn Bishop

Publisher's Interests
Established in 1989, this specialty publisher exclusively features
36-page stories for children between the ages of four and ten.
The majority of its titles are based on well-known fairy tales and
are developed from the company's radio show for children and
families. While it did not publish any new titles in 2003, it does
plan on releasing two new books in 2004. Writers interested in
working with this publisher are encouraged to send queries.

Freelance Potential
Plans to resume publishing in 2004. Receives 5–10 queries
each year.
Submissions and Payment: Query. Artwork improves chance of
acceptance. Accepts photocopies and computer printouts. SASE.
Responds in 2 weeks. Publication in 6 months. Royalty. Flat fee.

Story Time Stories That Rhyme

P.O. Box 416
Denver, CO 80201

Founder: A. Doyle

Publisher's Interests
Schools, community centers, and non-profit organizations are
among the readers of this publisher's material. Its stories for
elementary through middle-grade students educate, inform,
entertain, and rhyme. Topics covered on its current list include
nature, the environment, art, language, math, science, and
history. It is currently looking for submissions on the topics of
nature and the environment.
Website: www.storytimestoriesthatrhyme.com

Freelance Potential
Published 3 titles in 2003. Receives 250 queries yearly.
Submissions and Payment: Guidelines available. Query. No
unsolicited mss. SASE. Response time varies. Publication period
and payment policy vary.

Success Publications

3419 Dunham Road
Warsaw, NY 14599

Submissions: Diana Herbison

Publisher's Interests
This publisher targets middle-grade and young adult students. It publishes nonfiction only, offering how-to, self-help, and informational books on a wide range of topics, including crafts, hobbies, and entertainment. Writers are encouraged to study carefully the catalogue to determine whether their work will match this publisher's tightly focused list.

Freelance Potential
Published 6 titles (2 juvenile) in 2003: 2 were developed from unsolicited submissions. Receives 100 unsolicited mss yearly.
Submissions and Payment: Guidelines available. Send complete ms. Accepts photocopies. Availability of artwork improves chance of acceptance. SASE. Responds in 2 weeks. Publication in 3 months. Payment policy varies.

Sunburst Technology

400 Columbus Avenue
Valhalla, NY 10595

Submissions: David Wolff

Publisher's Interests
Sunburst Technology, a well-known resource for school technology products, develops and publishes multi-media educational software, videos, and printed supplements for use in kindergarten through high school.
Website: www.sunburst.com

Freelance Potential
Published 50 titles in 2003: 1 was developed from an unsolicited submission. Receives 150 queries, 20 unsolicited mss each year.
Submissions and Payment: Query with résumé and writing samples. Accepts product concept proposals with accompanying graphics. SASE. Responds in 3–6 weeks. Publication period and payment policy vary.

Sword of the Lord

P.O. Box 1099
Murfreesboro, TN 37133-1099

Editorial Dept. Supervisor: Dr. Terry Frala

Publisher's Interests
This publisher features titles that demonstrate Christian
growth. Its list includes fiction for early readers through young
adults, Bible stories, history titles, and biographies.
Website: www.swordofthelord.com

Freelance Potential
Published 20 titles (2 juvenile) in 2003: 2 were developed from
unsolicited submissions. Of the 20 titles, 3 were by unpublished writers and 4 were by authors who were new to the
publishing house. Receives 120 queries, 50 mss yearly.
Submissions and Payment: Guidelines available. Query or send
complete ms. Accepts photocopies, computer printouts, and
email to terryfrala@swordofthelord.com. SASE. Responds in 2–3
months. Publication period varies. Royalty; 10%.

Teachers & Writers Collaborative

5 Union Square West
New York, NY 10003-3306

Editor: Christina Davis

Publisher's Interests
Teachers & Writers Collaborative is a nonprofit organization that
publishes books on teaching writing, creative nonfiction, fiction
writing, and oral history. Founded as a forum for teachers and
writers to explore the connection between writing and reading, it
is interested in material for all age levels.
Website: www.twc.org

Freelance Potential
Published 5 titles in 2003: 1 was a reprint/licensed property.
Receives 100–200 queries yearly.
Submissions and Payment: Query with résumé, outline, market
analysis, and sample chapter. Accepts photocopies and computer
printouts. SASE. Responds in 3 months. Publication in 18
months. Royalty; advance.

Teachers College Press

1234 Amsterdam Avenue
New York, NY 10027

Acquisitions

Publisher's Interests
Books that focus on child development appear in this publisher's catalogue together with textbooks and titles on curriculum trends and special education. Its readers include teachers, practitioners, and researchers. 5% co-venture published material.
Website: www.teacherscollegepress.com

Freelance Potential
Published 60 titles in 2003: 1–2 were developed from unsolicited submissions and 5 were by agented authors. Receives 2,400 queries yearly.
Submissions and Payment: Guidelines available. Query with 2 copies of prospectus, outline, introduction, and 2 sample chapters. Accepts photocopies and computer printouts. SASE. Responds in 1 month. Publication period varies. Royalty.

Thistledown Press

633 Main Street
Saskatoon, Saskatchewan S7H 0J8
Canada

Submissions Editor: Allan Forrie

Publisher's Interests
Fiction for young adults and adults, poetry, and resources for teachers are available from Thistledown Press. It is devoted to publishing writing by Canadian authors only.
Website: www.thistledown.sk.ca

Freelance Potential
Published 12 titles (5 juvenile) in 2003: 2 were developed from unsolicited submissions and 4 were by agented authors. Of the 12 titles, 3 were by unpublished writers and 5 were by new authors. Receives 600 queries yearly.
Submissions and Payment: Canadian authors only. Guidelines and catalogue available with #14 SASE ($.98 Canadian postage) and at website. Query with outline and sample chapter. SASE. Responds in 1 week. Publication in 3 months. Royalty.

Tortoise Press

11016 127th Street
Edmonton, Alberta T5M 0T2
Canada

President: Phyllis A. Arnold

Publisher's Interests
Formerly known as Arnold Publishing, Tortoise Press specializes
in educational materials for use with students in grades three
through twelve. Topics covered by its textbooks and multi-media
resources include Canadian and international history, social studies, and geography. It seeks to provide materials that are educa-
tionally challenging as well as enjoyable for students to use. 10%
self-, subsidy-, co-venture, or co-op published material.

Freelance Potential
Published 10 titles in 2003. Receives 20 queries yearly.
Submissions and Payment: Query with outline and market
information. No unsolicited mss. Accepts photocopies and computer printouts. SAE/IRC. Responds in 2 months. Publication
period varies. Royalty, 10%.

Touchwood Editions

Suite 6, 356 Simcoe Street
Victoria, British Columbia V8V 1L1
Canada

Acquisitions Editor

Publisher's Interests
Touchwood Editions is a Canadian publisher based in British
Columbia. Its list focuses on titles in the areas of history, biography, nautical topics, and architecture and design. It has recently
expanded its list to include books of historical fiction. Both
young adults and adults are the target audience for the titles
published by this company.
Website: www.touchwoodeditions.com

Freelance Potential
Published 7 titles (1 juvenile) in 2003.
Submissions and Payment: Guidelines available. Query with
synopsis, table of contents, 2–3 sample chapters, and word
count. SAE/IRC. Response time, publication period, and payment policy vary.

TowleHouse Publishing

1312 Bell Grimes Lane
Nashville, TN 37207

Editor: Mike Towle

Publisher's Interests
New to the publishing world, this house presented its first list in
2000. It focuses primarily on books about various sports and
publishes no fiction. Its titles are read by young adults and
adults. New writers are encouraged to visit the company's website to review current titles and to become familiar with the
kinds of material it publishes.
Website: www.towlehouse.com

Freelance Potential
Published 9 titles in 2003: 3 were developed from unsolicited
submissions and 6 were assigned. Receives 600 queries yearly.
Submissions and Payment: Query with outline and 2 sample
chapters. Accepts photocopies. SASE. Response time varies.
Publication period varies. Royalty; advance.

Tradewind Books Ltd.

1809 Maritime Mews
Vancouver, British Columbia V6H 3W7
Canada

Submissions Editor: Tiffany Stone

Publisher's Interests
Easy-to-read books, middle-grade titles, and young adult books
appear on the list of this Canadian publisher.
Website: www.tradewindbooks.com

Freelance Potential
Published 5 titles in 2003: 1 was developed from an unsolicited
submission and 2 were by agented authors. Of the 5 titles, 1
was by an unpublished writer and 4 were by new authors.
Receives 1,500 queries, 1,000 unsolicited mss yearly.
Submissions and Payment: Query with résumé and sample
chapter for fiction. Send ms with résumé for nonfiction. All submissions must include an indication that authors have read a
selection of the publisher's works. Accepts photocopies. SAE/IRC.
Responds in 3 months. Publication in 3 years. Royalty; advance.

Turtle Books

Suite 525
866 United Nations Plaza
New York, NY 10017

Publisher: John R. Whitman

Publisher's Interests
Turtle Books specializes in illustrated children's books. It offers
titles in English as well as Spanish, and it targets children
between two and ten years of age. For the coming year, it is
interested in submissions of good stories for picture books.
Website: www.turtlebooks.com

Freelance Potential
Published 6 titles in 2003: 2 were developed from unsolicited
submissions and 3 were by agented authors. Of the 6 titles, 2
were by unpublished writers and 2 were by authors new to the
publishing house. Receives 1,000+ unsolicited mss yearly.
Submissions and Payment: Send complete ms. Accepts photocopies and computer printouts. SASE. Response time varies.
Publication in 1 year. Royalty; advance.

Two Lives Publishing

P.O. Box 736
Ridley Park, PA 19078

Editor: Bobbi Combs

Publisher's Interests
Established in 1999, the mission of this publisher is to bring
children of bisexual, transgendered, gay, and lesbian families
books that depict such families in loving ways.
Website: www.twolives.com

Freelance Potential
Published 2 titles in 2003: both were developed from unsolicited submissions. Of the 2 titles, both were by authors who
were new to the publishing house. Receives 30 unsolicited mss
each year.
Submissions and Payment: Guidelines available. Send complete
ms. Accepts photocopies, disk submissions, and email submissions to bcombs@twolives.com. SASE. Responds in 2 months.
Publication in 3 years. Royalty, 5%; advance, $500–$1,000.

Unity House

Unity School of Christianity
1901 NW Blue Parkway
Unity Village, MO 64065-0001

Editor: Michael Maday

Publisher's Interests
This publisher offers self-help and inspirational titles that express the Unity School of Christianity's philosophy of practical Christianity. It has temporarily suspended its children's publishing program.
Website: www.unityworldhq.org

Freelance Potential
Published 15 titles (2 juvenile) in 2003: 1 was developed from an unsolicited submission. Of the 15 titles, most were by unpublished writers and most were by authors new to the publishing house. Receives 450 queries yearly.
Submissions and Payment: Guidelines available by mail and at website. Query. SASE. Responds in 6–8 weeks. Publication in 11 months. Royalty.

VGM Career Books

Suite 900
130 East Randolph Street
Chicago, IL 60601

Editor: Denise Betts

Publisher's Interests
VGM Career Books is a subsidiary of McGraw-Hill that publishes books on careers and educational success for students in the middle grades through college and beyond.
Website: www.mcgraw-hill.com

Freelance Potential
Published 40 titles in 2003: 36 were developed from unsolicited submissions and 4 were by agented authors. Of the 40 titles, 39 were by unpublished writers and 1 was by an author new to the publishing house. Receives 200 queries yearly.
Submissions and Payment: Guidelines available. Query with résumé and clips or writing samples. Accepts photocopies and computer printouts. SASE. Response time, publication period, and payment policy vary.

Viking Children's Books

Penguin Young Readers Group
345 Hudson Street
New York, NY 10014

Editorial Department

Publisher's Interests
Viking Children's Books, a division of Penguin Young Readers
Group, offers high-quality hardcover books, including fiction,
nonfiction, and novelty books for preschool children through
young adults. It averages sixty titles a year and has published
several debut books within the last year. Due to the overwhelming number of submissions it receives, however, the company is
no longer considering unsolicited manuscripts or queries.
Website: www.penguin.com

Freelance Potential
Published 75 titles in 2003. Receives 3,000 queries and unsolicited mss yearly.
Submissions and Payment: Catalogue available at website. Not
accepting queries or unsolicited mss at this time.

Visual Education Corporation

Building #4
14 Washington Road
Princeton, NJ 08550

Acquisitions Editor: Jean Elkin

Publisher's Interests
This specialty publisher focuses on creating textbooks, ancillary
books, and reference titles for kindergarten through grade 12
educators. Its titles include custom-tailored publishing services
for nonfiction titles to be used in school libraries, including concept development, text research, and writing and editing.
Unsolicited manuscripts will be returned, as all work is done on
assignment only.

Freelance Potential
Published 12–15 titles in 2003: all were assigned. Of the 12–15
titles titles, 5 were by authors new to the publishing house.
Submissions and Payment: All work is assigned. Guidelines
available. Query with résumé and clips. SASE. Response time
and publication period vary. Flat fee.

Windswept House Publishers

P.O. Box 159
Mt. Desert, ME 04660

Manuscript Editor

Publisher's Interests
This small regional house offers books for all ages. Its list
includes children's picture books, novels for young adults, and
adult fiction. While its focus is on the state of Maine, it also
features titles on the environment and New England. Interested
writers are asked to send a query that includes publishing
credits, a detailed outline, the book's length, its title, and its
subject matter.
Website: www.booknotes.com/windswept

Freelance Potential
Published 2 titles in 2003.
Submissions and Payment: Guidelines available with SASE.
Query. No unsolicited mss. SASE. Response time varies.
Publication period and payment policy vary.

Winslow Publishing

P.O. Box 38012
550 Eglinton Avenue West
Toronto, Ontario M5N 3A8 Canada

President & Publisher: Michelle West

Publisher's Interests
This publisher's products include craft books, craft supplies, and
how-to titles, and all are marketed through direct mail. Although
many of its titles are commissioned, Winslow Publishing is interested in receiving queries for craft books for children. These
books should target children ages five through twelve and
include art.
Website: www.winslowpublishing.com

Freelance Potential
Published 2 titles in 2003. Receives 40 queries yearly.
Submissions and Payment: Query with sample illustrations.
Availability of artwork improves chance of acceptance. Accepts
simultaneous submissions if identified. SAE/IRC. Responds in 2
weeks. Publication in 2–3 months. Flat fee.

Wordware Publishing

Suite 200
2320 Los Rios Boulevard
Plano, TX 75074

Editor: Eileen Schuett

Publisher's Interests
Wordware Publishing offers a range of software, workbooks, and
other educational materials for students preparing for Texas
state and district exams. It also produces curriculum-related
nonfiction titles for students in grades three through twelve.
Website: www.wordware.com

Freelance Potential
Published 25 titles in 2003: 1 was by an agented author. Of
the 25 titles, 4 were by unpublished writers. Receives 100+
queries yearly.
Submissions and Payment: Guidelines available. Query with
résumé. Accepts photocopies, computer printouts, disk submissions, and simultaneous submissions if identified. SASE.
Responds in 6 weeks. Publication in 1 year. Royalty.

YMAA Publication Center

4354 Washington Street
Roslindale, MA 02131

Director: David Ripianzi

Publisher's Interests
Launched in 1982, this publisher features advanced titles
about the martial arts as well as in-depth books on Asian
health topics. Many of its titles are read by young adults.
Website: www.ymaa.com

Freelance Potential
Published 6 titles in 2003: all were developed from unsolicited
submissions. Of the 6 titles, 3 were by authors who were new
to the publishing house. Receives 72 queries, 240 mss yearly.
Submissions and Payment: Guidelines and catalogue available
with 6x9 SASE ($1 postage) or at website. Query with clips or
send complete ms. Accepts photocopies. Availability of artwork
improves chance of acceptance. SASE. Responds in 1–3 months.
Publication in 12–18 months. Royalty, 10%.

Zigzag Children's Books

The Chrysalis Building, Bramley Road
London W1O 6SP
United Kingdom

Editor: Steve Evans

Publisher's Interests
Informational books on a broad range of subjects are available
from Zigzag Children's Books. All of this British publisher's titles
include CD-ROMs or special Internet links that allow children to
explore subjects further on their own. It strives to create titles
that are both accessible and affordable.
Website: www.chrysalisbooks.co.uk

Freelance Potential
Published 15 titles in 2003: 7 were developed from unsolicited
submissions. Of the 15 titles, 1 was by an author who was
new to the publishing house. Receives 50 mss yearly.
Submissions and Payment: Send complete ms with résumé.
Accepts photocopies and Macintosh disk submissions. SAE/IRC.
Responds in 2 months. Publication period varies. Flat fee.

Zino Press Children's Books

P.O. Box 52
Middleton, WI 53701

Editor: David Schreiner

Publisher's Interests
Zino Press is interested in picture books for young children, both
fiction and nonfiction, that either tell an unusual story com-
posed in rhyme or that offer multicultural themes not covered by
other recent books. It strives to teach young children tolerance
and compassion toward others.
Website: www.zinopress.com

Freelance Potential
Published 2 titles in 2003: 1 was by an unpublished writer and
1 was by a new author. Receives 800 unsolicited mss yearly.
Submissions and Payment: Guidelines and catalogue available
at website. Send complete ms. Accepts photocopies, computer
printouts, and simultaneous submissions. SASE. Responds in 4
months. Publication period and payment policy vary.

Contests and
Awards ▶ ▶ ▶

Selected Contests
& Awards

Whether you enter a contest for unpublished writers or submit your published book for an award, you will have an opportunity to have your book read by established writers and qualified editors. Participating in a competition can increase recognition of your writing and possibly open more doors for selling your work. If you don't win and the winning entry is published, try to read it to see how your work compares with its competition.

To be considered for the contests and awards that follow, your entry must fulfill all of the requirements mentioned. Most are looking for unpublished article or story manuscripts, while a few require published works. Note special entry requirements, such as whether or not you can submit the material yourself, need to be a member of an organization, or are limited in the number of entries you can send. Also, be sure to submit your article or story in the standard manuscript submission format.

For each listing, we've included the address, the contact, a description, the entry requirements, the deadline, and the prize. In some cases, the 2004 deadlines were not available at press time. We recommend that you write to the addresses provided and ask for an entry form and the contest guidelines, which usually specify the current deadline.

Atlantic Writing Competition

Writers' Federation of Nova Scotia
1113 Marginal Road
Halifax, Nova Scotia B3H 4P7
Canada

Description
Established in 1975, this competition is open to all writers living
in the Atlantic Canadian provinces. It accepts books, plays, short
stories, and nonfiction. All entries are returned with written comments to help writers become ready for publication.
Website: www.writers.ns.ca
Length: Length varies for each category.
Requirements: Entry fee, $10 (members), $15 (non-members).
Writers who have had a book published may not enter in the
genre in which they have previously been published. Limit one
entry per category. Author's name must not appear on manuscript. Manuscripts are not returned. Send an SASE or visit
the website for complete guidelines and category information.
Prizes: Cash prizes ranging from $50 to $150 are awarded.
Deadline: August 1.

The Boston Globe-Horn Book Awards

The Horn Book
Suite 200
56 Roland Street
Boston, MA 02129

Description
The Boston Globe–Horn Book Awards honor excellence in literature for children and young adults. They are considered among
the most prestigious in the nation. A committee of three judges
evaluates books submitted by United States publishers and
selects winners on the basis of their overall creative excellence.
Website: www.hbook.com/bghb.html
Length: No length requirements.
Requirements: No entry fee. Publishers may submit up to 8
books from each of their juvenile imprints in the following categories: fiction or poetry, nonfiction, and picture books. Visit the
website for complete guidelines, or send an SASE.
Prizes: Winner receives $500 and an engraved silver bowl. Honor
books may also be named.
Deadline: May 15 of each year.

Marilyn Brown Novel Award

Association of Mormon Letters
125 Hobble Creek Canyon
Springville, UT 84663

Description

The Association of Mormon Letters presents this novel award for
a Mormon novel about, by, or for Mormons that celebrates the
religion. Held every other year, it accepts previously unpublished
manuscripts only.

Website: www.aml-online.org

Length: No limit.

Requirements: No entry fee. Accepts photocopies and computer
printouts. Author's name should not appear on manuscript.
Include a separate cover letter including author's name,
address, and phone number. Visit the website or send an SASE
for guidelines prior to submitting your work.

Prizes: Winner receives a cash award of $1,000.

Deadline: July 1.

CNW/FFWA Florida State Writing Competition

CNW/FFWA
P.O. Box A
North Stratford, NH 03590

Description

This annual competition presents awards in 11 categories including children's literature short story, children's nonfiction, novel
chapter, nonfiction book chapter, and poetry.

Website: www.writers-editors.com

Length: No length limitations.

Requirements: Entry fees vary for each category. Multiple
entries are accepted, as long as each entry is accompanied by
an entry fee. Use paper clips only. Author's name must not
appear on manuscript. Send an SASE for complete contest
guidelines, specific category information, and official entry form,
or visit the website.

Prizes: First through third prizes will be awarded in each category. Winners receive cash awards ranging from $50 to $100.

Deadline: March 15.

The Dana Awards

Mary Elizabeth Parker
7207 Townsend Forest Court
Browns Summit, NC 27214-9634

Description

The Dana Awards look to encourage emerging writers and honor quality writing in the categories of novel, short fiction, and poetry. All entries must be previously unpublished original work that contains clear, developed themes.

Website: www.danaawards.com

Length: Lengths vary for each category.

Requirements: Entry fees, one short story or five poems, $10; novel entries, $20. Multiple submissions are accepted. Email danaawards@pipeline.com for questions regarding the contest. Send an SASE for complete contest guidelines and official entry form, or visit the website.

Prizes: Winners in each category receive a cash prize of $1,000.

Deadline: October 31. Winners are announced in March.

Marguerite de Angeli Contest

Marguerite de Angeli Contest
Delacorte Press/Random House, Inc.
1540 Broadway
New York, NY 10036

Description

Named for the famous children's book author and illustrator, this competition seeks submissions of contemporary or historical middle-grade fiction set in North America. This contest is open to all writers who have not published a middle-grade novel.

Length: 80–144 typewritten pages.

Requirements: No entry fee. Limit 2 entries per competition. No simultaneous submissions or foreign-language translations. Accepts photocopies. Include a brief plot summary and cover letter. Send an SASE for return of manuscript. For complete guidelines, send an SASE.

Prizes: A book contract for a hardcover and paperback edition, including an advance and royalties. The award consists of $1,500 cash and $3,500 in royalties.

Deadline: Manuscripts must be postmarked by June 30.

Delacorte Press Contest for a First Young Adult Novel

Random House, Inc.
1540 Broadway
New York, NY 10036

Description

This contest looks to encourage the writing of contemporary young adult fiction. Held annually, it is open to all US and Canadian writers who have not previously published a young adult novel. Manuscripts must have a contemporary setting, and should be suitable for young adults from ages 12 to 18.
Length: 100–224 typewritten pages.
Requirements: No entry fee. Limit 2 manuscripts per competition. Accepts photocopies, if legible. Manuscripts under consideration for this contest may not be submitted to other publishers. Author's name should appear only on cover letter. Title of manuscript should appear on each page of the manuscript. Send an SASE for return of manuscript.
Prizes: $1,500 in cash and a $6,000 advance on royalties.
Deadline: December 31.

Gardenia Press First Novel Writing Competition

P.O. Box 18601
Milwaukee, WI 53218-0601

Description

This competition accepts previously unpublished fiction and non-fiction. It is open to authors who have not had work of any nature published for $500 or more within the last five years.
Website: www.gardeniapress.com
Length: Fiction, 45,000–175,000 words. Nonfiction, no length limits.
Requirements: Entry fee, $65. Multiple entries are accepted. Manuscripts will not be returned. Entries should include a cover letter including author's name, address, telephone number, email address, word count, and suggested genre.
Prizes: Grand-prize winner is guaranteed publication by Gardenia Press. First-place winner receives a late model Desktop PC, and second-place winner receives a $200 gift certificate.
Deadline: August.

Golden Kite Awards

Society of Children's Book Writers and Illustrators
8271 Beverly Boulevard
Los Angeles, CA 90048

Description
These annual awards honor the most outstanding children's
books written by members of SCBWI that were published during
the preceding year. Awards are presented in four categories:
fiction, nonfiction, picture book text, and picture book illustration.
Website: www.scbwi.org
Length: No length requirements.
Requirements: No entry fee. No anthologies or translations.
Submit 3 copies of each book per entry category. Books must be
submitted during the calendar year of original publication.
Request contest guidelines and addresses for the three judges in
each category.
Prizes: Winners in each category receive a Golden Kite statuette.
Honor plaques are also awarded. Winners are announced at the
SCBWI summer national conference.

The Barbara Karlin Grant

SCBWI
8271 Beverly Boulevard
Los Angeles, CA 90048

Description
The Society of Children's Book Writers & Illustrators encourages
excellence in children's picture books by presenting this annual
grant that provides assistance to both full and associate SCBWI
members who have never had a picture book published.
Website: www.scbwi.org
Length: 8 typed, double-spaced pages.
Requirements: No entry fee. One picture book manuscript per
applicant. Requests for applications may be made beginning
October 1 of each year. Instructions for mailing and written
material are sent with application forms.
Prizes: $1,500 Grant; $500 runner-up Grant, to be used on
items to encourage further writing.
Deadline: Postmarked between April 1 and May 15 of each year.
Request contest application for additional information.

Milkweed Prize for Children's Literature

Milkweed Editions
1011 Washington Ave. South, Suite 300
Minneapolis, MN 55415-1246

Description
Given to the best manuscript accepted for publication by Milkweed Editions during the current year for the 8–13 age group,
this award is presented annually. It looks to encourage writers to
turn their attention to this important age group.
Website: www.milkweed.org
Length: 90–200 typewritten pages.
Requirements: No entry fee. Entries must have been accepted
for publication by Milkweed during the calendar year by a writer
not previously published by Milkweed. Picture books and collections of stories are not eligible. All entries must follow Milkweed's
usual children's manuscript guidelines. Send an SASE for complete information.
Prizes: Winners receive a $10,000 cash advance on royalties.
Deadline: Ongoing.

National Children's Theatre Festival Competition

Actors' Playhouse at the Miracle Theatre
280 Miracle Mile
Coral Gables, FL 33134

Description
The National Children's Theatre Festival presents this competition that invites the submission of original scripts for musicals
targeting the 5-to-12 age group. It accepts previously unpublished entries and prefers plays that are appealing to children
and adults.
Website: www.actorsplayhouse.org
Length: Running time, 45–60 minutes.
Requirements: Entry fee, $10 per piece. Accepts photocopies
and computer printouts. Multiple submissions are accepted.
Include an SASE for return of manuscript. Complete guidelines
are available at the website or with an SASE.
Prizes: Winner receives a cash prize of $500 and a full produc-
tion of their play.
Deadline: August 1. Winners will be announced in October.

Native Writers' Circle of the Americas ☆ First Novel Award

Geary Hobson, English Department
University of Oklahoma
Norman, OK 73019-0240

Description
Since 1992, the Native Writers' Circle of the Americas and the University of Oklahoma has sponsored this award that accepts unpublished entries in the categories of prose and poetry. Open to writers of Native American background who have not yet published a novel, this contest is held annually.

Length: Prose, 100 pages minimum. Poetry, 50 pages minimum.

Requirements: No entry fee. Accepts photocopies and computer printouts. Include a brief biographical note with entry. Author's name, mailing address, phone number, and email address must be included with manuscript. Send an SASE for complete competition guidelines.

Prizes: Winner receives a cash award of $500 and a plaque.

Deadline: January 1.

Newbery Medal Award

American Library Association
50 East Huron
Chicago, IL 60611

Description
Named for the eighteenth-century British bookseller, this annual award is recognized as the most prestigious award in the US in the field of children's literature. It honors the authors of the most distinguished original contributions to children's literature during the preceding calendar year.

Website: www.ala.org/alsc/newbery.html

Length: No length requirements.

Requirements: No entry fee. Multiple submissions are accepted. All entries must have been published during the preceding calendar year; restricted to citizens or residents of the US. Send an SASE for guidelines and additional information.

Prizes: Newbery Medal. Honor books may also be named.

Deadline: December 31 of each year.

New Muse Award

Broken Jaw Press
Box 596 Stn A
Fredericton, New Brunswick E3B 5A6
Canada

Description
The New Muse Award is presented annually to a Canadian writer who has not yet published a short story collection or novel. Entries may be in any fiction genre including children's books, young adult novels, mystery, and adventure novels.
Website: www.brokenjaw.com/newmuse.html
Length: Varies for each genre.
Requirements: Entry fee, $20. Accepts photocopies and computer printouts. Author's name should not be included on manuscript. Include an SASE for return of manuscript. Send an SASE or visit the website for complete guidelines.
Prizes: Winner receives a cash award of $500 and publication by Broken Jaw Press.
Deadline: January 31. Winner will be announced in September.

New Voices Award

Lee & Low Books
95 Madison Avenue
New York, NY 10016

Description
This annual award accepts multicultural picture book submissions, both fiction and nonfiction, by writers of color who have not yet published a picture book. The competition is open to US writers only.
Website: www.leeandlow.com.
Length: 1,500 words.
Requirements: No entry fee. Limit 2 entries per competition. Accepts photocopies and computer printouts. Send an SASE or visit the website for complete guidelines.
Prizes: Winners receive a $1,000 cash award and publication. Honor winners receive $500 and possible publication.
Deadline: October 30.
Submissions Received: Receives 200 submissions each competition, 100% by unpublished authors.

New Worlds First Novel Award

Hyperion Books for Children
114 Fifth Avenue
New York, NY 10011

Description

This annual award is presented to the best work of contemporary
or historical fiction for ages 8 to 12, set in the US, that reflects the
diverse ethnic and cultural heritage of our country. It is open to all
US writers who have not yet published a novel.
Website: www.hyperionbooksforchildren.com.
Length: 100–240 pages.
Requirements: No entry fee. Entries must have an official entry
form to be eligible. Accepts photocopies, if legible. Send an SASE
for return of manuscript. No simultaneous submissions. Send an
SASE or visit the website for contest guidelines and entry form.
Prizes: Prizes include a standard book contract with a $7,500
advance, and a $1,500 cash prize.
Deadline: Entries are accepted between April 1 and August 31.

NWA Novel Contest

National Writers Association
3140 S. Peoria Street #295
Aurora, CO 80014

Description

This annual contest seeks to encourage the development
of creative skills, and to recognize and reward outstanding
ability in the field of novel writing. It accepts unpublished novel
entries only.
Website: www.nationalwriters.com
Length: To 100,000 words.
Requirements: Entry fee, $35 per piece. Multiple submissions
are accepted. Accepts computer printouts and photocopies.
Include an SASE for return of manuscript. Send an SASE or visit
the website for complete guidelines.
Prizes: First-prize, $500; second-prize, $250; third-prize, $150.
Fourth- through tenth-place winners receive a book and an
honor certificate.
Deadline: April 1. Winners are announced in June.

Once Upon a World Book Award

Museum of Tolerance
1399 S. Roxbury Drive
Los Angeles, CA 90035-4709

Description
This award recognizes children's literature with themes of tolerance and diversity. Submissions should reinforce mutual understanding and illustrate the effects of stereotyping and intolerance. Books should let children root for the underdog.
Website: www.wiesenthal.com/library/award.cfm
Length: No length requirements.
Requirements: No entry fee. All submissions must have been published in the year prior to the award. Submissions should be for children ages 6 to 10 and may be fiction, nonfiction, or poetry. A nomination form must accompany each submission. Send an SASE for complete competition guidelines and nomination form.
Prizes: Winners receive a cash prize of $1,000.
Deadline: April. Winner is announced in June.

Pacific Northwest Writers Association Literary Contests

PNWA
P.O. Box 2016
Edmonds, WA 98020-9516

Description
The Pacific Northwest Writers Association presents several contests annually in categories including juvenile/young adult novel, nonfiction book, juvenile memoir, short story, and adult short story. Only original, unpublished work will be accepted.
Website: www.pnwa.org
Length: Varies for each category.
Requirements: Entry fee, $35 for members; $45 for nonmembers. Multiple entries are accepted. Accepts photocopies and computer printouts. All entries must include an official entry form; available with an SASE or at the website. Submit 2 copies of each entry. Send an SASE or visit the website for complete information.
Prizes: Winners receive cash prizes ranging from $150 to $600.
Deadline: February 16.

Edgar Allan Poe Awards

Mystery Writers of America
6th Floor
17 East 47th Street
New York, NY 10017

Description

Sponsored by the Mystery Writers of America, this competition offers awards in several categories, including children's mystery and young adult mystery. It honors the best mysteries published in the year preceding the contest and looks to enhance the visibility of the mystery genre.

Website: www.mysterywriters.org

Length: Length requirement varies for each category.

Requirements: No entry fee. Entries may only be submitted in one category. Submit a copy of the entry to each member of the appropriate judging committee. Official entry form is required. Send an SASE for contest guidelines and official entry form.

Prizes: $1,500 in cash and a $6,000 advance on royalties.

Deadline: Deadlines vary for each category. Winners are announced in late April.

Skipping Stones Awards

Skipping Stones Awards
P.O. Box 3939
Eugene, OR 97403

Description

Held annually, this competition focuses on multicultural awareness and honors exceptional contributions to ecological and multicultural education. Books, magazines, and educational videos are considered in each of the four categories: Ecology & Nature, Educational Videos, Multicultural & International, and Teaching Resources.

Website: www.efn.org/~skipping

Length: No length requirements.

Requirements: $50 per entry. Multiple entries are accepted. Send 4 copies of each book and magazine entry; 2 copies of each video. Only entries produced in the preceding calendar year are eligible.

Prizes: Cash prizes are awarded to first- through fourth-place winners. Winning entries are reviewed in *Skipping Stones*.

Kay Snow Writing Contest

Willamette Writers
Suite 5A
9045 SW Barbour Blvd
Portland, OR 97219-4027

Description
This annual contest presents awards in several categories including juvenile short story or article, fiction, nonfiction, and student writer. It looks to promote new writers in memory of the group's founder, Kay Snow.
Website: www.willamettewriters.com
Length: Length varies for each category.
Requirements: Entry fee, $10 for members; $15 for non-members. Submit 3 copies of each entry. Author's name must not appear on manuscript. Request complete contest guidelines or visit website for additional information.
Prizes: Cash prizes ranging from $50 to $300 are awarded in each category. A Liam Callen award will also be presented to the best overall entry with a cash prize of $500.
Deadline: May 15th.

Southwest Writers Contests

Southwest Writers Workshop
Suite 106
8200 Mountain Road NE
Albuquerque, NM 87110

Description
This annual contest offers awards in several categories including middle-grade novel, young adult novel, children's picture book, and nonfiction book. It looks to recognize, encourage, and honor excellence in writing.
Website: www.southwestwriters.org
Length: Lengths vary for each category.
Requirements: Entry fee, $29 for members; $39 for non-members. Submit 2 copies of each entry. Each entry must be accompanied by an official entry form. Author's name should appear on the entry form only. Multiple entries are accepted. All entries must be typed. Send an SASE for complete contest guidelines and official entry form, or visit the website.
Prizes: Cash prizes ranging from $75–$100.
Deadline: May 1.

Tall Tales Press Hidden Talents Short Story Contest

20 Tuscany Valley Park NW
Calgary, Alberta T3L 2B6
Canada

Description
Tall Tales Press sponsors this contest that offers prizes in categories for adult and junior writers. It accepts previously unpublished short stories in any genre of fiction.
Website: www.talltalespress.com.
Length: To 5,000 words.
Requirements: Entry fees, $10 for adults; $5 for junior writers. Multiple entries are accepted, provided each is accompanied by the entry fee. All entries must include an official entry form (available at the website or with an SASE). Include an SASE for winners' list.
Prizes: Winners and honorable mentions receive cash prizes ranging from $10 to $500 and possible publication.
Deadline: May 31.

Peter Taylor Prize for the Novel

Knoxville Writers Guild
P.O. Box 2565
Knoxville, TN 37901-2565

Description
The Peter Taylor Prize is open to both published and unpublished writers living in the US. Held annually, the competition looks to identify and publish novels of high literary quality.
Website: www.knoxvillewritersguild.org
Length: 40,000 words minimum.
Requirements: Entry fee, $20. Multiple submissions are accepted provided that each is accompanied by an entry fee. Entries must be on standard white paper. Manuscripts will not be returned. Include an SASE for contest results.
Prizes: The prize includes a $1,000 cash award, publication of the novel by the University of Tennessee Press, and a standard royalty contract.
Deadline: Entries must be postmarked between February 1 and April 30.

Work-In-Progress Grants

Society of Children's Book Writers and Illustrators
8271 Beverly Boulevard
Los Angeles, CA 90048

Description
Each year, SCBWI presents 5 grants in the categories of General Work-In-Progress Grant; Grant for Contemporary Novel for Young People; Nonfiction Research Grant; and a Grant for a work whose author has never had a book published. The grants were established to assist children's book writers in the completion of a specific project.
Website: www.scbwi.org
Length: 750-word synopsis and writing sample from the entry that is no more than 2,500 words.
Requirements: No entry fee. Requests for applications may be made beginning October 1 of each year. Instructions and guidelines are sent with application forms.
Prizes: Cash awards of $1,500 and $500 are awarded in each category.

Writers Union of Canada Writing for Children Competition

24 Ryerson Avenue
Toronto, Ontario M5T 2P3
Canada

Description
This competition is open to Canadian citizens who have not yet been published in book format. It accepts fiction or nonfiction manuscripts for children.
Website: www.writersunion.ca
Length: To 1,500 words.
Requirements: Entry fee, $15 per entry. Accepts computer printouts and photocopies. Include a separate cover sheet with name, address, phone number, and whether the entry is fiction or nonfiction. Author's name should not appear on manuscript itself. Visit the website or send an SASE for guidelines.
Prizes: A cash award of $1,500 is presented to the winner. The winning entry and 11 finalists will be submitted to a Canadian publisher of children's books.
Deadline: April 24.

Indexes ▸ ▸ ▸

2004 Market News

New Listings ☆

Accord Publishing
ACTA Publications
Action Publishing
Alpha Publishing
Ambassador Books
Ambassador-Emerald
  International
AMG Publishers
Avocus Publishing
Baylor University Press
Bebop Books
Marilyn Brown Novel
  Award
Caddo Gap Press
Capstone Press
Children's eLibrary
Christian Focus
  Publications, Ltd
Clark City Press
Cornerstone Press Chicago
Corwin Press
Creative Paperbacks
Denlinger's Publishers
Encounter Books
Finney Company
Halstead Press
HarperCollins Children's
  Fiction
Health Press
I B Publications Pty Ltd
Journey Forth
Jump at the Sun

Learning Links Inc.
LifeSong Publishers
Llewellyn Publications
MacAdam/Cage
MightyBook
National Geographic
  Children's Books
Native Writers' Circle of
  the Americas First Novel
  Award
New Muse Award
New Voices Award
New World Library
Peter Pauper Press
Quest Books
Redleaf Press
Renaissance House
  Publishers
Scholastic Press
Sleeping Bear Press
Star Bright Books
Sword of the Lord
Tall Tales Press Hidden
  Talents Short Story
  Contest
Tortoise Press
Touchwood Editions
TowleHouse Publishing
YMAA Publication Center

2004 Market News
Deletions/Name Changes

Arnold Publishing: See **Tortoise Press**
Anchorage Press Plays: Unable to locate
Avon Books: See HarperCollins Children's Books
Challenger Publishing: Did not respond
The Children's Nature Institute: No longer publishing
China Books & Periodicals: Did not respond
Christian Publications: No longer publishes material for
  children
C.I.S. Publishers and Distributors: Did not respond
Doral Publishing: Removed at editor's request
Eager Minds Press: No longer publishing
E. M. Press: Did not respond
Fearon Teacher Aids: Did not respond
Gallopade International: Did not respond
Girl Press: Unable to locate
GT Publications: Did not respond
Guardian Press: See **MightyBook**
HarperTrophy Paperbacks: See HarperCollins Children's
  Books
Harvest House Publishers: Removed at editor's request
iPicturebooks: See **Children's eLibrary**
Bob Jones University Press: See **Journey Forth**
Majestic Books: No longer publishing
Tommy Nelson: Removed at editor's request
Pauline Books & Media: Did not respond
Pebble Beach Press Ltd.: Unable to locate
Ranchworks: Unable to locate
Frank Schaffer Publications: Unable to locate
SeaStar Books: Did not respond
Serendipity Systems: Removed at editor's request
17th Street Productions: Did not respond
Stoddart Kids Books: Unable to locate
The Story Place: Did not respond
J.N. Townsend Publishing: All children's titles are now
  subsidy-published
Two Bytes Publishing: Did not respond
What's Inside Press: Did not respond
Winslow Press: Company future uncertain
Wolfhound Press: Unable to locate

Category Index

To help you find the appropriate market for your query or manuscript, we have compiled a selective index of publishers according to the types of books they currently publish.

If you don't find a category that exactly fits your material, try a broader term that covers your topic. For example, if you have written a middle-grade biography, look through the list of publishers for both Middle-Grade (Nonfiction) *and* Biography. If you've written a young adult mystery, look under Mystery/Suspense *and* Young Adult (Fiction). Always check the publisher's listing for explanations of specific needs.

For your convenience, we have listed all of the categories that are included in this Index.

Activity Books
Adventure
Animals/Pets
Bilingual (Fiction)
Bilingual
  (Nonfiction)
Biography
Board Books
Canadian
  Publishers
Chapter Books
  (Fiction)
Chapter Books
  (Nonfiction)
Concept Books
Contemporary
  Fiction
Crafts/Hobbies
Current Events
Drama
Early Picture Books
  (Fiction)
Early Picture Books
  (Nonfiction)
Easy-to-Read
  (Fiction)
Easy-to-Read
  (Nonfiction)
Education/Resource
  Material
Fairy Tales

Fantasy
Folklore/Folktales
Geography
Gifted Education
Health/Fitness
High-Interest/
  Low-Vocabulary
Historical Fiction
History (Nonfiction)
Horror
How-to
Humor
Inspirational Fiction
Language Arts
Mathematics
Middle-Grade
  (Fiction)
Middle-Grade
  (Nonfiction)
Multicultural/
  Ethnic (Fiction)
Multicultural/Ethnic
  (Nonfiction)
Mystery/Suspense
Nature/Environment
Parenting
Photo Essays
Picture Books
  (Fiction)
Picture Books
  (Nonfiction)

Plays
Reference Books
Regional (Fiction)
Regional
  (Nonfiction)
Religious (Fiction)
Religious
  (Nonfiction)
Romance
Science Fiction
Science/Technology
Self-Help
Series
Social Issues
Social Sciences
Special Education
Sports (Fiction)
Sports (Nonfiction)
Story Picture Books
  (Fiction)
Story Picture Books
  (Nonfiction)
Toddler Books
  (Fiction)
Toddler Books
  (Nonfiction)
Travel
Western
Young Adult (Fiction)
Young Adult
  (Nonfiction)

Activity Books

Adventure

Animals/Pets

Bilingual (F)

Current Events

Crafts/Hobbies

Drama

Early Picture Books (F)

Early Picture Books (NF)

Fairy Tales

554

Middle-Grade (NF)

Multicultural/Ethnic (F)

Parenting

Self-Help

Series

Publisher and Contest Index

If you do not find a particular publisher, turn to page 539 for a list of deletions and name changes.

★ indicates a newly listed publisher or contest